W9-ADY-642

THE CINEMA OF CENTRAL EUROPE

First published in Great Britain in 2004 by
Wallflower Press
4th Floor, 26 Shacklewell Lane, London, E8 2EZ
www.wallflowerpress.co.uk

Copyright © Peter Hames 2004

The moral right of Peter Hames to be identified as the editor of this work
has been asserted in accordance with the Copyright, Designs and Patents Act of 1988

All rights reserved. No part of this publication may be reproduced, stored in a retrieval system,
or transported in any form or by any means, electronic, mechanical, photocopying, recording or
otherwise, without the prior permission of both the copyright owners and the above publisher of
this book

A catalogue for this book is available from the British Library

ISBN 1-904764-20-7 (paperback)
ISBN 1-904764-21-5 (hardback)

Printed by Antony Rowe Ltd., Chippenham, Wiltshire

THE CINEMA OF
CENTRAL EUROPE

EDITED BY

PETER HAMES

 **WALLFLOWER PRESS** LONDON & NEW YORK

11-22-2005
WW
$24.50

24 FRAMES is a major new series focusing on national and regional cinemas from around the world. Rather than offering a 'best of' selection, the feature films and documentaries selected in each volume serve to highlight the specific elements of that territory's cinema, elucidating the historical and industrial context of production, the key genres and modes of representation, and foregrounding the work of the most important directors and their exemplary films. In taking an explicitly text-centred approach, the titles in this list offer 24 diverse entry-points into each national and regional cinema, and thus contribute to the appreciation of the rich traditions of global cinema.

Series Editors: Yoram Allon & Ian Haydn Smith

OTHER TITLES IN THE **24 FRAMES** SERIES:

THE CINEMA OF LATIN AMERICA *edited by Alberto Elena and Marina Díaz López*

THE CINEMA OF THE LOW COUNTRIES *edited by Ernest Mathijs*

THE CINEMA OF ITALY *edited by Giorgio Bertellini*

THE CINEMA OF JAPAN & KOREA *edited by Justin Bowyer*

FORTHCOMING TITLES:

THE CINEMA OF SPAIN & PORTUGAL *edited by Alberto Mira*

THE CINEMA OF SCANDINAVIA *edited by Tytti Soila*

THE CINEMA OF BRITAIN & IRELAND *edited by Brian McFarlane*

THE CINEMA OF FRANCE *edited by Phil Powrie*

CONTENTS

INTERNATIONAL EDITORIAL BOARD

DUDLEY ANDREW Yale University, USA

KEITH BEATTIE University of Queensland, Australia

GIORGIO BERTELLINI University of Michigan, USA

BIRGIT BEUMERS University of Bristol, UK

MICHAEL CHANAN University of the West of England, UK

MARINA DÍAZ LÓPEZ Instituto Cervantes, Spain

GONUL DONMEZ-COLIN Independent film critic, France

RACHEL DWYER SOAS, University of London, UK

ALBERTO ELENA Universidad Autónoma de Madrid, Spain

PETER EVANS Queen Mary and Westfield College, UK

HECTOR FERNANDEZ L'HOESTE Georgia State University, USA

CAROLIN OVERHOFF FERREIRA Universidade Católica Portuguesa, Portugal

JOSEPH GARNCARZ University of Cologne, Germany

JULIAN GRAFFY SSEES, University College London, UK

LALITHA GOPALAN Georgetown University, USA

PETER HAMES Staffordshire University, UK

DINA IORDANOVA University of St Andrews, UK

KYUNG HYUN KIM University of California, Irvine, USA

JACQUELINE MAINGARD University of Bristol, UK

ERNEST MATHIJS University of Wales, Aberystwyth, UK

GEOFF MAYER LaTrobe University, Australia

BRIAN McFARLANE Monash University, Australia

ALBERTO MIRA Oxford Brookes University, UK

DORIT NAAMAN Queens University, Canada

CATHERINE PORTUGES University of Massachusetts, Amherst, USA

PHIL POWRIE University of Newcastle upon Tyne, UK

LAURA RASCAROLI National University of Ireland, Cork

PAUL JULIAN SMITH Cambridge University, UK

TYTTI SOILA University of Stockholm, Sweden

MITSUYO WADA-MARCIANO Carleton University, Canada

JERRY WHITE University of Alberta, Canada

NOTES ON CONTRIBUTORS

JIŘÍ CIESLAR is Head of the Department of Film Studies at Charles University, Prague, Czech Republic, and a member of the editorial board of *Literárni noviny*. His books include *Luis Buñuel* (1987), *Filmové zápisky* (*Film Comments*, 1993), *Concettino ohlédnutí* (*Concettina's Look Around*, 1996), *Démanty všednosti: Česky a slovenský film 60. let: Kapitoly o nové vlně* (*Diamonds of the Everyday: Czech and Slovak Film in the Sixties – Chapters on the New Wave*, with Stanislava Přádná and Zdena Škapová, 2002), *Kočky na Atalantě* (*Cats in Atalanta*, 2003) and *Hlas deníku* (*Voice of a Diary*, 2004). He is currently completing a book on the Czech director Alfréd Radok, director of *Dáleka cesta* (*Distant Journey*, 1949).

PAUL COATES is Professor of Film Studies in the Department of English and Film Studies at the University of Aberdeen, Scotland. His books include *The Story of the Lost Reflection* (1985), *The Gorgon's Gaze* (1991), *Lucid Dreams: the Cinema of Krzysztof Kieślowski* (as editor, 1999), *Cinema, Religion and the Romantic Legacy* (2003) and *The Red and the White: The Cinema of People's Poland* (2005).

JOHN CUNNINGHAM teaches Film Studies at Sheffield Hallam University, England and at the London Centre, University of Notre Dame, Indiana. He has taught extensively at a number of Hungarian universities including Pécs, ELTE (Budapest), Szeged and Debrecen. He is the author of *Hungarian Cinema: From Coffee House to Multiplex* (2004).

JANINA FALKOWSKA is Associate Professor in the Department of English and Film Studies in the University of Western Ontario, Canada. She has published extensively on Polish and East Central European cinemas. Her books include *The Political Films of Andrzej Wajda: Dialogism in 'Man of Marble', 'Man of Iron', and 'Danton'* (1996) and *National Cinemas in Postwar East-Central Europe* (as editor, 2000) and, *The New Polish Cinema* (with Marek Haltof, 2003). She is currently completing a biography of Andrzej Wajda and working on a project dealing with nationality and transculturalism in the European Union, focusing on Austria and Germany.

ZUZANA GINDL-TATAROVÁ is Professor of Script-writing and Vice-Dean of Foreign Affairs at the Film and Televsion Faculty at VSMU, Bratislava, Slovakia. A graduate of FAMU (the Prague Film School) she worked as a scriptwriter and script-editor at the Slovak Film Studio (Koliba) from 1981–91, and also wrote for television and radio. She has worked on ten feature films, including work by Štefan Uher, Juraj Jakubisko and Martin Šulík. A writer of short stories, journalist and film critic, her books include *Holly-woodoo: Filmove iluzie podla zarucenych receptov* (*Holly-woodoo: Film Illusions by Guaranteed Recipes*, 2001).

MICHAEL GODDARD has recently completed a PhD at the University of Sydney, Australia, on the relationships between Polish modernist writing, especially that of Witold Gombrowicz, and the aesthetic theories of Gilles Deleuze. He has published on Polish cinema, Raul Ruiz, film theory, European cultural studies and poststructuralist philosophy. He is currently writing on the Italian political philosopher Antonio Negri and is planning to extend his research through a postdoctoral project on Italian media and cultural subversion.

PETER HAMES is Honorary Research Associate and former Subject Leader in Film and Media Studies at Staffordshire University, England. He has published widely on Central European Film and is a programme adviser to the London Film Festival. His books include *The Czechoslovak New Wave* (1985), and *Dark Alchemy: The Films of Jan Švankmajer* (as editor, 1995). He has also contributed to *Post New Wave Cinema in the Soviet Union and Eastern Europe* (1989), *Five Filmmakers: Tarkovsky, Forman, Polański, Szabó, Makavejev* (1994), *The BFI Companion to Eastern European and Russian Cinema* (2000), *100 Years of European Cinema: Entertainment or Ideology?* (2000) and *Censorship: An International Encyclopedia* (2001). He is currently co-editing *Cinema in Transition* together with Catherine Portuges.

MARTIN KAŇUCH works in the editorial department of the Slovak Film Institute, Bratislava, Slovakia and is Editor in Chief of *Kino-Ikon*. He is co-editor (with Marián Brázda and Peter Michalovič) of *Svet v pohyblivých obrazoch: Martina Šulíka* (*The World in Moving Pictures: Martin Šulík*, 2000)

VÁCLAV KOFROŇ is a research fellow at the National Film Archive, Prague, Czech Republic, executive editor of the quarterly *Iluminace*, the journal of film theory, history and aesthetics, and lecturer in Czech film at Charles University, Prague.

ANDRÁS BÁLINT KOVÁCS is Head of the Film Department at ELTE University, Budapest, Hungary. He teaches the history of modern cinema and film analysis. He has translated Deleuze's *Cinéma 1-2* into Hungarian. His books include *Les Mondes d'Andrej Tarkovsky* (with Ákos Szilágyi, 1987), *Metropolis, Párizs. Az absztrakt szubjektiv stílus a filmben (Metropolis, Paris: The Abstractive Subjective Style in Film*, 1992) and *A film szerint a világ. Válagatott tanulmányok (The World According to Cinema*, 2003). He has also contributed to *The BFI Companion to Eastern European and Russian Cinema* (2000) and *The Brain is the Screen* (2001).

EWA MAZIERSKA is Reader in Contemporary Cinema, Department of Humanites, University of Central Lancashire, England. Her publications include numerous works in Polish and English about contemporary Polish and world cinema. Her books include *Człowiek wobec kultury, James Ivory i jego filmy (Man Against Culture: James Ivory and his Films*, 1999), *Uwiezienie w terazniejszosci i inne postmodernistczne stany: Twórczosc Wonga Kar-Waia (Trapped in the Present and Other Postmodern States: The Cinema of Wong Kar-Wai*, 1999) and, with Laura Rascaroli, *From Moscow to Madrid: European Cities and Postmodern Cinema* (2003) and *The Cinema of Nanni Moretti: Dreams and Diaries* (2004).

ĽUBICA MISTRÍKOVÁ is a graduate of the Philosophical Faculty of Comenius University (Slovak Language and Aesthetics) and the Academy of Music and Dramatic Arts in Bratislava (Theatre and Film Science). She works in the Slovak Film Institute, Bratislava, Slovakia, focusing mostly on international relations and politics in the audiovisual field. She is a member of the editorial board of the Slovak film magazine *Film.sk* and occasionally publishes analyses and reviews of films and interviews with filmmakers.

ELŻBIETA OSTROWSKA teaches film in the Department of Media and Audiovisual Culture, University of Łódź, Poland. She has published numerous articles on film history and women in cinema. Her books include *Kino ma sto lat (A Hundred Years of Cinema*, co-editor, 1998), *Gender in Film and the Media: East-West Dialogues* (co-editor with Elżbieta Oleksy and Michael Stevenson, 2000), *Przestrzeń filmowa (Cinematic Space*, 2000), *Gender w kinie europejskim i mediach (Gender in the European Cinema and Media*, 2001), *Gender-Film-Media* (co-editor with Elżbieta Oleksy, 2001), and *The Cinema of Andrzej Wajda: The Art of Irony and Defiance* (co-editor with John Orr, 2003).

CATHERINE PORTUGES is Director of the Interdepartmental Program in Film Studies, Curator of the Massachusetts Multicultural Film Festival and Professor and Graduate Program Director of Comparative Literature at the University of Massachusetts, Amherst, USA. She has published widely on Central European film in publications such as *Slavic Review, American Historical Review* and *Cineaste* and has also contributed to *Nationalisms and Sexualities* (1992), *Writing New Identities: Gender, Nation, and Immigration in Contemporary Europe* (1996), *Borders, Exiles and Diasporas* (1997) and *Comparative Studies and Central European Culture Today* (2001). Her books include *Screen Memories: The Hungarian Cinema of Márta Mészáros* (1993) and *Gendered Subjects* (co-editor with Margo Culley, 1983). She is currently co-editing *Cinema in Transition* together with Peter Hames.

MIROSŁAW PRZYLIPIAK is Professor of Film and Media Studies at Pomorska Akademia Pedagogiczna in Słupsk, Poland. He is also a translator, film critic and documentary filmmaker. He is mainly interested in documentary cinema and film narration. His books include *Kino stylu zerowego* (*Zero Style Cinema*, 1994), *Kino najnowsze* (*Contemporary Cinema*, with Jerzy Szylak, 1998), *Poetika kino dokumentalnego* (*Aesthetics of Documentary Cinema*, 2000) and *Poszukiwanie i degradowanie sacrum w kinie* (*Searching for and Degrading the Sacred in the Cinema*, co-editor with Krzysztof Kornacki, 2002).

TINA-LOUISE REID is a professional guitarist and vocalist, based in California, who works in audio production, music recording and sound collage. She has researched at the University of Kent at Canterbury, England, exploring the influence of Max Ernst's automatic techniques on the work of Jan Švankmajer and other experimental animated filmmakers, and has previously published on animation and on Van McElwee's multi-layered video art. She is a freelance lecturer and writer whose subjects include the influence of Ernst's automatic techniques on animation as well as transformative practices in art.

DAVID ROBINSON is a critic and historian, specialising in cinema pre-history, and director of the Giornate del Cinema Muto (Pordenone Silent Film Festival). He is the author of numerous books, including *World Cinema* (1972, 1980), *Chaplin: His Life and Art* (1985, 2001) and *From Peepshow to Palace* (1995). His interest in Eastern European cinemas goes back to 1957, when he first visited the Soviet Union to research Russian and Soviet film history at first hand.

ZDENA ŠKAPOVÁ lectures at FAMU (the Prague Film School), Czech Republic and previously worked as a script adviser specialising in the field of animation. She has written widely in magazines such as *Film a doba* and *Kino*. She has contributed to *Cinema cecoslovacco degli anni 60* (1994), *Le Cinéma tchèque et slovaque* (1996), *Marketa Lazarová* (1998) and is co-author of *Démanty všednosti: Český a slovenský film 60. let: Kapitoly o nové vlně* (*Diamonds of the Everyday: Czech and Slovak Film of the Sixties – Chapters on the New Wave*, with Stanislava Přádná and Jiří Cieslar, 2002).

CHRISTINA STOJANOVA is Associate Professor of English and Film at Wilfred Laurier University, Waterloo, Ontario, Canada. She is an independent programmer and curator for Cinémathèque Quebecoise, has served as a jury member at many international film festivals and writes regularly for *Balkanistica*, *Ciné-bulles*, *Canadian Journal of Film Studies* and other journals. She has contributed to *European Cinema in the Age of Globalization* (2003), *Alternative Europe: Eurotrash and Expoitation Cinema Since 1945* (2004), *Horror International* (2004), and is currently preparing her book *Dual Vision: The Eastern European Cinema and the Totalitarian State 1948–1989*.

ACKNOWLEDGEMENTS

Special thanks are due to the Slovenský filmový ústav (The Slovak Film Institute), Bratislava, and to its director, Peter Dubecký, for funding the translations of the three chapters translated from Slovak (*Obchod na korze/A Shop on the High Street*; *Vtáčkovia, siroty, a blázni/Birds, Orphans, and Fools*; *Zahrada/The Garden*). In addition, I am very grateful to Ľubica Mistríková for her work in co-ordinating the Slovak entries and translations, and to the translators: Zuzana Dudášová, Beata Havelska and Janet Livingstone.

A book of this kind is essentially a collaborative work and I would like to thank all the contributors not only for their commitment to the work as a whole but for the advice that many have given at various stages in its development. Particular thanks are also due to Yoram Allon, Renata Clark, John Cunningham, Nick Hames, Zdena Škapová and Michael Stevenson. For the provision of stills, thanks are due to Monika Braid (Polish Cultural Institute, London), Renata Clark (Czech Centre, London), Janina Falkowska, Zuzana Gindl-Tatarová, Martin Kaňuch, Václav Kofroň, Ewa Mazierska, Ľubica Mistríková, Národní filmový archiv (Prague), Elżbieta Ostrowska, Mirosław Przylipiak, Christina Stojanova, and Eva Vezer (Magyar Film-unió, Budapest).

Parts of the chapter on *Napló gyermekeimnek/Diary for My Children* by Catherine Portuges first appeared in her book *Screen Memories: The Hungarian Cinema of Márta Mészáros* and are reproduced here with the kind permission of Indiana University Press. The chapter on *Daleká cesta/Distant Journey* originally appeared in a slightly different form as 'Living with the Long Journey: Alfréd Radok's *Daleká cesta*' in *Central Europe Review* (4 June 2001) <http://www.http://www.ce-review.org./01/20/kinoeye20.cieslar.html>.

Only an hour away from Budapest there is a small Hungarian town called Kecskemét – famous for its apricot brandy. Its main square is surrounded by six churches. The Town Hall is flanked by a Catholic, a Greek Orthodox and a Calvinist church, and a Presbyterian School and chapel. Opposite, on the other side of the square, there is a synagogue, and to the right, on the corner of a small street there is yet another Catholic church and convent. The town's people did not build their churches away from each other, locked into small communities but all together, grouped on the main square. In the middle of the square there is a park, with one building only, a café: the only café for all the different churchgoers, where they could gather, read the papers, have coffee, play cards and billiards.

This is what Central Europe used to be before the First World War: a world of diversity and tolerance, a world of living together where dissimilarity was honoured. The common inner driving force had always been national pride and traditionalism. And then, like everywhere else, something else took over: instead of solving internal problems by self-examination, people began to search for an enemy image as an outlet for growing hostilities. Two world wars followed and a century of dictatorships based on ideologies – and maybe the area which was afflicted most was Central Europe. The lives of two or three generations of almost every family were seriously affected; almost every Central European family had its casualties.

This is why it is so difficult to find a film in Poland, the Czech Republic, Slovakia or Hungary which is not about lives crippled by politics and history, about victims and losers. This is what we have learned from our grandparents, and this is what we have experienced ourselves.

And yet, this Central European mentality nurtured Alexander Korda, Michael Curtiz, Pál Fejős and Béla Balázs, and though Austria and Germany are not included in this book, the same *Mitteleuropa* mentality has driven Billy Wilder, Fred Zinneman, Otto Preminger and Ernst Lubitsch in America, not to mention the latest generation of Central European immigrants, Miloš Forman, Ivan Passer, Roman Polański or the cinematographers like Vilmos Zsigmond, László Kovács – they all have their roots in the same soil. Thus it may not surprise the reader too much that I would call films like *The Private Life of Henry VIII* (1933), *Ninotchka*

(1939), *Casablanca* (1942) or *To Be or Not to Be* (1942), *Some Like it Hot* (1959) or *One Flew Over the Cuckoo's Nest* (1975) and *The Pianist* (2002) essentially Central European. In this list I would carefully and secretly include *High Noon* (1952) as well.

Even the founder of Paramount, Adolph Zukor, or the founder of Twentieth Century Fox, Vilmos Fried (William Fox) were born in Central Europe, in small villages in Hungary. Their secret was probably very simple: they knew how to address a multi-lingual audience of diverse identity because they had learnt it from their parents: how do you greet your neighbour if he happens to be Slovakian, Romanian, Serbian, Ruthenian, German; how do you call to the person across the street if he is Catholic, Jewish, Greek-Orthodox, Muslim or Protestant. A similar history, fate, similar challenges and life experience created this strange common identity or at least a likeness that we call *Mitteleuropa* or a Central European mentality. This notion emerges in the relationship of the protagonist and the surrounding world. In the historical and social dependence, in the 'circumstances' ruling over private lives.

In Central Europe we carry the past on our backs, sometimes it lifts us but more often it overpowers us. Once somebody asked me why I didn't make a film based on a simple love story. I thought about it and realised that in any story I could tell if there was a scene with a boy and a girl who sat in a café, holding hands, there would surely be a group of men wearing some kind of uniform, rushing into the café, asking for their papers. And the same thing would be true in Prague, Bratislava or Warsaw. Each generation has lived through the fall of a regime driven by some kind of ideology, each learned how life could be ruled by politics and ideology, how politics could interfere with private lives. This is our common experience. So where are our differences? They are also hidden in history and politics. For centuries, the Polish fate forced people to a much harder struggle to defend their mother-tongue, living in the claws of a ceaseless German and Russian influence; it was different from the lot of the Czechs or Slovaks. This is why Polish theatre, acting and the art of filmmaking is different. The survival technique of the Czechs more often than not was irony, or even sharp satire. Their best films often make us laugh but always with affection, we are always laughing at ourselves too. In Hungarian films one often finds a strong symbolism and poetry; the protagonists disregard reality and escape into fantasy. Yes, our differences are in our methods of survival.

This book speaks mainly about Central European films from the 1940s on. Naturally one volume is necessarily limited, the authors cannot mention every school or trend. It's a great pleasure to me that one of my films is amongst those discussed. But allow me to speak about a scene in a French documentary made in 1995 for the centenary of film. The authors asked several excellent and exceptional people about what films meant to them. The French president of the time, François Mitterand, said if he thought of what a film was, he thought of the laughing face of a girl. The girl is circling around in the seat of a village fair carousel, next to her there is a peasant boy in the other seat, they fly, they soar, sometimes they can touch, sometimes they get separated but the girl keeps on laughing and this laugh is unforgettable. He didn't know in which country the film was made, he didn't know the director's name but he could never forget the laughing face of the girl, and for him this image was the essence of film.

The film is called *Körhinta* (*Merry-go-round*, 1955), the director is Zoltan Fábri, and the girl laughing fifty years ago is Mari Törőcsik, one of the greatest Hungarian – or Central European – actresses of all time. Which means she is a little sad, she is often self-ironic but her smile is always genuine.

István Szabó
Budapest
July 2004

INTRODUCTION

Central Europe is not a state: it is a culture or a fate. Its borders are imaginary...
– Milan Kundera, 1984

Once upon a time I was East European. Then I was promoted to Central European
... There was a dream of Central Europe, a vision of its future ... Then, a couple of
months ago I became a New European...
– Péter Esterházy, 2003

Most studies of Central Europe begin with the opening question 'Where is Central Europe?' while one book is even entitled *In Search of Central Europe*. The answer is clearly not self evident. For most practical purposes (for example, from the perspectives of the European Union, the World Bank, and US foreign policy) the countries considered in this book – the Czech Republic, Hungary, Poland and Slovakia – are considered Central European. However, from those of the Western media and in popular perception, they remain 'East European' and they are described in a number of academic contexts as 'East Central European'.

This is not the place to consider these issues in detail but it is important to note that all such definitions carry their own ideological projects. Larry Wolff has suggested that the idea of 'Eastern Europe' was invented by the Enlightenment, 'a synthetic association of lands, which drew upon both fact and fiction', and has functioned in a manner analogous to that identified by Edward Said in connection with Orientalism. The countries considered in his book as 'East European' extend from Bohemia and Moravia (the present Czech Republic) to Russia, including Siberia. Throughout his account the legacy of the Roman Empire is apparent, with constant references to Sarmatians, Scythians, Tartars and other terms suggesting barbaric or uncivilised peoples. He makes a powerful link between these Enlightenment perspectives, Hitler's desire to impose a superior 'kultur', the post-war division of Europe at Yalta and Churchill's 'iron curtain' speech, all of which, he argued, mirrored the eighteenth-century division invented by Western Europe.

The importance of German culture in Central Europe has been fundamental (indeed, specialists might characterise Austria, Germany and Switzerland as constituting 'West Central

Europe'). Central Europe has also been the site for competition between the Habsburg Empire, the German Empire post-Bismarck and the various manifestations of Russian Empire. Centuries of Habsburg domination and the importance of German influences in Bohemia should not be easily forgotten nor should the role played by German-Jewish culture. The concept of Central Europe, in its German form of *Mitteleuropa*, was coined in the nineteenth century and connoted German or, at best, German-Hungarian, domination over other cultures, and the idea ultimately found its reflection in Nazi policies of imperialism.

For the first president of Czechoslovakia, Tomáš Masaryk, the concept of Central Europe excluded Germans and Austrians altogether. More recently, for countries like the former Czechoslovakia, Hungary and Poland, the term Central Europe has implied something else – the right to form part of an indivisible European culture. In the late 1980s, there was a great deal of debate around the issue, focusing in particular on the essay by the Czech émigré novelist, Milan Kundera, entitled 'A Kidnapped West or Culture Bows Out'.

The title gives a clear indication of his subject. For Kundera, the historical and, above all, cultural traditions of nations like Czechoslovakia, Hungary and Poland were 'European'. The Hungarian revolution of 1956, the Soviet suppression of the Prague Spring in 1968 and the institution of martial law in Poland in 1981 constituted 'a drama of the West – a West that, kidnapped, displaced and brainwashed, nevertheless insists on defending its identity'. Although the culture of Central Europe had sometimes followed a separate course, its history was basically that of constructive interplay with that of Western Europe. Echoing the Czech historian, František Palacký, Kundera regarded Central Europe as a 'family of small nations' united by its distrust of History but in which nations would cultivate the maximum variety and individuality.

Not everyone will agree with Kundera and many have pointed to the destructive role of nationalism in the area. If Czechoslovakia benefited at the expense of Hungary in the post-World War One settlement (Slovakia had previously been known as Upper Hungary), both Hungary and Poland seized land from Czechoslovakia in 1938–39 and Slovakia declared temporary independence. But, of course, nationalisms and conflict in Western Europe have not destroyed the notion of a common European inheritance. And, in Central Europe, there have also been proposals for federation (for example, the Sikorski-Beneš plan for a federation of Poland and Czechoslovakia of 1942).

Prior to the fall of Communism in 1989, there were important exchanges between the 'dissident' thinkers within the four countries in their confrontation with what were perceived as parallel problems. Independent Polish, Czech and Hungarian intellectuals, noted Timothy

Garton Ash, found themselves sharing 'a distinctive set of attitudes, ideas and values'. For them, he argued, the notion of Central Europe presented an organising principle for opposing the realities of Soviet domination (yet he notes, rather tellingly, that their personal encounters were invariably outside the area and that they read each other's works in 'West European' languages).

In the immediate post-Communist period, this led to meetings between political leaders in the Hungarian town of Visegrád in 1991. These political initiatives led to a qualified success in presenting the countries to the West as in the forefront of the transition from Communism and the term the 'Visegrád Four' came into common usage. At a conference held in Budapest in December 2002, there was still seen to be value in the Visegrád alliance and it was agreed that the notion of 'Central Europe' implied a shared historical experience and cultural affinity. In an everyday sense, it could be argued that the notion of Central Europe is increasingly focused on these four countries; in practical terms, Germany and Austria are placed in the traditional West while the Baltic countries and Slovenia and Croatia are further marginalised.

The magazine *Central Europe* defines the area as comprising those countries that were formerly part of the Habsburg Empire together with Poland-Lithuania. For Lonnie R. Johnson, the area comprises the Visegrád Four plus Germany, Austria, Slovenia and Croatia. These are logical demarcations, and it should not be assumed that a looking back to the idea of Central Europe is restricted to the former Warsaw Pact countries. However, even if one can agree on geographical delimitations, it is much less easy to agree on cultural and socio-political identities, which are frequently aspirational and contradictory.

In 1989, Claudio Magris described the Central European revival as 'often a flirtatious fashion or cheap formula' but pointed to aspects of a common culture. These included: a tendency towards analysis, the defence of the individual against totality, the defence of the margins against the centre, the supranational role of Jewish culture, the rejection of dogmatic philosophical systems and the sense that history could be different. While these elements did not constitute a unity, Central Europe had something to offer to the Western democracies, 'a human dimension, which was developed through Central Europe's tragedies and in resistance to them'.

The term 'East Central Europe' has also been used in a number of contexts to refer to the former 'Eastern Europe', describing the former Warsaw Pact countries (Bulgaria, Czechoslovakia, East Germany, Hungary, Poland, Romania) plus the former Yugoslavia and Albania. Various reasons have been given, including the notion that the original designation of 'Eastern Europe' carried the connotation of Soviet control. In addition, it has been suggested that the emergence of new states from the former Soviet Union – the Baltic states (Estonia, Latvia and Lithuania), Ukraine, Belarus, Moldova – created a new grouping of states that could 'more properly be described as 'Eastern Europe'.

The term 'East Central European Cinema' also emerged in the 1990s. In *The Oxford Guide to Film Studies*, the countries included are as above but represented only by examples from Poland and Czechoslovakia. Dina Iordanova uses the term to refer to the four countries discussed in this book while *The Oxford History of World Cinema* does the same with the addition of Yugoslavia (but ignores Bulgaria and Romania altogether). The *Encyclopedia of European Cinema* uses the inclusive category of 'Central and Eastern Europe' but *The BFI Companion to Eastern European and Russian Cinema* returns to the more traditional designation of 'Eastern Europe'. There is clearly no consensus.

The problem with the term 'East Central Europe' is that it can represent as few as three countries or as many as six using pre-Communist divisions and from four to thirteen or more, according to choice, using post-Communist divisions. Whatever category is used – 'Eastern Europe', 'East Central Europe', 'Central Europe' – they remain 'synthetic associations of lands' combined for a variety of reasons and objectives. All such divisions imply the separation of Europe 'as a whole'. Behind the need to group countries according to 'political and cultural similarities' one senses a desire to hang on to the certainties and simplifications of the Cold War. Editors and publishers also lack the space and/or markets to deal with cultures or cinemas considered to be small or 'minor'. However, I would prefer to preserve 'East Central European' for the more inclusive classification simply because it is the more usual.

While this book effectively identifies the notion of Central Europe with the Visegrád Four, this is not entirely by design. A number of Central European countries appear elsewhere in the *24 Frames* series because of their particular political and cinematic histories. Austria appears in the volume on German cinema, Slovenia and Croatia, as part of the former Yugoslavia, appear in the volume on Balkan cinema, and the Baltic countries are considered in the volume on Russian and Soviet cinema.

The grouping of countries according to certain assumed identities also relates to notions of national and regional cinemas. It is noticeable that, in film encyclopaedias, most English language and West European cinemas find themselves written about individually as 'national' cinemas while much of the rest of the world finds itself appearing under 'regional' categories. The concept of a regional cinema more often than not embodies a process of marginalisation with respect to cultures perceived as minor. This inevitably leads to the question of whether the cinemas of the Czech Republic, Hungary, Poland and Slovakia, however they may be defined as a group, together constitute a regional cinema. A regional cinema, one assumes, would reflect a common culture together with evidence of significant collaboration in the fields of production, exhibition and consumption.

It is perfectly possible to agree with Iordanova's argument that the area can be approached both nationally and regionally. She points to several convergences during the Communist period, most fundamentally joint membership of COMECON, which led to the mutual exchange and screening of films within the Warsaw Pact countries which, of course, also included the Soviet Union, Bulgaria, Romania and the German Democratic Republic. Thus, the countries would see each other's films and there were various co-production arrangements and exchanges of personnel.

On the other hand, such exchanges have been much less obvious in the pre- and post-Communist periods. In the 1930s, for instance, in Czechoslovakia, a regular percentage of films were produced in Czech, German and French versions, and exports to Poland and Hungary were probably less than those to Western Europe. In fact, if one takes the long view, it can be argued that the degree of cultural exchange within the area has been considerably less than that between France, Germany, Italy and other West European countries which are not normally designated as regional cinemas.

Despite the appearance of Slovak, Czech, Hungarian and Polish actors in films from other countries in the grouping (notably Jozef Kroner, György Cserhalmi, Jan Nowicki), the degree of co-operation was limited even in Communist times. For instance, prior to 1989, in the period 1972–89, the numbers of Czech and Slovak co-productions were dominated by the Soviet Union and West Germany respectively with minimal co-production with Poland and Hungary.

Also, the fact of economic exchange in the Communist period does not automatically convert into one of cultural exchange and impact. Key films (those deemed 'subversive') often received limited exposure while officially approved titles played to empty cinemas. Some research should also be conducted into the impact of the 'forbidden fruit' of US and West European cinema, politically-approved selections from which often played a significant role in subsidising the more ideologically correct exchanges. (Of course, since 1989, Hollywood's dominance has been established as effectively as it has in Western Europe. But this should not necessarily be equated with public demand.)

In 2000, the Bratislava Film Festival in Slovakia devoted one of its strands to pre- and post-1989 co-productions between the 'Visegrád Four'. With the exception of Czech-Slovak productions (and the rare example of 1930s Czech-Polish collaboration, *Dvanáct křesel/The Twelve Chairs*, 1933, co-directed by Martin Frič and Michał Waszyński) they proved to be relatively dull and unproductive. This is not to suggest that co-production could not become productive and there have been occasional post-Communist moves in this direction (for example, the Czech-Polish-Slovak-French *Je třeba zabít Sekala/Sekal Has to Die*, 1998). But it is fairly conclusive evidence that the area cannot be regarded as a 'regional cinema' in terms of production and, as indicated above, nor can it really be viewed as such in terms of the exchange and circulation of films. (However, one should accept that such exchange, especially for television, is greater than that between the four countries and Western Europe.)

The Czech and Slovak cinemas, of course, represent a special case. They co-existed as separate cinemas within a single state from 1945–93 (Slovak cinema was virtually non-existent in the 1920s and 1930s), producing films in different languages but at the same time enjoying major exchanges in personnel. Since 1989, Slovakia has been very much the poor relation in terms of production and, with the decline of its own technical laboratories, the relationship between the two countries continues on many levels. Czech and Slovak cinema culture, as Martin Kaňuch suggests in his chapter on *Vtáčkovia, siroty, a blázni* (*Birds, Orphans and Fools*, 1969), is both common and separate. With this exception, there is little case for regarding the four cinemas as constituting a 'regional cinema' or for identifying a common Central European or East Central European cinema.

It is much more logical to regard them as 'national' cinemas which, like Western Europe, enjoy a common geographical space and shared histories – 'a family of nations', as Kundera puts it, exhibiting a maximum of individuality. To do them adequate justice would require three separate volumes on Poland, Hungary and the Czech and Slovak Republics. But if this volume represents to some extent a marriage of convenience, it is important to recognise common historical experiences: Russian domination (all of the countries between 1948–89), German invasion and Habsburg domination in its various forms and combinations. In addition, one should add the importance of Jewish culture and the experience of the Holocaust. These historical themes are consistently implied or addressed in the films of all four countries. In this sense, to return to Iordanova's argument, the countries can be approached 'regionally'. It is also clear that filmmakers from the area have been aware of each other's work, and this was particularly true of the Communist period. Needless to say, common themes can also be found across West European culture, European culture as a whole and even extended to the USA.

If one considers the comparative development of the three pre-war industries, it is apparent that the histories of Czech, Hungarian and Polish cinema can be traced to the beginnings. Each can claim their pioneers of early cinema, each were responsible for early feature films in the 1910s and 1920s, and each has enjoyed regular production since (apart from Poland during the Second World War). While the early 1920s also saw the first Slovak feature, it was not until after 1945 that a separate Slovak feature industry was to develop.

In terms of quantity, Czech production has undoubtedly been dominant, especially if one considers relative sizes of population, achieving figures that were frequently double those of Hungary and Poland in both pre-war and post-war periods. If pre-war production in the three countries was overwhelmingly commercial, they were each influenced by their own political histories, and drew on the resources of national literature. Hungary established the world's first nationalised industry in 1919 under the Communist Republic of the Councils with Mihály Kertész (Michael Curtiz), Sándor Korda (Alexander Korda) and Béla Lugosi all playing central roles. They were among the many to leave the country after the right-wing reaction set in in the early 1920s. Hungary's highly promising early development was to drop to single figures until the mid-1930s when the government introduced a quota system, but also an approved agenda. By the 1940s, although privately financed, films were *de facto* 'state approved'.

István Nemeskürty points out that the expansion of Hungarian cinema in the mid-1930s to around 23 features was linked to the demand of Hungarian ethnic audiences in the US. The importance of the US as a market was also reflected in the development of Yiddish cinema in Poland. With a Jewish population of over 3 million, there were strong theatrical and literary traditions and, in 1936, the Polish-born Joseph E. Green, organised a production programme aimed also at the US market. Michał Waszyński, who directed *Der Dibuk* (*The Dybbuk*, 1937), his only Yiddish film, was the most prolific Polish director of the pre-war period.

Czech production was more consistently part of the European mainstream. One example of this was, of course, the success of the team of Anny Ondráková (Anny Ondra) and Karel Lamač (Carl Lamač), who based their production initially in Prague but subsequently moved to Berlin, making films for both the Czech and German markets. (Ondra appeared in Hitchcock's *The Manxman* and *Blackmail*, both 1929, and Lamač directed three British features during the Second World War.) 'West European' stars occasionally appeared in Czech films and a number of German firms, including UFA, maintained Czech production interests. In the 1930s, 28 Czech films were produced in German versions and around 8 in French versions.

When the Barrandov Studios were built in Prague in 1932–33, they were intended as a centre for international production which, of course, they finally became in the 1990s.

With the establishment of the Venice Film Festival in 1932 as the world's first festival dedicated to screening the best in world cinema, all three countries began to attract wider attention. A sequence of Czech films won awards between 1934–38 including films by Gustav Machatý, Josef Rovenský, Martin Frič and Otakar Vávra. Machatý's *Extase* (*Ecstasy*, 1933) was sold to over 30 countries. Karel Plicka's Slovak-produced feature documentary *Zem spieva* (*The Earth Sings*, 1933) was screened in 1934. Between 1935–37, the films of Poland's most distinctive filmmaker, Józef Lejtes (*Dzien wiekiej przygody/Day of the Great Adventure*, 1935; *Barbara Radziwiłłowna*, 1936) attracted attention as did the experimental *Trzy etiudy filmowe* (*Three Studies of Chopin*, 1937) by Stanisław Wohl and Eugeniusz Cękalski. In the last Venice Festival before its cancellation in 1942, it was the turn of Hungary and István Szőts' *Emberek a havason* (*People of the Mountains*, 1942), won the main prize. While the festival was now an Italian-German one, the ethnographic poetry of Szőts' film prompted an editorial manifesto in *Cinema* by the future neo-realist directors Giuseppe De Santis and Carlo Lizzani and critic Guido Aristarco: 'At long last, let the song of the Alps into our studio, the song that the Hungarian István Szőts was the first to sing, and let it chase the antiquated bigshots, the merchants and the hucksters, away from the festivals of Venice as well.'

During the Second World War Polish cinema was eliminated together with much of its past production but, under the Protectorate of Bohemia and Moravia, Czech production continued while, in Hungary, production averaged 40 films per year, reaching 54 in 1943, a level never again achieved. It attained significant exports, particularly in the Balkan countries.

The idea of nationalised industry was not, of course, a simple product of Communist ideology, and plans for nationalised film industries were proposed in both Western and Central and Eastern Europe following the Second World War. Hungary already had its precedent but the industry was not nationalised until the Communist takeover in 1948. In Czechoslovakia and Poland, however, the industries were nationalised three years earlier.

It is the nationalised cinemas that produced the great works of the three (now four, if we include Slovakia) cinemas. While they all suffered the brutalities associated with the application of the themes and styles of Socialist Realism in the 1950s, they have all enjoyed their periods of international acclaim. In the 1950s and 1960s, particularly following the death of Stalin in 1953 and Khruschev's denunciation of the Stalinist 'cult of personality' in 1956, developments often mirrored each other. Andrzej Wajda's *Pokolenie* (*A Generation*, 1954) heralded the arrival of 'The Polish School' (1954–63), which also included the work of Andrzej Munk and Wojciech Has. Ideological control was loosened in Hungary in 1955, leading to the international success of Zoltan Fábri's *Körhinta* (*Merry-go-round*, 1955), and was followed by a breakthrough in Czech cinema (1957–59). In the early 1960s, the new wave of Hungarian art cinema was inaugurated by films such as Miklós Jancsó's *Szegénylegények* (*The Round-Up*, 1965) and work by András Kovács, Márta Mészáros, Péter Bacsó, István Szabó, István Gáal and many others. The same period saw the early work of Roman Polański and Jerzy Skolimowski in Poland while the Czech and Slovak New Waves (1963–69) saw one of the most striking examples of the possibilities of a nationalised industry. Ján Kadár's and Elmar Klos' *Obchod na korze* (*A Shop on the High Street*, 1964) and Jiří Menzel's *Ostře sledované vlaky* (*Closely Observed Trains*, 1966) were the first films from the area to win Academy Awards, in 1965 and 1967 respectively. Miloš Forman's *Lásky jedné plavovlásky* (*A Blonde in Love* aka *Loves of a Blonde*, 1965) and *Hoří, má panenko* (*The Firemen's Ball*, 1967) were also Oscar-nominated. The 'wave' also saw the emergence of Věra Chytilová, Jan Němec, Jaromil Jireš, Juraj Jakubisko and many others.

The Czech and Slovak cinema was, however, linked to the developments leading to the Prague Spring of 1968, which was suppressed by Warsaw Pact troops. After 1969, over a hundred films were banned and culture (including film) was subjected to an extensive suppression that was to last twenty years. Many directors emigrated and others found their careers at an end. In contrast, Hungary was able to develop a substantive body of original work based on historical allegory and was directly addressing political themes by the late 1970s. Wajda again attracted international attention when his controversial *Człowiek z marmuru* (*Man of Marble*, 1976) heralded the arrival of the Polish 'Cinema of Moral Concern' (1976–81), which included the work of Krzysztof Zanussi, Agnieszka Holland and Krzysztof Kieślowski. After the suppression of the independent trade union, Solidarność (Solidarity), and the imposition of Martial Law in 1981, many Polish directors were also forced to work abroad.

The nationalised cinema at its worst produced propaganda and uninspired commercial cinema, but it also allowed for the development of an art cinema and a forum for critical debate. This, of course, had much to do with the privileged role of artists and intellectuals and their traditional role as the conscience of the nation. Developments within the three countries were both united and separated by major political developments such as the Hungarian revolution in 1956, the Soviet suppression of the Prague Spring and the institution of Martial Law in Poland. At its best, the nationalised cinema performed a public service role, something increasingly challenged by the commercialism of the Western media.

With the exception of a crisis-dominated Slovak cinema, where production has often dropped to one film a year (compared with ten per year under Communism), the cinemas have survived the transition to capitalism. With greater or lesser degrees of state support, Poland has continued to produce socially relevant films as well as lucrative national epics based on classic literature. Hungary has also turned to nationalist epics but has also maintained its distinctive record in the world of art cinema. The Czech Republic has continued with its tradition of ironic comedy but, like Hungary and Poland, its production is now 15–20 films a year, a significant drop on its previous output.

But the international (that is, 'Western') consciousness of these cinemas has seemed to fade since the arrival of the 'free' market as has knowledge of their previous attainments. This is, perhaps, understandable in the case of Czech and Slovak cinema, where most of the key films were banned in the years subsequent to the Soviet invasion of 1968 and the government seemed to be bent on liquidating its most significant cultural achievements. It is less understandable in the cases of Hungary and Poland. Where names such as Wajda and Jancsó once featured among the leading 'auteurs' of European cinema alongside Bergman, Fellini, Antonioni and Godard, their work and reputations have begun to fade from view. Here, one suspects that it is the 'East Europe' categorisation that is responsible and, of course, since the fall of Communism, the countries have also lost their 'exotic' attraction.

If 'East European' countries were once perceived as awaiting the benefits of the eighteenth-century Enlightenment, it is also possible to see such attitudes in the twentieth century. In his *Europe: A History*, Norman Davies has pointed to the ways in which the history of Europe has been conventionally written as the history of Western Europe, leading to significant distortions and misleading generalisation. He notes the ways in which the treatment of Central and Eastern Europe has been marginalised through the conventions of university programmes and enterprises such as the Chicago 'Great Books' scheme (151 authors of which 49 are English and American and only 3 East European).

The cultures of Central and Eastern Europe have similarly been presented as an undifferentiated 'other' and tend to be marginalised or ignored in anything other than specialised History of Art or Film Studies programmes. The profile of Central European literature focuses almost exclusively on novelists such as the Czechs Milan Kundera and Josef Škvorecký, who have emigrated to the West. Filmmakers like Miloš Forman, Roman Polański, István Szabó, Krzysztof Kieślowski and, somewhat earlier, painters such as Toyen or Mucha, became known because they worked in or located to the US and Western Europe. If one looks at the British

Film Institute's series of publications of 'Film Classics', there are no Central or East European films in a list numbering some seventy titles. Kieślowski and the Serbian director Dušan Makavejev appear in the BFI's Modern Classics series, but only via the *Three Colours Trilogy* (1993–94) and *W.R.–Misterije organizma* (*W.R.–Mysteries of the Organism*, 1971) – titles with explicit Western connections.

The selection of films in this book is designed to provide entry points into the cinematic cultures of the four countries. While all of the films are important, and many outstanding, the collection is not intended to represent the 24 'best films' from Central Europe. There is no balanced reflection of particular historical periods either within or between countries. Thus, for instance, there are only two films from the 1930s, three from the 1990s (two Hungarian and one Slovak) and nine from the 1960s. While all of the films are important in their own right, they have also been selected because of links to national cultures and histories, and to particular artistic tendencies. But while, on balance, I feel this to be a correct selection, it would be possible to select another 24 with almost equal justification.

Some of the major film makers missing from this collection include: from Poland, Agnieszka Holland, Jerzy Skolimowski, Krzysztof Zanussi, Andrzej Żuławski; from Hungary, Péter Bacsó, Zoltan Fábri, István Gáal, Péter Gothár, András Kovács; from the Czech Republic, Gustav Machatý, Miloš Forman, Vojtěch Jasný, Pavel Juráček, Ivan Passer, Evald Schorm, Jiří Weiss, Jiří Trnka, Karel Zeman; and from Slovakia, Peter Solan, Štefan Uher, Dušan Hanák and Elo Havetta. The absence of any Czech and Polish films from the 1990s selection does not imply that there are not important film makers or that the work of Saša Gedeon and Petr Zelenka, Dorota Kędzierzawska and Małgorzata Szumowska, and many others, is not deserving of attention.

The important focus is the extent to which the discussions of the films selected provide access to the cinematic traditions considered. In this connection, the selection includes the unfamiliar – *Hej-rup!* (*Heave-Ho!*, 1934), *The Dybbuk*, *People of the Mountains*, *Daleká cesta* (*Distant Journey*, 1949), *Marketa Lazarová* (1967) – alongside more traditionally-known titles. All too often, the best-known films are those that have been awarded or selected for West European festivals and have been subsequently bought for distribution. Many striking films have never emerged from the cultures that produced them. It is to be hoped that this volume will draw attention to some of the many remarkable achievements that, if they are allowed to reach international audiences, can still produce a powerful impact. There are many ways to read it, by chapters on individual films, by country or chronologically. Despite my reservations on the categorisation of the countries as a region, the films are organised chronologically so that parallel and sometimes unexpected insights may emerge.

Peter Hames

REFERENCES

Artmann, H. C., and Péter Esterházy, Danilo Kiš, György Konrád, Edward Limonov, Claudio Magris, Czeslaw Milosz, Paul-Eerik Rummo, Miklós Mészöly, Adam Michnik (1991) 'The Budapest Roundtable', in Ladislav Matejka (ed.) *Crosscurrents 10: A Yearbook of Central European Culture*. New Haven: Yale University Press.

Davies, Norman (1996) *Europe: A History*. Oxford: Oxford University Press.

Esterházy, Péter (2003) 'Reporting from the Moon', *The Hungarian Quarterly*, 44, 171, 3–6.

Garton Ash, Timothy (1989) 'Does Central Europe Exist?' in George Schöpflin and Nancy Wood (eds) *In Search of Central Europe*. Cambridge: Polity Press.

Hill, John and Pamela Church Gibson (eds) (1998) *The Oxford Guide to Film Studies*. Oxford: Oxford University Press.

Iordanova, Dina (2003) *Cinema of the Other Europe: The Industry and Artistry of East Central European Film*. London: Wallflower Press.

Johnson, Lonnie R. (2002) *Central Europe: Enemies, Neighbors, Friends*. New York: Oxford University Press.

Kundera, Milan (1984) 'A Kidnapped West or Culture Bows Out', Trans. Edmund White, *Granta*, 11, 93–118.

Nemeskürty, István (1968) *Word and Image: History of the Hungarian Cinema*. Trans. Zsuzsanna Horn. Budapest: Corvina Press.

Nowell-Smith, Geoffrey (ed.) (1997) *The Oxford History of World Cinema*. Oxford: Oxford University Press.

O'Connor, Cóilín (2003) 'The Status of Visegrád: A Report from a Budapest Conference', *The New Presence*, 5, 1, 33–4.

Schöpflin, George and Nancy Wood (eds) (1989) *In Search of Central Europe*. Cambridge: Polity Press.

Taylor, Richard, Nancy Wood, Julian Graffy and Dina Iordanova (eds) (2000) *The BFI Companion to Eastern European and Russian Cinema*. London: British Film Institute.

Vincendeau, Ginette (ed.) (1995) *Encyclopedia of European Cinema*. London: Cassell/British

Film Institute.

Wolff, Larry (1994) *Inventing Eastern Europe: The Map of Civilization on the Mind of the Enlightenment.* Stanford: Stanford University Press.

HEJ-RUP! HEAVE-HO!

MARTIN FRIČ, CZECHOSLOVAKIA, 1934

A sunny summertime day. There is a meadow, with an open horizon, rimmed with a road, where an assembly of people gathered under a 'Welcome!' banner is impatiently waiting. A truck slowly drives up. The people see it and shout: 'Hurray, hurray' – but their fervour withers and they grow silent. All the fun of expectation is gone when the poor little jolting truck pulls up.

'Hey, what's up, how come there is no cheer … just a tad?' asks Filip (Jiří Voskovec), standing on the truck bed among milk cans. 'After all, this is our first truck, we have delivered our first batch of milk,' he adds, taken aback.

'So come on, do some cheering,' entreats Jakub (Jan Werich), who is driving the truck.

'All right then. Hurray!' offers somebody in the waiting crowd, while the rest force themselves to express some enthusiasm, which is over almost as soon as it has started.

Filip unloads one milk can, while Jakub elaborates on the dubious qualities of the ancient truck. Then someone in the crowd discovers that the milk can holds no liquid but butter. Following a brief dialogue with Jakub, who is the first one to notice the unsuspected outcome of the truck's poor shock absorbers, Filip yells with a Russian accent: 'Maslóstroj!' [butter machine]. There then follows a rapid montage of the flabbergasted faces of individuals in the crowd and of the truck's parts, accompanying Filip's cheerful prodding, in quasi-Russian, of the bystanders to admire the butter-churning contraption. Soon they are all chanting: Da, da, da, da, da. Then the camera switches to a high angle as the accelerating 'da, da, da' slowly transmutes into the hard-to-hear din of the engine. The 'butter machine' keeps jolting along in circles in the now-empty area. The sequence provides a fairly clear reference to the 'cream separator' episode in Sergei Eisenstein's *Generalnaya linya* (*The General Line*, 1929) and the ranks of tractors that appear in its final scenes. Jiří Voskovec left a valuable personal testimony about this 'butter machine' sequence in a letter written more than thirty years later:

Ah yes, the 'butter machine' in *Heave-Ho!* A grand, bitter, absurd exuberance: When some years ago I spent nearly a year in captivity on Ellis Island as a suspect whose 'presence in the United States could be to the detriment of the States' security' – this Catholic sort of a fascist, a Mr. Chudoba …, testified how this scene in *Heave-Ho!* was actually pro-Soviet propaganda. I started laughing aloud in the courtroom and my defense counsel had to caution me. Of course, I then produced a witness, Dr Brumlík, with whose aid we managed to tear Brother Chudoba to pieces. For me, it is a bottomless well of private fun that when Jan and I made fun of that idiotic *'adoration of the tractors'* in the silly 1930s Soviet films – the 'progressives' and card-carrying Communist Party members were horrified – and later on in the America of the McCarthy era I got bumped on the head again, this time on the opposite side, mind you, yet it's still my head…

The lengthy (almost three minutes) 'butter machine' sequence turned out to be significant for *Heave-Ho!* and serves as a convenient starting point for discussions on the supposed bias of that film – and that brings us to Osvobozené divadlo (the Liberated Theatre), the home stage of Jiří Voskovec and Jan Werich.

Heave-Ho! is a 'theatre-holidays' film. It was made in the summer of 1934, between the seventh and the eighth Liberated Theatre seasons, when the theatre's principal performers, writers and protagonists, Voskovec and Werich, were enjoying their holidays. Back in the early 1930s, their comedy theatre constituted a Mecca on the cultural map of Prague to which faithful audiences, the integral 'co-creators' of its prominence, made repeated visits. At the centre of all Liberated Theatre productions was the team of Voskovec and Werich (popularly known as V+W), who built on traditional clowning principles, which they enriched with elements of contemporary absurd humour and poetic imagery, creating a poetics of sense in nonsense. The creative identity of the actor-poets V+W was crystallised in the originality of their closing speeches, prodded by the inspiration of the moment, removed from schematism, and in immediate touch with the audience. On the basis of its essentially democratic, 'dialogic' nature, the Liberated Theatre perceived social developments in the context of political change (the worldwide depression, unemployment, the growing threat of fascism in Europe). Lively and responsive, its performances gradually moved away from the poetic, exotic and general world of pure comedy toward political and social satire, which gained in importance as the era's political atmosphere became more acute.

In the seventh year of their stage collaboration, V+W wrote and produced a piece entitled *Osel a stín* (*Donkey and Shadow*). In this relentless anti-fascist satire, in which analogies were presented with political developments in Germany and the onset of the Nazi regime, Voskovec and Werich played the roles of plebeians. They poked fun at political dilettantism, demagogy and various types of fanaticism, and pointed to the funding of the Nazi movement, and the links between German big capital and the Nazi Party. Although the play was the Liberated Theatre's most successful and critically acclaimed production to date, and performances were usually sold-out, the authors unexpectedly withdrew it from the repertoire.

It was replaced with a 'mere' but extensive (as far as the changes were concerned) adaptation of *Slaměný klobouk* (*The Italian Straw Hat*), by Labiche. It was only the second time in their career that V+W had selected a play they did not write and one that had been staged many times before. They took the eight-act vaudeville play back to the year 1900. Here they combined beauty with revulsion, complicated attractions and the outdated, quaint fashions of the end of the century. The play's atmosphere was based on a combination of these contradictory elements, but audiences did not take to it. Theatregoers wanted live observations on contemporary affairs, up-to-date commentaries and current political anecdotes; they did not wish to be distracted by the retro spirit of the *fin de siècle*. Still, *The Italian Straw Hat* played until the end of the season. The classic farce gave Voskovec and Werich a certain kind of 'break' after the tense, emotionally-charged atmosphere of *Donkey and Shadow* where every night the audiences demanded new improvisations reflecting the latest political developments. Against the background of this contrasting dramaturgical divide, the definitive script for *Heave-Ho!* was being written.

In many aspects, the film comedy *Heave-Ho!* was successful as a kind of joyful parody. Its timely topic touched on many filmgoers' everyday lives; it responded to the pressing problem of the period – unemployment – and it presented (for the first time in Czech cinema, it appears) a capitalist who went bust. The major part of the plot takes place in working-class suburbs and does not gloss over the plight of the unemployed. For that reason, people expected it to provide a solution, a programme of action, a prescription, as the film's reception at the time reveals. Not a single review failed to include such demands. However, this serious topic was approached in a completely slapstick fashion in *Heave-Ho!* making it far removed from reality.

The critics at the time were unanimous in elevating *Heave-Ho!* to a level of European importance, ranking the movie – which was unlike anything else in Czech film production – alongside such masterpieces as René Clair's *A nous la liberté* (1931), Charlie Chaplin's *City Lights* (1931) and King Vidor's *Our Daily Bread* (1934): 'The first Czech social film ever was made by Voskovec and Werich in the comedy *Heave-Ho!* However, they did not depict our contemporary circumstances, but rather, on the circumstances' ruins, they attempted to build a new society of young people.' Jan Kučera wrote upon the film's release that *Heave-Ho!* restored confidence in the future and the joy of life, attempting, as Voskovec and Werich said in a 1937 interview, to be 'not only a comedy, but also a film, which within the conventions of comedy, defended the optimistic solidarity of young people against the woes of economic depression.' Its overall utopian flavour was a disappointment to some, or, at best, a mere inconsistency, even an irresponsibility. Others considered it to be fearless and outspoken. In any case, it was worth talking about as it not only provoked discussion but also embodied it, since, in itself, it did not create – or even attempt – any kind of rigid ideological analysis.

Heave-Ho! can be seen as a refined, balanced parody, pursuing a circular course beginning and ending in the interior of Mr. Worst's office. The film opens and ends there. The caricatures of black-clad shareholders are replaced by those of shareholders wearing white T-shirts. Actually, both groups are the subjects of parody, as are the characters of the protagonists – a factory owner and an unemployed man. Individual supporting characters leave that imaginary circle of parody at various points and for various lengths of time, since the circle is permeable, even unsustainable. Voskovec and Werich do not respect the outline of the circle. They do not wish to respect it, but they have to take it into account. The circle they are describing primarily serves their comic routines as they skip from subject to subject, in both words and situations. Functioning more or less in a stand-alone (parenthetic) form, the slapstick appearances of V+W become the dominant element of *Heave-Ho!*'s film style. In the individual sections of the circle, their clowning routines make limited use of the possibilities of film language, and cannot disguise their stage origins. They do not deny their links to a specific space and time, and this produces a certain kind of 'tour de force' – 'a cabinet', a centripetal comic style. The comic style (accompanied by parody and self-parody) rushes on into the film's first level. But the real space captured on the screen is centrifugal, referential.

The 'ruthless' realism of the film medium in many respects fails to sustain the illusion achieved by V+W's original onstage clowning (regardless of the extent to which the techniques of their comic play may be anti-illusory). In a nutshell, it can be said that all four of V+W's films provide a continuing search for the possibilities of how to adapt their original comic style (theatrical in principle, because based on improvisation) for the silver screen. *Heave-Ho!* is characterised precisely by this 'split', best observed if compared to their next movie, *Svět patří nám* (*The World Belongs to Us*, 1937), where the comic routines of V+W acquire a larger degree of 'autonomy' and the entire film is composed in a more illusory manner.

In summary, against the social-cum-optimistic ground plan of comedy in *Heave-Ho!*, one can see a parodic game plan – playing through film and playing with film. Regardless of whether we see this finding positive or negative, it has to be noted here that the paradoxical dual interpretation of the 'butter machine' sequence actually applies to *Heave-Ho!* as a whole.

Ze dne na den (*One Day at a Time*) is what the 'great feature slapstick comedy' was originally meant to have been called. As the magazine *Filmový kurýr* (*Film Courier*) predicted, it would achieve 'world renown' since in it 'Liberated comedians' Voskovec and Werich intended to delve into a topic everybody was interested in, namely the great depression. *Film Courier* went on to say that Voskovec and Werich would not play the characters familiar from their theatre productions but rather 'two of us, two regular civilians mercilessly pursued by the depression: an unemployed worker and a factory owner without a job, who eventually team up to cope with the depression in a unique way.' So said the first official press release about the forthcoming film as published on 27 April 1934, one day short of a half a year before the premiere.

The *One Day at a Time* project was financially underwritten by producer Emil Meissner. In early May it was still unclear who would direct the film. There were rumours it would be German director Erich Engel, but in late June the press reported that Martin Frič would direct Voskovec and Werich and that the shooting would begin in early July. The erection of interior sets begun at the Barrandov studios on 13 July 1934 and, on the same day, the new name of the film was announced: *Hej-rup! Chceme žít! (Heave-Ho! We Want To Live!)*. The shooting began in five days and all the interior scenes were completed in three weeks. Although the premiere was scheduled for late September (director Martin Frič and director of photography Otto Heller already had contracts for another movie and Voskovec and Werich were finishing a new play to open their eighth season), the shoot lasted until mid-October. Frič completed the final shots on 10 October and started editing the film. The film's opening credits, which are in Jiří Voskovec's writing, introduced the abbreviated and definitive name: *Hej-rup! (Heave-Ho!)* The music, composed by Jaroslav Ježek (who wrote the music for the majority of V+W's plays), was synchronised one week before the premiere. Destined to become hits, a blues song 'One Day at a Time', and the pivotal 'spirited song', the march, 'Heave-Ho! We Want To Live!', were recorded by Voskovec and Werich in a studio on 7 October so that the recording would reach the stores at the time of the premiere.

On Thursday, 25 October 1934, at the cinema Alfa in, Prague, the Liberated Theatre Orch-estra under the baton of Jaroslav Ježek opened the gala premiere of *Heave-Ho!* It was received positively by audiences and critics. In the first ten days, it was seen by more than 30,000 spectators, or an average of 875 per show (at that time, Cinema Alfa seated 1,100). Four weeks after the premiere, it was still going strong and Cinema Alfa added an extra week; some 70,000 moviegoers saw the film by the end of November. Seventeen prints were distributed across the country to appreciative audiences. Producer Emil Meissner left for Paris in early November to negotiate a French version of the film to be shot in Prague. Save for Voskovec and Werich, only French actors were to be cast in it. Articles reported that Jiří Voskovec was working on a French-language script. By the end of the year, a trial introductory scene was made where Voskovec and Werich introduced themselves in French, but the whole idea fizzled out.

In March 1935, *Heave-Ho!* was presented at the Moscow Film Festival (the first international festival in the Soviet Union, which was held to celebrate the Soviet cinema's first 15 years). Paradoxically, it won a prize. Although Voskovec and Werich parodied the style prevalent in Soviet films, they received a major award from the jury for their 'masterful' acting performances. In August 1935, *Heave-Ho!* was featured at the international film festival in Venice where its reception left more to be desired. It was shown in Paris, Brussels and London. Again, there were talks about producing English and French versions, but in the end, *Heave-Ho!* was not even dubbed into German that year. Within two years it was nevertheless sold to most European countries and to North America, as well as being shown in Palestine. The last pre-war mention, in the summer of 1938, stated that the film had been purchased by the Hunnia company, which intended to dub *Heave-Ho!* into Hungarian. In the summer of the following year, *Heave-Ho!* appeared on a list of films prohibited from public cinemas in the now German-occupied Protectorate of Bohemia and Moravia.

'Fresh milk beats canned milk'. With some exaggeration, this is how the slogan on a *Heave-Ho!* film poster might read. Mr. Worst, an older man confined to a wheelchair, and president of a company manufacturing canned milk, decides to ruin his competitor, dairy magnate Jakub Simonides (Werich). Supplied with lots of booze, Jakub is deliberately kept in a bar for several days at a card game, while his firm's shares are plummeting. Before Jakub learns that his company is finished, he hears a sincere (and uncensored) live speech on the radio by the unemployed Filip Kornet (Voskovec). The speech moves him so much that he goes to the radio station and offers Filip the position of secretary. Afterwards, Jakub has to withdraw the offer because he is insolvent, but Filip offers to be his guide through the life of the unemployed.

Together, they walk around the working-class suburbs; they sleep over at a shelter for the poor, and the next day, under more or less adventurous circumstances, they look for a job. In the evening, they see a discarded railway carriage, now inhabited by Miss Marta. Jakub soon remembers her as the barmaid from the drinking establishment where he went on that binge and where he lost his wallet. Marta has found it. There are no banknotes in the wallet but there is a letter confirming that Jakub has become a property owner and has inherited a half-built factory.

With enthusiastic assistance from other jobless people, the trio of Jakub, Filip and Marta complete the construction of the unfinished building. They set up a working co-operative which they call Heave-Ho, after the phrase used for encouragement in work. Now they also use it as a greeting. The manufacturing co-op's earnings are put into a common account. In a few months, Jakub, now a member of the collective leadership, and his Heave-Ho gang are competitors to Worst, as they supply fresh milk to the market and get more and more customers. Worst's renewed attempt to get rid of Jakub Simonides fails and, in the end, the Heave-Ho gang become shareholders in Worst's company.

Václav Wasserman wrote the first version of the *Heave-Ho!* script and an outline. The original script covers 63 scenes. In nine instances, there are individual scenes prefaced with a note in parentheses – 'as proposed by V+W'. This testifies to the fact that Voskovec and Werich prepared certain key scenes to initiate action regardless of the outer plot, 'their own' places with the atmosphere and ingredients for a film scene, exchanges to which the future action of the film was to be attached.

While the Wasserman outline only provided a basic plot for the film, the unemployed couple and the female protagonist – a barmaid – it also included several sketches for future scenes, already penned into the original version of the script. These included the radio speech given by Worker X, the bar scene, the doss-house arguments and disputes, the construction of the Heave-Ho gang's cooperative building, and the dangerous, Harold Lloyd-like scene on the 'Systém Březinův' scaffolding, including the jump into the firemen's jumping sheet.

Heave-Ho! is in many respects an uneven film: in the protagonists' acting, in its setting and in its approaches to filmmaking. The episodic structure provides room for the individual appearances of Voskovec and Werich in diverse settings. They always remain at the centre of what is happening, since the film would be nothing without them. Frequently, they undermine the dramatic parts of their film characters, parodying them to the maximum, or remain fragmentarily authentic (i.e. Voskovec and Werich in person).

There is a straightforward reason for this 'weakness' in their acting for the screen. It issues from the personality-based type of acting which had established their 'brand name' in comedy and was further developed and validated by performances at their theatre company. The ad-libbing clowns of their 'curtain speeches' provided the basis for the Liberated Theatre's success. They allowed a space for V+W's *spontaneous* humour and *inspired* acting: lyricism and absurdity, the daze of a brainwave, the fall into the abyss of words – the play with an idea, the play with a word, play in a play.

It is obvious that this method could hardly be transferred to the screen. While the incompatibility between the 'realism' of film images and the techniques of improvisation does blur the V+W acting style somewhat, it also turns *Heave-Ho!* into a singular encounter. It records fragments of such improvisations, providing evidence of a certain developmental phase in the work of V+W. Examples can be found in their dialogue during the opulent dinner next to the bizarre statue and, more especially, in the scene where Jakub tries to explain to Filip and Marta that he is the owner of the house.

Otto Heller's camerawork upholds the high standard of the period. In an interview, Voskovec and Werich assessed his work and saw it as certainly very good, if occasionally uneven. According to them, the photography's 'signature style' was supposed to reflect certain of the exterior scenes. Here the couple are featured with workers at the building being constructed, a high sky in the background, scenes overexposed to dark through a filter, the faces in front, and the scaffolding shot with the sun at the cameraman's back, with no backlighting, making use of the soft plasticity of lights and shadows. The co-authors would have liked the entire film shot in this fashion. The incongruity of certain images, as the film's co-creators saw it, followed from the diversity of individual scenes with different kinds of atmosphere and an unusual number of exteriors.

The combination of interjections, 'heave-ho', is used to indicate a rhythm when working together. Unlike the meaning of the original title, *One Day at a Time*, which expressed sudden change (maybe for the better), but also despair, hopeless waiting and melancholy, the encouragement-laden title *Heave-Ho!* demonstrates the fact that the ensuing form of the film is organised precisely by rhythm. This is no accidental development but a deliberate directorial approach.

The entire film is based on a compromise between the protagonists' spirited improvisation, their free-associating capabilities at a given moment, staking out claims to an undisputed space, and the direction of Martin Frič, who used a range of specifically film-related means reflecting the conventions of the period. Simply put: where V+W permit it, Frič can have his space too. Frič nonetheless fully uses up the space allotted to him. Here we are witnesses to a rare creative symbiosis. The innovative theatrical clowns and would-be film comedians found their ideal collaborator in the person of Martin Frič, an experienced director of film comedies with an instinctive understanding of the poetics of their humour. Frič filmed more than a hundred films during his career, many of significance, but his films with V+W are probably among the best.

The screening time is 104 minutes. Perhaps it is surprising how this span of time is allotted among the four segments. The first, which needs to convey the majority of the information, takes 22 minutes; the second segment, during which there is much travel during a single day of the film's story, takes 42 minutes; while the third and fourth sections take 20 minutes each. Another unimportant but interesting point can be discerned if we split the journey's time in half. Just at that time, at this divide, Jakub and Filip sing the 'One Day at a Time' blues. And – what a coincidence – it is precisely at this point, in one of the film's key comic sequences, that the steamroller (which they use to iron trousers) goes out of control.

A sunny summertime day. There is a meadow with an open horizon … In this way *Heave-Ho!* is recorded in the imaginary calendar of Czech cinematography.

Václav Kofroň

REFERENCES

Anon. (1937) 'Interview s Voskovcem a Werichem', *Pressa*, 157 (30 July), 3.

Kučera, Jan (1934) 'Kovsek bilance za pul roku', *Ceské slovo*, 300 (28 December), 12.

Voskovec, Jiří (1965) Letter to Petr Král (8 December), unpublished.

DER DIBUK THE DYBBUK

MICHAŁ WASZYŃSKI, POLAND, 1937

Der Dibuk (The Dybbuk), made by Michał Waszyński in 1937, is often claimed to be the finest accomplishment of Yiddish film produced in Poland before the Second World War. At that time the three-million strong Polish-Jewish community established not only significant centres of Jewish culture in all the main Polish cities of Warsaw, Kraków, Vilnius and Łódź but also contributed significantly to the development of Polish culture. Despite the antipathy toward this community or, more bluntly put, anti-Semitic attitudes in parts of Polish society, Polish Jews managed to create works of literature, theatre, film, music and painting of lasting importance.

The contribution of Polish Jewry to the development of pre-war Polish cinema is of particular importance and was by no means limited to Yiddish cinema (which was aimed both at local and international audiences, especially in the US). Polish Jews also produced Polish cinema's main artistic achievements (such as the films of Józef Lejtes) and included considerable box-office successes Among the many film studios and companies, there were two important Jewish studios, both located in Warsaw: Green Film and Kinior. Other film companies also produced for the local Polish-Jewish audience. However, due to the instability of the Polish film industry, they disappeared as quickly as they emerged. According to different historical sources, about 40 Jewish films (in Yiddish or Hebrew), both feature and documentary, were produced in pre-war Poland, accounting for a significant proportion of the world production of Jewish film, estimated at 170 films in this period. Among these, The Dybbuk is undoubtedly one of the greatest achievements.

The Dybbuk was produced by the Phoeniks Film Company run by Izydor and Fayga Fenigstein. The screenplay, based on the renowned play by Solomon Ansky (Shloyme-Zanvl ben Aaron Hacohen Rappoport), was written by Alter Kacyzne, the owner of the copyright to the writer's work. However, the idea of adapting the play came from Ludwig Prywes, who financed the famous production of it by the Vilna Troupe (Di Vilner Trupe). To collaborate on adapting the work, Kacyzne invited Mark Arnstein, renowned theatre director at that time, together with professor Meyer Balaban from Warsaw University, to oversee the historical background of the events represented. Waszyński, one of the most famous film directors of the popular cinema in pre-war Poland and known as an extremely efficient filmmaker (he was frequently acclaimed for his ability to make films below the estimated budget), was a perfect candidate for this assignment. Indeed, he responded to the opportunity with great enthusiasm. As noted in the Polish newspaper *Dziennik* (*Daily*):

> A year ago he [Waszyński] was asked to direct a Jewish musical comedy with the renowned American-Jewish actress [Molly Picon in the film *Yidl Mitn Fidl/Yidl with a Fiddle*, directed by Joseph Green and Jan Nowina-Przybylski, 1936]. However, at that time he rejected this offer, as he had not been very keen on the project. Yet, he grew enthusiastic when he was asked to direct *The Dybbuk*. He was fascinated with the monumentalism of the movie and the mystical romanticism of its content. The prospect of creating a film to be representative of Jewish cinema was so tempting that he could not resist. Besides, he found himself among zealots, who could not forget the overwhelming impression made on them by *The Dybbuk* as a mystery play. These zealots were for example a writer, Alter Kacyzne – a friend of Ansky and the publisher of his works – Henikh Kahn – one of the most intelligent of Jewish composers – and Avrom Marevsky, a renowned Jewish actor, who became famous as a *tsaddik* from Miropolye in the Vilna Troupe's production. Their enthusiasm passed on to the director, who still affectionately talks about his deep satisfaction with his work on *The Dybbuk*.

Avram Marevsky, an actor who played the role of the *tsaddik* from Miropolye (a *tsaddik* is a leader of the Hasidic community) all over the world for dozens of years, was one of the people to whom Ansky read his play for the first time in Vilnius. However, Ansky was to die soon afterward. Over the grave of the writer, Marevsky and David Herman, both members of the Vilna Troupe, decided to stage the play within the 30-day period of mourning for Ansky's death. They kept their promise, and the premiere took place on 9 December 1920 in the Elizeum Theatre in Warsaw. Six months later Marevsky staged it in Vilnius, which at that time as well as Lithuania was part of Poland. Thus, before Waszyński's film appeared on the screen, *The Dybbuk* was well-known to both Jewish and Polish theatre audiences. The first Polish translation was staged in 1925 in the Teatr Miejski (State Theatre) in Łódź, then in Warsaw, in the theatre Szkarłatna Maska (Scarlet Mask). These performances, made with the intention of 'breaking the wall between the two neighbouring cultures' met with an enthusiastic reception.

Waszyński's intention was to convey all the mysticism of Hasidism as expressed in Ansky's play. In addition, in his concern for the popular, he, along with the screenwriters, decided to make the original work more directly within the demands of mainstream cinematic form. This required a transformation of the existing form into a coherent narrative. To achieve this aim, Alter Kacyzne decided to re-work the story, beginning with events from the past that are only briefly related in the play in Act IV. It takes almost a third of film before the story reaches the point where the play begins.

This change not only allowed a narrative more appropriate for film but also resulted in an emphasis on an 'earthly prologue' that leads to the spiritual bonds of love that grow between Leah (Lili Liliana) and Khonon (Leon Liebgold). The earth-bound nature of their initial love had been marginalised in the play. To prevent this newly-developed part of the story from becoming too realistic and, as such, moving too far from the original, an introductory voiceover commentary was added: 'In the soul of the Jewish nation there is a deeply-rooted belief in magical forces and invisible ghosts. These dark ideas are expressed in the Kabbalah, a work devoted to the fantastic which is full of miracles. The belief in the wandering of souls acquired a special character here. The figure of the Messenger looks after the fulfilment of fate. Though he takes a human, yet uncanny, form, it is easy to recognise from his words and deeds that he is an emissary of the spiritual world.' These words are followed by a long shot of the wanderer walking along a valley. He disappears at a point that allows the viewer to identify him as the Messenger (Isaac Samberg). By means of these devices the first part of the story, though mostly realistic in terms of its mode of representation, is laced with elements of spirituality and the fantastic, locating it 'between two worlds,' and introducing the viewer to the ideas of Hasidism, a mystical strand of Judaism that developed in Eastern Europe in the eighteenth century.

The main story begins with a scene at the *tsaddik* of Miropolye's house. A panning shot shows a row of Jews sitting at a table and singing, the *tsaddik* in the centre of the group. In the next exterior shot, the strange, dark figure of a Jew enters the crowd of poorer Jews who try to look through the window into the *tsaddik*'s house. Then he says: 'One should see the way he is going on.' One of the Jews answers: 'How can I see it, if nobody has opened my eyes yet?' This small episode can be seen as a mould according to which the fictional world is to be developed throughout the film, that is, a realistic situation (the Jews crowding next to the window) is disrupted, or contradicted, by the element of the symbolic or fantastic (here, the dialogue). Then the camera returns to the interior and singles out two men in medium close-up, Nissen (Gershon Lamberger) and Sender (Moyshe Lipman), who try to say something to the *tsaddik*.

Just before they approach him, the strange Jew enters the room and introduces himself as the Messenger. He greets the *tsaddik* and offers him a bottle of wine. Nissen and Sender try again to approach the *tsaddik* and are again unsuccessful. However, later, in the synagogue, they manage to make a pledge to marry their future children if these should be a boy and a girl. Witnessing this, the Messenger says: 'One cannot make such a reckless plea. One cannot decide about the fate of children who are not yet born', and then adds: 'My mission is over.'

A dramatic twist of events then ensues: Sender's wife dies while giving birth to her daughter, Leah, and Nissen drowns in a lake at the same moment that his son, Khonon, is born. Nissen says just before his death: 'Sender, remember!' The following montage sequence is aimed at showing that, with the passing of the years, Sender gradually becomes more focused on the material aspects of life and seems unlikely to remember the pledge. There are three scenes in which the viewer sees him counting money at his desk, asking his daughter Leah not to disturb him. However, the past inevitably returns to enter the present. An apparently accidental encounter of Sender and Khonon is actually due to the intervention of the Messenger. When Sender finally invites Khonon to his home, destiny is fulfilled. The meeting of Leah and Khonon is presented as a 'romantic love' that overwhelms the couple at first sight. Of course, cultural conventions demand that the sudden and unrestrained emergence of such love has to be accompanied by an instant appearance of the obstacles that will bring about its disastrous end. Here, Leah's father seems to be one such obstacle. In a medium shot we see Leah and Khonon sitting at the right and left sides of a table, opposite each other, while Sender stands between them. They do not begin talking to each other until the father falls asleep at the table (which again makes the situation itself fit melodramatic conventions).

The tragic possibility of this love is marked even more conspicuously in the following scene, in which Leah walks Khonon to the porch, from which he notices with surprise the grave in the middle of the street just opposite Sender's house. Leah explains to him that this is 'a holy grave' of a bride and groom killed by the Cossacks in one of the pogroms in 1648 just as they were being led to the wedding canopy. As Leah tells the story of the tragic couple they approach the grave and stand on its right and left side respectively. Suddenly the figure of the Messenger appears behind the grave between them, a repetition of the visual pattern used in the earlier scene with the father at the table.

This initial scene of the couple's first encounter, as well as Sender's consequent efforts to find a husband for Leah, shifts the story away from the symbolism and spirituality of Ansky's original. In place of these, patterns of melodrama and 'family romance' are used to a significant extent. (Another generic affinity of *The Dybbuk*, the horror genre, could be taken into account, but, as Ira Konigsberg notes, the play comes from the tradition of 'Hasidic Gothic', far from the tradition of horror as developed in classical cinema.) Time is spent presenting Sender looking for a proper husband for Leah and arranging the marriage as if it were a business enterprise. This mercantile attitude to marriage is contrasted with the highly spiritual one represented by Khonon and Leah. The scene in which Sender explains to Khonon that the future husband of his daughter has to be rich fits into melodramatic structures particularly well. At the same time, this scene triggers a spiritual strand of the plot previously marked by the figure of the Messenger. The next scene takes place in a synagogue where, for the first time, Khonon tries to get unearthly help to unite him with his beloved. In the presence of his *yeshiva* colleague, Henekh, he says: 'I want … I want to seize a clear and brilliant diamond … to dissolve it in tears and to draw it into my soul! I want to seize the rays of the third Temple, the third divine emanation. I want … Yes! There are still two barrels of gold coins that I must get for the one who can count only gold coins.' Although Henekh warns him that this is not the way to achieve this aim, Khonon leaves the synagogue and goes to take a ritual bath during which he falls into a state of ecstasy. This is observed through the window by a terrified Henekh who is suddenly approached by the Messenger, saying, 'The Devil can be summoned only by uttering the mighty double name of God whose flame dissolves the highest mountain crests and melts them into the deepest valleys … The danger is … that the vessel might shatter because of the great intensity of the spark's longing for the flame.' He also adds that any effort to warn Khonon is in vain, 'Let everybody go their own way.'

Khonon's idea of eternal love transcends the earthly dimension of the young lovers' mutual fascination. Although the love scene that takes place in the synagogue is included in the play, Kacyzne and Waszyński transformed it and added new elements to create one of the most impressive and original love scenes in cinema. It begins in the *yeshiva*, when Khonon says to his friend, Henekh, that everything in this world is God's creation, hence even evil contains an element of holiness. Then, through parallel editing the scene follows of Leah coming to the synagogue to see the old embroidered hangings on the Ark. In the *yeshiva* Khonon continues, 'What sin is the most powerful? What sin is the hardest to conquer? The sin of lust for a woman. But if the sin is purified in the heat of a strong flame this vilest uncleanness is transformed into the greatest holiness, into the *Song of Songs*.' And now, all of a sudden, the *yeshiva* students begin singing the *Song of Songs*. Khonon takes a leading part as if it was addressed directly to Leah, who he does not know is in the adjacent space of the synagogue. The following shot shows her listening to the song as if it were the confession of love she had so longed for. Khonon walks in a trance to the door leading to the synagogue where he can see Leah. He approaches Leah, who remains motionless until her auntie takes her hastily away. Waszyński's usage of parallel editing and off-screen space allowed him to achieve in this scene an emotional tension of exceptional strength.

The *Song of Songs* is used in the film as a recurrent motif. In the first sequence, Nissen sang it for the *tsaddik*. Now Leah sings it in the presence of her father who responds to it with a sudden astonishment for, as he admits, only his old friend Nissen could perform it in that way. Then he learns from Leah that Khonon must be his friend's son who should marry his daughter. Although terrified by this unexpected discovery, he does not change his mind regarding his marriage plan for Leah, which is a change in relation to the play, as in the original Sender does not learn of Khonon's identity. In the play, the misery of the couple is the result of fate, whereas in the film, it is the result of deliberate action undertaken by Leah's father, allowing us to see him as a variant of the melodramatic figure of the villain. Moreover, Leah's father, with his emphasis on money, clearly represents the rich and powerful, whereas Khonon with his concern for spiritual values, belongs to the poor and powerless. This accords with the emphasis in melodrama that it 'sides with the powerless'. These changes partly shift the story towards the melodramatic structures virtually absent in Ansky's original.

This dramatic conflict resulting from Sender's action reaches its climactic point in the next sequence, in which Khonon dies. Again, parallel editing provides the flow of events with an emotional and dramatic tension. After learning about Leah's forced engagement, Khonon decides to use Kabbalistic spells to change the situation and finally conjures up Satan for help. Low camera angles, expressionistic lighting, smoke effects and exaggerated acting move the scene from the realist mode. Images of Khonon are juxtaposed with rhythmically inserted images of Hassidim ecstatically dancing at Leah's engagement. Khonon's emotions are intertwined with the movement of the dance, and this rhythmical path finally reaches its peak when Khonon falls dead on the synagogue floor.

Waszyński's film expands the original story in relation to diegetic space. Two scenes occurring in the cemetery are typical in this regard and add to the film's visual power. The first is the melodramatic scene of Khonon's funeral at which Leah, according to generic conventions, faints at the grave of her beloved. The second precedes Leah's wedding ceremony. She comes with her auntie to invite her mother's soul to her wedding, but in the end the scene turns into her passionate confession of love. The image of Leah sitting at the grave, gently holding the tombstone, and saying, 'Come to me, my beloved. Sleep my baby', epitomises the idea of eternal love as transcending the limits of earthly reality. The darkly-lit image of the lonely grave surrounded with wild trees and bushes immersed in a mysterious mist recalls romantic painting in its conjunction of horror and beauty.

Elements of surreal horror pervade the following, probably the most spectacular, scenes in the film, that is, the 'Dance of the Beggars' and the 'Dance of Death'. The amazing effect gained in these scenes is due to Judith Berg's choreography and Albert Wywerka's cinematography. The first dance is the customary dance of a bride with poor people. The second one takes place during the prenuptial ceremonies. After the words, 'everything that's alive must pass away. Human life is like a dance of death' a crowd of the beggars begin their 'Dance of Death', pulling Leah into their circle. Her inert body is rapidly passed among the dancers until she is caught by the figure with the Death mask. The couple start whirling in a rapid movement that is reinforced through the fast circular camera movement. The crowd dissolves into a shapeless mass and a close-up of Leah is followed by her point-of-view of the Death mask. The mask gradually dissolves into Khonon's face, at which Leah looks tenderly. The scene epitomises the close relationship of love and death variously elaborated in many cultures.

This visionary appearance of Khonon anticipates the moment when his persona as 'dybbuk' enters Leah's body and possesses her. (In Ansky's play the Messenger defines the dybbuk in the following words, 'There are also souls who belong nowhere, who find no peace anywhere; they take possession of another person's body in the form of a dybbuk, and this is way they achieve their purification.') This happens as the engaged couple stand beneath the marriage canopy. Asked to repeat the words of the marriage vow, Leah screams, 'You are not my bridegroom!' She runs to the 'holy grave', falling on it and crying, 'Holy bride and groom, protect me!' Then she slowly stands up, looks far away, and says with Khonon's voice, 'You have buried me! But I have returned to my promised bride and will not leave her!' Finally, the Messenger announces to the terrified crowd, 'A dybbuk has entered the body of the bride.' The crowd flees in horror.

In the last part of the film, when the exorcisms occur, the fictional world conspicuously oscillates between the real world and the world of spirits (as suggested by the initial title of the play, *Between Two Worlds*). However, in the film these events, which were substantial in the original (they are represented in two of four acts) are significantly compressed, and all the monologues of the rabbis significantly shortened. What should be emphasised here is that elements of the spiritual world are placed into the world of the real. Whereas the moment of the dybbuk entering Leah's body is marked by a particular usage of *mise-en-scéne*, lighting and music, the rabbinical court requested by the dead Nissen, and the exorcisms, are presented in a more realistic way. It could generally be said that in the last part of the film all the elements from the 'other' world, due to their recurrence and multiplication, gradually become more familiar and as such permeate the realm of the real in an unrestrained way. In sum, though those two worlds are separated, there are some connections between those who are dead and these who are alive. The events in the rabbinical court as well as the act of exorcism, although fantastic, are motivated by the sense that they are necessary for earthly life to regain its order.

The 'naturalisation' of the fantastic allows the final scene to attain an extraordinary emotional dynamism. After the dybbuk is excommunicated from the community of Israel by the *tsaddik* from Miropolye and finally leaves Leah's body, she loses her consciousness, to regain it after a while. She is left on her own, as everybody has gone to welcome the bridegroom and his father. When she regains consciousness, a genuine poetic dialogue occurs between the lovers:

Leah: Who is here sighing so sadly?

Khonon's voice: It is I.

Leah: Tell me who you are.

Khonon's voice: I had forgotten. It is only through your thoughts that I can remember who I am.

Leah: It was you my heart I was longing for. Why did you leave me again? [line added in the film]

Khonon's voice: I left your body in order to enter your soul.

Leah: Take my soul. My bridegroom, my husband. [line added; after uttering this line she falls dead]

The poetic tenderness of the above lines transforms Leah's dialogue with the soul of the dead Khonon into a genuine expression of true love, understood as eternal, due to its ability to transcend earthly limits and resist human efforts to restrain it. Otherwise, the melodramatic resolution of the narrative through its extrapolation to the realm of the spiritual opens itself up to the ambiguity of the poetic and the mysticism of Hasidic ideas. In the end, the souls of the star-crossed lovers merge with each other, achieving a unity of the psychological and spiritual.

The Dybbuk received mostly positive reviews ranging from those focusing on issues of Jewish culture and mysticism to those in which the influence of Polish culture on Jewish culture was examined. The latter, which I find symptomatic of Polish-Jewish relationships before the Second World War, is represented by the review written by the renowned pre-war Polish film critic Stefania Zahorska. She made a comparison between *The Dybbuk* and *Dziady* (*Forefathers' Eve*, 1823), parts II and IV, by Adam Mickiewicz, the iconic figure of Polish Romantic literature. Although both works share the idea of the duality of the world and both construct ambiguous fictional realities consisting of the elements of real and fantastic, it is certain that Polish Romanticism is not the cultural tradition Ansky was using. Zahorska's critical stance is symptomatic of the cultural mechanism of 'familiarising the Other', that is the strategy of interpreting an 'Other's' text through the blindfold that proposes that it is really another example of 'Ours' after all. Another example of criticism worth mentioning here is the opinion of the Nazi propaganda chief, Joseph Goebbels, who saw *The Dybbuk* as unintentionally anti-Semitic. Apart from these aberrant readings the film was received positively in its day, and is now universally acclaimed as one of the major accomplishments of Jewish film.

The newly restored version of the film was presented at the Festival Theater in New York in September 1989. To a contemporary audience *The Dybbuk* carries a different message than it did in 1937, shortly before the outbreak of the Second World War and the Holocaust that followed. As Ira Konigsberg wrote:

> It is impossible to regain the historical purity of a work and see it through eyes innocent of events that have happened since its creation … *The Dybbuk* is a Kaddish, a prayer for the dead, which asks us to remember the dead. But along with our nostalgia, we bring to the film a sense of the tragic that may not have fully been there to begin with but that makes the film more beautiful and painful to watch. And yet the film dramatises death and loss ultimately to get beyond them, to suggest other paths, other realities that we may not see or understand but that we may certainly sense and feel.

Elżbieta Ostrowska

REFERENCES

Konigsberg, Ira (1997) '"The Only 'I' in the World": Religion, Psychoanalysis, and *The Dybbuk*', *Cinema Journal*, 36, 4, 22–42.

Zahorska, Stefania (1937) 'Dybuk', *Wiadomości Literackie* 44, 6.

EMBEREK A HAVASON PEOPLE OF THE MOUNTAINS

ISTVÁN SZŐTS, HUNGARY, 1942

István Szőts, despite a long career in filmmaking, directed only two feature-length films, *Emberek a havason* (*People of the Mountains* aka *People on the Alps*, 1942) and *Ének a búza-mezőkről* (*Song from the Cornfields* aka *Song of the Cornfields*, 1947); it is a remarkable testimony to his talent, therefore, that Philippe Haudiquet, writing in *Image et son*, declared him the equal of Dovzhenko, Ford or Renoir. Fellow French writer Jean-Pierre Jeancolas thought Szőts fused a realist perspective with a poetic vision in a fashion similar to Jean Vigo, while back in 1942, young, nascent Italian Neorealists such as Francesco Pasinetti and Carlo Lizzani had nothing but praise for *People of the Mountains*. In Szőts' homeland, director Márta Mészáros paid homage to it in *Napló gyermekeimnek* (*Diary for My Children*, 1984) when her protagonist, Juli, watches it in a cinema. Perhaps also to its credit, among other audiences, the film evoked less favorable reactions, such as when the Nazi Minister for Propaganda, Joseph Goebbels, refused it a distribution license. Although it is appreciated mainly by cinephiles outside of Hungary, it is clearly a film that merits attention.

Born in southern Transylvania, then part of Hungary, in 1912, István Szőts grew up in a moderately wealthy family where a longstanding tradition of army service meant enrollment in a military academy. However, through a family connection, he made contact with the popular writer Lajos Zilahy who was also involved in film production, and Zilahy was able to help Szőts find his first work in the film industry. As was standard practice at the time, the newcomer started at the bottom of the studio ladder and worked his way up, gaining valuable experience on films such as László Kalmár's *Halálas tavasz* (*Deadly Spring*, 1939), which featured the Hungarian heart throbs of the day Pál Jávor and Katalin Karády.

His first major break came in 1940 as assistant director on István György's film *Göre Gábor visszatér* (*Gábor Göre Returns*), released by the small Szivárvány Company. More work as assistant director followed, including two films with Endre Rodriguez, one of which, *Néma kolostor* (*Silent Monastery*), released on 22 December 1941, involved the great Hungarian cinematographer István Eiben. In the following year he directed a 15-minute film, *Látogatás Kisfaludy Stróbl Zsigmond műtermében* (*A Visit to Stróbl Zsigmond Kisfaludy's Studio*), about the sculptor Zsigmond Stróbl Kisfaludy, whose famous work 'The Liberation Monument' still adorns the Budapest skyline, on the western bank of the Danube.

The early 1940s was a time when Hungary's relatively small film industry was at its most accessible for newcomers. Numerous small production companies sprang up in Budapest only to disappear towards the end of the war, and many names appear on film credits that had not been seen before or since. However, this situation partly arose because Jewish film personnel were banned from working in the film industry by anti-Semitic legislation. The outbreak of the war, which Hungary would enter as an ally of Nazi Germany in June 1941, also sparked off a growth of filmmaking as the supply of foreign films, invariably more popular than the home product, became increasingly restricted. Another development was the territorial increase in the domestic market, as Hungary finally achieved its long-term goal of occupying those areas it had lost after the First World War, including a large part of Transylvania (Erdely in Hungarian), in the notorious Treaty of Trianon.

But although film production increased, it is true to say that there was, overall, little improvement in quality. Most of the films were undemanding romances, melodramas or adventures, differing little from the films on offer in the 1930s. In such an environment it was not long before Szőts, a real talent in contrast to the many novices and mediocrities around him, began to make his mark. He was offered the chance to direct a project for the Modern Film Company, using the facilities of the Hunnia Film Studio. Based on a collection of stories, *Kopjafák*, by the novelist József Nyírő (1889–1953), this was originally intended to be a short film, shot on a small budget in the Carpathian Mountains, in Transylvania. As the project developed it grew into a feature film taking the title *Emberek a havason* (*People of the Mountains*) with a running time of 103 minutes.

The Hungarian army reclaimed the northern area of Transylvania in August 1940, thus restoring a sense of national pride and much of 'Historical Hungary' (that is, Hungary prior to 1920). Without this manifestation of Hungarian irredentism, achieved under Nazi patronage, Szőts probably could not have made his film. Relations between the Hungarian and Romanian governments were frosty, to say the least, and it is highly unlikely the latter would have granted permission for a Hungarian crew to film in such a sensitive area – the object of claim and counter-claim for much of the twentieth century and home to 2,557,260 Hungarians or 52.1 per cent of Transylvania's total population, according to the 1941 census. Szőts' film therefore appeared at a particular and crucial time in Hungarian history, filmed in an area considered by many to be the heart of a resurrected and reunified Motherland.

Nyírő, a Transylvanian like Szőts, was a popular author of novels and short stories and worked with Szőts on the screenplay. The title of Nyírő's collection of stories, *Kopjafák*, is untranslatable in English, but a *kopjafa* (singular form) is a wooden, ornately carved grave marker or post favoured in certain areas of Transylvania. *People of the Mountains* is set in the region of Transylvania known as the Székelyföld (literally, land of the Székelys), and the Székely people are related to those early Hungarians who settled in the Carpathian Basin; they still speak Hungarian but also have a specific identity and culture. Although their origins or relationship to the broader Magyar entity remain a matter of debate, the Székelys have a particular place within Hungarian mythology, folklore and legend, being seen as a repository of Magyar-ness (in an area now belonging to Romania), and holding on to aspects of a life-style that goes back to the original Magyars. They have a reputation, partly connected to their mountainous habitat, as hardworking and dour, and historically many of them earned their living as herders, subsistence farmers or woodcutters. Paradoxically, the recovery of northern Transylvania by the Hungarians in 1940, rather than creating favourable conditions for the Székelys, probably made their situation worse. In 1921, the Romanian government instituted a range of modest land reforms, but with the territory now returning to Hungary, a number of landowners were able to reclaim their estates. These and other changes created difficulties for the Székelys, whose semi-migratory lifestyle (particularly that of woodcutters and herdsmen) became restricted.

The film concerns a family who live in the high mountains of the Carpathians: husband, Gergő Erdei Csutak, his wife Anna, and their infant son, also called Gergő. Casting for the various parts caused problems, and it was finally decided to give the two leading roles to the relatively unknown János Görbe and Alice Szellay. Görbe, who was to become an enduringly popular film actor after the war, had only appeared in a few films prior to *People of the Mountains*. He first came to the attention of the public with his 1940 performance in *Földindulás* (*Landslide*), directed by Arzén Cserépy. Szőts' feelings toward the actor were contradictory: he found him both crude, with an almost brutal roughness – and mild mannered. But while Görbe had limited film experience, the female lead Szőts chose, Szellay, was a complete novice. Szőts was taking a risk casting these relative unknowns, but it paid off; both turned in compelling performances in spite of their lack of experience – as did the winter weather of early 1942. (In his memoirs Szőts reflected on whether or not established stars would have put up with such conditions). Further, to keep costs down, the production team was reduced to the minimum; there were no painters, hairdressers and make-up artists.

Most of the mountain scenes were shot in and around Gyilkostó (Lacu Rosu in Romanian), approximately 180km directly east of Kolosvár (Cluj). Photography was directed by Ferenc Fekete who, at the last minute, replaced Árpád Makay, a friend of Szőts who had worked with him on the Kisfaludy short film. Fekete was one of a number of brilliant Hungarian cinematographers – a tradition which continues to this day – who rarely had a chance to display their talent due to the tendency for studio shooting, unimaginative storylines and generally low production values. As his first major assignment, he acquitted himself superbly. Away from the confines of the studio, Fekete exploits to the full the brilliant mountain light streaming through towering trees and fog-shrouded valleys which make the mountain tops look as if they are floating on a milky sea. Visually, this is one of the most beautiful films in the history of Hungarian filmmaking. In the end, although the potential for disaster was huge – a shoe-string budget, two novice leads, a debut for the cinematographer, first feature film for the director and a skeleton production team – it somehow all came together to produce an undoubted classic.

The plot of *People of the Mountains* is simple. The couple, Gergő and Anna, and their child live a simple, happy life close to nature guided by their devout religious beliefs. However, poverty forces Gergő to take employment with a lumber contractor while Anna works in the local tavern. The contractor attempts to rape Anna while Gergő is away; she escapes into the mountains and falls into a stream. Found by a search party and close to death, she is taken by Gergő to the city (Kolosvár) to procure medical treatment. With Anna's health failing, they tramp around the city. However, with their money running out, they cannot pay for a doctor, and eventually Anna dies in a cheap boarding house. In a harrowing scene, Gergő, who cannot afford to have her body transported home, carries her onto the train claiming she is asleep. On his return he finds the contractor and kills him; he is then arrested, and although the wood-cutter community come to testify on his behalf, they arrive at the court too late and Gergő is sent to prison. At Christmas, Gergő escapes in a forlorn attempt to see his son and is shot by gendarmes. Although he finds refuge in the hut of a fellow woodcutter, he is fatally wounded. But before he dies, he is able to convince the woodcutter to claim the reward for capturing him and by doing so look after his son. He dies, but his son will be cared for.

The most memorable scenes in the film are those when Gergő, Anna and little Gergő set out from their mountain home to Kolosvár. Anna is seated on a cow, and as the trio wind their way through the mountain tracks they are shot against the backdrop of the cloud-filled valleys. The effect is stunning and exudes the sentiments of a nativity scene, reinforced by their struggle to find accommodation when they reach the city. On the way they hear church bells and join a village congregation to pray for help. Here the film uses archive footage of a religious procession, adding to the sense of realism of the film. At various points, Szőts inserts actuality footage; of woodcutters at work, horses pulling carts of logs and a timber yard – in a number of scenes (the search for Anna, for example) real woodcutters from the mountains were used. The effect is that despite its lyrical beauty and the religious elements, including the occasional paganism (Gergő carves a wooden doll-like figure which he offers to the Virgin Mary in the church scene), *People of the Mountains* is always grounded in a very firm sense of place, environment and culture.

The film, at one level, is an indictment of the conditions of the population, in particular how their traditional way of life is destroyed by the rapacious capitalism of the lumber company who, in contrast to the artisanal way of the woodcutters, cut great swathes through the rich verdant forests of Transylvania. In this respect one could perhaps suggest that *People of the Mountains* is also one of the first 'Green' films. It is also possible to trace elements of William Morris' stress on the maintenance of handicraft versus industrial mass production, Tolstoy's utopianism and even Guild Socialism. Certainly these ideas were popular in the late nineteenth and early twentieth century, at least among certain artistic and intellectual circles in Hungary. The writings of William Morris influenced the establishment of some artist and craftworkers' colonies in Hungary (at Gödöllö for example), while Tolstoy was widely read, and the ideas of Guild Socialism were studied by adherents (such as Karl Polanyi) of the Galilei Circle – an intellectual discussion group – in Budapest in the first decades of the twentieth century. It is true that the film posits a romantic, idyllic notion of rural life, infused with an intense religious belief, but these were powerful trends in Hungarian thinking around this time, as many Hungarians wrestled with alternatives to, on the one hand, fascism (in both its Nazi and home-bred versions) and on the other, the bowdlerised Marxism of the Soviet Union (although this was limited due to the outlawing of the miniscule Hungarian Communist Party). The ethics of the film could thus be usefully seen as an articulation of what was often vaguely referred to as the 'Third Way', however much its 'romantic anti-capitalism' was not to everyone's liking.

The film was released in Hungary on 29 January 1943, around the time the Hungarian Second Army was being slaughtered on the Russian Front at the Battle of the Don. It was, therefore, hardly the most auspicious time for national release, as Hungarians began to realise the consequences of their government's disastrous foreign policy. However, it was reviewed with gusto both by those who liked and disliked it. For example, it certainly made an impact at the 1942 Venice Film Festival. It impressed a number of participants, particularly those associated with the Italian journal *Cinema*, some of whom would later be involved in the Italian Neorealist movement. It was also awarded one of the festival's Biennale prizes, but although *People of the Mountains* no doubt deserved an award, the circumstances need qualification. First, the Venice Festival in 1942 was little more than a jamboree for the Italian fascists, the Nazis and their allies; there was no meaningful competition, and many of the films ranged from the mediocre (Augusto Genina's *Bengasi*) to the truly dreadful (Veit Harlan's *Der Grosse König*). Besides Szőts' film, the only other offering of quality seems to have been *Noi Vivi* (*We the Living*) by Goffredo Alessandrini. Second, the judges (who included one Hungarian, Aladar Haase) seemed keen to please everyone; no less than seven films received the Biennale Award, with another four winning Biennale Medals. Indeed the judges' criteria seemed to be: if it flickers on a screen, give it an award. Under such circumstances, critical response speaks more than winning a somewhat spurious award at a questionable event of limited artistic merit in rather dubious company (Goebbels attended some of the festival).

And what critical response there was. An editorial in *Cinema* (signed L., most likely Carlo Lizzani) headed 'The young teach us' (*I giovani insegnano*) praised the film and its 20-year-old director:

> It proves that young people have a message to convey by means of the cinema. They want to, and do, create and fight in the spirit of art, because they reject all mercenary claims … Let the song of the Alps, the song sounded for the first time by István Szőts' finally penetrate our own studios, and chase away the senile notables of film, the traders and profiteers – and from the Venice Film Festival, too. We believe in the young who will fight and win their own cinema battles.

Other writers and critics were equally enthusiastic. In the same issue of *Cinema*, Francesco Pasinetti praised the film, as did Antonio Pietrangeli in the September issue of *Bianco e nero* (the official publication of the Centro Sperimentale di Cinematografia, the Rome Film School). Not to be outdone, the film critic for *Il Messagaro* waxed lyrical, 'This film is beautiful, unique and inimitable'. Without a doubt the film made an impact, but how influential it was in the development of Italian Neorealism remains a matter for conjecture

The group centred around *Cinema* contain a virtual Who's Who of future Italian cinema, in particular those associated with the rise of Neorealism: Michelangelo Antonioni, the Puccinis, Giuseppe De Santis, Mario Alicata, Luchino Visconti as well as the already mentioned Pasinetti and Lizzani. Dissatisfied both with contemporary Italian film, with its 'blanco telefono' (white telephone) melodramas of high-class life and panegyrics to past Italian glories, and with the policies of Italian fascism (ironically, Vittorio Mussolini, the dictator's son was the editor of *Cinema*), the *Cinema* group were searching for a new direction. Alicata and De Santis, almost a year before seeing *People of the Mountains*, argued passionately for 'a cinema that seeks things and facts inside a definite time and within a realistic space in order to redeem itself from the facile conventions of stultifying bourgeois taste', a prescription which *People of the Mountains* satisfied.

Certainly in Italy it appeared at the right time and in the right place. A number of films which were precursors of Neorealism came out around the time of the Venice Festival. There was Alessandro Blasetti's *Quattro passi fra le nuvole* (*Four Steps in the Clouds*, 1942), Visconti's *Ossessione* (*Obsession*, 1943) and Vittorio De Sica's *I bambini ci guardano* (*The Children Are Watching Us*, 1944). It is tempting therefore to make a number of easy connections. However, the truth is that there is little mention of Szőts and his film in the readily available literature on Neorealism, nor does the 1942 Venice Festival receive much coverage. (For example, the historical section of the official Festival website dismisses it in a few sentences.) It seems likely, then, that *People of the Mountains* acted more as an encouragement than a model for a group of filmmakers, critics and cinephiles who had already taken their first steps in defining a particular trajectory.

In Hungary the reception of the film was mixed. Right-wing critics liked its overt Christianity, which they saw as an affirmation of Christian as opposed to 'Cosmopolitan' (read: Jewish) values, while perhaps conveniently ignoring its pagan elements. The right-wing daily *Új Magyarország* (*New Hungary*, 31 January 1943), for example, praised the film for its 'complete separation of meaning between the Jewish past and a Christian present'. Left critical opinion was equivocal about its 'romantic anti-capitalism' (a phrase initially used by György Lukács earlier in the century). The left-leaning *Népszava* (*People's Voice*, 24 January 1943) criticised the film 'because there was no civilisation, no school, no hospital and other cultural institutions, only a romantic fog which covered reality' and for its 'fake popular character'. Nowadays, the film can be seen, at one level at least, as an example of a wider trend, popular in Hungary prior to the end of the Second World War, of agrarian or rural populism, where the organic values of the honest, unsullied peasantry were pitted against those of the corrupt city and big business. In many instances, however, this collapsed into crude populism and, in its more extreme form, anti-Semitism – the Hungarian countryside representing the true Magyar spirit while the city (particularly Budapest) was denigrated as some curious hybrid Judaeo-Bolshevik/big business Sodom and Gomorrah. *People of the Mountains* avoids this crudity, partly because Szőts simply does not appear to be the type of person who would want to make such a film, and because the powerful performances of Szellay and Görbe infuse their characters with a degree of humanity and decency impossible to detect in films such as *Doctor Kovács István* (*Doctor István Kovács*, Viktor Bánky, 1944), the quintessential Hungarian 'Blut und Boden' film.

The film does, however, completely elide any Romanian presence – this is a completely Hungarian Transylvania, and Szőts must have been aware of this having grown up in the region and being fluent in both Hungarian and Romanian. This no doubt pleased the Hungarian authorities, although one suspects that the Dickensian labour conditions shown were not to their liking, particularly in this newly liberated heartland. The Romanian authorities were, predictably, less than elated. However, they were in no position to do much about this until the war was over, when Transylvania reverted back to Romanian sovereignty. In a delayed retaliation, a 1947 request by Szőts and the Hungarian government to allow him to make a film in Transylvania about the composer Béla Bartók and his famous field research (much of which Bartók undertook in Transylvania) was obstructed by the Romanians and the film never materialised.

Events overtook the film. Within a year of its release, Soviet troops had entered Hungarian territory and elements in the Hungarian government secretly tried to negotiate for peace, to no avail. Hungary was occupied by the Red Army, with Budapest and much of the country in ruins. This brilliant, beautiful film was thus confined to a twilight existence. Szőts, like all Hungarian artists, found working conditions increasingly difficult. In 1944 he made, in collaboration with the composer Zoltán Kodály, an 11-minute short, *Kádár Kata* (*Kata Kádár*), as his contribution to *Szerelmi szivek* (*Loving Hearts*), a film of six episodes, each by a different director. In the last months of the war he devoted himself to a major study of the Hungarian film industry, film art, and the way forward in the post-war period. *Röpirot a Magyar filmművészet ügyében* (*Pamphlet on Behalf of Hungarian Film Art*) was published in Budapest in 1945, and a number of his proposals, such as a film archive, a laboratory and a regular film journal, were eventually adopted.

The rest of his career is chequered to say the least. His second major project, *Song from the Cornfields*, was due for release in early 1948. But the political changes affecting Hungary as it was sucked inexorably into the long night of Stalinism, meant that the film was shelved. Romantic anti-capitalism and poetic lyricism were no longer in favour; Socialist Realism was the order of the day. A third project, *Talpálatnyi föld* (*The Soil Under Your Feet*), was taken from him and given to Frigyes Bán. Szőts spent the next ten years making documentaries, mainly for the Budapest Ethnographic Museum film programme.

In the 1956 Hungarian Uprising, Szőts had the last word – it was mainly his footage of the street-fighting and destruction that was smuggled out of the country by, amongst others, the young László Kovács (later the cameraman on *Easy Rider*, 1969). Szőts himself became part of the 1956 exodus and made his home in neighbouring Austria. Hungarian cinema thus suffered one of its greatest losses; this talented, visionary director spent most of the rest of his life on various projects including short films and documentaries on such subjects as the artists Gustav Klimt, Egon Schiele and Otto Wagner. But despite Szőts' and its own troubled history, *People of the Mountains* still holds a firm place in Hungarian film culture. As one of the first Hungarian films of the 1930s and 1940s to be shot almost entirely on location, with its strong representations of a real place (rather than the previous idealised pastoral Arcadia that too frequently passed for rural Hungary), its deployment of a number of non-professional actors and its commitment to a critique of prevailing conditions, this was a groundbreaking film. The realist trajectory in Hungarian cinema was held up by the war and the post-1945 recovery but was back on track by 1949 with Géza Radványi's gritty portrayal of homeless war orphans in *Valahol Európában* (*Somewhere in Europe*). The promise of *People of the Mountains* and *Somewhere in Europe* did not immediately materialise, however, as Socialist Realism became the state policy. With the more relaxed policies of the 1960s the cultural agenda again began to shift. In 2000, a panel of judges placed it fourth in their twelve best Hungarian films. One question remains and is unanswerable: what if the Hungarian authorities had allowed Szőts to work unhindered? Ultimately, we can only wonder (with dismay) about what might have been.

John Cunningham

REFERENCE

Jeancolas, Jean-Pierre (1989) *Miklós, István, Zoltán et les Autres*. Budapest: Corvina. Magyar Filmintézet/Hungarian Film Institute

DALEKÁ CESTA DISTANT JOURNEY

ALFRÉD RADOK, CZECHOSLOVAKIA, 1949

Daleká cesta (*Distant Journey* aka *The Long Journey*, 1948–49), the first feature film by the Czech theatre and film director, Alfréd Radok, was also the first Czech film to deal with the Holocaust and remains one of the most important. The *New York Times* critic Bosley Crowther described it as 'the most brilliant, the most horrifying film on the Nazis' persecution of the Jews that this reviewer has yet seen'. But while admired by New York film critics in the early 1950s, in Czechoslovakia, it was granted only marginal screenings in the Prague suburbs. Banned for forty years, Czech audiences were only able to see the film again when it was screened on television on 6 May 1991.

Until this time, the film itself had been known only to film historians but, because of its banning, it had acquired a legendary reputation. Its enthusiastic reception in the US and France, where it was the subject of André Bazin's 1952 article, 'Le Ghetto concentrationnaire', remained unknown to the public and Radok himself only heard of these responses at second-hand. But the authorities had achieved their objectives. In Czechoslovakia, the film was suppressed and, in the world at large, it became virtually forgotten.

Distant Journey was filmed in a very difficult and dark time – the autumn and winter of 1948–49. The Communist regime had been established in February 1948 and *Distant Journey* can be seen as one of the last manifestations of cultural freedom preceding the dogmatism that was to be applied in the 1950s. But this freedom was already limited by Communist controls, a factor that was to influence the film's final shape.

The inspiration for the film was personal. Alfréd Radok (1917–76) was half-Jewish on his father's side and many members of his family died in concentration camps. His father and his 90-year-old grandfather died in the ghetto town of Terezín (Theresienstadt), where the last part of *Distant Journey* is set. His father was murdered in the Little Fortress – a special prison within the ghetto that was reserved for political prisoners. When shooting his film on the authentic locations in Terezín, he avoided the Little Fortress, setting the film in other areas.

During the war, Radok worked in the theatre under an assumed name, but later hid in Southern Bohemia before being imprisoned in the detention camp at Klettendorf, near Wrocław, in Poland, from where he escaped. The film was made only three years after the destruction of his own family and, as many witnesses have testified, filming on actual locations at Terezín was very difficult and painful for him. It was an act of great human and artistic courage.

Distant Journey has a special and complex structure that works on three levels. On the first level, it is a melodramatic story about a 'mixed' marriage between two young doctors from the same Prague hospital, the Jewish Hana Kaufmannová (Blanka Walewska) and her 'Aryan' colleague, Antonín ('Toník') Bureš (played by the future theatre director, Otomar Krejča). Their wedding takes place in virtual secrecy during the dark atmosphere of the newly-enacted anti-Semitic laws. Already, the first call-up papers for Terezín are being issued and the word 'transport' is repeated on many lips. The 'distant journey' of the film's title will end mainly in death.

The first part of this love story takes place in Prague, 'a ghetto without walls', an environment full of fear and anxiety. It begins when Hana is dismissed from her position. It is a sad truth that the first order for the Czech government of the so-called Protectorate of Bohemia and Moravia, only two days after the occupation, was for the enactment of the anti-Semitic laws, which were enforced in the Protectorate from 1 September 1941. When Hana and Toník plan to go to the theatre, they remember that Jews have been excluded. A montage of posters and denunciations ends with the instruction 'Jews and dogs forbidden'. They are required to wear the Star of David.

The film's attention gradually shifts to Terezín when Hana's family and, finally, Hana herself are located there. Terezín, a small town about 60km from Prague, was built as a military fortress town in the reign of the Habsburg Emperor Josef II between 1780–90 but it is a historical irony that it only served this purpose during the Nazi occupation. During this time, Terezín was established as a ghetto from November 1941 to the end of the war in May 1945. It was not an extermination camp but a transit camp from which Jews were to be transported to their fates further East – to Auschwitz, Bergen-Belsen, Buchenwald and Treblinka. Its true objectives were to remain secret and it was to be represented to the Jews as a labour camp.

Living conditions in this ghetto town with its very high red-brown brick walls were mild compared with those in the extermination camps. But this statement is relative. During the war, 150,000 Jews were imprisoned in this small and enclosed area. The majority of them (about 60,000) were from Bohemia and Moravia but they were also transported from France, Holland, Belgium and other countries. About half of them were transported to the East – mostly to their deaths. In Terezín itself, 35,000 Jews died of starvation, disease, mental distress and other causes.

In the Terezín ghetto, the Nazis granted the Jews a limited but dependent self-government in order to create an illusion of freedom. After a time, they even permitted a degree of cultural freedom. So Terezín developed its own specific culture. Many concerts, cabarets and operas (for example, Verdi's *Tosca* and Smetana's *Prodaná nevěsta/The Bartered Bride*) were performed in lofts and cellars. The premiere of Hans Krása's children's opera *Brundibar*, was also held in Terezín. In *Distant Journey*, we see a group of children singing a song from the opera. Many examples of Terezín's culture have survived – drawings, compositions, poems, secret diaries – for instance, those by Alisah Shek and Erich Kassler.

The Germans pretended, in the words of the Nazi propaganda film *Der Führer schenkt den Juden eine Stadt* (1944) that Hitler 'gave the town to the Jews'. Also, under international pressure, they allowed a visit by the International Red Cross. The inhabitants had to 'prepare' the town for its international visitors in a process of 'beautification'. In Radok's film, we see an echo of these preparations as women absurdly wash the pavement of one of Terezín's streets.

Terezín's reality was very specific, complex and full of contradictions – a closed world that was at the same time hallucinatory and incredible. Radok, who had served his stage apprenticeship with the avant-garde director, E. F. Burian, was particularly influenced by his use of metaphor and lighting and in *Distant Journey* this led to the use of an unambiguously Expressionist approach. He viewed Terezín from a very subjective viewpoint, as a terrible dream, a nightmare in which the personal experiences of the former prisoners would be emphasised.

In contrast to the almost documentary approach of the Polish director, Wanda Jakubowska, in her film about Auschwitz, *Ostatni etap* (*The Last Stage* aka *The Last Stop*, 1948), made in the same period, he created a vision of Terezín that resembled a large, crazy and grotesque railway station, a waiting room or antechamber for the extermination camps – a world of chaos. The lofts of the houses are constructed like a stage set, without visible floors or ceilings, made up of steps, oblique walls and black wooden bars, in which it is impossible to orientate, with many unexplained sounds from off-screen. It is a complex labyrinthine area of enclosed spaces and pools of light. Radok also emphasises the unusual image – a peg leg, a puppet descending the steps, combining this with the incongruous use of jazz and the sound of the saxophone. When Terezín is introduced, we see Jews entering one gate with their packs as coffins are carried out the other. The musical accompaniment is a grotesque variant on Ravel's 'Bolero'. It is truly, as the novelist Josef Škvorecký observed, 'a terrifyingly poetic "danse macabre"'. When I screened the film to a former inmate of Terezín, he did not accept Radok's artistic style or licence at all. Terezín, he said, was not like that, it was characterised by order, not chaos.

But Radok was, above all, an artist and not a witness. While many things came from his own imagination, he also drew on the dreamlike reality of Terezín itself. In the film, for example, we see the night train travelling along the narrow street in the town centre. It appears as something from an absurd dream but it was reality and, for Radok, it was a metaphor for the madness of Terezín.

Radok's deliberate use of Expressionist techniques was one of the main reasons for its limited release and subsequent banning. In Czechoslovakia after 1948, it should be remembered that words such as 'expressionism', 'formalism' and 'structuralism' were not just aesthetic or technical terms – they carried the weight of a political accusation and verdict. Because of his 'degenerate art' (what the Nazis had called 'entartete Kunst'), Radok was to be effectively excluded from the development of Czech cinematography. Oddly enough, the French critic, André Bazin, whose distaste for Expressionism and support for realism is well known, commended the film on the grounds that 'this "world of Kafka, or more curiously of de Sade" had an internal fidelity which made it clearly not the whim of an artist but a result of the logic of a political machine. Expressionism here exists not in cinema but in history.'

The tragic and disturbing nature of Jewish life in Prague and in the Terezín ghetto makes up the film's second narrative level. Many of these scenes take on the role of ceremonies or rites within the primary narrative. The protagonists in these strange scenes lose their individual character and take on the function of symbols, with the meaning of a particular moment or situation gaining in emphasis.

The number of these metaphorical scenes increases in the second part of the film as the action moves to Terezín. One of the most hallucinatory scenes is that in which a Jewish band standing on a funeral coach play as a procession of Jews is herded past in the night rain towards a transport bound for the East. It immediately follows the incident in which a woman is taken to one side and we hear her disembodied scream. In contrast, at the end of the film, a train of typhoid victims arrives from the East. Hana waits for the train on a ramp dressed in black. The black silhouette of her body is like death itself. Then there is the almost geometrically constructed scene of dying prisoners where Hana, dressed in white, appears as a doctor and symbol of hope.

One of the most developed of these ritual scenes occurs in the first part of the film when the action is still centred on Prague. Following the wedding of Hana and Toník, there is a scene in which Professor Reiter (Eduard Kohout) commits suicide. The scene is composed with radical camera angles, depth of field shots and an impressive use of soundtrack (the increasingly rapid playing of piano scales in an adjacent room). Radok focuses on a variety of symbolic objects – the Jewish rucksack packed for the transport (with the number 402), a globe on the desk, which has previously been introduced as a symbol of the world to which he has refused to escape, and the clock, where the hands have come to a stop. His hand, holding a lit cigar, is held to the side of his chair, and then placed in an ashtray. There is a pause after the piano scales stop.

We do not see the professor's jump from the open window. Everything is achieved through the use of off-screen sound (the sound of squealing brakes). The net curtains in the window shift in the breeze. The scene does not only illustrate the fate of one professor but conveys the reality of the general Jewish situation and functions as a symbol of the Holocaust itself. It also shows the exceptional courage of someone who chooses his own death in place of the future suffering of transportation and the camps.

The third narrative level of *Distant Journey* involves the use of documentary inserts. One example follows the scene of Reiter's suicide when we are forced to link it to outside political realities. We see Himmler, Reinhard Heydrich, and K. H. Frank. Heydrich was the Reichsprotektor of Bohemia-Moravia, who issued the instructions for the creation of the Terezín ghetto (as Hitler's deputy, he was later assassinated by Czech paratroopers). Frank, a former leader of the Sudeten German party, was *de facto* controller of the Protectorate of Bohemia-Moravia throughout the war. Himmler was, of course, head of the SS.

The film's opening sections make a powerful statement. Before the credits, we see the shadows of figures (Jews) moving from right to left across the screen to the accompaniment of the *Bolero*. These images are juxtaposed after the credits with the marching feet of a German military band. Nazi promises of an improved future are juxtaposed with the anti-Semitic speeches of leaders, National Socialist justice equated with the image of the guillotine and execution by machine gun. Fictional images of Terezín are intercut from the film's later narrative. We are in the grip of the progressive and relentless progress of an ideological machine. The film's prologue is narrated in a strange, sometimes ironic, sometimes weary voice that gives the film a very personal quality.

Radok uses the device of small images in the right-hand lower corner of the screen, a frame within a frame. He uses images from the German propaganda newsreels of the time and also from Leni Riefenstahl's *Triumph des Willens* (*Triumph of the Will*, 1935) to create a sense of the larger historical events that are, on one hand distant from the lives of the characters, but nonetheless determine their fates. He thus juxtaposes the broader political history with the smaller personal history.

Radok filmed some of the apparently documentary shots himself and *Distant Journey* is therefore a mixture of real documentary work and intentional mystification. This is linked to Radok's idea of the ideal film as an 'artistic report', a multidimensional structure in which different points of view can be compared.

The small image (frozen or moving) sometimes represents the following scene and sometimes the previous one but, crucially, presents an effect of duality. This simultaneous recognition of the political and the personal, combined with the use of Expressionism, denies us the consolations of realism, attempts to maintain multiple levels of cognition and is in direct descent from the political objectives of the pre-war avant-garde.

In an interview with Antonín J. Liehm, Radok has spoken of how the origins of much of what he wanted to communicate in film and theatre derived from Hitler. The name, he said, evoked for him the image of a little girl offering Hitler a bunch of wild flowers, as he bends over her with a benevolent smile. 'To me, this image is linked with the awareness of what National Socialism meant, just because the image conceals something'. He further stated:

> [In *Distant Journey*] I wanted to stress the paradox that so many people – and this was true later of many in Communist Czechoslovakia – simply don't see things, don't want to see them, or see only the picture of Hitler and the little girl. And that is the horror of it. Everything that they wrote about in the newspapers was depicted as the best … Hitler promised Czechoslovakia the only possible salvation … If you really want to get a picture of that period, you have to see the one and the other, not one but two, both sides.

This mixture of feature film and documentary, together with the Expressionist use of lighting and sound was quite probably influenced by Orson Welles' *Citizen Kane* (1941). In a newspaper questionnaire published in *Mladá fronta* in December 1947, Radok cited *Citizen Kane* as his greatest artistic experience of the year. Without Radok's knowledge of Welles' film, it is likely that *Distant Journey* would have taken a different form.

While the two films emerged from different historical and cultural contexts, there are nevertheless some interesting similarities. Both directors came to the cinema from theatre. But their inexperience in cinema liberated them from convention and allowed an almost exhibitionist endeavour to demonstrate what could be achieved in film. Both drew on experienced collaborators and, above all, their directors of photography. Welles used Gregg Toland and Radok used Josef Střecha. One has only to look at the use of depth of field, the low angle shots in which ceilings form part of the composition, and the concern with composition across several planes, to see the similarities. *Distant Journey*, however, represents only part of Radok's original intentions. He based his film on a synopsis by Erik Kolár, who had experienced Terezín as a prisoner during the war. Together, they wanted to show not only the evil 'in the others' (that is, the Nazis) but also the evil 'in us', in hidden or open Czech anti-Semitism.

From these intentions, only a small number of scenes and characters remain. There is, for instance, the character of the caretaker who shamelessly steals Jewish possessions and the character of Toník's father, who represents 'everyday' anti-Semitism and refuses to attend his son's wedding. But Toník's father and brother, like Hana's family, also die in the camps. In the original screenplay, Radok and Kolár had wanted to contrast a scene in which German students watch the execution of Jewish professors with one in which Czech nationalist students fight with Jewish sympathisers. It is very probable that the Communist censorship did not approve of this kind of insight into domestic anti-Semitism.

In spite of the director's inexperience (the acting styles are somewhat dated), *Distant Journey* remains an important and outstanding film. It explores the topic of evil on many levels, both as a universal tragedy and as a metaphor for the inner prison that threatens each of us. At a conference on the Holocaust and the Moving Image held in London in 2001, one of the participants noted that the Holocaust was not just history but was still present, it was a present state of mind. But the Holocaust also reflects profound archetypes, to use Jung's terminology. It draws on the archetypes of violence, fear and anxiety but also, as in the case of Terezín, self-defence and creativity.

Radok's vision of Terezín is the vision of an inner experience from which nobody can escape. When, at the end of the film, the commentator reports from the post-war cemetery that 'man was victorious', Radok's *mise-en-scène* indicates that this was a historically specific experience that cannot be dominated or overcome. The experience remains as does the question of what we should do about it. It is not only a question for the survivors but for everyone.

Radok and his leading actor, Otomar Krejča, were to become two of the leading figures in the post-war Czech theatre. Krejča later founded the famous Divadlo za branou (Theatre Beyond the Gate). Radok worked for the Národní divadlo (National Theatre), from which he was twice dismissed and, in 1958, presented his Laterna magika (Magic Lantern) at the Brussels Exposition. Together with his brother, Emil Radok, and the scenographer Josef Svoboda, he was able to continue a commitment to experiment. Miloš Forman, who worked with Radok at the time, described Laterna magika as a kind of cybernetic machine combining multiple projection, live action and stereophonic sound. Forman later remarked in *The Miloš Forman Stories* that 'at a time when we were forced to talk about nothing, he [Radok] discovered how to do it so it was enjoyable'. Besides Forman, other film directors who later worked with Laterna magika included Evald Schorm and Jan Švankmajer and, of course, the Laterna magika has become a permanent fixture in Prague.

But Radok was only able to make two further films, *Divotvorný klobouk* (*The Three Cornered Hat*, 1953), a mediocre musical, and *Dědeček automobil* (*Grandpa Automobile* aka *Old Man Motor Car*, 1958), a whimsical film about motor car and motorbike racing at the turn of the century filmed in the style of art nouveau. Forman was his assistant director and helped him in the creation of artificial machines such as the butterfly catching machine. Radok continued his combination of documentary with live action. But Radok never overcame the problems of *Distant Journey* which Škvorecký aptly described as a 'tragically premature and anachronistic work of art'. Although he had initially wanted to work in cinema rather than theatre, the times did not permit it. As he himself commented, in the 1950s he was regarded as a 'cosmopolitan' and a 'formalist', characterised by the Stalinist cultural watchdog, Ladislav Štoll, as 'a person who is standing on the other side'.

Only three days after the Soviet occupation in 1968, Radok emigrated to Gothenburg in Sweden. He worked with minimal success on the stage and faced many problems with actors and the use of a foreign language. He died of a heart attack during a short stay in Vienna in 1976. Václav Havel, his former assistant and friend, who had written some important analytical essays on Radok's theatre work in the 1960s, wrote an impressive obituary.

Jiří Cieslar

REFERENCES

Bazin, André (1952) 'Le Ghetto concentrationnaire', *Cahiers du Cinéma*, 9, 60.

Cieslar, Jiří, (2001) 'Living with the Long Journey: Alfréd Radok's *Daleká cesta*', in *Central Europe Review* (4 June). Available at http://www.ce-review.org./01/20/kinoeye20-cieslar.html

Liehm, Antonín J. (1974) *Closely Watched Films: The Czechoslovak Experience*. New York: International Arts and Sciences Press.

_____ (1975) *The Miloš Forman Stories*. New York: International Arts and Sciences Press.

Škvorecký, Josef (1971) *All the Bright Young Men and Women: A Personal History of the Czech Cinema*. Trans. Michael Schonberg. Toronto: Peter Martin Associates.

EROICA

ANDRZEJ MUNK, POLAND, 1957

Andrzej Munk, the director of *Eroica*, is regarded, together with Andrzej Wajda, as the main creator of the Polish School, which in the late 1950s put Poland on the cinematic map of Europe for the first time, mainly thanks to films about the Polish experience during the Second World War. He is also the most distinguished Polish filmmaker to die young – in 1961, at the age of only 40 years (Munk lost his life in a car accident, while returning from the set of his film *Pasażerka/Passenger*). Despite his relatively short period of artistic activity, his work reveals an extraordinary maturity and consistency, which continues to fascinate critics and film historians in Poland and abroad. The most recent testimony to this interest was the retrospective of his work at the Venice Film Festival in 2001.

Eroica belongs to the strand of the Polish School described as 'rationalistic', or 'plebeian' and is opposed to its 'romantic-expressionist paradigm', of which Wajda's *Kanał* (*Kanal*, 1956) and *Popiół i diament* (*Ashes and Diamonds*, 1958) are the main examples. This paradigm, of which other examples include *Wolne miasto* (*Free City*, 1958) and *Swiadectwo urodzenia* (*Birth Certificate*, 1961) by Stanisław Różewicz, *Krzyż Walecznych* (*Military Cross*, 1958) and *Ludzie z pociągu* (*People from a Train*, 1961) by Kazimierz Kutz and *Kwiecień* (*April*, 1961) by Witold Lesiewicz, is characterised, amongst other features, by the choice of ordinary, working-class and peasant main characters, a realistic style and critical attitude towards a certain ethos which is identified with Polish Romanticism. Consequently, in Polish popular consciousness, Munk's film functions as a kind of 'anti-*Kanał*' or 'anti-*Ashes and Diamonds*'. Yet, if we take a closer look, we will find more meaningful similarities than differences between these respective films. In particular, both contain criticism of the idea that a Pole's holy duty is to be heroic, even if in practice it means acting against common sense, recklessly or in a way that jeopardises the lives of fellow countrymen. At the same time both show much sympathy and understanding of their doomed heroes, although *Eroica* comes across as a more disillusioned film than Wajda's movies of the Polish School period. Some Polish critics, the most important of which was Ewelina Nurczyńska-Fidelska, the leading expert on Munk, argued that in spite of the critical, even cynical attitude to some national myths, Munk's film deserved to be situated inside the borders of the Polish romantic paradigm. The reason for that is the richness and complexity of Polish Romanticism, which contains many motifs and attitudes which contradict each other, including elevation and condemnation of abstract patriotism and heroism, realism and symbolism, pathos and irony.

In Munk's film the theme of heroism is conveyed by the very title of the film and its subheading *Symfonia bohaterska w dwóch częściach* (*A heroic symphony in two movements*), which is borrowed from Beethoven's masterpiece, the Third Symphony, whose subtitle is 'Heroic'. The Beethoven composition consists of three movements and Munk originally shot three parts, all based on short stories written by Jerzy Stefan Stawiński, the most accomplished scriptwriter of the Polish School films, who also collaborated with Munk on other occasions. Eventually, however, only two parts were included in the final version. The third part, initially entitled *Con bravura* and based on Stawiński's story *Zakonnica* (*The Nun*), remains in the Polish film archive in Warsaw and has never been exhibited in cinemas. However, in 1995 it was shown on Polish state television with a commentary by Stawiński, causing some upset amongst friends of Munk, including the cinematographer, Jerzy Wójcik and Jerzy Kawalerowicz, who was the head of Studio Kadr which produced Munk's film. They regarded it as a violation of the director's artistic testament. Some critics, however, felt that the third part matched the two which were included in the original 'director's cut' of *Eroica*.

The plots of the respective stories were all inspired by authentic events from the Second World War, but have different settings and characters. The first part, entitled *Scherzo alla pollacca* and based on *Węgrzy* (*The Hungarians*) by Stawiński, is set during the 1944 Warsaw Uprising. It casts as the main character a Warsaw fixer, Dzidziuś Górkiewicz (Edward Dziewoński) who admits that during the war he supported himself by trading on the black market, and presumably also with the occupiers. At the time of the uprising, he finds himself in Mokotów (in common with the characters of Wajda's *Kanal*), as a member of a group of the Armia Krajowa (Home Army) insurrectionists. The Home Army was the main military organisation supporting the anti-Soviet Polish government in London and the principal force organising the uprising, whose purpose was to liberate Warsaw before the Soviet Army could enter. The commander of the group is so committed to transforming the recruits into elite fighters, that he fails to notice an enemy plane approaching. Only Dzidziuś who is utterly bored by the routine sees the plane and probably saves the lives of his fellow partisans, as well as his own, drawing their attention to the danger. Hence, already in this early scene Munk counterpoints the heroic and 'blind' idealism, typical for the bulk of partisans with the healthy and selfish common sense of Dzidziuś. As the film progresses, we observe more and more absurdities, ineptitudes and inconsistencies in the behaviour of the insurgents. For example, we learn that the commanders of two groups in different districts of Warsaw telephone each other via London. On another occasion, Dzidziuś who brings some important information to pass to the uprising's commander is first treated as an enemy and imprisoned and then kept waiting for a long time for a meeting with the commander. The whole uprising is represented as an irrational activity, doomed to failure from the very start. It is best conveyed in the conversation Dzidziuś has with one of the Polish officers of the Home Army, who admits that in the end it will be Russians, not Poles who liberate Warsaw. The officer describes it as the 'Polish fate' – tragic and absurd at the same time.

After the incident with the plane, Dzidziuś leaves Warsaw for Zalesie, a resort near Warsaw, where he left his attractive wife in a spacious villa. He finds her there with a Hungarian officer. The Hungarians are nominally on the side of the Germans, but expecting the imminent end of the war and the Nazi defeat, change sides to ally themselves with the Russians. Accordingly, the officer proposes to provide the Home Army with a large supply of weapons to be used in the uprising in exchange for a guarantee of safety from the Russians. Dzidziuś agrees to transmit this offer to the Home Army command, which means passing through heavy German patrols, which prevent anyone from entering or leaving Warsaw. Dzidziuś, however, manages to enter the capital, bribing the German guard with a golden coin. During the course of the film, he travels from Warsaw to Zalesie and back several times. Although such trips were regarded as extremely dangerous, they are represented by Munk in a humorous way. The director gives the impression that Dzidziuś is too down-to-earth, ordinary and crafty, and loves life too much, to fall prey to the Germans. However, it is suggested that his last trip to Warsaw, when he leaves peaceful Zalesie for no particular reason, will be fatal for him.

Polish film historian, Bronisława Stolarska, compared Dzidziuś to Hermes, quoting Kopaliński's definition – 'a guardian of a household, messenger to the gods, god of communication in his capacity as guide to the dead, taking them down to the Underworld; from his primitive association with roads he is patron of all wayfarers, traders, travellers and thieves, of things found and those taken into possession as well as of the stealing of such things, god of profit and riches'. Indeed, Dzidziuś takes the role of a messenger, bringing news and advising people and he remains faithful to this role until the very end. However, the reasons for his return from the 'Arcadia of Zalesie' to the 'hell of Warsaw' have been disputed by the following generations of Polish critics. According to one view, his act is a testimony to the heroic and romantic atmosphere pervading Warsaw during the Uprising. As a result, even the ordinary folk and people whose war activities were morally dubious felt as if they had to 'live for a legend', rather than for their own welfare. Stolarska also suggests that by his last return to the burning capital, Dzidziuś completes his mission as Hermes. Moreover, by inscribing the Polish sense of 'everything or nothing' into the Mediterranean mythology, Munk made the Polish myth universal.

Dzidziuś' decision to join the doomed uprising can also be read as placing his story in the context of another Mediterranean myth – that of Odysseus. In common with Odysseus, or at least Homer's famous interpretation of this mythical character, Dzidziuś leaves his wife and his house full of suitors (there is only one suitor at the time – the Hungarian named Kola, but it is suggested that there were others in the past), to look for adventure and encounters with other women. We also learn that plenty of attractive girls took part in the uprising; to one of them, nicknamed Berry, who is a liaison officer in one of the squads of the Home Army, Dzidziuś confides that he wished she was his wife, rather than his real spouse. Unlike Dzidziuś' wife, Berry prides herself on being faithful to her fiancé. On the whole, the moral contrast between Dzidziuś and the male insurrectionists seems to be less than between his wife and the young women, who fought Germans during the war. Although a reluctant and unlikely insurrectionist, Dzidziuś ultimately proves to be a brave and patriotic man. His wife, on the other hand, seems to think only about comfort and material goods and is even unable to distinguish between enemy and ally.

The musical term 'scherzo', which in Italian means joke, alludes to the light character of the first part of the film. *Scherzo alla pollacca* is full of funny situations, the most memorable being one in which Dzidziuś gets drunk after consuming a supply of foreign alcohol found in the Uprising headquarters. However, laughter is often caused by the contrast between the serious situation of Warsawians during the uprising, including that of Dzidziuś, and a light-hearted approach to what happens.

By contrast, the word 'lugubre' in *Ostinato lugubre*, the title of the second part of *Eroica*, based on Stawiński's short story Ucieczka (*Escape*), meaning lugubrious, sad, dispirited, suggests that its tone will be more sombre. Indeed, the humour of this part is almost exclusively black. Superficially, the situation depicted by Munk in this part is less tragic than in *Scherzo alla pollacca*. His characters, who find themselves in a POW camp (or Oflag, as Poles used to call it), somewhere in the Alps, are not condemned to an imminent death, but to a relatively peaceful, even humane existence. This life is guaranteed by the Geneva convention which ensured that prisoners of war should be treated humanely. The relative comfort of their existence is signified by the influx of parcels from the Red Cross, containing food and cigarettes, which the prisoners dutifully divide amongst themselves. Yet, life in the camp proves in the end to be less bearable to these ex-soldiers, than the time when they were actually fighting.

The story begins at the end of 1944, when a new, small group of prisoners, consisting of Warsaw Uprising fighters, join those who have been in the camp since the September Campaign of 1939. Amongst the newcomers we see for a short while a major, with whom Dzidziuś Górkiewicz has returned to Warsaw for the third time. Dzidziuś, however, is missing, which suggests that he died in the uprising. Soon the new prisoners discover that the overall mood in the camp is bad and prisoners cultivate some bizarre habits. The aura of eccentricity results primarily from the fact that the prisoners have no sense of time, and as a consequence, no sense of reality. For them, time stopped in 1939. They are hardly interested in the news concerning the Warsaw Uprising, nor are they awaiting the end of the war, which will take place in a few months. Their manner of thinking is shaped by the moral values which were valid before the beginning of the war, but in 1944 seem desperately outdated. For example, the officers, who fought in the September Campaign of 1939, question the validity of military insignia for those who gained them in Warsaw Uprising. The most important issue in the 'oflag' is that of the officer's honour, which must be asserted by committing an act of extraordinary bravery. In the given circumstances this equates to a successful escape. According to the prisoners' testimony, one of them, Lieutenant Zawistowski (Tadeusz Łomnicki), managed to escape from the camp. Thus, he proved himself a hero and provided an example for those who remained incarcerated. Yet, this example is difficult to emulate, as the ex-soldiers are perfectly aware that it is virtually impossible to escape from the camp, as it is not only heavily guarded by German soldiers, but by many natural barriers, including high mountains. In reality, Zawistowski did not escape, but lives hidden in the roof of the 'oflag', virtually over the heads of the fellow prisoners. He perpetuates this fiction in order not to disappoint them. Two other prisoners who know about his real situation, and share their food rations with him at night when other prisoners are sleeping, help to keep his legend intact.

One might expect that preserving a heroic legend would boost the morale of the prisoners and give them hope for their own imminent freedom. Munk, however, shows that the legend has the opposite effect on the prisoners: it makes them feel inadequate, almost cowardly. Zawistowski's 'heroism' has the most destructive effect on Lieutenant Żak (Józef Kostecki), who was his best friend in the camp. Envying his friend his courage to escape, and suffering from the claustrophobia of life more than the others, he decides to escape himself and is shot by the prison guard. The news of Żak's fate has a devastating effect on Zawistowski, who feels guilty for his friend's death and commits suicide. Hence, it can be argued that both Zawistowski and Żak become victims of the expectations of heroism, rather than of their own motivation. This paradox leads to a terrible waste of young lives, which was also a theme of such Polish School films as Wajda's *Ashes and Diamonds* and Wojciech Has' *Jak być kochaną* (*How to Be Loved*, 1962). This is also a motif Munk explores in some of his remaining films, including *Zezowate szczęście* (*Bad Luck*, 1959).

Although *Ostinato lugubre* is set during the war, some critics regarded it as a metaphor for the situation in which Poles found themselves after 1945. Hence, the POW camp signifies the whole of Poland under communist rule, from which it was almost impossible to escape due to numerous visible and invisible barriers, including great difficulties in acquiring a passport. Similarly, one can notice a similarity between the claustrophobic atmosphere of the camp and the apathy and hopelessness, typical for large sections of Polish post-war society, particularly pre-war intelligentsia, who found it especially difficult to adjust to the new socio-political order of communist Poland. Even the absurd and black humour, immortalised by Munk, is reminiscent of the view that Poland was the jolliest prison in the whole Soviet camp.

While Wajda's films appear to be highly conscious of their own cinematic character and heavy with symbolism, in *Eroica*, art is assiduously avoided, except when it is useful to convey the characters' personalities and situations. Similarly, the symbols and metaphors in Munk's film appear to be inherent in the reality represented, rather than added to it, as was often the case in films such as *Kanal* and *Ashes and Diamonds*. For example, the bottle, thrown by Dzidziuś in the direction of a nearby tank, is not only the bottle of a drunkard who does not know what he is doing, but also carries associations with the home-made missiles used by the Warsaw insurrectionists. Another important difference between Wajda and Munk's Polish School films concerns the position of the camera. Wajda uses many close-ups and subjective shots, which convey the compassionate attitude of the film's author to his characters and facilitate the viewer's identification with the protagonists. Munk, on the contrary, avoids such devices, preferring to place the camera further from the characters. This allows him to present the characters in a wider context and also creates a certain distance between the viewer and the protagonist. Moreover, the second part of *Eroica* does not really have a main character, and different characters take on the main role one by one. Such a narrative structure, which accurately captures communal life in the POW camp, also hinders our identification with any individual portrayed in the film.

It must be emphasised that the overall impression of unaffected artlessness, given by *Eroica*, was achieved through many sophisticated technical and artistic means, including deep focus and zooming, some of which were used in Polish cinema for the first time. The most important was the use of deep focus. The cinematographer, Jerzy Wójcik, admitted that in *Eroica* he was strongly influenced by the work of Gregg Toland on *Citizen Kane* (Orson Welles, 1941). In common with *Citizen Kane*, this device in Munk's film allowed the condensing of the action, and the inclusion of more information in a scene than in films which do not use this technique. Take, for example, the scene in *Ostinato lugubre*, in which the prisoners assemble in the foreground and the water-cart, containing the body of Zawistowski, is shown in the background. More importantly, as Jerzy Płażewski observed, deep focus allowed the director to emphasise the incompatibility of certain events taking place at the same time. Hence, the foreground often includes an event which is ordinary or banal, such as Dzidziuś drinking alcohol when the backdrop contains a very dramatic scene, like German tanks attacking civilians; or vice-versa – the mood of the first plane of action is elevated, that of the second plane banal or comical. Accordingly, it could be argued that the use of deep focus in Munk's film is a vehicle for irony.

The music of Jan Krenz fulfils a similar function of revealing and accentuating the ironic positions of the protagonists. Only a few instruments play in *Eroica*, including piano, trumpet, xylophone and drums. In the first part of the film, these instruments, some normally used in marches, on the one hand convey the military character of the events represented, and on the other seem to sneer at what we see. In the second part, the music mainly emulates the sounds of sobs, sighs and distant cries, in this way adding to the atmosphere of claustrophobia and paranoia pervading the camp. The music by Krenz is also so powerful because it is used very sparsely.

Of all the visual symbols Munk uses in his film, the most significant is the circle, which is the structural principle of the whole film, as well as an important visual element in *Ostinato lugubre*. In *Scherzo alla pollacca*, Dzidziuś keeps returning to the same place, albeit using different routes, as if he was moving on a circular road. In *Ostinato lugubre*, we see the soldiers taking their daily exercise by walking in a large circle, which is shot from a point high above their heads. Obviously, the circle conveys the fruitlessness and hopelessness of the characters' heroism and patriotism. The circularity and by extension, the futility of the efforts of the prisoners, is also suggested by the title of the second part: 'ostinato' is a musical work, which is by definition repetitive.

At the time of its premiere in 1958, *Eroica* divided the critics. While many regarded it as a very honest film about the war, Polish history and fate, others maintained that it offended patriotic feelings, particularly of those who took part in the Warsaw Uprising, going so far as to claim that it was anti-Polish. Accordingly, *Scherzo alla pollacca* was more criticised than *Ostinato lugubre*. Yet, Polish critics were almost unanimous in praising the technical/artistic side of the film and the acting, especially of Edward Dziewoński in the part of Dzidziuś. *Eroica* received even worse press in the countries of the Soviet bloc where the film's content and message was criticised as well as its form. As Jerzy Płażewski testifies, at the Prague conference in 1958, attended by filmmakers and film critics from the socialist countries, the film was accused of pessimism and formalism. The first reproach was epitomised by the opinion of the well-known Russian critic, Rostislav Iureniev, who wrote, 'The film shows how a drunkard and profiteer joined the Warsaw Uprising. Although it could happen in reality, the filmmaker's duty is to represent what was typical in the given circumstances.' Iureniev also attacked Munk for pessimism and an eclectic mixing of incompatible styles, such as comedy and tragedy. It is easy to dismiss such opinions as the last symptoms of the East European disease known as Socialist Realism. However, Iureniev also captures the mood of the Polish critics of *Eroica*, who argued that Munk was reckless in playing with the feelings of the Polish war veterans.

Over twenty years later, Bożena Janicka in an insightful and balanced essay, published in the Polish magazine *Film* in a series commemorating the most important Polish films made since the Second World War, attempted to summarise and analyse the reasons why *Eroica* encountered much hostility in the Polish press when it was released. 'Perhaps the attacks on Munk', she wrote, 'were a sign given by the critics, that more films, uncritically acknowledging the bravery of insurrectionists were needed.' From this perspective, *Eroica* appeared in the Polish cinemas too early, when not enough discussion was devoted to the issue of the Warsaw Uprising. It must be added here that before the beginning of the Polish School in the mid-1950s, it was virtually impossible to have any honest discussion about the Warsaw Uprising in Poland. Due to its political controversy (the uprising was regarded as not only aimed at the German occupiers, but also the Russian liberation of Warsaw and political control of the country) the subject was virtually taboo.

According to Janicka, the criticisms of *Eroica* could also reflect a certain intellectual 'heaviness' amongst some reviewers. Similarly, in common with Nurczyńska-Fidelska, Janicka does not contrast *Eroica* with Polish Romanticism, but places it firmly in the Romantic tradition, along with such works by Andrzej Wajda, and the books *Siedem polskich grzechów głównych* (*Seven Polish Cardinal Sins*, 1962) by Zbigniew Załuski and *Bić się czy nie bić* (*To Fight or Not To Fight*, 1978) by Tomasz Łubieński, which all avoided the simplistic vision of national culture, according to which Poles were always a nation of heroes who died for their country without the slightest resentment or doubt. The fact that Dzidziuś was the focus of the greatest hostility from the reviewers was also explained by Janicka by the fact that he was essentially a civilian, with little 'inborn' respect for the uniform and life in the barracks. By contrast, in Polish official culture, military affairs are treated with the highest and most uncritical respect. Paradoxically, many of the factors which, in the late 1950s, put many critics off Munk's work, such as his unsentimental vision of Polish history, extensive use of irony and mixing of comedy with tragedy, also assured *Eroica* an enduring place in Polish and European cinema. Along with *Ashes and Diamonds* it remains to this day the most widely viewed and cult film from the Polish School period.

Ewa Mazierska

REFERENCES

Janicka, Bożena (1984) '*Eroica*', *Film*, 20 (13 May), 11.

Nurczyńska-Fidelska, Ewelina (1982) *Andrzej Munk*. Kraków: Wydawnictwo Literackie.

Płażewski, Jerzy (1958a) 'Pomnik z piołunu', *Przegląd kulturalny*, 3 (16–22 January), 3.

_____ (1958b) 'O optymizmie, czyli ćwierć racji Rościsława Jureniewa', *Przegląd kulturalny*, 4 (23 January), 3–7.

Stolarska, Bronisława (1995) 'In Search for Hope: On the Films of Andrzej Munk', in Ewelina Nurczyńska-Fidelska and Zbigniew Batko (eds) *Polish Cinema in Ten Takes*. Łódź: Łódzkie Towarzystwo Naukowe, 21–38.

ANDRZEJ WAJDA, POLAND, 1958

Popiół i Diament (*Ashes and Diamonds*, 1958) is honoured by many Polish critics as being the best Polish film ever made, and has also been considered by critics abroad to be one of the best Polish films. It is generally thought of not only as the highlight of Andrzej Wajda's early career, but also as his finest film. It is regarded as the best example of the Polish School's 'romantic-expressionist paradigm', as noted by Ewa Mazierska. Critical responses aside, *Ashes and Diamonds* has provoked intense emotional and intellectual reactions both in Poland and abroad. Its structure and aesthetics have also been scrutinised at length. Wajda repeatedly describes the film as his best work, despite being quite sceptical about his other accomplishments.

Among those general themes most frequently acknowledged in discussing *Ashes and Diamonds* are its tragic heroism, historicism (that is, Wajda's probing of history as a factor in dictating human fate), romanticism and nationalism – issues of nation-building, and its examination of Polish political dilemmas. The film has also been analysed for its aesthetics: to some critics, it reveals surrealist, neo-realist or baroque traits and influences, while to others it is a realistic and accurate portrayal of the post-war realities of Poland. Some attempt will be made here to correlate this extensive body of literature, but of course a full analysis of all these sources falls beyond the scope of this introductory chapter.

In her article 'Romanticism and History', Ewelina Nurczyńska-Fidelska, a Polish authority on Andrzej Wajda, claims that *Ashes and Diamonds* together with *Pokolenie* (*A Generation*, 1954), *Kanal* (1957) and *Lotna* (1959) 'were the first manifestations of the set of problems and themes which are basic to Wajda's cinematic accomplishments'. It is *Ashes and Diamonds*, however, which alone encapsulates all the greatest accomplishments in both theme and form that can later be traced throughout all of Wajda's films. *Ashes and Diamonds* is based on Jerzy Andrzejewski's novel of the same name, the action of which takes place over the course of one day, 8 May 1945, at the end of the Second World War.

The film's protagonist is Maciek Chełmicki (Zbigniew Cybulski), a young Home Army soldier who on this first day of peace is ordered to kill a communist activist, Szczuka (Wacław Zastrzezyński). However, the first assassination attempt fails, and, because the wrong man has been assassinated, Maciek has to try again later. In the meantime, he begins to fall in love with a young woman, Krystyna (Ewa Krzyżewska). Once Maciek realises that he cares for her, he becomes reluctant to participate in the second assassination attempt. Faced with a difficult choice between duty and love, Maciek chooses the former, although he does so only half-heartedly; he obeys the orders of his superiors and, as a good soldier, kills the man – his ideological enemy. Although he is not punished for this crime, he is later killed by Polish soldiers as he tries to flee from them. This tragic story bears witness to Maciek's search for an answer to the questions of how to live after the war and how to negotiate a painful past with the hope for a new life and love in a liberated Poland.

Wajda, who was nineteen when the Second World War ended, considers the film a personal story of sorts that he had to relive. The film refers to his personal war experience (Wajda lost his father to the war) and incorporates influences from many areas of his life. Here, Wajda is the artist embracing a cultural tradition of Polish Romanticism, that of Poles brought up on classical Polish art and literature and the acknowledgement of the quintessentially Polish love for politics and history. The film is not only a story of love and lost chances, but also a palimpsest revealing the complexities of history and society in post-war Poland. It is a text rich in political, historical and social allusions, vibrating with cultural references in which every scene means something to a Polish audience and confirms the director's love for and understanding of his people and his country's traditions.

Considering this textual density, it seems reasonable that an analysis of *Ashes and Diamonds* should follow the natural flow of the narrative, which not only reveals the course of events, but also uncovers complex historical and cultural questions. In this selection of some of the film's most important sequences, I will try to show a few examples of this interweaving of the personal and the public as it unfolds in both the images and the dialogue. This analysis will also point to several artistic choices that have become Wajda's trademark: the brisk, quickly moving narrative; the film diegesis saturated with historical details, character complexities and ambiguities; and, finally, a rich film aesthetics abounding with references to European art.

Ashes and Diamonds starts with a bucolic scene set near a small country church, birds chirping, the sun shining brightly. Maciek and Andrzej (Adam Pawlikowski), officers in NSZ (a unit of the Home Army), wait for Konrad Szczuka's car to arrive. Drewnowski (Bogumił Kobiela), a third Home Army member, stands guard nearby. These three young men plan to assassinate Szczuka, who is District Secretary of the regional party committee of PZPR (The

Polish United Workers' Party), along with his assistant, Podgórski. The historical context of the film is of course dictated by the specific situation of Poland after the Second World War, when the country became a Russian satellite. During the war, the entire country was embroiled in the doomed effort to fight the Nazi invaders, and members of all political parties were generally united. After the war, however, these same factions fought each other in ideologically grounded guerrilla wars. The very first scene in the film plunges the spectator, especially a Polish spectator already familiar with the situation, into the middle of this ideological conflict.

The scene begins from an idealistic, and in this context surrealistic, series of images. A ploughman works the field in a scene reminiscent of a well-known painting by Ferdynand Ruszczyc, called *Ziemia* (*The Earth*). A little girl approaches the men and asks them to open the church; standing against the pristine birch trees overlooking the scene, she represents the innocence of youth, unaware as she is of any political tensions. Meanwhile, Maciek and Andrzej engage in small talk, but they are soon interrupted by Drewnowski, who whistles to them as a car approaches. Rapid shooting ensues, during which the older man in the car is killed instantly. The young driver tries to escape but, after a short run, is killed mercilessly by Maciek in the church, with the Madonna ironically looking on. This first sequence introduces several elements that will reappear throughout the film: the youthful, reckless behaviour of the assassin Maciek; the contrast between the pastoral and innocent character of the *mise-en-scène* and the ominous and terrible events that occur; and the iconoclasm of the scenes in the Catholic church. Wajda incorporates here his deep love for and understanding of painting, which he studied at Kraków ASP (Academy of Fine Arts) as a young man. His allusiveness to Polish art, whether conscious or subconscious, has been discussed extensively by Tadeusz Miczka in his seminal work on the artistic inspirations of Andrzej Wajda.

The next scene in the film refers meta-theatrically to other events in Wajda's life, primarily to his contact with the ideas and aesthetics of Socialist Realist filmmaking, contacts that he made at both ASP in Kraków and Film School in Łódź. After the Home Army assassins have fled, another car approaches the scene of the murder. Comrade Szczuka gets out of this second car, quickly deducing what has happened. Approaching workers also witness this scene and hear Szczuka mourning the fallen comrades in a propagandist monologue redolent of Socialist Realist 'new-speak': Szczuka informs the workers that the real fight for Poland has only recently begun and that it will necessitate the elimination of their (read: his) political opponents. The scene is surprisingly bold in its ideological tone, ostensibly condemnatory of the Home Army. It alludes to similarly-styled scenes in well-known propaganda films of the 1950s in Poland, to the extent of having Szczuka appear against the open sky in the background, shot with a low-angled camera.

The parodic delivery of Szczuka's somewhat too grandiose speech refers to the rigorously implemented modes of Socialist Realism, an artistic trend introduced and enforced by followers of Stalin in the early 1950s, rather than to the importance of struggle for a new Poland in the 1940s, a Poland free of Germans and capitalists alike. This discrepancy between the substance of the speech and its counter-effective mode of delivery directs the knowing spectator's attention to the context of the film's production, post-1953, at the beginning of 'the political and artistic thaw' enthusiastically embraced by Wajda and other artists in Poland.

After Szczuka's speech, the film shifts to the Hotel Monopol Restaurant in the nearby small town of Ostrowiec, near the Soviet border, where the end of the war is being celebrated at a special banquet. Here begins the brief love affair between Maciek and Krystyna, a waitress there. Initially playful, their flirtatious exchanges quickly change into more serious dialogue. In this first scene of a charming subplot, Maciek plays at hide-and-seek with a vodka glass, finally taking out the military mug he would have used during the underground fighting; the *menażka*, a soldier's mug, is a potent symbol of the perils and hardships of the warrior's life. By putting his mug on the bar in this way, Maciek symbolically acknowledges the end of the war but also signals that he remains deeply entrenched in it. The *menażka* is one of the many symbols that Wajda, with full awareness, introduces into this film and into his cinematic discourse later on in his life. Other such symbols are that of the white horse, the church – with all its cultural and religious connotations – the communal dance and the party. All of these symbols, each steeped in meaning to the informed Polish viewer, reappear later in most of his films. This symbolist trend might arise from Wajda's affinity for symbolist art, acknowledged through his love of Andrzej Wróblewski's deeply symbolist paintings.

In another important sequence of the film, set in the bourgeois apartment of the Staniewicz family – Home Army sympathisers – the iconography of a traditional Polish home is fully present. Although presented as ironic in Tadeusz Lubelski's work on authorial strategies in Polish fiction film, this iconography clearly refers to the paintings hanging in the vast majority of Polish homes, Wajda's own childhood home included. These famous patriotic paintings, depicting army parades, horses and battles, were eagerly copied or lovingly imitated by Wajda's father, Jakób. Due to Jakób Wajda's interest in such historical art, his son became well acquainted with such art in his own home (as attested in Wajda's unpublished biography). The film then documents this home tradition in the ironic portrayal of Mrs Staniewicz's residence.

Several sequences among the scenes from the banquet attest to Wajda's insightful treatment of Polish society, a vision that is both realistic and sceptical. The guests at the Monopol Hotel reception represent many spheres of Polish society: Communist Party officials, members of the security, official press, smalltown opportunists and members of the Soviet army. As in Wajda's later films *Wesele* (*The Wedding*, 1972) and *Pan Tadeusz* (*Mr Thadeus*, 1999), in which aristocrats and commoners, artists and intelligentsia intermingle freely with Russians, Jews and Ukrainians in an evidently harmonious ceremony, this scene ignores those ever-present historical conflicts and tensions which would make this heterogeneity almost impossible. As Marek Hendrykowski has commented, 'everybody participates in this historical drama *nolens volens*'. Such a reluctantly idealistic portrayal would attest to Wajda's deep wish to see Poland as a tolerant and united country, a wish so openly proclaimed in his two most recent films, *Mr Thadeus* and *Zemsta* (*Revenge*, 2002), and so cynically subverted in *The Wedding*.

As the banquet scene unfolds, Hanka Lewicka, a young singer, begins the song 'The Red Poppies of Monte Cassino', a moving lyric about the heroism of the Polish Second Corps soldiers who fought the Germans at the Battle of Monte Cassino. Historians have recognised that this battle in Italy was won largely thanks to the Poles who sacrificed themselves there. The pain and despair of this passionate song constitutes an apt background for the next scene: Maciek and Andrzej stand at the bar listening and reminiscing about dead comrades. In a famous scene later revisited in *Pierścionek z orłem w koronie* (*The Crowned-Eagle Ring*, 1993), Maciek lights numerous glasses of vodka on fire, each intended to represent one fallen comrade. Asking Andrzej, 'Do you remember Haneczka … Wilga … Kossobudzki … Rudy … Kajtek?' he moves from glass to glass, recalling the names of their deceased compatriots. The camera moves with him, changing positions and points of view, as if identifying singly with each name in the long list of the dead.

As if to downplay the morbidity of this scene and the young men's consequent conversation about Szczuka's assassination, Wajda next introduces a long comic sequence presenting Drewnowski, who stood watch for Maciek and Andrzej in the opening scene, and Pieniążek (Stanisław Milski), the representative of the democratic press. Straight from the assassination near the church, Drewnowski has come to the banquet hall. He is, we find, a mere caricature, a shady career opportunist who cooperates with the Home Army while at the same time acting as secretary to the Communist bureaucrat in Ostrowiec. He and Pieniążek get ridiculously drunk while cynically discussing career prospects: new positions, new money and new influence in post-war Poland. Through comedy, Wajda is able to approach the sensitive issues of opportunism and careerism. Drewnowski thus characterises the two dominant, contradictory, yet impossibly entwined views in Polish society at the end of the Second World War – like Drewnowski, uncertain as to which political orientation would prevail, many Polish citizens were virtually forced to cooperate with the winning party against their inner wishes. The humorous sequence is one of Wajda's modest attempts at comedy, an area into which he has rarely ventured.

Still, here moving freely between comedy and tragedy, Wajda again leads the spectator to a scene full of symbolic connotations. In this scene, Maciek goes to his hotel room to check his gun. In the process, he loses his eyeglasses: symbolically he has lost the clarity of vision required to assess properly his role in the assassination of Szczuka. As he fumbles and drops a piece of his gun on the floor, Krystyna knocks on the door. Distracted and confused, yet trying to appear relaxed, Maciek invites her into his room while simultaneously looking for the gun part and his glasses, on the floor. His relief at finding the missing part is matched by his relief at finding that she will stay, culminating in a sudden burst of boyish, liberating laughter. In an amusing scene, shot from above, the young protagonists realise that they have begun to fall in love. Their budding romance is contrasted by solemn dialogue, in which Maciek tells her that his dark glasses symbolise his unfulfilled love for his motherland and, more practically, the darkness he experienced in his long wadings through the sewers.

Symbols and emotional references to cultural icons abound in the following scenes, as well. Maciek decides that he wants to leave the hotel, and he and Krystyna go for a walk. Soviet soldiers pass them on their way; it begins to rain, and Krystyna and Maciek decide to hide in the ruined church. Krystyna notices a poem inscribed on the wall (Cyprian Norwid's 'Ashes and Diamonds', from which the title of the film comes).

Norwid's poetry is highly romantic and sophisticated. It is full of hidden meanings, the poetry of worldly intellectuals, but it is important to the film for another reason: Norwid was a nationalist who believed in and categorically supported Poland's freedom, not a future obfuscated by Poland's relations with the Soviets. His words express the aspirations of Maciek himself and, by extension, the deep convictions of young Polish people about their nation's fate. Here Wajda's romanticism is most palpable. In reading the poem, Maciek bears out his conviction that he must sacrifice his happiness to national duty. As Marek Haltof explains, 'The Polish romantic protagonist always solves such a dilemma by considering national matters as having topmost priority … Like other Polish romantic characters, Maciek is a prisoner of fate that he is powerless to escape.'

This romanticism, however, is scarred by cynicism in the next scene. The young people walk about the church full of debris, in which the figure of Christ hangs upside-down from the ceiling. As she moves around, Krystyna breaks her high-heeled shoe, and Maciek decides to repair it. In search of a hammer, he goes to the altar and finds a small church bell. In one of the most startling scenes in the film – one frequently commented upon by reviewers – Maciek repairs the shoe on the altar. This blasphemy is interrupted by an older man who is guarding the corpses of the two men Maciek and Andrzej slew earlier. The guard, unaware of the irony of the situation, scolds Maciek, telling him that he offends the memory of the dead people with his recklessness and insensitivity. This scene signifies the young man's lack of respect, his apostasy, his cynicism and his immorality, all of which have been brought about by his immersion in the war. In a deeply Catholic Poland, this blasphemy, along with the opening murder near the church, offended the audience in its insolence, and was in many eyes an attack on Polish values and tradition. The figure of the Christ hanging upside down in the Church signifies this new disorder, candidly revealed not only in cluttered *mise-en-scène*, but also in Cybulski's nervous portrayal of Maciek. The cynicism of this scene is later recaptured in a different context in *Krajobraz po bitwie* (*Landscape After Battle*, 1970), which also shows the cynicism of war in a religious context.

One of the most hotly debated symbols in the film is the surreal image of a white horse. On the way back to the hotel, Maciek passionately kisses Krystyna good-bye. As he turns away from her, he is approached by a white horse running loose in the streets. The horse, particularly the white horse, is an enduring symbol of virginity, innocence and chivalry present in many of Wajda's films – *Lotna, Wszystko na sprzedaż* (*Everything For Sale*, 1968), *Landscape After Battle*, *The Wedding*, and others. This symbol has multiple connotations: in *Ashes and Diamonds*, it seems to signify the unfulfilled dreams of the young fighter, leading to a transformation in Maciek, who, feeling that he is in love, now begins to think of a bright and peaceful future. Back in the hotel, now a reluctant assassin, Maciek questions Andrzej about the necessity of killing. The war is suddenly behind him; he wants to live, to study, perhaps to start a family. But Andrzej, his fellow soldier, is a man of resolute principle; he counters that they both have a duty that cannot be abandoned.

In a cross-cut to the party scene, Drewnowski, now completely drunk, does mischief at the banquet: he makes a fool of himself by climbing on to the banquet table and covering the other guests with foam from a fire extinguisher. Career and reputation thus ruined, he leaves the hall in shame. In a chaotic barrage of quickly ensuing scenes, we see Szczuka approached in the main hall of the hotel by an officer who knows the whereabouts of his son, Marek. Maciek overhears this conversation and waits under the staircase. In an elaborate sequence, the legs of Szczuka descend slowly down the ornate staircase, reflecting inversely the mounting tension, and we see as well the frightened face of Maciek, who is aware that his moment has come. When Szczuka leaves the hotel hurriedly, Maciek follows him and asks him for a light – and then, when offered it, shoots the older man in the heart. Szczuka staggers and slumps against the immobile Maciek. Just then the fireworks celebrating the end of the war erupt, illuminating Maciek and Szczuka standing still, seemingly crucified, clearly invoking the religious connotations and also tying this scene to that of the Crucifixion in the church.

When Maciek afterward washes the blood off his hands in the hotel room, we hear the banquet going on uninterrupted by the tragic event. In fact, Frédéric Chopin's Polonaise in A-major leads the tired banquet participants in a solemn dance of celebration. (A similarly austere dance will later reappear, with a slightly different tone, in *The Wedding*.) The film concludes with Maciek's attempted escape and subsequent death. He plans to leave by train, but when he approaches the tracks, he sees Andrzej beating Drewnowski for betraying the principles of the Home Army and for playing to two masters. Drewnowski notices Maciek and calls his name. As the startled Maciek begins to flee in an effort to catch the train, he accidentally runs into some Polish soldiers who, alert for saboteurs and members of the outlawed Home Army, shoot at him and fatally wound him. The famous 'laundry scene' follows, during which the bleeding Maciek tries to hide among the hanging sheets, unable to believe that he has been shot. He then lurches to the railway, but there his strength finally fails and – slowly, reluctantly, kicking – he dies on a pile of dirt. In this deeply symbolic scene, Wajda may have utilised some images from Andrzej Wróblewski's paintings, presenting the convoluted bodies of dying prisoners of war.

In the meantime, through brilliant cross-cutting, the spectator is led back to the banquet at which the polonaise continues into the early hours of the morning. Here, music itself carries a double meaning. The polonaise starts with the A-flat major polonaise by Chopin, but then turns into 'Pożegnanie ojczyzny' ('Farewell to the Homeland') by Michał Kleofas Ogiński, an ironic rewriting of Chopin's composition. This was Wajda's signal to his Polish audience that after 1945 the past had gone, never to be repeated, and dispelling illusions about Poland's political future. In the final sequence, the death of the young fighter is juxtaposed with the old porter taking out the Polish flag and with the last chords of the polonaise; these two accents provide a bitter commentary on Maciek's death.

The analysis of some of the film's sequences gives an insight into the structure of the narrative and the complexity of the historical and social issues presented. The conflict is already clearly delineated at the beginning of the film, which then unravels with an internal rhythm that moves briskly toward the tragic conclusion. Wajda himself credits the pace of the film to the well-written screenplay and, especially, to the acting of Zbigniew Cybulski as Maciek, who was able to stimulate and fascinate audiences with his onscreen presence. Called by Paul Coates 'the Polish James Dean, the existential representative of every young *"homme révolté"* in 1956', Cybulski easily conveyed a tragic hero who, while transforming from a cold-blooded assassin into a young man in love, must kill once again in the name of the Romantic notion of Idea. With his internal dilemmas, Maciek represents the generation torn by wartime events and forced to make specific choices. He was the reluctant hero, or rather anti-hero with whom Polish audiences could identify. With his doubts and almost hysterical reactions, with his uncertainty and strong desire to live and love after the Second World War despite or against any political dilemmas and struggles, Maciek is a deeply human figure. His death on the heap of rubbish symbolises the senselessness and pointlessness of his sacrifice and thus of similar sacrifices of countless other young people.

Maciek's story is portrayed against a rich social tapestry that presents itself in all its subplots: the political dilemmas of the post-war Polish society; the emerging new powers; the creation of new segments in the now communist society, in which the spoils of the war will come to those associated with the Communist Party (for example, Drewnowski); the presence of the new oppressor, the Soviet Union (the army officer at the party); and the presentation of traditional and aristocratic elements constituting remnants of the past (as represented by Mrs Staniewicz and her party). All these characters are linked by one predominant theme – that of the Second World War, in all its horror and sadness. The polonaise at the end of the film aptly illustrates these feelings of sadness and despair after the war, but it also illustrates, in its cynical ending, the war's political consequences.

Upon its release, *Ashes and Diamonds* triggered an unprecedented emotional response from young audiences who could identify with Maciek and his dilemma. Critics both in Poland and abroad realised immediately that they were dealing with a true masterpiece. Even in official party papers, such as *Trybuna ludu*, critics were generally full of praise. Aleksander Jackiewicz, then the official film critic of *Trybuna ludu* and editor of the weekly *Film*, states 'It is rare indeed – and not only in film art – for a young artist like Andrzej Wajda, at the start of his creative life, almost at its inception, to undertake a work which well may be the most outstanding work in his life'. Although the authorities officially condemned the romanticisation and glorification of the characters' clandestine activities, most Poles, young or old, clearly identified with their fight for Poland's ultimate independence. Young people especially, both those in 1958 and even today, understand Maciek and his intense emotional entanglement in the events surrounding the war. This appeal to human emotion and experience makes *Ashes and Diamonds* universally captivating, and appreciated for its honesty in the presentation of human emotions.

Janina Falkowska

REFERENCES

Coates, Paul (1996) 'Revisiting *Ashes and Diamonds* with Andrzejewski and Wajda', *Canadian Slavonic Papers*, 38, 3–4, 288–303.

Haltof, Marek (2002) *Polish National Cinema*. New York and Oxford: Berghahn Books, 87–8.

Hendrykowski, Marek (1984) 'Styl i kompozycja *Popiołu i Diamentu* Andrzeja Wajdy', in Alicja Helman and Tadeusz Miczka (eds) *Analizy i Interpretacje. Film Polski*. Katowice: Uniwersytet Śląski, 72–92.

Lubelski, Tadeusz (1992) *Strategie autorskie w polskim filmie fabularnym lat 1945–1961*. Uniwersytet Jagielloński: Rozprawy Habilitacyjne, 154–84.

Miczka, Tadeusz (1987) *Inspiracje plastyczne w twórczości filmowej i telewizyjnej Andrzeja Wajdy*. Katowice: Uniwersytet Śląski, 41–6.

Nurczyńska-Fidelska, Ewelina (1995) 'Romanticism and History: A Sketch of the Creative Output of Andrzej Wajda', in Ewelina Nurczyńska-Fidelska and Zbigniew Batko (eds) *Polish Cinema in Ten Takes*. Łódź: Łódzkie Towarzystwo Naukowe, 7–19.

Płazewski, Jerzy, Grzegorz Balski and Jan Słodowski (1996) *Wajda: Filmy*. vol. 1. Warsaw: W.A.i.F.

Wajda, Andrzej, unpublished biography, presented to the author in 2000.

NÓŻ W WODZIE KNIFE IN THE WATER

ROMAN POLAŃSKI, POLAND, 1962

07

Nóż w wodzie (*Knife in the Water*, 1962) is a tense, stripped-down story of the brief encounter between a couple, Andrzej and Krystyna, and a young hitchhiker. The couple's car screeches to a halt when a young man leaps in front of it, as they drive to the Mazurian lakes to sail their yacht. Andrzej challenges the hitchhiker to sail with them, then adopts the role of autocratic captain. The psychological duel of the two men is joined above the body of Krystyna, whose shedding of glasses and donning of bikini rejuvenate and transform her, placing her as close to the younger man as the older. An on-deck altercation in which Andrzej allows the hitchhiker's prized knife to fall overboard culminates in the young man himself landing in the water. It seems he cannot swim, and Andrzej and Krystyna cannot find him and fear he has drowned. While Andrzej searches, the hitchhiker – who has hidden behind a buoy – boards the boat, and he and Krystyna make love, after which he disembarks. On Andrzej's return, Krystyna tells of her betrayal, but Andrzej cannot or will not believe her. The film ends with the car immobile at a junction, reflecting his dilemma over whether or not to go to the police: reporting the hitchhiker's disappearance could see him indicted, while a turn the other way would indicate acceptance of the truth of Krystyna's words, and hence of his own cuckolding.

Writing in 1965, Al Alvarez elegantly situated *Knife in the Water* on the map of European cinema in the following terms: 'With less formal chastity and more invention, Godard might have directed it; with more formality still and no humour at all, Antonioni.' Polański's film had been the eagerly-awaited feature début of a director already well-known for his surreal short *Dwaj ludzie z szafą* (*Two Men and a Wardrobe*, 1959), a story of men emerging from the waves bearing a wardrobe, then returning to the sea from an inhospitable world. In a sense, *Knife in the Water* can be seen as giving a digressive rather than diagrammatic conjugation to the key elements of two of Polański's other, then-unreleased shorts, *Ssaki* (*Mammals*, 1962) and *Le gros et le maigre* (1961), which are Beckettian stories of duels between the strong and the weak. It can also be seen as remarkably Hitchcockian, particularly in its focus of tension upon the movement of small objects. Unusual in a film from an Eastern bloc country, its imaginative extraterritoriality helped promote the young director to the cover of *Time* magazine, win the FIPRESCI

(Fédération Internationale de la Presse Cinématographique) prize at the 1962 Venice Film Festival, and gain a nomination for the Oscar for Best Foreign Film in 1963. It also prompted the Alvarez comparisons with the gurus of vanguard Western narrative cinema, despite Polański's denials that his trips to France suggested any link with the *nouvelle vague*. The denials were well-founded, for in many respects *Knife in Water* was very much of its Polish time, justifying Alvarez's reference to its reading in Poland as 'a parable of the generations', though not his slightly sniffy irritation at the allegorical habits whereby Poles infiltrated relevant messages into officially sanctioned works of art: 'This perennial Polish game of Hunt-the-Symbol may at times be all very intriguing, but it is equally often irritating and sometimes debilitating.'

The film resembles a knife, with its many possible uses and use-values. The degree to which it is not simply localised in time or place can be gauged – for instance – by its status as the main, unspoken intertext of Michael Haneke's *Funny Games* (1997), to which it is linked by the provocative use of the knife, the summer sailing and bourgeois idyll, the pressure-cooker use of a time-limit, the older male's mocking as 'captain' and – last, but perhaps most importantly – the preoccupation with games. Whether or not Polański's film could also be an object of Haneke's stark critique of filmic violence is more debatable, as this is not yet the Polański of Hollywood, nor even of *Repulsion* (1965). Indeed, as noted – and despite official Polish criticisms – it is deeply rooted in contemporary Polish reality and concerns. It may well be that the combination of densely-registered social actuality (the likelihood with which windscreen wipers will be stolen) with the coolly-observed abstraction of an emotional triangle is what gives the film its continued appeal.

That social element has a great deal to do with the scriptwriting presence and preoccupations of Jerzy Skolimowski, whose inventive contribution Polański acknowledged. The dyeing and cutting of the hair of Jerzy Malanowicz, a young Method actor cast as the hitchhiker, to suggest a resemblance to Skolimowski is perhaps the most genuinely *nouvelle vague* element of the work – one of *hommage,* in-joke and brazen autobiography. His voice was dubbed by Polański himself, who also toyed with the idea of playing the boy, before Jerzy Bossak – the head of Polański's 'Kamera' film unit – dissuaded him. The genesis of this performance suggests the two directors' unification within a single body, rendering this almost as much a Skolimowski film as a Polański one. Thus another source of the film's authority may be its virtual dual authorship, as it combines the early 1960s most brilliantly gifted Polish directors, each of whom – of course – would find himself an exile before the decade's end. Skolimowski's films, revolving autobiographically around generational conflict and its symbolisation and ritualisation through games, are all 'cruel stories of youth'. Their young people, like so many young Poles, were energised by the Western jazz that represented political freedom precisely because of its coolness, flow and condemnation by rigid twentieth-century totalitarians of all stripes. That youthful spirit becomes quietly sophisticated in the marvellous jazz sax score of Krzysztof Komeda, the other main collaborator. The tight, inventive photography of Jerzy Lipman, meanwhile, may be arresting but arguably not quite so crucial.

Polański's title for the film was stunningly simple and elegantly Hitchcockian. On one level, it suggests a variety of crimes or primal confrontations culminating in a Macbethian need to cleanse a blade steeped in blood. Grażyna Stachówna notes how the boy's knife seems to outweigh all the gadgets possessed by Andrzej, usefully cross-referencing the statement by Balzac's Rastignac that 'one has to have a knife to go through life'. The knife has this status because it is not merely symbolic of power (though it is that also, of course, being – inevitably – 'phallic' in the senses of both Freud and Lacan) but is itself a form of power, outweighing all other objects through its ability to determine life and death. The knife can trump Andrzej's many gadgets because it is itself already a multiplicity of objects, something made explicit in the invention known as the Swiss Army knife, of which it is the poorer Polish cousin. Its usefulness in the forest – underlined by the boy – is primal efficacy. The concentration of power in this one object suggests the possible success of the boy's challenge to the older man, for all the latter's yachting know-how. We cannot know at the outset that the blade will fall into the water rather than be dipped there deliberately to cleanse it. It clicks open with great *éclat* when first brandished, like a winning hand slapped down triumphantly in a card game.

'If two men are on board, one's the skipper', says Andrzej. As noted above, *Knife in the Water* is a study of power relations. It can be read as dramatising what the French literary and social theorist René Girard would term a crisis of 'mimetic desire', in which Freudian Oedipal rivalry becomes a game of mirroring or imitation between rivals. Not for nothing does it unfold in the strictly delimited time period of the classical tragedies Girard studied. Andrzej's efforts to humiliate the boy seek to bolster his own prowess in the eyes of the sceptical Krystyna. His fear and jealousy become patent as he wakes to find her not below deck and his immediate appropriation of the knife lodged in the breadboard indicates a determination to take the matter – and the boy – in hand, which he does by ordering him to swab the deck. Anything and everything can stage the symbolic drama of rivalry. Andrzej's amusement at the boy's discomfiture when the latter tries to steer becomes shamefacedness whenever he is caught taking over something from the younger man, be it whistling the same tune (a mistake he is lured into by Krystyna whistling it before him) or imitating the boy's movement of the blade among his outstretched fingers. Rivalry even extends to the speed with which each can inflate a lilo.

Questions of relative power are woven deeply into the techniques of shooting on a small boat, usually from one of its ends to the other. The camera is almost always required to be behind one or other of the men, looking up or down the yacht, thereby rendering one or the other *smaller*. Their situational interchangeability is inscribed in this movement, from, say, behind Andrzej at the helm to behind the boy, near the prow, looking back at him. The proximity to the body in this tight space emphasises the sensuality of exposed flesh, the risk and promise of contact and the usual distance, or middle-distance – 'in-play' status – of the most attractive body, that of the bikini-clad and even twice topless (shot from behind) Krystyna. The interchanges follow a musical rhythm that also marks the dialogue with mutually dependent inversions and repetitions, such as when the boy asks Andrzej if he can anticipate a storm 'in his bones' (*po kościach*) and Andrzej comments, shortly thereafter, that he knows it's lunchtime 'by his stomach' (*po żołądku*).

This musicality is that of Beckettian dialogue. The film is defined neither by any putative relationship with the French *nouvelle vague* (Polański himself being trenchantly critical of the inadequacies both of the term and the movement) nor by its relationship with such works as Andrzej Wajda's *Niewinni czarodzieje* (*Innocent Sorcerers,* 1960) or Janusz Morgenstern's *Do widzenia, do jutra* (*Be Seeing You, Tomorrow,* 1960). It is, rather, a successful transposition into a realist feature context of the absurdist sketches of power relations of such Polański shorts as *Mammals* or *Le gros et le maigre*. This passage from short to feature is smoothed by the work's structuring as a set of 'variations on a theme'. As Marek Hendrykowski rightly notes, this involves a jazz-like improvisation. Here Krzysztof Komeda's jazz score becomes crucial. It performs two functions. On the one hand, it works briefly in the traditional manner of film music, be it for dramatic heightening (when the hitchhiker holds the hot soup-pan in his bare hands or when he goes overboard near the end) or for comic relief (as the two men pull the yacht away into the distance). On the other hand, and much more importantly, its more extended passages evoke a cool release of tension that may be called utopian, as the characters' confrontations subside and they simply tune-in to the sun and lapping water. The alternation may be described as one of ideology and utopia; confrontational games and relaxing in the sun. In the latter sections, the camera movements and positions become cool and playful, calling attention to themselves: the hitchhiker's finger shifts from one side to the other as he opens and closes his eyes; Krystyna dominating the foreground, with a string of small shoreline trees. There is indeed a jazz-like rhythm of improvisatory variations on a theme, of confrontations sizzling then fizzling, usually whenever Krystyna intervenes to discharge a tension of which she is to some extent the unacknowledged catalyst. The casual, jazz-like sections never become desultory, spiced, as they are, with rising tension. The unpredictable interweaving of these two registers help generate the film's interest, its continuing freshness and the consummate feel for cinematic rhythm.

If Alvarez's impatience with allegorical reading suggests an incompatibility of 'Eastern' and 'Western' hermeneutics, it is worth concluding with words from a review by the Polish critic Zygmunt Kałużyński who seems to some extent to have enjoyed a jester's licence to tell the truth, and who describes the film in terms that could have been used either side of the Iron Curtain, as well as after 1989: '*Knife in the Water* is the story of a banal weekend, somewhere on the Lakes, as performed by three such average people that it could have occurred anywhere: one has to say, not just in Poland, but throughout the Europe of the period of social go-getting, of the trend to embourgeoisement and fast profits. It is possible that *Knife in the Water* has a broader resonance than the local, addressing the moods of 1961 wherever the slogan "make the most of life" is heard.' He further claimed that 'the film unmasks the characteristic feature of contemporary wealth; its relativity, nervousness, limitations. If the aim of wealth is supposed to be independence, as it was generally judged to be in the nineteenth century, one has to say that the protagonists of *Knife in the Water*, for all their material success, are still a long way from achieving that.' No wonder Polański could move with such ease to the West, or that his film – for all its local colour (that Polish bourgeois of 1961 who justly fears the theft of his windscreen wipers) – remains profoundly relevant to our own aspirational world.

Very few materials concerning the approval and post-shoot vetting of Polański's film are extant, the only relevant document in the Warsaw Filmoteka Narodowa (National Film Archive) being the protocol of a meeting of the Script Assessment Commission. Its close inspection reveals the divisions aroused by Polański's project, and it is remarkable for the absence of the two scriptwriters, who would usually have been present (their interests are represented by Jerzy Bossak, head of the 'Kamera' film unit that produced the film).

Generally speaking, the members of the film industry on the commission were in favour of making the film, while the political appointees had considerable objections (the sole exception to this being Aleksander Ścibor-Rylski, future scenarist of *Man of Marble*, who disliked it intensely). Łódź Film School Director Jerzy Toeplitz's faint advocacy was on the grounds that 'a summer adventure' would be 'a popular hit', though he worried whether the film should be classified as serious or as a comedy and would have preferred 'a more mocking view of the well-heeled representatives of the upper levels of our people's Fatherland'. Where the well-known critic, cultural commentator and scriptwriter Krzysztof Teodor Toeplitz discerned an excellent study of generational conflict compromising both male protagonists, the political opponents saw it as favouring the hitchhiker. The most vocal of them was Wincenty Kraśko, who initially deemed it the worst script he had encountered. Kraśko felt that the work's pedagogical dimension required 'far greater significance for a positive example than a negative one'. One of his remarks is chillingly prophetic of later reaction at the highest Party levels: 'If certain viewers were outraged after seeing *Innocent Sorcerers,* there'd be real cause for outrage here.' Several opponents likened the work to the *nouvelle vague,* deeming it an empty, bourgeois entertainment film, contrasted it unfavourably with Tadeusz Konwicki's *Ostatni dzień lata* (*Last Days of Summer,* 1957) and felt there was too little material for a film. This last criticism would be a leitmotif of reaction to screenplays with which Skolimowski was associated, though it rings somewhat ironic in the context of the comparison with Konwicki's film, which is in fact shorter than *Knife in the Water.* Only the film industry representatives mentioned Polański's name and derived confidence from it. Where the script's detractors floundered in their efforts to categorise it, one representative of this group saw it as resisting pigeonholing, and was one of several to term it a psychological drama. Summing up, Culture Minister Tadeusz Zaorski confessed that the script read well, but wondered what its authors meant to say. He recommended that the Commission meet again, with them present, to consider the next step.

Once approved, the film encountered a mixture of obstacles, some comic, some more serious. Those involving the non-professional Jolanta Umecka, cast as Krystyna on the basis of her shapeliness in a bikini, were simply comic, as she forgot her lines and her excessive eating changed her shape during the shoot. Actual shooting on the yacht was also problematic, be it because of the need to hang from a safety harness or because the changing breeze shifted the light and disturbed background continuity. More serious was the visit to the set by a reporter from *Ekran,* whose hatchet-job on the high life of a film crew disporting itself between a luxury yacht and Polański's Mercedes prompted Bossak to engineer its replacement with a Peugeot. The media further darkened Polański's mood with shots of his wife clubbing in Italy with director Gillo Pontecorvo. Most devastating of all was the death during this period of Andrzej Munk, the black comic master of the Polish School, to whom Polański had felt particularly close.

Nor was post-production smooth, as the recorded sound proved useless and the actors' voices needed post-synchronisation (only Leon Niemczyk, the professional who played Andrzej, synchronised his own). The film was then almost shelved by the Ministry of Culture, one of whose senior officials reportedly demanded a clear-cut ending: 'either have them go home or go to the police – one of the two.' Bossak suggested one or two cuts to reduce the ambiguity, however, and the film was released to an ambivalent press.

If, as one reviewer put it, 'mixed feelings' characterised the Polish press reception of *Knife in the Water*, the mixture was usually one of praise for its form and scepticism of its content; the usual formula for dealing with artistically impressive but politically sensitive material. Most reviews begin by lauding its formal virtuosity, thereby establishing their freedom from political bias and apparent primary commitment to the aesthetic, with subsequent declarations of discontent with the work's ostensible 'unreality' representing attempts to blunt its genuine socio-critical thrust. Although Grażyna Stachówna has argued against the notion of any critical conspiracy, the way in which a specialist film journal like *Ekran* echoes the criticisms of the Party daily, *Trybuna ludu*, is somewhat suspicious. Each attacks fashionable French influences ('Yachting on the new wave' being the *Trybuna ludu* title); each adds that a real French work would have been more realistically grounded; and the phrase 'terrifying nihilism' recurs. Perhaps the most amusing critical move is found in a review paralleling the film with *Lady and the Tramp*, distributed in Poland as *A Mongrel in Love* (*Zakochany kundel*).

Given the widespread early 1960s Party preoccupation with the putative decline in youth morality, it is noteworthy that the review of *Głos nauczycielski* (*The Teacher's Voice*) refers to a large number of schoolchildren attending even during school hours, adding that 'this film is not appropriate for the young, particularly under-sixteens', while 'the older young need to realise that the protagonists are not typical'. This search for 'typical' protagonists was, of course, central both to socialist aesthetics, which sought to define characters as 'reflective' of their class origins, and also to Polish audiences, used to reading texts for allegorical relevance to the state of the nation. The recurrent critical denials of typicality indicate that the film was being read – as intended – precisely in these terms.

These denials were reinforced by a tendency to take Krystyna as the film's *porte parole*, voicing a critique of 'buffoonery' (*kabotizm*). Reviews then pronounced an attack on this phenomenon to be a rather minor matter, ignoring the fact that only Krystyna describes the hitchhiker as essentially akin to her husband – rather than situationally similar, like the mimetic rival of the theories of René Girard. In any case, this does not obviate the critique of the consumerist and potentially criminal bankruptcy of the older generation. After all, it is Andrzej who initiates the deadly game. In any case, there may well be a stronger resemblance between the boy and Krystyna, each with little power *vis-à-vis* Andrzej, each briefly asserting power over him by fictionalising reality (the boy pretends to have drowned, and Krystyna pretends to Andrzej that this did indeed occur, relenting only just before the end). Their youth and relative powerlessness link them. Perhaps unsurprisingly, one of the very few laudatory high-profile reviews appears in the Catholic *Tygodnik powszechny*, where the well-known and widely-respected Jan Józef Szczepański emphasised the importance of the ethical problems treated by the film, praised its avoidance of the easy artistic option of 'getting by by bringing a large number of elements into play', and welcomed it as 'a harbinger of a new, promising generation of artists'.

However, that generation and its preoccupations would be lambasted shortly thereafter in a notorious speech by the Party leader, Władysław Gomułka, whose patronage of the 'thaw' of the Polish October of 1956 had revealed itself as temporary. On 4 July 1963, his speech 'On Current Issues in the Ideological Work of the Party' named *Knife in the Water* as one of several films that 'considered separately may even possess certain artistic or technical values, but their striking feature is a detachment from the concrete and the real social conditions of a Poland engaged in building socialism, as well as a pessimistic approach to human fortunes'. The dovetailing of the terms of this critique and that of the earlier reviews does indeed suggest a concerted campaign against Polański's work (though, even more against that of Jerzy Skolimowski, whose hand was in two of the offending films and who – not coincidentally – may be viewed as the source of their irritatingly hard-hitting social criticism). The foundations of the Party's worries about the youthful response becomes obvious when one considers Czesław Michalski's review in *Walka młodych* (*The Struggle of the Young*), which contrasts it favourably with the 'literariness' of another work condemned by Gomułka, Kazimierz Kutz's *Nikt nie woła* (*Nobody Calls*, 1960) as well as with others rendered hermetic by the modernity of their form. The very *accessibility* of Polański's generational critique was surely the reason why so many reviewers sought to denigrate it as a merely snobbish aping of Western, particularly *nouvelle vague,* trends.

The ending, with the car immobile before the road sign, may be less an example of modernist openness than a devastating image of a culture with nowhere to go. That image becomes modernist to a degree, however, when juxtaposed with Krystyna's question about the ending of Andrzej's anecdote about the sailor who danced on broken glass. The issue of how stories ought to end is linked to that of the viability of communication in general, as the marriage is deadlocked by the refusal of one party (Andrzej) to accept what the other is saying, either because Krystyna's confession of infidelity with a 'pup' (Andrzej's word for the boy – *szczeniak*) would wound his pride if believed, or because truth and falsehood have become inextricable. In either case, of course, their relationship (on the allegorical level, that between Poland and its rulers) is bankrupt, literally going nowhere.

Paul Coates

REFERENCES

Alvarez, Al (1965) *Under Pressure: The Writer in Society; Eastern Europe and the USA*. Harmondsworth: Penguin.

Hendrykowski, Marek (1997) 'Modern Jazz', *Kwartalnik filmowy*, 17, 85–96.

Kałużyński, Zygmunt (1966) *Salon dla miliona*. Warsaw: Iskry.

Michalski, Czesław (1962) '*Nóż w wodzie*', *Walka Młodych*, 18 March.

Stachówna, Grażyna (1987) '"*Nóż w wodzie*" Romana Polańskiego czyli: jak debiutować w kinie?', *Kino*, 242, 4–7, 24–6.

Szczepański, Jan Józef (1962) '*Nóż w wodzie*', *Tyganik powszechy*, 8 April.

ŖEKOPIS ZNALEZIONY W SARAGOSSIE THE SARAGOSSA MANUSCRIPT

WOJCIECH J. HAS, POLAND, 1964

Wojciech Has' film Ŗekopis znaleziony w Saragossie (*The Saragossa Manuscript* aka *The Manuscript Found at Saragossa*, 1964), recently restored to its original version by the Pacific Film Archives of San Francisco, would seem to be an unlikely candidate for the kind of international cult interest it has sustained to the present day. In order to clarify the surprising contemporaneity of an apparently anachronistic film by an internationally little-known director, this chapter will examine the aesthetic strategies at work within the film and how they transformed the early nineteenth-century novel by Jan Patocki upon which it is based.

The distinguishing feature of Potocki's novel *Le Manuscrit trouvé à Saragosse* (*The Manuscript Found at Saragossa*) is its particular use of a *mise-en-abyme* structure in which multiple levels of narration are superimposed, generating a labyrinthine text highly resonant with more contemporary forms of literary experimentation such as the work of Borges. While the use of *mise-en-abyme* was a key element of Baroque aesthetic practices, Patocki extended this structure to such an extent that distinguishing between different levels of the text at times becomes impossible and the book becomes a potentially infinite text extending into the cosmos itself. The modernity of this text is, however, not limited to this *mise-en-abyme* structure but extends to a novel treatment of the fantastic. While clearly inspired by such tales of the fantastic as the *1001 Nights* and *The Decameron*, *The Manuscript Found at Saragossa* distinguishes itself through a unique tension between the telling of fantastic tales, and the demystification of these tales through a rational interpretation influenced by the Enlightenment. In fact, as Barbara Giżycka has pointed out, the novel is characterised by the '"supposed supernatural", by the constant hesitation between a rational or supernatural interpretation of events'. Here the role of the intercalated stories is crucial as they provide examples that either reinforce the supernatural or else deflate it through narratives that reveal examples of the 'false supernatural', in which apparently supernatural events are revealed to in fact have rational explanations. Furthermore, this 'supposed supernatural' leads to a novel manner of representation in which it is through variation that the supernatural is both suggested and thrown into doubt, through the repetition of key scenes, as well as via the multiple echoes of similar events in different narratives.

Both this tension and its labyrinthine construction through multiple levels of narration are not only maintained but emphasised by Has' cinematic adaptation, which while maintaining a 'pragmatic fidelity' to the original text, also contains significant alterations to the original. In fact, it would be more correct to consider the film as a transcription of the novel serving to generate an entirely new text, in the markedly different sign system constituted by the cinema. Has' treatment of the text is to render it both more unstable and more productive, by emphasising and extending the tendencies towards undecidability already present in the novel.

Before analysing the film itself it is worth looking briefly at Has' cinematic production more broadly, in order to give some idea of the enigmatic and atypical place it holds in Polish film culture. Coming from an art school background, Has' cinematic career began in the 1950s, at the same time as the more well-known filmmakers Andrzej Wajda and Andrzej Munk, whose work of this period became known as the 'Polish School'. However Has' subjective and expressionistic cinema was so divergent from the social and national preoccupations of these filmmakers that it would be tempting to view it as an equivalent of 'art cinema', in relation to the mainstream of Polish filmmaking. However, any such distinction is problematic in relation to a non-capitalist production system, where the dominant tendency embodied in filmmakers like Wajda was in fact a politically engaged *cinéma d'auteur*. Inasmuch as this dominant cinema of the Polish School, informed as it was by aesthetic as well as social intentions, was nevertheless a realist, socially engaged cinema, the cinema of Has clearly departs from this paradigm in the direction of an expressionist, aesthetically experimental cinema.

This divergence can clearly be seen in Has' first feature film *Pętla* (*The Noose*, 1957) in which the originally realist story concerning the last days of an alcoholic was transformed by Has into an expressionist and metaphorical film, where all fixed social and historical references are suspended in favour of an aesthetic universality. From these beginnings, Has' work as a whole can be characterised as the transformation of real elements into a highly subjective and personal vision of the world, whatever its apparent subject matter. This is why Has' decision to adapt literary works with a fantastic dimension, such as *The Saragossa Manuscript*, was hardly a break in his career, and far from invalidating his auteurism was, in fact, its culmination. *The Saragossa Manuscript* was in many ways the perfect way for Has to develop his cinematic aesthetics in the direction of the Neo-Baroque. This understanding of Has as an auteur is necessary to counter the original reception of the film in Poland where, while appreciated, it was usually reduced to questions of whether it faithfully adapted the original novel rather than being evaluated in its own terms.

08

In Has' film, Patocki's sprawling and polyphonic novel is broken down into two contrasting parts, corresponding respectively to the adventures of Alphonse Van Worden in the Sierra Morena and the tales of the Gypsy Avadoro, largely taking place in Madrid. This contrast was certainly present in the original text, and both these components of the novel were in fact published separately during Patocki's lifetime. Nevertheless, their presentation in the film highlighted their incommensurability as two contrasting approaches to the supernatural. Whereas in the first, the supernatural is presented in terms of inexplicable experiences, accompanied by a highly Baroque and 'Orientalist' aesthetics, in the second part numerous overlapping stories, of a much more urbane nature, serve to demystify the apparently mysterious as merely the result of false perceptions and misguided beliefs. However, the embedding of the second series of stories within the first, disallows any simple account of the film as a narrative of demystification, as many of the earlier events are never fully explained, and even in the second series of tales, there still remain gaps and inconsistencies that elude any complete rationalisation. Furthermore, as both parts of the film are contained within the same framing narrative, both the mysterious and rationalist interpretations are called into question, or relativised as interlaced elements of an infinite process of invention. However, in order to clarify how the film functions as a whole, it is necessary to first disentangle these three components of the film.

Following the opening, framing sequence, which more or less recapitulates Patocki's *mise-en-abyme* preface to his novel as two opposing officers begin to read the text itself, we see Alphonse Van Worden (Zbygniew Cybulski) lying on the ground in the desolate environment of the Sierra Morena. This posture, apart from echoing Cybulski's most famous role in *Ashes and Diamonds*, also serves as a visual indication of a descent or disorientation, in which action and consciousness are suspended. When Alphonse does act and speak, in order to insist to his two servants that they will take the most direct route to Madrid, through the Sierra Morena, as his honour dictates that he pay no attention to their superstitions, his performance establishes a strong vein of comic absurdity. In Has' film, despite the identificatory powers of the medium, there is a considerable distancing from this central character who is presented as being rash, foolish and far more susceptible to fear and superstition than he presents himself to be. Although the spectator accompanies Alphonse on his journey, it is less through identifying with him as a heroic figure than through Alphonse's tendency, as played by Cybulski, to become a substitute spectator, an everyman who lives his experiences ineptly and as if they hardly concerned him.

The journey into the Sierra Morena is presented explicitly as a journey into both the supernatural and the unconscious, by means of a Baroque iconography of skulls, snakes and hanging bodies, as well as a series of rapid stages in which Alphonse finds himself abandoned by both his servants, the first of whom has run off with his supplies, and then arrives at a seemingly deserted inn, the Venta Quemada. However, it is when he falls asleep that he fully arrives in the realm of the fantastic; after being startled out of his sleep by a semi-naked black woman, he is informed that two foreign women request that he dine with them. The black woman leads Alphonse through a passageway into a hidden room where he meets two 'Muslim' sisters, Emina and Zibelda who, apart from informing Alphonse that he is their cousin and that they have an erotic relationship with each other, also indicate that they have been waiting for him as he is to be their husband on the condition that he renounce his Christianity, symbolised by the locket he wears around his neck.

The Orientalism of this scene is clear, and is in part explained by Patocki's fascination with *1001 Nights*, but there is also a use, by Has, of scenic and aural components in order to effect a metamorphosis into the realm of the fantastic. First of all there is the construction of a seemingly infinite room, which loses all sense of being part of its setting of the inn, to become a virtual space where all kinds of transformations are possible. This is partly done through visual means, but also through the use of abstract electronic music and the echoing of footsteps as if taking place in a vast space. In fact, the highly fluid camera movements, the scenic alterations – so that what begins as a dining room suddenly becomes a bedroom – and the circling of the characters around each other, all give the sense of an induction into a realm where rationality is suspended, which affects the viewer directly rather than through the medium of the narrator's interpretations. Alphonse is rendered almost speechless by these events, and is more like a spectator than an interpreter; a crucial difference between the film and the book. The result of this is to completely suspend any questions of the truth or falsity of the supernatural in favour of a direct entry into a form of surreality.

This scene culminates in another key sequence in which the two sisters encourage Alphonse to drink from a cup in the form of a human skull, after which he awakes under the gibbet of two hanged brothers, the same setting that he had passed on his way to the inn and where his servants disappeared. When Alphonse returns to the inn, there is no sign of the two women, and the room has been transformed from a space of enchantment into a space of decay, complete with rotting food and rats.

The remainder of this section of the film is a series of variations on this scenario. For example, when Alphonse encounters a hermit who is attempting to exorcise a deformed creature called Pasheco. Pasheco recounts a tale in which he too is subject of an erotic enchantment by two sisters at the same inn, in this case his father's new wife and her sister, after which he also awakens under the gallows. But when Pasheco returns to the inn, he is pursued by two 'demons', who turn out to be none other than the two hung bandits, who eventually succeed in gouging out his eye. Finally, after Alphonse drinks from the skull-cup again, only to awaken once more under the gallows, he finds himself in the company of a Kabbalist who seems to know everything about his experience, but to whom Alphonse refuses to impart any more information.

What is at stake in these repetitions and variations is a presentation of the fantastic at once strange and familiar, as entirely plausible and defying explanation. In fact, what is most striking is the erotic quality of these scenes, in which desire and death are intertwined, rather than any conventional representation of the supernatural. There is a dream logic in which the impossible is directly related to desire and the unconscious. From the opening scenes of Alphonse lying on the grass, through multiple images of the loss of consciousness, to the cyclical experience of time, much of this part of the film seems concerned with access to the unconscious and an attempt to master it rather than present a conventional representation of the fantastic. While this 'psychoanalytic' dimension was already anticipated in the novel, Has' film clearly draws on psychoanalysis in its presentation of this unconscious logic. In this respect, Alphonse's reluctance or inability to articulate his experiences of otherness and erotic plenitude, would seem to correspond to the psychoanalytic model of the dream, for which several film theorists such as Christian Metz have claimed, cinema forms an analogous mechanism. However, it is necessary to be a little more precise; in this film, this 'other' scene is not presented as completely other to conscious experience, but rather as a process of induction, or the opening up of another world within the existing one. As such, it corresponds more closely to a process of hypnosis, in which the subject is led to perceive and act differently, but not without losing all capacity for action, except at the limit of unconsciousness. Furthermore, despite the presence in Has' film of objects that could be interpreted symbolically, such as snakes, skulls and jewels, there is no real meaning behind these elements except as Baroque emblems of desire. In short, the experiences of enchantment are presented as the opening of a virtual, utopic realm within the real, a form of surrealism, in which the question is more how this desire functions and what affects it provokes, than whether the scenes represented are true or false, or what their meaning is.

The formal construction of this section of the film, while more linear than the second part, already consists of a series of overlapping stories told from a variety of perspectives. There is a marked contrast in tone between the story narrated by Alphonse about his father's marriage and that told by Pasheco, under the monk's orders, even if both concern the possibility of a demonic possession at the hands of a beautiful woman. However, it is in the second part of the film that this proliferation of overlapping stories is carried to the point of delirium, despite the fact that this is the part of the film that apparently seeks to demystify the 'supposed supernatural' expressed by the first section.

Rather than attempt to disentangle the multiple narratives recounted in the second part of the film, it is more fruitful to concentrate on the scene of their elaboration, and the very different aesthetics that are used to recount them. All action on the primary plane of the narrative ceases, in favour of a scene of storytelling, conducted exclusively by an entirely new character, the Gypsy Avadoro. It is as if the hypnotic enchantment of the first section has served as the induction into a world of multiple interlocking stories that take up the space where the action has been suspended, emphasised by the fact that even the storyteller tells not his own story so much as a network of other stories that have been told to him, and according to which he is obliged to re-orient his actions. In a different, yet related manner to the deserted inn, the Kabbalist's castle where this storytelling takes place is also a virtual space, but a space of fabulation rather than of sensory enchantment.

This shift is expressed by both the difference in the content of the narratives and the aesthetics of how they are presented. First of all, these stories, all set in Madrid, are broadly comic tales of betrayed and betraying lovers, secret trysts, absurd conventions, romance and eroticism. While this comic tone was already anticipated in Cybulski's performance and the story concerning his father's duel to near-death with a stranger, simply because the latter had overtaken his carriage, in this part of the film this kind of comedy of manners completely replaces the Baroque iconography of the Sierra Morena section. This is expressed through scenes that are as well-lit as a Hollywood historical romance; moreover, this section looks as if this was indeed the model being emulated. However, this apparent conventionality is deceptive. If on one level, there is a simplification of visual style, there is also an accompanying complication of narrative levels, at times relaying four or five individual stories, frequently moving between each with little notice, generating a dizzying effect of narrative instability.

At the same time, since most of these stories concern an unmasking of false perceptions and beliefs in the name of enlightenment values, there is a direct reversal of the aesthetics of the first section to correspond to this logic. If the first part of the film followed a hypnotic or oneiric logic to present a journey into the supernatural, it makes sense that the passage from superstition to reason should be presented by means of a comic and realist aesthetics, in which human ignorance is deflated through broad parody and satire.

For this reason, many of the elements of the first part of the film reappear but in an entirely new light. For example there are effects of horror, such as the husband who believes he is visited by a ghost in the form of a disembodied head, but this is revealed to be no more than the result of the comic and scheming activities of his unfaithful wife and her lover. There is also the recourse to Christian faith of the character Toledo, to counter the demonic forces of the afterlife, but this spiritual conversion is shown derisively to be no more than a case of mistaken identity; immediately reversed once its true cause is revealed. Finally, there is the figure of the potentially demonic woman, especially in the character of Frasquita. But her 'evil' is shown to be an all too earthly will to pursue her carnal desires rather than the result of any occult forces. In short, the mystery evoked in the first part of the film is subjected to an entirely worldly treatment through the derisive humour of the second, reflected in the well-lit aesthetics and fluid movements, in which even murders are presented as comic events.

Nevertheless, there are several factors that undermine this narrative of enlightenment, even before taking into account its placement within the film as a whole. First of all there is the undecidability of the narrative; there are just too many narrative threads on too many different levels for complete resolution to take place. Even if it is arguable that at the end of this section, all the stories have been explained, gaps and inconsistencies nevertheless remain, and there are simply too many stories to be retained by the spectator at any one time.

Secondly, there is the unreliability of many of the narrators. Not only are some of the storytellers, such as Bousqueros, shown to be unreliable and self-serving rogues, thereby casting doubts upon their stories, but the multiple levels of stories within stories adds to this unreliability, in that any of these multiple narrators could easily be lying or inventing things, including Avadoro himself.

Finally, there are the cuts back to the scene of the storytelling in the castle, which not only reminds the viewer that these are all just stories being told within a completely different narrative, to which their demystifications may not apply, but also show the psychological effects of this storytelling on its audience, especially Alphonse, who notably says on reviewing a particularly dense moment of intercalated tales, 'but this could drive one mad'. As this is the direct echo of something said earlier by the Kabbalist in relation to attempting to understand Alphonse's own story, the delirium of this apparently rational section of the film is clearly emphasised.

This brings us to the ending of the film, which as the greatest departure from the novel is also the most controversial component of Has' adaptation. The ending begins when Alphonse is suddenly called away on business, back to the inn where he once again encounters the two sisters, this time in the company of their father who is revealed to be the hermit and hands him the book in which all his adventures are inscribed, telling him it is up to him to write the rest. He expresses his regret that he will not see the Princesses again, but this time, when he falls asleep he awakens in the inn, and through a hole in the wall sees himself leaving with the two sisters. His double turns back and for a brief time the two Alphonses mirror each other, before separating again. This ending is a departure from the novel and inscribes the story as an infernal doubling closed in upon itself. It seems to imply that despite Alphonse's apparent freedom to write his own story, he has become, in part, a prisoner of the book. In addition, Alphonse's uncanny doubling in which he becomes the alarmed spectator of himself tends to retrospectively recast the entire story as a descent into madness, an effect that is only increased by the final scene.

After another return to what appears to be the beginning of the narrative in which he assures his servants that they will reach Madrid by nightfall, the final scene shows a seemingly mad Alphonse frantically scribbling in the book and mumbling. When he is informed that two strangers request that he dine with them and sees them once again through the window with a mirror between them, he puts his fingers to his lips, throws the book against the wall where it lands in its original position in the beginning of the film, before riding off against the familiar Sierra Morena backdrop. While it would be a mistake to analyse this overdetermined ending too narrowly, it certainly seems to reinforce the sense of enclosure within the world of the film, both through the repetition of the motif of mirroring, and through the fact that even Alphonse's escape is only once more within the world of the manuscript. Of course, this enclosure could be interpreted either in terms of madness or of demonic possession, but this really makes little difference as the effect is to give a sense that there is no escaping the world of the film, that Alphonse will perpetually be plagued by an alternation of enchantment and disenchantment within a maze of overlapping narratives.

All through this analysis, it has been clear that Has' film, even more than Patocki's novel, is characterised by an indecision that undermines both romantic beliefs in a central hero, and enlightenment aspirations towards total clarity. This indecision points in two seemingly disparate directions. One of these is a type of modernism, based on the multiplication of narratives, the paradoxical, open ending and the psychoanalytic dimensions of the film, which are all key components of a modernist aesthetics in both literature and film. The film clearly resonates with the works of such modernist writers as Jorge Luis Borges, Bruno Schulz and Witold Gombrowicz, along with modern filmmakers such as Raul Ruiz, not to mention the aesthetics of Surrealism. Has' subsequent adaptation of Bruno Schulz's stories, entitled *Sanatorium pod klepsydrą* (*Sanatorium Under the Sign of the Hourglass*, 1973), usually taken as a project directly linked to this film, would seem to confirm this hypothesis.

But at the same time, both the novel and the film also draw on a clearly Baroque aesthetics, which distinguishes itself from both Romantic and Enlightenment strategies through the excessive proliferation of signs, which function more as paradoxical allegories than as symbols with clear univocal meanings. It is this Baroque proliferation that creates a bridge between Patocki's and Has' aesthetics in the articulation of a Baroque Modernism, or a Neo-Baroque aesthetics, which sidestep the intervening contestation between Romanticism and Rationalism that was still very popular in Polish film culture at the time the film was made. Hence, if there is a political dimension to this film, it arguably resides in its contestation of the dominance of these tendencies, in favour of a Neo-Baroque aesthetics of invention, which goes beyond any 'art for art's sake' aestheticism. Instead, there is, throughout all Has' work, an ethical presentation of the neglected and virtual dimensions of the past, presented in order to contest and render strange the 'codes' of the present. This kind of Baroque modernism is equally present in the work of Bruno Schulz, which Has would subsequently adapt, as well as in that of the Polish avant-garde theatre practitioner, Tadeusz Kantor, who similarly resorts to Baroque proliferations of allegorical objects. Has' related tendency to fill his shots with assemblies of dead or discarded objects, without any clear narrative purpose, abundantly demonstrated in *The Saragossa Manuscript*, tends to support this interpretation, and to give some indication as to why this apparently anachronistic film should have such a strong sense of contemporancity, and a continued popularity well beyond the usual channels of East European film reception.

Michael Goddard

REFERENCE

Giżycka, Barbara (1976) Le Fantastique dans le 'Manuscrit trouvé à Saragosse' de Jean Potocki et dans le film de Wojciech Has. Warsaw: Master's Thesis, Department of Romance Philology.

OBCHOD NA KORZE A SHOP ON THE HIGH STREET

JÁN KADÁR AND ELMAR KLOS, CZECHOSLOVAKIA, 1965

For a number of reasons, *Obchod na korze* (*A Shop on the High Street* aka *The Shop on Main Street*, 1965) is among the most extraordinary films of Czecho-Slovak cinematography. When it was released, the film caught the interest of public and critics alike with the strength and drama of its story, looking back at the history of the wartime Slovak State (1939–45). Made during the expansion of 'new wave' cinema, its formal simplicity was surprising and it was the first of Czech and Slovak films to win an Academy Award. What is also interesting is the fact that it was made by two older directors: Ján Kadár, a Slovak, who had made his debut in 1945, and Elmar Klos, a Czech, originally a screenwriter and script supervisor, who had made his debut before the war. *A Shop on the High Street* is considered part of Slovak cinema while at the same time belonging to the history of Czech filmmaking. It is an adaptation of a Slovak topic, tells a story taking place during the Slovak State, was filmed in Slovakia, and contains dialogue written and spoken only in Slovak. It was created during the era of Czechoslovakia by two Czecho-Slovak artists, together with a Czecho-Slovak film crew. Finally, the closing titles tell us that it was produced at the Barrandov Studios in Prague. All of this means it can be found in both Czech and Slovak film encyclopaedias and, for the same reasons and criteria, it may have been deleted from one source or another. At a time when the term had not even been coined, this was one of the first Czecho-Slovak co-productions made based on close historical and cultural ties, on the relationship between Slovak and Czech artists, and on the interconnectedness of historical themes.

In addition to Kadár and Klos's varied and rich cinematography and the artistry of individual scenes, there are several key characteristics that are central to the film as a whole. The film's poetic appeal is traditional and without any tendencies towards visual and formal experimentation. It is based on strongly-conceived characters that carry the story, an approach that requires realistic and psychologically-oriented acting by experienced actors. Kadár and Klos's films can be dubbed 'engaged art' in that the medium interests them above all else as a means of examining an issue, especially if related to a wider social problem. In the case of *A Shop on the High Street*, the issue under examination is Slovak society's attitude toward the

Nuremberg laws and the deportation of Jews during the Second World War. The dramatic development of their stories is typically based on an internal conflict of some kind. Often this translates into a dilemma for the characters arising from the collision of strong ethical attitudes and differing opinions.

An extraordinarily well-functioning artistic team, Kadár and Klos worked together for 17 years, making eight films that are among the outstanding works of that time. They understood each other well despite the fact that Klos was older than his colleague and had been involved as a screenwriter and director of documentary films since the latter half of the 1930s. His role in the collaborative relationship with Kadár was to oversee the script development of the film while Kadár concentrated more on directing the action on the set.

A Shop on the High Street is their most acclaimed film. In terms of genre, it is a tragicomedy about the unsuccessful efforts of an ordinary person who is insignificant within the regime and personally opposed to it. It takes place in an unspecified, small Slovak town in 1942, during the period of the Slovak State when the government openly collaborated with Nazi Germany and acted according to the Nuremberg Laws. A kind-hearted carpenter, Tóno Brtko, is living a quiet life, working, having petty arguments with his wife, Evelyna, and walking around town with his dog, when his peace is suddenly disturbed by a visit from his sister-in-law and her husband, Kolkocký, head of the local fascist militia. The latter, out of a desire to heal long-strained relations between the two men, offers Brtko the opportunity to become the Aryan controller of a Jewish shop on the town's high street. Tóno, in a drunken state and under strong pressure from his wife, accepts.

Difficulties emerge when Brtko discovers that the owner of the small button shop is an elderly, deaf Jewish woman, Mrs Lautmannová. He is unable to explain to her that times have changed and that the shop is no longer hers. She mistakes Brtko for an assistant and a relationship of mutual respect develops between them. Among other things, Brtko discovers that his role as Aryan controller means nothing financially when he finds that the shop is not full of Jewish gold, but of half-empty boxes of buttons, strings and lace. The more the sad truth about the deportation of the Slovak Jews and their condemnation by society reveals itself to Brtko and the more he falls into a tangle of lies about his new position as shop owner, the more he is consumed by guilt. This increasing pressure turns to tragedy when Brtko, in an attempt to save 'his Jewish woman' from another wave of deportations, throws her so roughly into a hiding place that the injuries from the fall result in her death. Brtko, out of despair, hangs himself in the shop.

The story of Tóno Brtko is one in which big historical events interfere in the life of a small person. If the temptation of owning property had never crossed his path, Brtko would never have had to face such a difficult dilemma. His fate is firmly planted in the concrete historical and political circumstances of the so-called Slovak State and the Second World War, a period considered to be one of the darkest times in the history of twentieth-century Slovakia. As early as 1939, Slovakia had officially adopted Germany's Nazi ideology. Officially, the country was the Slovak Republic and was constantly referred to as the independent Slovak State. The word 'independent' was added, in fact, because the autonomy of the new, wartime European state was questionable from the very beginning. According to Ľubomir Lipták, 'On 18 March 1939 in Vienna, the Germans forced on the Slovak government an "agreement on the protective relationship between the German Reich and the Slovak State". Via this agreement, the Germans "took responsibility for preserving the political independence of the Slovak State and its territorial integrity", on condition that they had the right to install a military base along the Carpathians anywhere from Bratislava north to the Polish border.' Slovakia was at the time dependent on Hitler's good will and, therefore, was required to accept orders from Germany within the framework of its domestic politics. New laws were passed that liquidated political and personal freedoms in Slovakia. The regime was brutally harsh in its treatment of Jews. To this effect, Lipták claims, 'it was as if the government and the state apparatus concentrated all of the brutality of its frustrated ambition for power [on the Jews] and thus compensated for its servility to its German protectors'. The government registered all the Jews individually, then gradually confiscated their property and all their civil and human rights. Hiding behind Christian liberalism, the Slovak regime intensified its persecution, later increasing the number of deportations of Slovak Jews, their final destination in the concentration camps littered across the occupied or allied territories no longer in doubt. The film portrays and gives life to a specific historical period and time while its gentle appeal and human quality work on a universal level. Jan Žalman remarked that 'Without heavy-handed picturesque local colour, the authors of *A Shop on the High Street*, in a few subtle strokes, captured the physiognomy of the time when a society, dancing on top of a volcano, knows only one imperative: *Carpe diem!* Scenes of drunken excess, corruption, political bluster, the arrogance of jackboots among some and the pandering humility of others – this is how the "New Europe" presents itself, a conceited dream that has become a caricature of the petty provinciality of smalltown life.' Tóno Brtko has no desire to cause harm to anyone – he is a simple and kind-hearted man. The film illustrates how, despite Tóno's 'caste-less' approach to people as he walks his dog through the town, the most innocent involvement with evil itself generates more evil. With this motif, the film unapologetically demonstrates that oppressive regimes will never hesitate to involve small, insignificant citizens – essentially pacifists – in the decline of moral values and the destruction of society. Brtko becomes a part of the majority, watching events develop, and with the spreading of the fascist mood, this act of observation becomes an act of *de facto* participation. He has accepted a double game: he is not capable of refusing a tempting offer to profit from the bitter fate of the Jews and attempts, at the same time, to ease his conscience by helping them. Both his worlds are threatened and then begin to approach each other until they actually come together directly in front of his 'shop' on the high street, where another deportation of Jews is being organised.

Throughout the film's development, the narrative ingeniously – and subtly – moves between subjective and objective perspectives. The introduction already foreshadows this when, above the city, we see a nest where the storks are 'dancing' to brass band music written for a walk on the promenade. Filmed from their perspective high above the city, the introductory scene shows us everything essential to the film's subject. From above, we see the main square, the high street with a church, the prison yard, and we then pause on the small figure of Tóno Brtko. He is seen walking his dog along the railway track, where he crosses paths with a military cargo train carrying an accordion-playing soldier. These first scenes already introduce the main conflict of the film – the tension between the objective transformation of an entire society, with the intimate drama of an individual person. We know at once from clues in the introduction what we are talking about and in what tone. From above, we see the city, the main scene of the drama, with its 'High Street' and prison behind the film's titles, which reveal that we are in the year 1942, in the Slovak State, one of the first countries to voluntarily adopt the Nuremberg Laws. The shot of prisoners exercising in the yard reveals that, during this period, Slovakia was not its own master, but a vassal of Germany. In addition, during the first few minutes of the film, we find out that the town's main street is named after Andrej Hlinka, the founder of one of the strongest political parties that, with the help of its militia, supported the fascist regime after 1939. Then we meet Tóno Brtko who is forced to stop for the military transport vehicle. A waltz plays in the background. As we learn later, it is the same music played by the local band, giving the scene a relaxed, caricature-like mood. Even after this short sequence, one begins to feel the style and pace of Kadár and Klos's narrative, their work with leitmotifs, analogies and metonyms. These images – the main street (the promenade), the storks, the brass band, Brtko and the transport trains (used for the deportation of Jews) reappear throughout the film in numerous forms and with various meanings.

09

One of the fundamental characteristics of the tragicomic genre used in the film is the alternation of serious or even tragic scenes with more comical ones. For the film to feel realistic, the inevitability of the tragic ending must be believable, so that the audience can feel for the main characters. Most of the time, the action appears comical, but at the same time, each scene potentially feeds a tragic ending. The underlying assumption of the tragicomic effect is that the main characters get into trouble *pars pro toto*, due to the actions of higher powers and run up against insurmountable obstacles, leading to a tragic ending that seems unavoidable. This is exactly how the viewer feels about Brtko's futile fight with high politics and his entanglement in history. Alone he has no chance of winning, but if there were many Brtkos and they found greater courage within themselves, perhaps the world would be different. In an interview with Antonín J. Liehm, Ján Kadár described the film's genre as a 'comedy with the classic structure of an ancient tragedy' and later added, 'I found two other things fascinating. First, a comic, grotesque, tragic scenario that grows wholly out of a misunderstanding. And second, the possibility of showing the whole problem from the inside out, in one drop of water. Talking about millions is, indeed, always easier than showing one human fate!'

At times, some of the film's comic moments border on the grotesque and absurd. The main source of this is Brtko's inability to extract himself from his tangle of lies and go his own way. When his wife reproaches him about money and pushes him to act like a businessman, he withdraws into his own world, playing deaf. His deafness very much resembles the deafness that prevents old Mrs Lautmannová from understanding that the world has changed and she no long owns her shop. The first time they meet, in her blithe, hard-of-hearing state, the old woman dubs Brtko 'krtko'; a clever play on words, 'krtko' also means mole – like Brtko, a small, seldom-seen animal who lives underground. Even Brtko's real surname, with its diminutive suffix 'tko' evokes the image of something small and meaningless rather than a real hero. This feeling is simply magnified by the nickname 'mole'. There is a sense of this and a useful inter-textual message when Brtko puts on a black suit previously worn by the widow's husband. He adds to this a hat and an umbrella and takes to the promenade like a newly-fashioned Charlie Chaplin. In this way, the directors draw other contextual material into the film, including similar tragicomic figures, such as those in Chaplin's *The Great Dictator* (1940).

The film's comic side recedes, replaced by a darker tone in which the truth about the condemnation of the Slovak Jews is made clear. The Jewish barber packs and prepares for his mandatory departure, the band leader is called upon to send the Jews off with music, the authorities catch Mr Kuchar, branding him a 'white Jew' for helping Jewish citizens and then beat him up, displaying him in the main square for public ridicule. The film, gathering natural momentum, becomes a horrible tragedy that mirrors history just as the 'seemingly excusable' confiscation of Jewish property transforms itself into mass murder.

A Shop on the High Street uses several motifs, which frequently work in stark contrast to each other. For example, there is a theme evident in the details – the dog's leash and the tangled ball of clothesline in Brtko's yard seem to represent for him his tangled web of problems as well as the rope that awaits him at the end of the film. Another example is the figure of the town drummer, the announcer of town news. At a certain point, he is replaced by a large loudspeaker that, with extreme volume and distorted sound, disseminates official messages that have nothing to do with the will of the people. The loudspeaker also represents higher power. It hangs high above the town and, in the film's concluding scene, as Brtko watches the deportation of Jews from his shop, announces in alphabetical order the names of the families being sent to their death. This loudspeaker also appears in sharp contrast to the large speaker of the gramophone on which Mrs Lautmannová plays her favourite old Jewish songs, in a scene filled with tenderness and nostalgia.

The film takes place against the backdrop of a small Slovak town. The choice of this particular milieu, with all of its contextual meanings is useful for many reasons. Firstly, the main theme of the clash of the individual with higher politics – would be hard to portray in a non-urban setting. Here the town represents the smallest unit of a larger society, where a relatively strong hierarchy of citizens exists and where, with the help of the national state apparatus, the reality of power and the higher interests of society prevail. The town is a model for a part of society that, as a whole, supports a criminal regime. This support is provided by individuals whose future victims will come from the ranks of their neighbours, customers and perhaps their friends. The choice of an anonymous small town provides an environment where there are no strangers and everyone 'has something' on each other. For this reason, it is almost impossible for Tóno Brtko to mask his dilemma.

In a microcosm where life is disrupted by the estrangement of an entire part of the population, it is impossible not to declare one's position. The place in town where one goes to be seen, to masquerade and to display membership of one class or another, is the main street or the promenade. It is here, mostly on Sundays, where figures in uniform and members of the *nouveau riche*, in stylish clothes, stroll up and down. The promenade is the place where the different classes and groups mix and where the transformation of class relations unfold. Some, such as Brtko's brother-in-law and his wife, who have risen in the fascist hierarchy, revel in it, flaunting their newly-acquired status in public. Brtko's wife, Evelyna would love to join them, but Brtko, rather than walk beside a member of the fascist militia, would prefer to sit hidden in his carpenter's workshop. The same promenade serves as a venue for the display of symbols of state power. Directly in front of the entrance to Brtko's shop a huge, tacky, wooden monolith of victory is being erected. One Sabbath day, right in front of this monstrous monument and of Brtko's eyes, the deportation is organised.

The acting contributes significantly to the film's feeling of authenticity. Clearly, the most important of the film's performances are those of the two main characters played by Jozef Kroner ('Tóno Brtko') and Ida Kamińska ('Rozália Lautmannová'). During the making of this film, Kroner was already one of the most experienced and sought-after actors in Slovak theatre and film. Because of his physiognomy, he was often cast as an older man, but in *A Shop on the High Street* he plays a role which corresponds to his real age at the time. Kroner's Brtko appears as the only character in the film who undergoes any real development. From the initial innocent state of an observer who strolls through the town, talks to himself, finds joy in small things, is childlike (he recites rhymes and plays hopscotch), we follow him through his flirtation with profiting from the liquidation of Jewish property to the final sacrifice.

Two exemplary scenes where the tragedy of Brtko's character is expertly brought out by Kroner's mastery of psychological realism are worth examining. The first is the dinner scene where his brother-in-law and wife visit and offer him the certificate of ownership. Everyone is rejoicing and encouraging Brtko to accept the offer. Brtko, before responding, chooses to get drunk. He begins to shout about Kolkocký's sins as a fascist only after he is truly drunk and standing on the table, doing an imitation of a speech by Hitler. A second instance of Kroner's brilliance comes at the conclusion of the film where he painfully hesitates and is filled with panic at the prospect of what will happen to Mrs Lautmannová or to him for being the 'white Jew' who helped her. He once again chooses to drown his mood swings and waves of emotion in alcohol. Through this drunken state, Kroner brings out the tragic essence of his character – a sober mind could not accept or understand this reality and a drunken one is transformed into aggression and despair. His state of extreme drunkenness is the only thing that allows him to speak the truth. We witness the transformation and tragedy of an entire historical period through his story.

Kroner's female counterpart is Ida Kamińska, a Polish actress who, at the time, was director of the only functioning Jewish theatre – the State Jewish Theatre in Warsaw. Lautmannová was her first important film role in a long, predominantly theatrical acting career. Her age was suitable for the role and it was decided that her real voice would be used, resulting in a mixture of Slovak and Polish, spoken with a strong Polish accent. This adds an intentional feeling of otherness that is substantiated by her role as a Jew in a world where Jews were considered to be increasingly 'different'. It is essential to understand that Brtko's and Mrs Lautmannová's dialogues are often two simultaneous monologues. The conflicts and comical moments come out of the lack of communication caused by Mrs Lautmannová's deafness and failing eyesight. This supports the main motif of the film – the period in which the story takes place is one where new societal norms are introduced that can neither be explained nor accepted by anyone with common sense.

In terms of the visual conception of the film, it is important to remember that despite the film's traditional creative character, one of its essential elements is the combination of objective and subjective perspectives. The intentional juxtaposition of the external events on one hand, with the internal drama of Tóno Brtko on the other, is fundamental. The morning after the drinking session with his brother-in-law he wakes up, opens his eyes and we see the room through his eyes, upside down. In the last scene, just before the tragic ending, the screen shows Brtko's rising internal anguish as his head spins and he desperately looks for a place in the room where he can hide or hide Mrs Lautmannová. There are two other creatively contrasting moments in the film that also bear certain similarities. One is dreamt by Brtko and the second is the concluding scene. In both, Brtko and Lautmannová are strolling together on the town's main street. The picture is awash in bright, white light as the two main characters, dressed in their Sunday best, smile blissfully at each other. The sound carries their dialogue, but in the picture their mouths are closed. Both of these 'unreal' scenes are intended to show that a walk by Brtko and Lautmannová down the promenade is possible only in a dream or in the 'other world' and a conversation can only happen between their souls.

The film's score was composed by Zdeněk Liška, a leading personality in the Czechoslovak film music revolution. His work included many well-known films of the 1960s, when he worked with both the older (Karel Zeman, František Vláčil, Jiří Krejčík, Juraj Herz, Stanislav Barabáš, Martin Hollý, Kadar-Klos) and younger (Juraj Jakubisko, Elo Havetta) generations of directors. Despite the large number of films he worked on, he gave each one individual attention, and his extraordinary sense of intuition turned the previous Slovak tradition of film scoring on its head. Liška works with two main musical leitmotifs. The first is the introductory promenade waltz where there are elements of 'caricature', and the residue of social dances and military marches. This music plays each time we return to the social scene of the promenade where the elite figures of the city display themselves in their 'costumes' and newly-donned 'masks'. The second is the intimate motif of Tóno Brtko, a dissonant, out-of-tune violin melody. This melody appears as Brtko's song of temptation whenever doubts or crises of conscience arise in him.

As Liška's film scoring philosophy dictates, these musical motifs have a purpose and are not meant only to create atmosphere. Their role is to bring out the meaning of the scene, not to make it sound 'attractive'. In addition to the metaphors expressed through the visuals, there are also hidden meanings in the soundtrack. In Brtko's case, there are often internal monologues that comment on what is happening with the character. On the surface he is quiet, but inside he responds to his grumbling wife and says what he feels. In contrast, when, for example, in the concluding scene he feels like screaming, we see him from outside through his shop window as his mouth opens, his voice drowned out by the noise of the deportation being organised on the square.

The value and quality of *A Shop on the High Street* springs from its complexity. The authors have succeeded in translating an excellent and emotionally evocative topic into a film experience. In addition to a screenplay that displays an evident knowledge of a local small-town atmosphere during the period of the Slovak State, the final result includes outstanding acting, sound and visuals. The authors were successful in bringing to life a forgotten piece of the past and making its atmosphere authentic: the apocalypse of the Third Reich in the guise of a horrible, grotesque farce.

Ľubica Mistríková

Translated from the Slovak by Janet Livingstone

REFERENCES

Liehm, Antonín J. (2001) 'Ján Kadár-Elmar Klos', in *Ostře sledované filmy*. Prague: Národní filmový archiv, 111–42.

Lipták, Ľubomír (1998) *Slovensko v 20. storočí*. Bratislava: Kalligram.

Žalman, Jan (1993) *Umlčený film: Kapitoly z bojń o lidskou tvář československého filmu*. Prague: Národní filmový archiv.

MIKLÓS JANCSÓ, HUNGARY, 1965

Miklós Jancsó is the most important representative of modern Hungarian cinema of the 1960s and 1970s. For more than twenty years he was the most internationally renowned Hungarian filmmaker, whose name was mentioned together with that of Antonioni, Fellini or Godard. During the 1980s and 1990s however, his international fame faded somewhat and the films he made during this period had very limited distribution outside of Hungary.

He started his career in the 1950s, working on documentary newsreels. His first feature film, *A harangok Rómába mentek* (*The Bells Have Gone to Rome*) was made in 1958. His next film, *Oldás és kötés* (*Cantata*, 1963), showed the considerable influence of Antonioni's modern films, particularly *La notte* (1961). Jancsó never denied his attraction toward Antonioni's cinema. However, critics soon realised that Jancsó had developed a genuine style of his own from the modernism of Antonioni, which itself has become a powerful model for both modern and postmodern filmmakers in Europe.

For most film historians and critics, the essential part of Jancsó's work consists of the films he made during the late 1960s and early 1970s. Among these films, two are considered as outstanding in the creation of Jancsó's particular style which, in turn, is based on a peculiar general vision of history and of political power systems: *Szegénylegények* (*The Round-Up*, 1965) and *Csillagosok, katonák* (*The Red and the White*, 1967). *The Round-Up* was the first film where all the important features of his style appeared and, with *The Red and the White*, this style reached unconditional international acclaim.

One of the defining characteristics of the modern cinema of Central and Eastern Europe is its focus on historical and political issues. Jancsó is no exception. His career has been dominated by an investigation of the nature of political power. Due to the political censorship in socialist countries of the time, in his first and second period – until the mid-1980s – this could be only be realised through a focus on historical themes. Jancsó admits turning to historical topics because he could not express his ideas about politics in any other way. Disguised as history, social and political criticism was more acceptable for the representatives of political power than direct criticism. Thus, for example, *The Round-Up* could be released in Hungary on the condition that Jancsó explicitly stated in an interview that this film was not about the retaliations following the 1956 revolution, it was instead about the retaliations following the 1848 revolution. It was clear for everybody that the historical setting was only a disguise, yet this explicit statement helped in calming the consciousness of the censors themselves. In this way, Jancsó's film became the first representative of a whole genre in Hungarian cinema, the historical parable, that was to become fashionable in Hungary especially during the early 1970s.

At the beginning of the film Jancsó makes the historical context appear very important. A voiceover commentary explains the historical background of the story as if it were indispensable for its understanding. He shows contemporary drawings and photographs, to evoke the historical atmosphere and to suppress all ambiguity about the period the story is placed in. However, the effect of this procedure is just the opposite of what it seems to achieve: the more the film emphasises its historicity, the more it becomes generalised. It is very hard for the viewer to avoid the question, why is it so important to evoke this particular point in Hungarian history where nothing really important happened and no major social or historical upheavals took place? Why pick a relatively unimportant story from the rich history of the nineteenth century which tells of a police mission? The story evokes the historical past, but history appears as an everyday 'business-as-usual' situation, with no outstanding characters and no events that change the life of a nation. Even the text emphasises the regular and systematic nature of the events depicted. All this suggests that it is the general picture about how an oppressive system works rather than a particular historical moment that will become relevant. Added to the appearance of historicity is another element, which is much more difficult to detect – that of a coherent narrative.

The plot appears to tell the story of a systematic investigation. As the voiceover commentary explains, after the 1848–49 revolution, when the fight for freedom had failed, the remnants of the rebellious national army were scattered all around the country, hiding from the Austrian authorities. Over the years, these groups had lost much of their revolutionary spirit and, in many cases, were little more than gangs of criminals, committing robberies and murders. While in popular legend they remained the last heroes of the war for freedom, in the eyes of the authorities, these groups became an important obstacle to pacifying the country and their elimination became a top priority. The film's plot is located in a fortress in the Hungarian Plain, the Puszta, where a number of common criminals and/or former fighters are rounded up and being interrogated. The voiceover defines the mission: to identify and neutralise the members of the rebel groups. However clearly the general goal of this mission is stated, the precise objectives of the specific steps taken by the authorities will never become entirely clear. And the logical relationship between these steps is even more obscure.

What is immediately apparent to the viewer is the restricted nature of the narration. Very few narrative details are revealed in the beginning. The story starts in the middle of an investigation, the goal of which seems to be finding the murderer of two shepherds. However, it turns out that the investigators know who the murderer is. The questioning of the suspect is part of an unknown game, as they know when he is lying and when he is telling the truth. Thus, what the viewer sees is not a real investigation, rather a ritual version of an investigation, the result of which is known in advance.

This is well illustrated by a parallel event. Heavy rain is falling. One of the inmates is isolated from the others. He finds himself in an empty courtyard, with several doors in one of the walls. He tries to open them, but finds they are all closed. Then he turns away and, on turning back, finds that one of the doors is wide open. He goes into the chamber behind the door, and the door closes as if it has been shut from the outside. After a while, the door opens again and a prosecutor signals him to step out. The rain has stopped and the sun is shining, so we do not know how much time has passed in the chamber. He follows the prosecutor leaving the fortress. He is then handed over to another prosecutor. The only thing this person tells him is not to be surprised if his parents do not see him again. The man says he is not surprised, as he knows that the authorities dislike his kind of educated people who can speak four languages and have been abroad. That is all we learn about him. Then he is ordered to leave. As he walks away, he is killed by a gunshot, but we do not know where it has come from.

This event contains all the most important elements of the way in which the narrative of the film is constructed: (i) very little or no information is revealed about why things are happening the way they do; (ii) important acts come from unrevealed locations through unseen agents   (the door opens, the shooting); (iii) questions are not posed in order to gather information, since all the information is already in the hands of those asking the questions; (iv) the events preceding the last act in a series of events do not make up a necessary process leading to this outcome (there is no particular reason for bringing him into the empty courtyard, for having the doors of the chambers first closed then opened, for making him wait, and so forth). All this leads to the most important conclusion about Jancsó's narrative style. What we can see in the plot is not a chain of events leading to a necessary result. The result could be reached right at the beginning, and the events are only part of a *symbolic ritual* which, according to

Jancsó, varies in its form during history, but with its essence and results always remaining the same: oppression and humiliation.

In the above-mentioned episode, the acts cannot be explained as part of a realistically depicted series of events. They derive sense only when they are given a symbolic interpretation: the scene is a highly abstract and symbolic representation of the ritual of execution. The sentenced person is first isolated, then taken to a special chamber to wait for execution. All human contacts are already cut here, which is why there are no humans around. Doors open and close as if by an automatic mechanism. The time one has to wait before execution is an irrational time. It can last from a couple of hours to many years, which is why it is not specified how much time elapses while the man is locked in the chamber. Then he is taken to the location of the execution where the last identification check is made and the sentence is declared. The executioners are not personalised. Until the last moment, it is uncertain what is happening. No one can foresee the events. Retrospectively, one realises that the aim of the events is basically psychological: to put the subjects of power into a state of uncertainty, humiliation and inability to act. The final goal of the ritual of power is not to arrive at a certain point, but to humiliate and to inactivate those located on the low levels of the hierarchy. Each Jancsó film can be considered a formal variation on the main patterns of the ritual of power, which is why one can call Jancsó's visual and narrative style fundamentally *ornamental*.

However consequential the events in the narrative of *The Round-Up* may seem, in reality they construct only a chain of juxtaposed events with little logical coherence. Most importantly, the long-term goal of the investigation is never revealed throughout the story, so the viewer can never predict the next step. In fact we hardly know more about what is happening than any of the inmates. Many things happen unexpectedly, which confuse not only the detained but also the viewer. The most important characteristic of the narrative that creates the effect of confusion is the fact that decisions are never made on screen. What we see and hear are only the results of decisions. Discussion, arguments, plans about what to do and how to proceed are never disclosed. When somebody says something on screen, it is already an order for the execution of a decision and the viewer never learns how and why it was made. In this way the viewer's knowledge is reduced to that of the inmates. Not only is the decision-making process concealed, but also the source of the orders. It is seldom clear exactly whose orders are executed on screen. We cannot see the entire military and political hierarchy, only its lower levels.

The plot consists of six separate episodes. Four of them are linked together through a single plot element: the story of János Gajdor, who has to find someone who has killed more people than he has. János Gajdor turns out to be the murderer of the two shepherds. Because the execution of the 'educated person' in the beginning runs parallel with the identification of the bodies, it initially appears that he is the person executed for the murder. Shortly after, it becomes clear that we will never know why this man was executed other than for what he reveals: the authorities dislike educated people smuggling revolutionary writings into the country. Instead, János Gajdor is revealed to be the murderer. Unlike the first man, who was not charged with murder, he is told that he will not be executed provided that he finds someone who has committed more murders than he has. The reason for this offer seems to be rational: the authorities want to find the most serious criminals, and they use all kinds of blackmailing and manipulative techniques. Gajdor indicates one of the inmates, Varju, as 'one of those', and he is kept in an isolated single cell. Instead of being interrogated, however, this person is brought back to the big courtyard among the other prisoners, which is a relief for him. The viewer will never learn why. He tries to escape, he is caught and executed. At the last moment he admits to Gajdor that he had killed more men than Gajdor, but he has no time to reveal all the names, so his confession will not solve Gajdor's problem.

The third episode in Gajdor's story is that of Veszelka. A gendarme is deprived of his military rank and thrown into the courtyard among the inmates. He tells Gajdor that he is suspected of being the criminal, Veszelka, who is believed to have killed seven people including the gendarme whose place he apparently took. This is another chance for Gajdor, but before he can report to the officer, the ex-gendarme is cleared, taken out of the court and his rank is given back. After this, Gajdor recognises the real Veszelka in the court, played by the same actor as the gendarme, which makes it clear that facial similarity was the main cause of the confusion. This raises the question of why, if the authorities knew what Veszelka looked like, they could not find him themselves? Why did they let Gajdor find him? They did not simply want to find Veszelka, they wanted Gajdor to pick him out in the presence of his fellow criminals. They wanted to make him guilty in the eyes of the inmates too. Again, their main goal is not to reach a result that is rational from the point of view of the investigation, but to morally break those who are detained.

It is here that the trajectory of the investigation shifts for the first time. When Veszelka is singled out, he is asked to tell how many of Sándor's men are kept in the fortress. There was no mention of Sándor before, while it seems now as if finding Sándor or his men has been the main object of the whole process. However, to achieve this goal the process preceding this question seems unnecessary. If they needed Veszelka to find Sándor, why did they need Gajdor to find

Veszelka, when they knew who Veszelka was? And if they needed Gajdor to find Veszelka, why did they not tell him in the beginning? And why did they need to have Gajdor kill the two shepherds in order to force him to work for them, if they knew that he was guilty of other murders as well? All these acts are not part of an investigation; they belong to the process of breaking morale and confusing the inmates.

As the goal of the investigation changes, they do not need Gajdor any longer, so they have him killed. But they do not execute him. Just as they had Gajdor kill the two shepherds, they have two other people kill Gajdor. Now the whole investigative ritual starts again. They ask questions, but they know the answers. They do not only want to 'find' the perpetrator, because they know who it is. But they want the inmates to point him out. Three men are selected in this way. They are isolated from the others as the most dangerous ones and chained to one another by the neck. At this point, the investigation is as far from any final result as at the beginning. It is hard to foresee what the next step could be. In fact, there is no next step.

The plot takes another shift. All the men kept in the prison are enlisted for military service except those three chained to one another. Suddenly, the whole story shifts direction. The investigation is discontinued and the inmates are turned into soldiers, as if everything that has controlled the plot so far has lost all importance. Only the three men remind the spectator that an investigation has taken place, the result of which amounts to no more than their isolation. A little later another officer arrives and orders the three men to join the army. Now everything that determined the previous plot events becomes irrelevant. What is more, the two men considered the most dangerous are given a chance to show their fighting skills in a duel. They are given weapons and horses, and the winner of the duel is given the task of organising a mounted squadron with other expert fighters. He selects Sándor's men from among the soldiers, and when he is done, an order comes from the high commander in chief granting Sándor mercy. The soldiers start to cheer Sándor, but the officer continues: the rest of his squadron will nevertheless be punished as deserved.

When it seems that the plot has moved to the furthest point from its original goal, it suddenly turns back, and the goal that was hidden in the beginning, and seemed to have lost all its relevance in the middle, is reached quite unexpectedly. In this last part of the film, the plot takes several sharp turns. Firstly, the three men are not enlisted, then this order is overruled. They are given a chance to organise a squadron, but only in order to disclose themselves to the authorities. Sándor is granted mercy, but not his men. This last turn seems particularly inexplicable. There is no rational explanation for letting the leader go and arresting the ordinary men. The only explanation is that, eventually, this order will also be changed, just like any order before it. It is noteworthy that all the orders are overruled or altered by another person in the film. Each officer gives out one kind of order, and never changes it. Other officers come and change the orders of each other. In this hierarchic structure the supreme will or the ultimate goal is fundamentally incalculable. Not only do those placed on the lowest level of the hierarchy not understand what is happening; everybody on any level is constantly faced with the incalculable dynamics of power. The narrative suggests that no individual initiative controls the events. Nothing depends on any one person in the hierarchy. Everybody executes a particular element of an order, but the whole system is fundamentally unknowable to anybody.

Jancsó's vision of the functioning of power is fundamentally Kafkaesque. Not only are the highest levels of the power hierarchy hidden from ordinary people, but so is its sense and rationale. The law of the hierarchy seems to be a secret that is never revealed to anyone. However, this 'secret' has lost the seriousness and metaphysical mystery it had in Kafka's times. After the horrors of the Second World War and after the experience of the Nazi and Communist dictatorships, the 'secret of power' seemed to Jancsó nothing more than a cruel ritual, the main goal of which is to assure the survival of the hierarchic power system itself.

Jancsó's extremely minimalist and symbolic visual style is an adequate form for expressing these ideas. He begins with a conception of fundamentally alienated human relationships. He chose Antonioni as his model, whose style seemed to be best suited to represent people whose relationship to one another and to their environment is essentially broken. Antonioni's characters wandering aimlessly in an environment in which they have no contacts created a feeling of emptiness that was one of the main novelties of modern cinema at the time. The main motivation for Antonioni's characters was a search for the lost contact with their environment, which is why there is always an illusion of a linear plot development, but in fact, the stories always lead to nothing. Jancsó radicalised Antonioni's style in two ways.

Although he still keeps the illusion of a linear plot development in *The Round-Up*, he makes it clear that this will not lead out of the situation from which the story begins: once the men are captured they will all be liquidated one by one with no further argument. Thus, the linear plot development is basically circular. Second, the constant movement of the characters motivated by a search typical of Antonioni's films becomes in Jancsó's films the central element of expression, and they are entirely self-contained, as the starting point and end result is essentially the same. A character's movement cannot possibly lead him out of the situation from which it starts. Movement of the characters as well as that of the camera therefore becomes increasingly ritualised and ornamental. The ornamental nature of these movements makes it necessary for the camera to follow them at length, like a dance or a ballet, driving Jancsó to create a style based on the extreme long take. Everything is subordinated to the ritualisation of movement, which is why the sets of the film are very abstract and minimalist. Jancsó uses very few ingredients so that nothing can block the way of the characters and the camera. Antonioni's space is the big city where the labyrinth of the streets determines the random movement of the characters. In *The Round-Up*, the space structuring the characters' movements is absolutely open and no exterior constraint controls the direction and choreography of their movement.

Jancsó's representation of alienation is radical in yet another way. While Antonioni's novelty was to break the contact between the environment and the characters, Jancsó eliminates the difference between characters and the environment, but in a way that results in an even more radical representation of alienation. The characters lose their autonomy and by their ritualised movements become mere elements of the environment. While Antonioni's heroes are individuals psychologically suffering from their loneliness and loss of contact with the outside world, Jancsó's heroes are deprived of their individuality too. They have no private lives, no emotions, and the only thing they are determined by is their position in the power hierarchy. Their acts and movements are determined not by their inner desires but by the necessities and logic of their power position. They are entirely absorbed by their environment. Here is what Yvette Biró, one time collaborator of Jancsó writes in this respect: 'The characters belong to a universe which abolishes their personal existence. They can keep of their personality only what the nature of the society around them lets them represent: the open or hidden antagonisms which constitute the tissue of the society and assure its organic dynamics.' That is why there are no real dialogues in the film. Usually dialogues characterise the protagonists and provide information about their goals and inner motivations. But Jancsó's characters are entirely driven by their position in the power hierarchy, their feelings and personal motivations are irrelevant to what they do.

András Bálint Kovács

REFERENCE

Biró, Yvette (1977). *Jancsó*. Paris: Editions Albatros.

OSTŘE SLEDOVANÉ VLAKY CLOSELY OBSERVED TRAINS 11

JIŘÍ MENZEL, CZECHOSLOVAKIA, 1966

When it won its Oscar for Best Foreign Language Film in 1967, Jiří Menzel's *Ostře sledované vlaky* (*Closely Observed Trains* aka *Closely Watched Trains*, 1966) was only the second Czech film to do so (the others have been Ján Kadár's and Elmar Klos' *Obchod na korze/A Shop on the High Street* aka *The Shop on Main Street*, 1965, and Jan Svěrák's *Kolja/Kolya*, 1996). Others to reach the final shortlist have included Miloš Forman's *Lásky jedné plavovlásky* (*A Blonde in Love* aka *Loves of a Blonde*, 1965) and *Hoří, má panenko* (*The Firemen's Ball*, 1967), Menzel's *Vesničko má středisková* (*My Sweet Little Village*, 1985), Svěrák's *Obecná škola* (*The Elementary School*, 1991) and Jan Hřebejk's *Musíme si pomáhat* (*Divided We Fall*, 2000). They have all contained large measures of comedy, although some, such as *A Shop on the High Street* and *Divided We Fall*, mix comic and tragic modes. In fact, all of them could be described as comedies with an 'edge'.

This suggests not only that the Czech industry is pretty good at producing comedies but that they also 'travel' to the outside world. In fact, Czech cinema has often been defined in terms of its contribution to comedy, a development conveniently linked to Jaroslav Hašek's classic comic novel about the First World War, *Dobrý voják Švejk* (*The Good Soldier Švejk*, 1921–23), and the many film adaptations that began as early as 1926. It could even be argued that foreign critics, audiences and film festivals have sought out comedies and helped to promote this view at the expense of work in other genres.

In an article written in 1983, the Hungarian theorist and screenwriter, Yvette Biró, identified the particular characteristics of Czech cinema in the 1960s as focusing on anti-heroes and dreamers: 'They are weird mixtures of sedate fools and successful survivors, and the secret of how they manage it all remains hidden.' *Closely Observed Trains* is a virtual embodiment of this description. Antonín J. Liehm also links Jiří Menzel's film and theatre productions explicitly to the Švejkian tradition – with one addition – a capacity to deflate the serious, the tragic and the conceited.

However, before discussing the film, we should consider the unusual position in which Czech cinema found itself in the mid-1960s, the heyday of the Czech New Wave, or 'Czech

Film Miracle'. The Czechoslovak film industry had been nationalised as early as 1945, three years before the Communist takeover. While there had been strong elements of socialism in President Beneš's post-war government, there is also little doubt that many saw a nationalised film industry as not merely rational but as a way of promoting the art of cinema. Although this ideal was hijacked by the ideological demands of state socialism, in the 1960s, the cinema began to fulfil some of the ideals of its founders.

Although many filmmakers had begun to expand cinema beyond narrow ideological criteria, the Czech New Wave was identified with a group of new directors who began their careers in 1963 – Miloš Forman, Věra Chytilová and Jaromil Jireš. The group was soon joined by Jan Němec, Evald Schorm, Ivan Passer, Jiří Menzel, Pavel Juráček and many others. While they shared no particular style or theoretical position, their work was created with a great deal of freedom and social relevance, winning many international awards. From the perspectives of many 'Western' directors, they enjoyed a freedom of creativity that the commercial system could never permit.

Alongside French, Italian and British influences could be found that of contemporary Czech literature. Of particular significance were the novels and stories of Josef Škvorecký (*Zbabělci/The Cowards*, 1958, banned and then republished in 1965) and Bohumil Hrabal (*Perličky na dně/Pearls of the Deep*, 1963). In the context of the conventions of Socialist Realism, *The Cowards*, with its loose and improvisational style and links to the vernacular and the life of young people, was a major breakthrough and Hrabal's work, with its emphasis on the absurdities and eccentricities of everyday life (mixed with elements of surrealism and existentialism), was even more radical. In 1965, Jireš approached Hrabal on behalf of the 'wave' to suggest adapting stories from *Pearls of the Deep*. They were released as a feature with contributions from Chytilová, Němec, Jireš, Schorm and Menzel. The film demonstrated their admiration for Hrabal and, in its obstinate investigation of an everyday reality free of ideological distortion, it was the nearest they came to a manifesto. Hrabal, who had walk-on parts in all of the episodes, became interested in developing his work for cinema, beginning a collaboration with Menzel that was to continue through *Closely Observed Trains*, *Skřivánci na niti* (*Skylarks on a String*, 1969, released 1990), *Postřižiny* (*Cutting it Short*, 1980) and *Slavnosti sněženek* (*The Snowdrop Festival*, 1983).

In his monograph, *Jiří Menzel and the History of the Closely Watched Trains* (1982), Škvorecký gives a fascinating account of how Hrabal's story moved from underground manuscript to Oscar-winning film. The original story *Legenda o Kainovi* (*The Legend of Cain*) was first written in 1949 and not published until 1968, when it appeared in the collection *Moritáty a legendy* (*Macabrosa and Legends*). Set during the Second World War and preoccupied with the subject of suicide, the subject is certainly existentialist, with its hero suggesting that 'the suicide will become the ethical and aesthetical measure not only of the individual, but of families, of nations'. In one chapter, which reappears in the reworking of the story for the novel and in Menzel's film adaptation, the hero is captured by the SS. The chapter, entitled 'Cain is Afraid', tells of a hero whose one desire is 'to get out of here safely at any price! Even if I should deny my nation, if I should spit on the national emblem'. In the new version of the story, *Closely Observed Trains*, first published in 1965, Hrabal wove himself a 'braid' consisting of humour, cruelty and tragedy, but with the humour dominant. The new version, which emphasised his hero's quest for sexual initiation, nonetheless retained much of his taste for morbid imagery. The close relation between beauty and horror is a major constituent, often manifested through cruelty to animals – part of Hrabal's gallery of martyrs. However, as is evident from his later work, Menzel's films are nothing if not humanist. It is not surprising therefore that, in the film version, the hero no longer sits down to rest on a dead horse with the head of its partner gazing at him 'with bulging eyes', and his sexual triumph is no longer lit in the night sky by the allied firebombing of Dresden. But Menzel did finally accept Hrabal's original concept of an 'unhappy' ending (the death of the hero).

The film focuses on a young man, Miloš Hrma (played by pop star Václav Neckář), who becomes an assistant at a sleepy railway station. Although he wants a successful career, he is mainly preoccupied with the problems of making love to his girlfriend, Maša, a conductor on one of the local trains. After a failed night in bed during a weekend visit to her uncle's, he attempts to commit suicide in a brothel. While he is in hospital recovering, his doctor (played by Menzel), advises him that he is suffering from problems of premature ejaculation, and that, at the moment of excitement, he should think about football. He should also seek the help of an older woman. Eventually he achieves success with the help of the glamorous resistance fighter, codenamed 'Viktoria Freie', a peacetime circus performer.

This theme is complemented by the film's observation of the station staff: the station guard, Hubička, a 'filthy fellow' (according to the stationmaster) who entertains young ladies at night; the stationmaster, Lánský, who keeps pigeons and dreams of becoming an inspector; the telegraphist, Zdenička Svatá, who engages in a midnight game with Hubička in which he is permitted to stamp her backside with the station stamps; and the old porter, Novák, who assiduously leaves minor jobs undone and dreams of the past. They are typically Hrabalian manifestations of the everyday. Believing that the direct life experience could become a poetic act, Hrabal always searched for what he called 'the little pearl at the bottom', pearls from the deep.

The subject of the war and the German occupation is not foregrounded – it is simply the context within which the characters live. Despite the visit of the head of the railways, to ensure compliance with a directive on the 'closely watched trains', references are oblique, and the blowing up of Maša's uncle's house functions almost like an act of God. There are references to the inhuman ways in which the Germans transport cattle, an SS train approaches the station and Miloš is temporarily arrested, but the activities of the resistance emerge as if by chance. Since Hubička, who is asked to plant a bomb on an SS munitions train, is undergoing a disciplinary hearing, Miloš takes on his role, and accident or fate leads to his death. Heroism is accidental. As Jan Žalman has written, 'the hero's brave deed comes somewhat unexpectedly and, moreover, is presented in an extraordinarily unheroic manner'.

The Czech novelist Karel Čapek once observed that Czech names often exhibit a sense of the comic, and that while common names translated as 'happy' (*šťastný*) or 'merry' (*veselý*), the language also abounded in joke names or names based on the remains of what had once been funny incidents. While names become detached from their original meanings, there is little doubt that Hrabal's meanings are intentional, if frequently based on the names of people he knew. Thus we have Hubička ('Smallkiss'), Svatá ('Saint'), Brabec ('Sparrow'), Viktoria Freie ('Victory-Freedom'), Slušný ('Polite') and, in Old Czech, Hrma means *mons veneris*.

It is the anti- (or rather non-) hero that is immortalised in Menzel's and Hrabal's film, and the pre-credit sequence provides an admirable summary of its position. It is also a model of its kind and a precise visual equivalent of Hrabal's text. The film opens with a fade-in to a room where we see small pictures of the hero's great grandfather, grandfather and father. A voiceover announces: 'My name is Miloš Hrma. People often laugh at my name, but ours is a famous family.' A montage of still photographs and old etchings illustrate the family history. Great-grandfather Lukáš had fought on the Charles Bridge in Prague and retired early after a student threw a stone at him with 'devastating effect'. Grandfather Vilém was a hypnotist, 'widely considered an idler', who unsuccessfully tried to hypnotise German tanks as they advanced to 'liberate' Prague. His father, an engine-driver, was able to retire at the age of 48 because engine-drivers were credited with double time. His father, who appears at various intervals in the film, is never shown as anything more than a shadowy figure reclining by a window, checking his watch to see that the trains are running on time. (He keeps 'a close watch on the trains' but it is not the one intended by the authorities).

In an ironic balance, Miloš is then dressed in his new uniform. The camera moves from polished shoes, up his trouser legs, past shining buttons, to his cap, which his mother lifts ceremonially above his head. The scene recalls the coronation in Sergei Eisenstein's *Ivan Groznyi* (*Ivan the Terrible*, 1944/46) or Laurence Olivier's *Richard III* (1955), the cap isolated in close-up between two hands: 'It is common knowledge in our town that like all my family … my one desire is to stand on a platform and avoid hard work, while others have to slave and slave and slave…'

Miloš's entry into the world and adulthood is reflected by the uniform, although this also symbolises the responsibilities of officialdom and the objective of social respect. The stationmaster also shares this obsession. His new uniform, for which he is specially measured, is prepared for his anticipated promotion to the role of inspector and is kept waiting in his cupboard. It reflects his deference to authority, nobility and traditional values. Herbert Eagle points to the ways in which Miloš's cap, which functions as a 'crown' in the film's opening and is caught by Maša at its end, links to motifs of bureaucracy, heroic action and sexual success: "The important dichotomy depends on what Miloš is capable of when he has his hat on (i.e. when he is under the control of impulses toward conformity, when he is repressed) as opposed to what he does when his hat is off.' At the beginning of the film, Miloš's mother puts the hat on while, at the end, when Hubička thrusts him into a room with Viktoria, Hubička removes it for him. On the other hand, he wears it for his heroic deed, when the crown has been earned.

If Miloš's search for sexual fulfilment, linked to 'manhood', provides the film's narrative interest, the film is also and, in many ways, primarily, about the characters he meets. It is here, as mentioned, that we encounter Hrabal's 'poetry of the everyday', not only in the characters who immediately affect his fate, but also in a wide range of subsidiary characters who, in any summary of the film, frequently go unremarked. As Ivana Košuličová suggests, 'Miloš looks at the other characters in the story with respect and admiration and makes ordinary people beautiful and magnanimous poets of everyday life'.

His role model is undoubtedly Hubička, the 'youngest' of the adults he meets and, arguably, the least eccentric. His main interest lies in his nighttime activities, entertaining the 'cousin' with the pretty ears or playing 'it flies, it doesn't fly' with Miss Svatá. His station patrol in the morning, chest out, fingering his ear and whistling the popular song, 'Noční motýl' ('Night Butterfly'), is one of the film's repeated motifs. But it is also Hubička who undertakes the 'male' activity of saluting the trains, and who is entrusted with the bomb by the resistance.

It is he who organises Miloš's initiation with a word in Viktoria's ear. Miloš effectively replaces him when he salutes an SS train, imitates his behaviour after the successful night with Viktoria and plants the bomb in his place.

The stationmaster (played by dramatist and screenwriter Vladimír Valenta) is presented as the personification of authority and respectability. Locked into a marriage dominated by convention and habit, he can only howl his disapproval of Hubička's activities down the ventilator shaft of the station lavatory. Here, he talks of Armageddon, and suggests that all pornographic writers should be shot. Fascinated by the nobility, respectability (and sexuality) of the Countess, he listens with avid attention to her tales of fornication behind the high altar. In the original novel, he had been a member of the Society for Public Regeneration. But he is an essentially kind man, who takes an almost paternal interest in Miloš.

Another major figure is the Nazi controller of railways, Zedníček. Zedníček is described in the screenplay as 'an inconspicuous human being, inspired throughout with the great ideas of Nazism, Mission and Providence sparkling from his eyes'. As played by Vlastimil Brodský, with his characteristic sense of controlled uncertainty, Zedníček remains both human and comical.

When he first appears, he brings with him a document concerning the need to keep 'a close watch on the trains'. Everyone is required to sign it, noting that the minimum sentence for non-compliance will be ten years. In some cases, people might be sentenced to death – or even life! Before that point, he sets out a map illustrating the various tactical moves that the Germans are taking to 'liberate' Europe and demonstrates 'the masterly tactical retreat of our armies'. The station stamps, that are later to be put to a more interesting use, are used as markers. Throughout his ideological address, the camera switches to Zdenička poking a pencil down her cleavage.

He next appears in the scene where Miloš reports to him from hospital after his failed suicide attempt. When Miloš confides to him his problems with premature ejaculation and, at Dr Brabec's suggestion, asks that he find him a woman, Zedníček resorts to the German language and throws him out. Zedníček's final visit is for the hearing of the case against Hubička. After discovering that Zdenička Svatá had willingly consented to their games, he concludes that there has been no crime against personal freedom, but there has been an abuse of official stamps and of the German language. Faced with the 'Švejkian' attitudes of Miloš and Hubička, observed by Lánský covered in pigeon droppings, he can only conclude: 'We all know that the Czechs are laughing hyenas.' When Zedníček departs in the novel, he does so on a rail trolley.

In the film, this has become a car mounted on rolling stock. The screenplay describes his earlier entry as 'somehow reminiscent of Lohengrin on the swan or Field-Marshal Keitel entering the great conquered cities'.

We have already mentioned Novák the porter, and Miloš' father and mother (although they are virtually offscreen figures). But there is also Maša's uncle, a professional photographer who cannot keep his hands off his young female clients (who scream with laughter), the bemused and unreassuring Dr Brabec, and the engine driver who holds an impromptu exhibition of his paintings propped on the engine. Then there are the judges and the policeman who examine Zdenička's backside and discourse on the nature of 'Pelikan' ink, her mother, the priest who 'knows about psychoanalysis' and promises to find a woman to help Miloš 'as a Christian duty', the man arrested for stealing a goose, and many other figures, who appear fleetingly, but are precisely observed.

The role of these characters could well be linked to the stereotype of 'the little Czech' – what Ladislav Holý describes as 'the embodiment of ordinariness and healthy common sense'. There are also, of course, negative elements in this stereotype (envy, conformity, egoism, laziness) but here they are largely absent or converted to positive ends. Many of these characters are transparently linked to Hrabal's own memories of life under the occupation when he too trained as a train dispatcher and had worked at Kostomlaty, the station portrayed in the film. Interestingly, the film contains many characters not in the novel, and the roles of others have been significantly expanded. While the film denies us the stream of consciousness approach adopted in much of Hrabal's prose, the onward flow of stories and associations, there is scope for both Novák's and Lánský's stories and Hubička's speculations about the countess. Lánský's story about the butcher who hid a cow's udder in his fly but left a nipple protruding has been repeated in a number of Hrabal's writings.

The portrayal of women, with Menzel's predilection for 'magical females', would not pass the test of political correctness. They are transparently cases of male enchantment and wish fulfilment. The well-upholstered countess is the explicit focus for Hubička's lechery, as he confesses his dream of being a cart which she grabs by the handle and takes to a shed ('Look at those limbs, more like a dream than a woman'). Maša, who invites Miloš to her uncle's for the night, is innocently forward and eventually forgiving of his failures. Zdenička provokes Hubička's misdeeds. Viktoria, with her white socks and heavy eyelashes, is a figure of self-assured power. But if these soft and attractive creatures are the stuff of male fantasy, it is they who, in every instance, take the initiative and possess the power. The subject of sex was, notes

Škvorecký in a 1984 article, 'extremely provocative [since] sex has always been the most dangerous enemy of puritanical revolutions'.

As already suggested, the Nazi occupation itself is experienced as a fact of life and is never discussed as an issue. In an early scene, a truckload of soldiers passes Miloš on his way to the station. It is an everyday event. Zedníček's appearances (save for his 'inner light') could be those of any figure in authority. The German soldiers who appear in the film are ordinary people, and climb into a hospital train to make love to the nurses with the same enthusiasm as would their Czech counterparts. But perhaps the strangest representation is that of the two SS officers, who arrest Miloš and take him for a brief and life-threatening ride on the footplate. (The film's equivalent of the 'Cain is Afraid' chapter in the original novel.) They are described in the screenplay as being 'as beautiful as gods' – indeed, their blond appearance and black uniforms grant them an unearthly and contradictory aura reflecting, perhaps, the erotic attractions of power. However, after Miloš's sexual success, the tensions are resolved. He is shot and killed, but the munitions train is blown up, and the powerful force of the explosion blows his cap into the hands of Maša. Hubička and the others dissolve into a gale of laughter. (Miloš's sexual failure had coincided with a bomb attack on Maša's uncle's house and a similar response of laughter.) The 'anti-heroic' emphasis on the everyday is not just a means of survival but a strategy that will, in the end, outlast empires and conquerors.

While Menzel maintained a deference to Hrabal's work, Hrabal has also noted that he rewrote the screenplay six times to reconceive it visually and ended up preferring the film to the novel. Škvorecký has pointed out that Menzel was a great admirer of his tutor at FAMU (the Prague Film School), Otakar Vávra, who believed that since film was a relatively new art form, it should defer to the rules of conventional dramatic construction (although his pupils, who include Věra Chytilová and Emir Kusturica, do not always seem to have followed his lead). Yet, unconventional characters create their own needs, and the script is anything but conventional. The range of characters is in itself extraordinary, as is the fact that, no matter how small the part, they remain precisely defined and constitute part of an overall vision. The central storyline also serves to stitch together a highly unusual and complex web of associations, and this takes it away from the simplicity and hierarchy of classical narrative.

Eagle points to the film's conscious use of analogy and metaphor (its paradigmatic axis). In fact, it is precisely this level of meaning that enabled Czech cinema to make its subversive points, because it is over and above the literal meanings of storylines. The importance of the uniforms and the stamps have already been discussed, but Eagle points to other important devices: the use of animals as a link to virility; the linking of these sexual references to impending death; the parallel usage of close-ups of body parts. The film is not only divided into scenes but also segments divided by the passing of trains, and the striking of the station clock (each occurs on twelve occasions), occurrences which interfere with the conventional progression of the narrative.

Menzel has frequently been criticised, particularly in recent years, for working primarily with his actors, for making films that are 'theatrical' (focused on actors) rather than 'cinematic'. Throughout this time, he has consistently worked with the same director of photography, Jaromír Šofr. But no one could make this accusation in the case of *Closely Observed Trains* – it is a film in which visual imagery asserts a considerable power.

On perhaps the most obvious of levels, there is a constant eroticisation of the scenes and objects that surround Miloš: the levers that he must handle while Hubička pesters him about what Maša is like in bed; the coffee grinder gripped between the 'cousin's' thighs; the swelling mound of ticker tape; the goose's neck (which manages to give him an erection); the coat rack after his failed night of love; the lone signal among the clouds of the final explosion. There is also the film's strong sense of texture: the cloth of uniforms, the leather of the sofa, the skin of the women. The sense of touch no doubt mirrors Miloš's own sensibilities. This extends to the unnerving effect of the suicide scene where two cutthroat razors are placed side by side in the cracks of a wooden stool, aligned with the grain of the wood. When Miloš cuts one wrist, and brings the other down on to the stool, a pool of blood is released and the image is strongly felt.

A great deal of the film's most potent imagery is reserved for the trains themselves, grand and impressive engines that pass through the station spouting sparks and shrouding Miloš and Hubička in steam. It is a train (a friendly, local one) that brings Maša, the great engines that bring death and destruction. Perhaps one of the film's most curious poetic sequences is that in which Miloš is kidnapped by the SS. He stands with his hands above his head as cheerful and lyrical music is played on the soundtrack. The countryside literally slips away behind him – a girl walking along a path; farm buildings; cottages; trees in blossom – the constant movement of the train evoking a physical sensation of beauty and of life slipping away. It is a sequence of extraordinary sensitivity and poetry.

The scene is taken from the novel, as is the sense of life slipping away. Indeed, a striking aspect of the film is the way in which Menzel finds a visual form for the original imagery: 'the twittering of telegraphs and telephones', the chime of the clock (a motif in the film but not the book), the image of the scissors when Miloš 'cuts off' his relationship to the past. Indeed, it could be argued that, with *Closely Observed Trains*, Menzel and Hrabal have weaved another braid, or as one critic suggested, you cannot distinguish where one of them ends and the other begins. Hrabal himself has said, 'we keep complementing each other, like two mirrors flashing at each other with the reflections of our poetic vision'.

If Hašek's *The Good Soldier Švejk* provides the classic Czech statement on the last years of the Habsburg Empire and the experience of the First World War, it is the film version of *Closely Observed Trains* that does the same for the Second. It is the best film adaptation of Hrabal's work, and a testimony to his multi-faceted take on the human comedy. Particularly for its time, the mixture of genres was unusual and its 'unhappy' ending (in a comedy) virtually unprecedented. But while it was probably the first time that premature ejaculation had been mentioned on screen, for Czech critical voices, it was not that sort of issue that caused concern. It was, wrote Jan Žalman, the 'daring link between the sexual theme and the "sacred" subject of the fight for national liberation' that gave the film its absurd dimension. In other words, it exposed the false pathos of the traditional war film and its failure to recognise the heroism of ordinary people. Although Menzel was not popular with the post-invasion regime, he continued to work, providing some of the few high points in Czech cinema in the next twenty years. After the Soviet invasion of Czechoslovakia in 1968, his film *Skylarks on a String* was banned, together with over 100 features by other directors. *Closely Observed Trains* was better treated but its subject matter was condemned, coming within that category of film that had debunked 'officially proliferated myths', as Jan Jaroš has described. The authorities suggested that its Oscar should be returned.

Peter Hames

REFERENCES

Biro, Yvette (1983) 'Pathos and Irony in East European Films', in David W. Paul (ed.) *Politics, Art and Commitment in the East European Cinema*. London: Macmillan, 28–48.

Eagle, Herbert (1977) 'The Syntagmatic and Paradigmatic Axes in *Closely Watched Trains*', in Ben Lawton and Janet Staiger (eds) *Film Studies Annual, Part 1*. New York: Redgrave, 45–57.

Holý, Ladislav (1996) *The Little Czech and the Great Czech Nation: National Identity and the Post-Communist Transformation of Society*. Cambridge: Cambridge University Press.

Hrabal, Bohumil (1990) *Closely Observed Trains*. Trans. Edith Pargeter. London: Abacus.

Jaroš, Jan (1990) 'A Retrospect', in Oldřich Černý and Gerald O'Grady (eds) *The Banned and the Beautiful: A Survey of Czech Filmmaking, 1963–1990*. New York: The Public Theater, 11–14.

Košuličová, Ivana (2001) 'The Ceremony of the Everyday: Jiří Menzel's Adaptations of Bohumil Hrabal's Prose', *Central Europe Review*, 3, 9. Available at http://www.ce-review.org/01/9/kinoeye9-kosulicova.html (accessed 5 March).

Liehm, Antonín J. (1974) *Closely Watched Films: The Czechoslovak Experience*. New York: International Arts and Sciences Press.

Škvorecký, Josef (1982) *Jiří Menzel and the History of the Closely Watched Trains*. Boulder CO: East European Monographs; New York: Columbia University Press.

____ (1984) 'Jiří Menzel', in Christopher Lyon (ed.) *The International Directory of Films and Filmmakers: Vol. 2: Directors/Filmmakers*. London: Firethorn Press, 366–7.

Žalman, Jan (1968) *Films and Filmmakers in Czechoslovakia*. Prague: Orbis.

SEDMIKRÁSKY DAISIES

VĚRA CHYTILOVÁ, CZECHOSLOVAKIA, 1966

Nine young filmmakers appear in the photograph that used to accompany articles on 'The Czechoslovak New Wave'. Among them, there is only one woman, Věra Chytilová. A director, screenwriter and an important representative of *auteur* filmmaking, she had, in the 1960s, already made her mark on the Czech and wider European film scene. She was not the only woman filmmaker, and other remarkable personalities such as Ester Krumbachová, Drahomíra Vihanová and Věra Plívová-Šimková (who worked solely on films for children) had also appeared on the scene.

But none of these demonstrated such a unique approach to filmmaking or were able to accumulate such a rich body of work. While it may seem contradictory, and despite the evidence of a firm directorial signature in both the themes and ideas for her films, she was always experimenting with form.

We can already see that Chytilová was concerned with the inner life of women in her graduation film, *Strop* (*Ceiling*, 1962) and her first feature, *O něčem jiném* (*Something Different*, 1963). Yet she avoids the subtlety and lyricism normally associated with women directors. In her medium length film, *Pytel blech* (*A Bagful of Fleas*, 1962), made between these two films, she showed that she was also interested in 'public affairs' and that dealing with women's issues did not prevent a strong critique of a society in a state of crisis and moral decay. In this film, she looked deeply into the cheerless and limited world of young factory trainees. In her portrayal of their everyday reality, she revealed the emptiness of the communist slogans about the care provided for working-class youth. Here she successfully merged her strong interest in women's characters, quite different from those typically portrayed on the screen, and her concern with themes reaching beyond the private sphere. She was to develop this tendency in important ways in the future, especially in the second half of the 1970s, when her return to filmmaking was permitted after a seven year ban. (Chytilová was one of the artists who became a victim of tough political oppression after the Soviet invasion of 1968.)

Her moral tales attacked the abuses of a deformed social system and, as her anger increased, irony and spitefulness became her most frequent weapons. No political lies fed to the population were spared. She also began to combine documentary-like observation with an exaggerated stylisation, the result of which is a distorted and grotesque portrait of reality. All the abuses that were supposed to be hidden were boldly exposed. This highly critical voice, which dominates in her films from this period, culminates in *Panelstory* (*Prefab Story*, 1979). This film has an unusually large number of characters and a wide range of episodes, but they are anchored in one day (from dawn until dusk) and one location – a construction site for apartment buildings on the edge of Prague. The inhabitants move in the dust and mud of unmade roads against the bleak grey of buildings containing box-like apartments where nothing works. People are neurotic and aggressive, there is a lack of communication between them and vandalism and burglary are rampant. After a time, the viewer realises that the real protagonist of the film is the housing development itself which, in Chytilová's view, is the modern-day equivalent of the Inferno. In the twenty years that passed between the Soviet invasion and November 1989, no other filmmaker created such complex testimony to the material and spiritual poverty of what passed for socialism.

Yet in both of her films from the second half of the 1960s, the allegorical *Sedmikrásky* (*Daisies*, 1966) and *Ovoce stromů rajských jíme* (*The Fruit of Paradise* aka *We Eat the Fruit from the Trees in the Garden of Paradise*, 1969), the reflection and critique of social conditions in Czechoslovakia is absent. It is as if she made a decision similar to that of the Polish director Krzysztof Kieślowski, when he made *Dekalog* (*The Decalogue*, 1988): 'I do not want local conditions to veil the broader horizons of thinking about human existence. I do not want, because of neverending queues in front of our stores, to avoid identifying the key moments of human Fate.' In this approach, Chytilová had a strong ally in Ester Krumbachová, who had the original idea for the latter film and co-wrote the scripts for both of them. Krumbachová was an influential intellectual and screenwriter, as well as graphic designer, whose name appeared on some of the best films of the period. As set and costume designer for both films, she balanced an attractive eccentricity and refined decoration that matched Chytilová's desire to disguise her work as a charming and playful spectacle.

To find his or her way through the subject matter of the films, the spectator cannot rely on a knowledge of reality since the artistic design of the sets and locations creates a gap between the films and any recognisable environment. In *The Fruit of Paradise*, the allegorical structure is already made apparent through the biblical reference in the title. In *Daisies*, the opening sequence presents a contradictory montage of shots, in which each provides different information. It is obvious from the beginning that the film will demand the audience's interpretative participation.

In *Daisies*, Chytilová does not examine specifically Czech social problems but warns us of ailments common to the world. She turned against the trends of the time, which had replaced morality with psychology. She demands that the individual follow the rules of high moral principle, which cannot be questioned and will lead to unavoidable punishment if not obeyed. Punishment cannot be evaded through psychologically-defined extenuating circumstances. This attitude is apparent throughout *Daisies* and influences the treatment of the characters.

The two protagonists and all the other characters (who are of only marginal importance) are portrayed as 'types', without psychological depth or individual personality. In this respect, the film is not unlike a medieval morality play, in which each protagonist exhibits one exaggerated character trait to sharpen the drama of the story, which is followed by a moral warning. Chytilová too works with 'models' who personify and demonstrate the stereotypes of human behaviour. Around the same time, Jean-Luc Godard was working in a similar way with his angry attacks on the status quo. He created flat poster-like characters that allowed him to play out numerous variations on the theme of 'man as a victim of cancerous social mechanisms'.

But Chytilová's critique takes her in an opposite direction – particularly in *Daisies*, where the characters personify negative qualities deserving public criticism. She portrays the relationship between the individual and society in a very different way from that of other 1960s film-makers and Godard before them. In a world in which everyone blames society (institutions, media, technology, advertising, consumerism, competition) for the deforming and manipulation of the ordinary citizen, Chytilová stubbornly attacks the individual. She points to the individual's lack of conscience, and claims that positive changes can only occur in society when each individual stops excusing his behaviour 'because of circumstances'. Not everyone is able to accept this reverse perspective, which corresponds to the raised arm of a preacher asking for mature moral engagement. There is a further character trait that Chytilová regards as infantile: passivity and resignation with respect to the search for knowledge. In the final analysis, these are 'communicating vessels' because those who are not actively trying to discover the substance of reality will soon be caught in its surface reflections, asking both themselves and others for excuses, blaming its blinding light.

If we consider the entire work of Věra Chytilová, we find that the bearers of positive character traits are invariably her heroines. None of them are understanding, patient and devoted wives, daughters or mothers whose life is fulfilled by living quietly next to a husband or lover. Instead, we are presented with women who courageously face a variety of obstacles and actively take charge of their own lives and the world around them. One of these women is Eva in *The*

Fruit of Paradise, who traces a killer on her own while her husband flirts with every woman in sight. Another is Anna in *Hra o jablko* (*The Apple Game*, 1976), who opts to be a single mother rather than marry a lover who has turned out to be immature and weak. Soňa, the young student in Chytilová's next film *Prefab Story*, could almost be Anna's younger sister. Despite the moral decline of that period and the lack of any prospect of improvement, she decides to be responsible for her life and that of her unborn baby. The director's concern to present examples of high moral courage and emancipation was most recently reflected, in extreme terms, in her film *Pasti, pasti, pastičky* (*Traps* aka *Traps, Traps, Little Traps*, 1998). The heroine's sense of justice is cruelly tested and culminates in the drastic and symbolically expressive gesture in which she castrates the two men who had previously raped her.

It has to be admitted that the men in Chytilová's films are often laughable, awkward, pitiful and of questionable moral quality. Also, in comparison with her women characters, the portraits of men are sketched with less precision. But, despite her liking for her female characters, she cannot be accused of adopting a narrowly pro-female or feminist attitude. She can also poke fun at women and presents them with an ironic anger. This is especially the case if they have a narrow view of the world around them and seek to gain undeserved advantages.

The character of Věra in Chytilová's first film, *Something Different*, is hit by the realities of life before she realises that taking a young lover will not solve her marital problems. The same happens to Marta in *The Apple Game* who, because of an affair, neglects her small children. It is boredom and vanity rather than lack of love that leads to her situation. The viewer is both lectured and entertained when Chytilová mocks the weak and uncritically vain attributes of her female characters. This is evident throughout the wide range of women she examines in *Prefab Story*, *Kalamita* (*Calamity*, 1980), *Kopytem sem, kopytem tam* (*A Hoof Here, A Hoof There* aka *Snowball Reaction* aka *Tainted Horseplay*, 1988) and, most recently, *Vyhnáni z ráje* (*Expulsion from Paradise*, 2000).

But it is in *Daisies* that her critical examination of women places her characters in a unique position. What is going on in this highly stylised spectacle? In the original screenplay, written by Pavel Juráček (a classmate of Chytilová at FAMU, the Prague Film School, and himself an important figure of the New Wave), two young students from a small provincial town are punished for their failure to resist the temptations of the big city. The screenplay by Chytilová and her co-screenwriter Krumbachová is much less tangible. The viewer does not know what realities the girls are engaged with and the daily routine of life in Prague ceases to be an important setting. Their situation depends more on invention than on realist observation. In the film, we follow two girls (the 'daisies' of the title) whose personalities and behaviour are interchangeable, and differ from each other only in their external appearance. They remain nameless in order to indicate that even this level of identification has no significant meaning. The environment they inhabit is highly stylised and non-specific to show that similar individuals can be found anywhere.

Chytilová's liking for characters that match her interest in specific problems and moral issues has already been mentioned. But her other heroines, whether negative or positive, and however schematic, were always linked to specifically female concerns. Through these characters, she addressed the previously submerged subjects of female sensibility, and women's destiny and role in society. This is apparent whether she approved or criticised their behaviour. And the 'girls-daisies'? What is feminine about them and how do they fit in to Chytilová's vision of modern woman?

They are in no way passive. They do not stand shyly to one side. On the contrary, they act with obvious self-confidence. They assert themselves with a voracious energy and, in a reversal of the norms, take great pleasure in manipulating others, especially men. Above all, they show an almost animal desire to satisfy their needs whatever the cost. They generally behave in a negative and selfish way and are subjected to Chytilová's criticism. They are less an example of emancipation than a warning of the direction that emancipation might take.

The two girls are exhibitionists and love to show off the most superficial attributes of femininity (they worship exaggerated make-up and clothing). But who could not admire their youth and spontaneity and who would wish to blame such whimsical little creatures? Only an exceptionally attentive viewer will notice the significance of the opening sequence. The girls appear in the Garden of Eden but instead of tasting the Apple of Knowledge, they jump around childishly. Amongst the rich flow of episodes and escapades, not many will notice the scene in which they rob the washroom attendant. She is their friend, helps them with little dress adjustments and works to supplement her pension. But they still steal her money because 'it doesn't matter'. Their seemingly harmless games allow no opportunity for emotional attachment. Not only do they consciously poke fun at the man who declares love to one of them over the phone but, as soon as one expresses interest in an admirer, she is humiliated by the other.

Chytilová's objective is to gradually reveal the harm caused by the girls' activities despite the superficial attraction of their mischievous behaviour. Because of this, she is unwilling to withdraw from the position of providing entertainment and an elaborate aesthetic framework. She continues this approach even when the girls turn their aggression and destruction on each other with pairs of scissors. This cruel act is presented as an effective and inventive collage in which the image is fragmented into small coloured pieces that cluster like the rapidly changing patterns of a kaleidoscope.

The film has no storyline, avoids any gradual progression of scenes, and has no dramatic arc. Instead, it juxtaposes different situations in which the girls constantly take advantage of what's around them and eliminate boredom through their endlessly destructive antics. The climax to their destruction occurs towards the end of the film. Frustrated by the indifference of those they try to provoke, they end up at a large banquet. The scene in which they throw cream cakes at each other was not the only reason that contemporary reviews described the film as 'philosophical slapstick'. Chytilová found many connections with her forerunners from the silent era. In these films, the public laughed at the destructive and malicious deeds of playful and child-like comics. Like *Daisies*, they had no significant plot and presented a series of acts each ending in a trick or a gag.

Yet Chytilová's girls not only destroy and provoke with vitality – they also have an endless appetite. They are able to devour one course after another and indiscriminately mix different foods together. When there is nothing to eat, they chew pictures of food cut from magazines. They poke each other with a fork, but this is only a symbolic gesture. In fact, they are willing to consume anything whether it be food, relationships, beauty, or the results of someone else's labour. The world around them is like the beautifully set banquet that they eventually destroy. A table to be emptied and consumed – and when they cannot consume anymore – destroyed.

Chytilová is a sophisticated director and she does not want to patronise the audience with a directly moralistic work. She confuses the viewer with her multi-layered aesthetics in both form and content. Her heroines are fresh and attractive. Their greed and aggressivity combines with an attractive frivolity – the sense of playful souls uncontrolled by conventions. She is consistent in her ambiguity and the 'disguising' of her message. What the girls plunder and destroy seems to deserve it or to be of no real significance. They do not do harm to old or defenceless people and important citizens or destroy paintings in an art gallery. They have fun at the expense of older men who want to seduce them, they humiliate an 'ordinary' guest in a cabaret, and they convert an elaborate feast into a heap of garbage. It was more than likely that the banquet was for a pretentious and self-serving group of people. The snobbish feast symbol-ises a decadent materialism and the gluttony of consumer society, against which the girls are revolting; they represent a new generation of revolutionaries. This is how some European and

American critics still interpret the message of this film. Małgorzata Radkiewicz, for instance, combines this analysis with her commitment to gender studies.

Through visual means, the film suggests a work of unchained imagination and an invitation to participate in an irresponsible game. Exaggerated sound effects, a mixture of modern musical motifs and classical music, dynamic straight-cut editing, the juxtaposition of unrelated shots, optical printing to modify movement, a constantly changing use of camera – in Chytilová's vision, all of this is combined to provide a real assault on the viewer's perception. Apart from the extremes of lavish colour and monochrome, many shots have specific colour emphases. The content of shots is organised in such a way that an aesthetic summary of their elements would inevitably outweigh any practical or functional content.

In one of her interviews, Chytilová said that she, and especially her cinematographer, Jaroslav Kučera (then her husband) based the film on the principle of collage: 'Collage in its own way expresses destruction, and that's what my film is about.' This visual approach is apparent in every moment of the film and is inseparable from Chytilová's overall objectives. The foregrounding of the film's formal elements makes it one of the most powerful examples of an anti-illusionist, intellectual film in the history of Czech cinema. The film does not attempt to imitate a reality in which the 'meaning' emerges automatically. On the contrary, Chytilová lets the audience know that she is presenting them with her own vision and that the meaning of that vision has to be deciphered.

Collage is, in a certain sense, a kind of game, and the structure of *Daisies* is based on the game. The first time that the girls appear, they agree to play the game '*vadi nevadi*' ('Does it matter? No it doesn't'). The play appears to be trivial and innocent. The winner will be the one who lasts the longest and can face any provocations with indifference. But they are not only testing each other, they are also testing their surroundings. Here, it seems that they can do anything. Whatever they attack or destroy, they will remain unpunished. Any game or diversion is acceptable provided it drives away the boredom that results from doing nothing. The audience is similarly tested and challenged in its eagerness to admire and enjoy their explosions of destructivity. But the chain of exploits is linked to documentary shots that frame the film at the beginning and the end. They show the frightening results of destruction in war. Exploding bombs, the atomic mushroom cloud, an air raid on a city, collapsing blocks of apartment buildings … this is where the indifference of people to the 'games' of others leads – the dreadful game of apocalypse. 'Everything in the world is getting spoiled, why not us as well?' argue the girls. Thus they provide an alibi against any attack of conscience.

They have no conscience and there is nobody to suggest they should, no one to criticise their behaviour. It is almost as if the world acknowledges that it really is spoiled. Finally, at the end of the film, it is 'providence' that intervenes when the girls are ducked in the water (maybe they flew out of the window after swinging on the chandelier above the devastated feast). There is a suggestion that they might put right the damage that they have caused. But it is no longer possible to lay the table with the broken dishes and the food they have trampled on. And what of the world? What will happen when it is inhabited by such soulless beings? In one scene, when the girls are moving, their limbs and joints squeak as if they were puppets. In another, one asks 'Are you a virgin?', but the Czech word '*panna*' has a double meaning, both virgin and doll. What will happen when, on the surface, the world is covered by fragile 'daisies' that are, in fact, stubborn and indestructible weeds?

Zdena Škapová

REFERENCES

Crespi, Alberto (1989) Interview with Krzysztof Kieślowski and Krzysztof Piesiewicz, *L'Unita* (Milan), 19 September.

Radkiewicz, Małgorzata (2002) 'Angry Young Girls: Gender Representations in Věra Chytilová's *Sedmikrásky* and *Pasti, pasti, pastičky*', *Kinoeye*, 2, 8. Available at http://www.kinoeye.org/02/08/radkiewicz08.php (accessed 29 April).

O SLAVNOSTI A HOSTECH THE PARTY AND THE GUESTS 13

JAN NĚMEC, CZECHOSLOVAKIA, 1966

In the 1960s the Czech and Slovak cinemas astonished the world and won a plethora of international awards. The new directors to emerge on the international scene included Miloš Forman, Ivan Passer, Jaromil Jireš, Věra Chytilová, Evald Schorm, Jan Němec, Jiří Menzel, Antonín Máša, Pavel Juráček, Jan Schmidt, Juraj Jakubisko, Dušan Hanák, Elo Havetta, Drahomíra Vihanová, Zdenek Sirový and many others. Older directors – Ján Kadár and Elmar Klos, František Vláčil, Karel Kachyňa, Vojtěch Jasný, Štefan Uher, Ladislav Helge – were also to make their contributions.

This extraordinary cultural rebirth was rapidly suppressed following the Warsaw Pact invasion of Czechoslovakia in 1968 and the liquidation of the reform Communism introduced by the Prague Spring regime headed by Alexander Dubček. Western critics, more stimulated by the challenge to capitalism represented by the May Events in Paris the same year and by Godardian notions of 'counter cinema' found it a difficult cinema to accommodate. Not only were its criticisms not directed at capitalism but at what passed for 'socialism' in Central and Eastern Europe – but many of the films fell within the category of what came to be termed 'art cinema', films deemed inherently elitist and bourgeois in their appeal. Yet this was to ignore the influences of Godard and the Soviet avant-garde on the Czech and Slovak cinemas. There were also links with the 'socially progressive' British New Wave (Lindsay Anderson, Karel Reisz) and Ken Loach has always acknowledged his admiration for the realist style and subject of Forman's *Lásky jedné plavovlásky* (*A Blonde in Love* aka *Loves of a Blonde*, 1965).

While it is true that a number of Central and East European films have achieved fame in the West because of their attacks on the Communist system, this was largely untrue of films from Czechoslovakia. Whatever might be read between the lines, the Oscar-winning *Obchod na korze* (*A Shop on the High Street*, 1965) and *Ostře sledované vlaky* (*Closely Observed Trains*, 1966) were seen to be primarily about the Second World War. Forman's and Passer's films were received as realist comedies while Chytilová, Němec and Juráček were seen as art cinema directors.

More explicitly political directors such as Evald Schorm and Ladislav Helge made little impact abroad. It was only after the Soviet invasion that films such as Jasný's *Všichni dobří rodáci* (*All My Good Countrymen*, 1968) and Jireš' *Žert* (*The Joke*, 1968), which dramatically exposed Stalinist realities, reached international audiences.

But the internal situation was somewhat different. As the Marxist philosopher Karel Kosík put it, the reason that philosophers devoted time to the interpretation of films, plays, novels and poems was because they embodied the same problems they themselves were encountering. He saw culture, and in particular cinema, as attacking the existing bureaucratic regime in its core and essence. But this was not achieved by direct attacks on the government and veiled political allusion but by emphasising 'such basic aspects of human existence as the grotesque, the tragic, the absurd, death, laughter, conscience and moral responsibility'. For Ester Krumbachová, whose unpublished novella provided the basis for *O slavnosti a hostech* (*The Party and the Guests* aka *Report on the Party and the Guests*, 1966), the roots went deeper than the post-war experience of Stalinism: 'I believe that the current cultural activity goes much deeper, and that it is an attempt to resolve problems that have been present in our cultural life for the past century and a half.'

After the suppression of the reform Communism of 1968, the collaborationist government set about the elimination of a culture. In the cinema well over a hundred feature films were banned for the next twenty years and four which were deemed especially subversive were banned 'forever'. These were *All My Good Countrymen*, *Farářův konec* (*End of a Priest*, Evald Schorm, 1968), *Hoří má panenko* (*The Firemen's Ball*, Miloš Forman, 1967) and *The Party and the Guests*. While the first two subjected the Communist Party to explicit criticism or ridicule, the second two adopted more oblique approaches. To foreign audiences, Forman's comedy about incompetent firemen failing to organise a village dance was not immediately interpreted as a satire on the Party and even *The Party and the Guests*, deemed the most controversial of all, was more often linked to absurdist drama and the surrealist visions of Luis Buñuel.

Jan Němec has always made it clear that he had no desire to make 'realist' or what we would now call 'classical narrative' films. He used his education at FAMU (the Prague Film School) very much for his own purposes, developing his notion of 'pure film', and discovering such films as Robert Bresson's *Un condamné a mort s'est echappé* (*A Man Escaped*, 1956). He also speaks admiringly of his tutor Václav Krška, a champion of film as an independent art, who he describes as a forerunner of Antonioni. (Krška is perhaps best known for his adaptations of Fráňa Šrámek's *Měsíc nad řekou*/*Moon Over the River*, 1953, and *Stříbrný vítr*/*The Silver Wind*, 1954.)

Němec has also been close to Surrealism although without any formal links to the Czech school. His first film *Démanty noci* (*Diamonds of the Night*, 1964), his hallucinatory account of the escape of two Jewish boys from a Nazi death train, includes several references to Buñuel's *L'Âge d'Or* while *Mučedníci lásky* (*Martyrs of Love*, 1966), a homage to the pre-surreal world of Czech Poetism, won a French award for best surrealist film. After the fall of Communism, similar interests can be detected in his adaptation of Ladislav Klíma's proto-Surrealist novel *Utrpení knížete Sternenhocha* (*The Sufferings of Prince Sternenhoch*) as *V žáru královské lásky* (*In the Flames of Royal Love*, 1990), influenced by the style of rock opera; his reflections on alchemy and politics in *Jméno kódu Rubín* (*Code Name Ruby*, 1996); his digitally-shot personal diary *Noční hovory s matkou* (*Late Night Talks With Mother*, 2001), inspired by Kafka's *Letters to the Father*, which won the video Grand Prix at the Locarno Film Festival; and his most recent project, *Toyen*, inspired by the lives of the painters Toyen and Štyrský.

Němec first met Ester Krumbachová when she was costume designer on *Diamonds of the Night* and they subsequently married. An author of many unpublished stories, he suggested that one of her novellas could be turned into a film and this was to become *The Party and the Guests*. Its story of a group of 'guests' who are invited to the birthday party of a powerful political leader and of the ways in which they adjust to or, in one case, escape from the world of power, was interpreted as an attack on the Communist state. Němec, however, maintains that it was never intended in this way – it was intended rather as an exposure of the ruling Mafia that exists in any society. In fact, references to any specific time or place were deliberately omitted. Today, he says, the characters would simply 'be wearing different clothes'.

The film begins with a group of well-dressed people taking a picnic in the woods – the scene recalls Manet. The opening scenes then introduce the characters and establish the basis of their later interaction. Their professional identities seem obscure but they all appear to be well-dressed and materially ambitious. After washing and deodorising themselves, the picnic group begins to walk up a forest track where they are surprised from behind by Rudolf (Jan Klusák), a man dressed in an open-necked shirt and plus fours who begins to ask disconcertingly personal questions. They are approached from all sides by casually-dressed thugs. When Karel (Karel Mareš) protests at their action, he is seized by the arms and frogmarched along with the other members of the group to a forest clearing.

As the guests speculate on the identity of their captors, a wooden table is set up and they are kept waiting. Rudolf eventually enters with a file under his arm and sits behind the table. Josef (Jiří Němec) volunteers to represent the group and to do all the talking and Rudolf proceeds to interrogate him on such topics as the weather and his attitude to women. Josef eventually lines up his fellow guests alphabetically to assist with the investigation. An imaginary prison is created when a circle is drawn round the group and a 'door' designated by rocks evenly spaced on the ground. At one point, Rudolf seizes Josef's arm, marches him round the outside of the circle, and launches into a modified goosestep. When Karel rejects this absurd charade and steps outside of the circle, he is immediately set upon as Rudolf desperately cuts the decorative fringe from his bag.

The disorder is brought to an end by the arrival of the host (Ivan Vyskočil), a diminutive man dressed in a white dinner jacket. He criticises Rudolf's behaviour but also notes that Karel has failed to keep to 'the gentlemen's rules'. He calls for a brush and a towel, kisses the hands of the ladies, and puts his arms round the shoulders of the men. 'Brother shouldn't stand against brother', he announces. But, he observes, Josef (unlike Karel) has kept to the rules. Karel responds that he is 'simply a democrat' to which the host responds that he is as well. All of the guests agree with this sentiment except one, played by film director Evald Schorm, who remains virtually silent throughout.

The host welcomes the guests to his party by the lakeside. Dinner tables are set out by the lake with waiters in attendance and a boat at anchor. Before dinner, he tells František (Pavel Bošek) that he will make the necessary arrangements for the 'special favour' they had discussed on the way. He also expresses the hope that Karel is no longer annoyed with him. Indeed, the promise of a new cigarette lighter and penknife seems to quell his democratic rebellion. Schorm's wife (Jana Prachařová) whispers to her husband that he will never again get an opportunity like this. As the dinner begins, Josef is invited to sit on the right hand of the host and Rudolf on the left.

Suddenly, it is revealed that one of the guests (Schorm) has disappeared. He has apparently run away because, as his wife puts it at the end of the film, he did not want to be 'here at the party'. The host covers his eyes as Rudolf's men run in from the sides to sit among the guests. When the wife discovers that she is sitting in the wrong place, the feast is turned into turmoil as everyone searches for his named place. The host refuses to eat as his birthday celebration has been ruined.

After speeches by Josef and Rudolf, the host agrees that Rudolf should take 'the boys' and hunt down the missing guest. There are to be no 'jokes' but he will be allowed to fire a gun when Schorm is found. Josef persuades everyone at the feast that it is their collective responsibility to join the hunt for the missing guest and the host decides to join the hunt since he has never been on one before and is impressed by the alsatian – 'a magnificent animal' – that will be used in the chase. Josef and the remainder of the picnic party remain behind at the tables in case the husband should decide to return. Like Rudolf, Josef will also fire a gun. The wife, who had originally planned to join the hunt, has been ordered to stay behind. One of the women returns to the wine, another to the food, and the wife expresses concern about her husband's new suit. The candelabra is doused (an economy requested by the host) as a dog barks in the distance. There is a shot of a smoking candelabra and crossed hands. The growling of the dog is magnified on the soundtrack as the screen turns black. The film concludes with the jaunty sounds of fairground music.

While the film suggests several lines of interpretation, it seems to be fairly clear that the host is a political leader and Rudolf head of the secret police. The guests represent a community or society that is won over through the invitation to the party and various private promises and incentives. To assist them, there are 'the boys' of the secret police, who sit next to them at dinner, escort them on their journey and will 'carry' them if they fail to make themselves comfortable for the ride. Those who refuse to join the celebration will be hunted down with dogs. Josef, who becomes the spokesperson for the guests and the host's 'right-hand man' is quite possibly a 'plant' from the beginning. We are also looking at an ongoing process since we encounter previous guests on the way to the party, who join together with the new contingent.

Already there are certain themes specific to Central and East European communism – the role of the secret police, the hunting of those who try to escape with police dogs. But, in the spirit of active interpretation, it is possible to find more. While the host's resemblance to Lenin was certainly accidental, his false assertions of faith in 'brotherhood' and 'democracy' are not. He often pauses in poses reminiscent of Socialist Realist portraiture and the references to the conversion of rocky ground into a future playground echo the bland tones of a political newsreel (as well as the 'radiant heights' of Soviet propaganda). Why should the air seem much better when it 'blows from the East'? When the bridegroom joins the hunt for the missing guest, the singing and tears satirise the conventions of the Russian war film. And why should Eva be forced to remain behind if she does not fulfil the familiar role of the wife as an incentive or hostage?

These are personal observations and they can certainly be questioned. Other viewers might quite rightly find different points and make different interpretations. But, at the same time, like Pavel Juráček's and Jan Schmidt's *Postava k podpírání* (*Josef Kilián*, 1964), it is a film whose insights can be applied in a variety of contexts. While the secret police may not function in precisely the same way in non-Communist societies, similar structures of power and accommodation can be found in a variety of institutions and need not be restricted to the example of government. Ultimately, it is people who help to create (read: acquiesce) in the systems of which they are apparently the victims. In this sense, *The Party and the Guests* retains its universal validity.

But in Czechoslovakia in the 1960s it seems unlikely that the film could not have been interpreted politically – if only because anything that was not for the system was assumed to be against it. One factor that made this inevitable was the casting. With the exception of the police dog handler (who lost his job as a result), all of the cast was made up of Němec's and Krumbachová's friends. Members of the Prague intelligentsia, they were selected precisely because they would never be suspected of the kinds of collaboration represented in the film. Consequently, Němec ended up with what was regarded as a 'rogue's gallery' of counter revolutionaries.

As Němec later put it, the only person missing was Václav Havel. They included the film director Evald Schorm (who was banned from the industry after 1969), the novelists Josef Škvorecký and Zdena Salivarová (Škvorecká), who later emigrated to Canada where they set up 68 Publishers in Toronto, the psychologist Jiří Němec, who became a spokesman for Charter 77, and Dana Němcová, who was sentenced to prison in 1979 as a member of VONS (Committee for the Defence of the Unjustly Prosecuted). Because of this irony or 'joke', the film was to be equated with a kind of collective subversion.

But the film is also of considerable formal interest. Němec's films have never conformed to the rules and expectations of the conventional narrative film. In *Diamonds of the Night*, there was one line of dialogue and in *Martyrs of Love* there was none. In *The Party and the Guests*, on the other hand, people never stop talking, leading to what Josef Škvorecký has described as 'a strange deafness, and appalling apathy, and a peculiar alienation'. Krumbachová insisted that the dialogue contained no secret code and no hidden meanings:

> The main creative element was distorted dialogue. I tried to create conversation in which the characters said nothing meaningful about themselves. The audience heard only isolated fragments of sentences, as if they had walked suddenly into the midst of a sophisticated party and had no idea what the conversation was about … it was my intention to demonstrate that people generally talk only in terms of disconnected ideas, even when it appears that they are communicating with one another. I tried not to mimic real speech but to suggest the pattern, to find a language for the sort of phenomenon that [Eugène] Ionesco discovered in drama.

Unlike Ionesco, she argued that she tried to use paradoxes and absurdities to depict her characters, but did not regard the world itself as absurd. Němec has observed that the characters mostly talk nonsense in a 'highly stylised, unrealistic dialogue' that is rather like a censored soundtrack. While he acknowledges the parallels with Kafka and Havel, he notes that their thinking was influenced more by the Camus of *L'Étranger* (*The Outsider*), the story of a man who was executed not for committing murder but for failing to cry at his mother's funeral. As Dina Iordanova notes, the group's misdeeds remain unidentified and everything revolves around elusive hints of culpability. The world of the absurd, even if, as Němec observes, the humour is closer to Hašek than to Kafka.

While the omnipresence of dialogue may seem strange in a film by a director with strong visual concerns, one suspects that Němec was drawn to it by its highly unusual use. In Hollywood films, dialogue is normally used to confirm and clarify the meaning of images. Here, however, it is the image that tells the truth. As Krumbachová puts it: 'In the past, heroes used words to describe tragic situations. Now tragedy is revealed by pictures, and our words have no relationship to what we see.'

The pure examples of dialogue as snippets from a cocktail party conversation occur only in the first and last sections of the film. But, given the human tendency to try to make sense of conversation, even these exchanges provide incentives to interpretation. But if the dialogue is 'mostly nonsense', it is not unrelated to the power games and adjustments that are being elaborated. The discussion about material goods is really about how they can continue to be acquired and the discussion with Josef about the countryside, birds and women is really about collaboration. Thus, like the dramatists of the absurd, Němec and Krumbachová recognise that language represents only one level of human interaction.

If the film's approach to dialogue is unorthodox so also is its approach to characterisation and narrative. Like many Czech films of the late 1960s (Forman's *The Fireman's Ball*, Jasný's *All My Good Countrymen*, Menzel's *Skřivánci na niti/Skylarks on a String*, 1969), there are no central characters. The guests constitute a 'collective hero' and they are examined both in terms of their individual characteristics and their group interaction.

The film can be divided into three more or less self-contained sections or 'acts': the introductory picnic, the interrogation and the banquet. The guests simply walk from one location to the next and, at the end of the film, the 'hunt' departs from the last location. Physical action is de-emphasised and takes a minor role in a film that emphasises group interaction. The ending remains open. A conventional narrative would almost certainly have concentrated on the figure of Schorm, the dissident guest who refuses to accept the dominant ideology, escapes and is to be hunted down. But, significantly, he is given no name, has scarcely any dialogue (he tells his wife to shut up when she raises the issue of 'human rights'), and his escape takes place off-screen. The wider community however, his fellow guests, talk incessantly as they attend to the necessities and conformities of everyday life.

The collective hero of six characters denies not merely the normal forms of audience identification but also the usual forms of narrative exposition. If the dialogue does the reverse of 'anchor' the meaning, the images mainly indicate relations. The 'significance' of what is happening emerges almost subliminally.

The film also has a very specific visual style. Its images are drawn partly from the influence of photojournalism and partly from the history of art. The scene of the beating of Karel was taken from a news shot of a political riot while many scenes seek to emulate the style of the French photojournalist, Henri Cartier-Bresson. Other images were drawn from Goya's *Capriccios* while Dutch still-life painting was the origin of images of food and tableware. All such influences were designed to 'lift' the film out of any specific time, a technique also used in Němec's and Krumbachová's following film *Martyrs of Love*. The seating arrangements for the banquet were based on the dinners for the Nobel Prize but each chair was deliberately selected from a different style. All of this gives the film a slightly 'static' quality quite at variance with Němec's other work.

Curiously, given its emphasis on character and dialogue, the film is developed principally through montage and the cross-cutting between faces. This establishes a strong sense of claustrophobia broken only by the occasional panning shot (for example, the approach of the thugs during the first section, the drawing of a circle round the group in the second). In the second section, Rudolf's interrogation of Josef often takes the form of a direct address to the audience.

To produce the resonance of the news shot, characters often look off-screen, and the image has to be held long enough to establish an impact. In the interrogation scene there are three occasions when there is a strange montage of faces – almost still shots, against a soundtrack that is virtually silent except for the sound of birds.

Krumbachová's hand as set and costume designer is fairly evident in both *The Party and the Guests* and *Martyrs of Love* as well as on Chytilová's *Sedmikrásky* (*Daisies*), made the same year, and *Ovoce stromů rajských jíme* (*The Fruit of Paradise*, 1969) and Jireš's *Valerie a týden divů* (*Valerie and her Week of Wonders*, 1970), all of which she co-scripted. She undoubtedly enjoyed a special role in the films of the Czech New Wave. As Michal Bregant has observed:

Ester revives that part of us that is the refuge of game. In this way, she provokes by art, intellect and imagination ... She was the art director as well as patron of the Czech New Wave ... she was the charming conscience and supporter of a generation of filmmakers.

The 'theatre of the absurd', interpreted as such because Martin Esslin's book had proved particularly influential in Prague in the 1960s, also provided an important context. Apart from Beckett and Ionesco, the Czech dramatists Václav Havel and Josef Topol had also made their contributions. It was inevitable, observed Kenneth Tynan, that the symbolism of such plays would be applied to contemporary politics. It is possible to regard *The Party and the Guests* as a product of the same cultural climate. (When Němec emigrated in 1974, police impounded Havel's screenplay *Stolen Hearts*, which he had hoped to film.)

Parallels have also been drawn between *The Party and the Guests* and Buñuel's *El Angel Exterminador* (*The Exterminating Angel*, 1962), in which a group of guests enter a house and find themselves unable to leave because of their own inertia. The easy adaptability of Němec's characters could also be linked to the heroes of Buñuel's *Le charme discret de la bourgeoisie* (*The Discreet Charm of the Bourgeoisie*, 1972). As an admirer of Buñuel's work, Němec is happy to be placed in his company although he did not see the first film until after he had made *The Party and the Guests* and the second did not appear until later. More recently, Němec noted parallels with Jean Renoir's *La Règle du Jeu* (*The Rules of the Game*, 1939), which he had also not seen.

When Němec and Krumbachová had prepared the screenplay, they thought that they would never be allowed to make the film. It was made because of the influence of Jan Procházka, head of the production group that had produced *Diamonds of the Night*. According to Němec, he was very supportive and said that, although it was not his type of film, it could be a nice 'time bomb' and could be smuggled into the production programme without publicity.

All well as being head of one of the Barrandov production groups, Procházka was a novelist and screenwriter whose work included a whole sequence of films made with the director Karel Kachyňa. Procházka was a member of the Communist Party's Central Committee where he set about enlightening the establishment. He saved some films from the wrath of President Novotný but not others since, as Kachyňa once put it, Novotný's support was in the final analysis a matter of mood, tactics and despotism. Procházka was expelled from the Central Committee in 1967 and became an outspoken supporter of the Prague Spring. He wrote the script for Kachyňa's film *Ucho* (*The Ear*, 1969), an explicit exposé of Stalinism that was suppressed until 1990. Accused by the KGB of heading an anti-Party group aimed at the destruction of socialism, he died in 1971.

When Novotný saw *The Party and the Guests* he was, according to Procházka, literally jumping with rage and demanded that it be destroyed, the director arrested and never allowed to work in the film industry again. Both Němec and the film were indeed banned but, given the workings of the bureaucracy, Němec had three months to complete *Martyrs of Love* before the ban came into effect. *The Party and the Guests* acquired a strong underground reputation and was eventually released in 1968, the year of the Prague Spring liberalisation, and was invited to both the Cannes and Venice Film Festivals. Unfortunately, in a year when Czechoslovakia had three films in the official competition at Cannes (*The Party and the Guests*, *The Firemen's Ball*, and Menzel's *Rozmarné léto/Capricious Summer*), the festival was closed down, by Godard and others, as a temple of bourgeois culture. Although it was not a film for 'wider audiences' and was made cheaply in a five-week period, it had a strong influence both before and after the Soviet invasion, when it was often, at great personal risk, shown privately.

Peter Hames

REFERENCES

Bregant, Michal (1992) 'Ester Krumbachová', in *Karlovy Vary International Film Festival Catalogue 1992*, 89–90.

Esslin, Martin (1962) *The Theatre of the Absurd*. London: Eyre and Spottiswoode.

Iordanova, Dina (2003) *Cinema of the Other Europe: The Industry and Artistry of East Central European Film*. London: Wallflower Press.

Kosík, Karel (1973 [1968]) Interviewed in Antonín J. Liehm, *The Politics of Culture*. Trans. Peter Kussi. New York: Grove Press.

Krunbachová, Ester(1973 [1966]) Interviewed in Antonín J. Liehm, *The Politics of Culture*. Trans. Peter Kussi. New York: Grove Press.

Liehm, Antonín J. (1973) *The Politics of Culture*. Trans. Peter Kussi. New York: Grove Press.

Škvorecký, Josef (1971) *All the Bright Young Men and Women: A Personal History of the Czech Cinema*. Trans. Michael Schonberg. Toronto: Peter Martin Associates.

Tynan, Kenneth (1967) 'The Theatre Abroad: Prague', *New Yorker*, (April), 103

MARKETA LAZAROVÁ

14

FRANTIŠEK VLÁČIL, CZECHOSLOVAKIA, 1967

Marketa Lazarová was undoubtedly the greatest work by the Czech director František Vláčil. Although it was completed in 1967, at a time when there was much interest in the 'New Wave' of Czech cinema (Miloš Forman, Věra Chytilová, Jiří Menzel and many others), it attracted relatively little international attention at the time. Vláčil was not one of the new generation – its theme was historical and it was a film outside of any fashion. As the Czech critic Jaroslav Boček wrote at the time, it was like an apparition, an enormous block of stone that not only changed critical and aesthetic criteria but our ways of thinking and perceiving. In a poll of Czech film critics taken in 1998 it was voted the best Czech film ever made.

Unlike other directors of his generation, Vláčil was not educated at FAMU (the Prague Film School). In fact, he originally studied art history and aesthetics at the Masaryk University in Brno, funding his studies by working on animation and educational films. As a student, he also undertook an exercise in which he drew Sergei Eisenstein's *Bronenosets Potëmkin* (*The Battleship Potemkin*, 1926) frame by frame. All of this, combined with his early work as a painter, reflects the instinctive concern with visual composition that was to characterise his film work. When he undertook his national service in the Army Film Unit, he worked there alongside the first FAMU graduates such as Karel Kachyňa, Vojtěch Jasný and cinematographer Jan Čuřík. They all shared a strong interest in film as a visual form.

In his medium-length film *Skleněná oblaka* (*Glass Skies*, 1957), which won an award at the Venice Film Festival, his interest in flight was constructed principally through images of glass and reflected surfaces. This emphasis on visual composition and rhythm was to become a defining characteristic of his work, a concern with 'pure film'. As he once stated, 'I wanted film to act like music and poetry'. This emphasis was also apparent in his first two feature films, *Holubice* (*The White Dove*, 1960) and *Ďáblova past* (*The Devil's Trap*, 1961).

Set in the thirteenth century, *Marketa Lazarová* was based on motifs from Vladislav Vančura's novel (first published in 1931) and also his *Obrázy z dějin národa českého* (*Pictures from the History of the Czech Nation*, 1939–40). Vančura, who was one of the leading Czech novelists of the interwar period, was a member of most experimental movements of the time,

THE CINEMA OF CENTRAL EUROPE   151

and had been chairman of the avant-garde Devětsil (Nine Strengths) group. Vančura's work, which focused on the poetic and experimental use of language, was described by one critic as an art of 'pure literary display'. For obvious reasons, his novels have never been translated into English and *Marketa Lazarová* was deemed to be unfilmable. But Vančura had also been fascinated by film and himself directed or co-directed five features in the 1930s, three of which took cinema in new formal directions. Concerned to expand and sometimes undermine existing realist notions of narrative and psychological involvement, his films experimented with both sound (*Na sluneční straně/On the Sunnyside*, 1933) and montage (*Marijka nevěrnice/Faithless Marijka*, 1934), the second film also featuring Bohuslav Martinů's only film score.

The links with Vančura are not accidental – both Vláčil and screenwriter František Pavlíček had been inspired to film the novel – and Vláčil's formal innovations can be regarded as an extension of the author's own inclinations. But while it is an adaptation, it is in no sense a 'film of the novel'. Vláčil has converted a short and unified text into a vast and sprawling two-part epic that evokes comparison rather with Akira Kurosawa's *Shichinin no Samurai* (*Seven Samurai*, 1954) and Andrei Tarkovsky's *Andrei Rublëv* (1966). Vláčil and Pavlíček can be said to have re-imagined Vančura. Zdena Škapová argues that the film marks a turning point in Czech cinema for three reasons: first, as a historical work; second, for its contribution to the Czech tradition of the poetic film; and third, as an outstanding adaptation in its own right. In the second instance, she is referring to works such as Gustav Machatý's *Extase* (*Ecstasy*, 1933), Josef Rovenský's *Řeka* (*The River*, 1933), František Čáp's and Václav Krška's *Ohnivé léto* (*Fiery Summer*, 1939) and Vojtěch Jasný's *Touha* (*Desire*, 1958).

The film deals with the conflicts between the rival clans of the Kozlíks and the Lazars, and the doomed love affair between Mikoláš Kozlík (František Velecký) and Marketa Lazarová (Magda Vašáryová). Interwoven with this is the conflict between paganism and Christianity, fierce clan loyalties and struggles with the central power of the king. Vláčil's approach to history is distinctive, and contrasts strongly with what Škapová has called the work of 'ideological mystification'. While she mentions no names, one assumes that she may have Otakar Vávra's Hussite trilogy in mind, inspired by Alois Jirásek's patriotic novels, in which history was reconstructed in simplified terms to suit the required mixture of nationalist and Soviet ideology. Vančura's novel was itself designed as a polemic with the Czech conception of history and Czech historical prose, with its sentimental emphasis on how the nation suffered for its faith, language and conviction. His characters were, in turn, possessed and tormented.

While Vančura's novel provided no historical clues and was designed as an 'autonomous' work, Vláčil strove consistently to recreate a sense of the thirteenth century, even locating the film in a specific reign, that of Václav I, when church dignitaries were attempting to arrange for his son, Přemysl Otakar II, to reign alongside him. The original screenplay located the action between 15 February and 1 August 1250, and a detailed calendar specified the time and place of the action. In fact, the royal sequences from the script did not appear in the final film, strengthening the sense of a more generalised determinacy. As Vláčil has said, although very little was known about daily life of the time and Theodor Pištěk, for instance, had a free hand in his design for the costumes, his historical advisors complemented him on his likely accuracy.

Vláčil wanted to express the spirit of the times as if the film were a contemporary document, 'to provide a testimony about people six, seven hundred years ago, as if they were our contemporaries … I wanted to understand them, see through the eyes of their lives, their failings, their desires – in short, I wanted to drop back seven centuries.' In order to approach this authenticity he studied groups of people living at 'the level' of the Middle Ages, including the lives of Brazilian Indians, and ensured that implements and weapons were made from the correct materials and by original methods. He took his cast to the Šumava forest where he encouraged them to live their parts in a shoot that extended over two years. Thus, while the film evokes a generalised political reality (the establishment of central control), the emphasis is rather on psychological and economic realities. It was a world in which the dominant emotion was fear and in which pagan myths provided a potent source for 'explanation'. As the American critics Emory Menefee and Ernest Callenbach wrote:

> The film is initially as confusing as it would be to actually arrive in such an alien culture. We don't at first have the slightest idea what the people are up to … yet it is powerfully clear that the primitive world they live in is coherent, alive, real, menacing…

While Vančura's novel was constructed on the basis of the characters' interweaving destinies, Vláčil has recomposed its themes adopting a structure closer to Vančura's *Pictures from the History of the Czech Nation* and *Tři řeky* (*Three Rivers*). The narrative is based on a series of short episodes or tableaux, which Vláčil has likened to the chapters in a romanesque novel, the structures of a poem or the movements in a musical work. In this way, he sought to remain faithful to the spirit of Vančura. The structure is also very close, he argues, to that of Janáček's *Sinfonietta*, describing the finished work as a 'Film-Opera'.

The film is divided into two major sections, *Straba* (*Straba the Werewolf*) and *Beránek Boži* (*The Holy Lamb*). In *Straba the Werewolf*, the two Kozlík brothers, Mikoláš and Adam, launch an attack on a Saxon noble and his followers in a sequence of merciless violence. We are also introduced to the treacherous and obsequious head of the rival Lazar clan, who robs the corpses in their absence. The sombre opening, which introduces the film's hero, Mikoláš, is shot in a kind of winter half-light, and is contrasted with bright sunlight for the visionary introduction of Marketa Lazarová, the heroine of the film and daughter of Lazar. After the Kozlíks have brought the noble's son, young Kristián, to their camp, there is a major conflict between Old Kozlík (Josef Kemr) and Mikoláš, centring on the latter's supposed lenience (allowing the escape of Kristián's father and the capture of Kristián and his servant). The sequence also introduces us to Alexandra, sister of Mikoláš and Adam. In a flashback/fantasy sequence, she is shown making love to a man in a pagan sanctuary. It is, in fact, her brother Adam although this is far from clear in these early images. The mutual attraction of Kristián and Alexandra is readily apparent. The section continues as Pivo, commander of the king's army, brings his soldiers in an attempt to make Old Kozlík account for his crimes. Kozlík, however, escapes, after knifing the commander, and a proclamation is issued calling for the pursuit of his clan.

Since the Lazars had shared in the proceeds from the attack on the Saxons, Mikoláš goes to Lazar in search of an alliance. Under the watching eyes of Marketa, he is savagely beaten and thrown out of the camp. In retaliation, the Kozlíks attack the Lazar settlement and carry off Marketa by force, leaving Lazar nailed to the gates of his burning fortress. The Kozlíks move to a secret hideout in the woods. Old Kozlík's wife, Kateřina, tells the story of Straba, who we learn, is 'from the line' of men, and the section ends with the rape of Marketa by Mikoláš. In a reversal of the norms, Kateřina's 'explanation' of the film's first half comes at its end and not at the beginning.

The Holy Lamb introduces us to the character of the wandering monk, Bernard (Vladimír Menšík), accompanied everywhere by his pet lamb, a new character who, Boček suggests, serves as a counterpoise to the pagan Alexandra. The lamb is caught and devoured by the Kozlíks, who leave Bernard with only its head. The simple-minded Bernard introduces a comic element to the story and serves as a narrative link between the film's increasingly diverse plot elements which here include the death of Adam at the hands of the king's troops, and a horrific battle with the Kozlíks, ending in Kristián's insanity.

The film's final section begins with scenes of the remainder of the Kozlík clan fishing. The relationship between Mikoláš and Marketa has developed into one of love but the insane

Kristián is killed by Alexandra. Released by Mikoláš, Marketa returns to her father's fortress but is rejected by him. She is undergoing her vows to enter the convent when she recognises the hypocrisies of the institution: 'Lead me in your justice from those who watch over me, for there is no sincerity in their words.' Hearing that Mikoláš has attacked the prison at Boleslav, where Old Kozlík is being held for his crimes, Marketa joins him and they are married, shortly before he dies from his wounds. The captain and Kozlík survive Mikoláš, but the landscape is strewn with the bones of the dead. Kozlík's survival is shortlived as he is taken to a place of execution.

From this, it is possible to extract two general thematic elements: the struggle between central authority and the clans, and between Christianity and paganism. The old men (Kozlík, Pivo) who embody the conflict show little weakness in their relentless struggles for dominance and little pity for their rivals (despite this, they exhibit the 'heroic' qualities missing from the calculations of Lazar). Mikoláš himself appears to differ little in essence and it is only in the context of unremitting violence that he seems less extreme, concerned only with what is essential. Significantly, Kateřina's tale of Straba the Werewolf, links all men to a heritage of blood with the exception of the seventh son.

Christianity and paganism are presented as parallel forces. Christianity, as a formal institution, is represented as a repressive force, an attitude that has sometimes been criticised. But Vláčil certainly saw the dogmas of Christianity as a parallel with those of 'socialism', 'in which the dogmas and principles are untouchable'. The repression is presented predominantly in visual terms, with an emphasis on the geometric lines of the convent, the nun's habit, bodies stretched out in angular patterns on a hillside, Marketa lying prostrate before the cross. The closing door of the convent contrasts with the fleeing of a deer, the shape of the building with the disorderly flight of birds. The first sequence in which Marketa's entry into the convent is proposed is contrasted with the scene between Alexandra and Adam.

Just as the scene with Marketa begins with the impact of blinding white light, the scene with Alexandra begins with a forward tracking movement through grass. A naked girl hangs charms on a tree and walks forward with a bird, cutting its throat. The woman is seen against the tree in various close-ups of sexual intercourse. A raven and a snake are seen in the tree but a man kills the snake, piercing it with a knife. The snake has bitten the man. At this stage of the film, we are scarcely aware of the identity of the two characters. Alexandra, who was a minor figure in Vančura's original novel, here represents 'a symbol of femininity without limitation'. In this *Rajská sonáta* (*Paradise sonata*) we also find the pagan ingredients of the myth of the

Garden of Eden. Adam is punished for his transgressions by the bite of the snake, which results in the loss of his arm.

While both sequences exhibit parallels, it is possible to see here Vláčil's admiration for the spontaneous passions of the period. While Mikoláš's rape of Marketa has a certain sense of inevitability, it is also accompanied by Kateřina's 'commentary', in which Mikoláš is viewed as a descendent of Straba (who had killed his wife on their wedding night and was consequently expelled from the world of both beasts and men). The development of their relationship into one of love is a reversal of expectations and reveals both Mikoláš's ability to reflect on his actions and Marketa's forgiveness. This positive force, although in no way simplistic, also presents a Christian – non-institutional – perspective, and reflects Vláčil's interest in the interpenetration of the Christian and the 'primitive'.

The representations of women in these scenes remain the central focus, seen through male eyes, relations that may promote liberation or madness. Here, it is important to recall Vláčil's objectives, to represent the psychology of a period. If one were to try to draw conclusions about Vláčil's view of Christianity (reflected especially in his following film *Údolí včel/ Valley of the Bees*, 1967), its purpose would seem to be social control, and its principal target, the disruptive role of sexual passion.

But the most important aspect of Vláčil's work is its extraordinary aesthetic charge and formal originality. Appearing against a background of the more overt stylistic radicalism of Godard, Antonioni and Jancsó, it was perhaps a radicalism that was seen to be too close to narrative conventions. In fact, its narrative is highly unconventional, and together with its *mise-en-scène*, promotes an unusual relationship with the viewer amplified by the archaic language of its bardic intertitles. The use of cinematography (Bedřich Baťka), music (Zdeněk Liška) and editing (Miroslav Hájek) combine with the *mise-en-scène* to promote new and unusual combinations.

The denial of narrative as the primary point of interest allows an emphasis on the reaction and interplay of character and on the subjective and psychological world (witness the number of scenes dependent on observation, voyeurism and reaction). The intertitles, which function much like the chapters in an old chronicle, provide succinct summaries of what we are about to see (and often the only explanatory clues). They are grouped graphically with Gothic lettering for the opening phrase 'O tom' ('About'), as in the second 'chapter': 'About Kozlík, Lord of Roháček, who had eight sons and nine daughters, and about the captive chosen to become Bishop of Hennau.'

While the titles are the predominant mode for organising narrative progression, Vláčil also uses the voice of a narrator, stories and monologues. At the beginning of *The Holy Lamb*, for instance, Bernard's monologue is at the same time a dialogue with the narrator. Dialogue and dramatic exchange off-screen frequently overlaps or interacts with the staging of a quite separate action. The distinction between flashback and parallel action is sometimes confused. The techniques of narration obscure what is fundamentally a simple story.

The conventional narrative interest, the kidnapping and rape of Marketa and the subsequent 'romance' and marriage is anything but central. In fact, the only dialogue exchange between Marketa and Mikoláš comes toward the end of the film after the defeat of the Kozlíks and, while there is reference to conscience, Mikoláš's childhood, and their forthcoming marriage, it is anything but 'explanatory' in any conventional sense. It is mainly devoted to a story about a deer and 'the solitude of death'. The plot elements only assume their normal priorities in the final stages of the film. Battles and action scenes remain fragmented and incomplete, selections of images that tell us about the psychological state of the participants.

The film's use of composition within the frame may reflect Vláčil's early studies of Eisenstein and he freely admits painting as a main source of inspiration. The published script of *Marketa Lazarová* contains much of the storyboard material, drawings and monotints that Vláčil produced during the course of production together with an exemplary range of frame enlargements. They serve to illustrate one of the most dramatic and original uses of the cinemascope format achieved anywhere.

Vláčil makes extensive use of deep space (and depth of field), for instance, Marketa's head in the foreground as she approaches the distant convent. Sometimes the frame contains 'contradictory' images (such as Adam facing the camera with horsemen approaching in the distance from behind him). This extension of the possibilities for dramatic focus and simultaneous action marks a sophisticated progression from the work of Orson Welles (some interior shots also use ceilings as part of the composition and recall *Citizen Kane*). Vláčil is also prepared to use extreme close-ups of eyes and devote the whole of the frame, for instance, to a close-up of Marketa against a wall, in which the qualities of stone, flesh and hair are emphasised.

But, as Vláčil has explained, despite his concern with composition, the camera is almost never still and there are frequent changes in focal length. There is also an extensive use of subjective camera – Mikoláš's view of a victim seen from over the head of his pursuing horse, Bernard's disoriented stumbling with the head of his beloved sheep, Kristián's journey to madness across a flattened landscape of grass. Many sequences are shot almost exclusively through the eyes of a particular character, recalling Robert Montgomery's experiment with *Lady in the Lake*. Thus the camera may progress along corridors or down staircases with only the hand of the character intervening between the character and what they perceive. This is the case, for instance, in the sequence where Marketa observes the beating up of Mikoláš at her father's fortress. Similarly, Old Kozlík's attack on the Hetman is filmed this way (as well as functioning in flashback). When Pivo is staying with the Lazars, he is not seen at all but his voice participates in the action, and includes a flashback of Old Kozlík's attack seen in reverse subjectivity.

Škapová argues that Vláčil's use of narrative is very much a response to Vančura's original, where the narrator is an active participant in the action. Thus the titles, the narrator ('the Voice of God' in the opening to *The Holy Lamb*), the subjective viewpoints, the stories and monologues, the contradictions between word and image, recreate the immediacy of a novel where 'the whole' remains hidden. It is similarly the case with Vláčil's emphasis on the expressive power of the image, a concern for intensity and atmosphere – direct experience – at the expense of narrative cohesion. This communication of meaning through the poetry of the image, of course, parallels Vančura's concern for the emotional significance of words.

As a 'Film-Opera', the role of music is paramount, and Zdeněk Liška was to prove an ideal collaborator. Liška's music, a familiar ingredient of many Czech and Slovak films, has featured in the work of a wide range of directors including that of Ján Kadár, Karel Kachyňa, Juraj Herz, Juraj Jakubisko, Elo Havetta and Jan Švankmajer. His extraordinary facility and use of unusual instruments is something of a trademark but sometimes, one feels, a little too powerful for his collaborators. But here (as in his other 'film-opera' collaboration, Věra Chytilová's *Ovoce stromů rajských jíme/The Fruit of Paradise*, 1969), his work is in perfect balance. Given the film's musical inspiration, Vláčil worked closely with Liška during the shooting to produce some remarkable sequences. Unusual at the time, his use of solo female or male voice and choral background is often remarkable, the solitary echoing effects mirroring those of the characters in the narrative against the wintry air. The female voice, of course, is specifically linked to the heroine and could perhaps be dubbed 'Marketa's theme', although it is closer to the calling female voice in Vaughan Williams' score for *Scott of the Antarctic* (1948) than to conventions of Hollywood romance. Liška's use of echoing percussive instruments (notably the xylophone) and electronic effect is disturbing and evocative and some instruments were even invented for the film. The music is, of course, also linked to the early traditions of church music. This 'musical' approach extends to particular qualities of voice in the actors.

The interaction of these elements becomes clear in the film's evocative and sustained opening. It begins with the introductory titles accompanied by choir:

> This tale was told by chance, so it hardly merits praise.
> But that does not matter.
> There are many others like it waiting to be penned.

Over images of a snow-covered landscape, a voiceover narration begins:

> Our tale takes place during a severe winter with frosts as passionate as Christianity at the time. Better to huddle by the fire and remember times past. Foolish deeds are scattered at random. Why listen? Is there sense in what was written?

A female singing voice is joined by a male voice as the landscape is penetrated by a party of wolves struggling through the snow from right to left. A hawk hovers above reeds and then lands on Mikoláš's gloved hand. The credits describe the film as a 'film rhapsody'. The narrator continues:

> By chance, haphazardly. For poetry's sake, at the behest of a wandering echo, and because the oldest things carry over into the present.

Already, we have a distinctive mood, and a precise summary of the film's objectives: the severe winter, the commitment to poetry, its musical form, its link to medieval Christianity and its contemporary relevance.

As the hawk flies in the sky, the credits for *Part I: Straba the Werewolf* appear:

> How two Kozlík brothers hunted on the royal road.
> How the neighbour, whose life was saved by a miracle,
> turned this to good account.

The opening sequence, the attack on Kristián and his father, is extraordinarily effective. It combines the progression of Kristián's retinue, the circling Kozlíks, the hovering of the hawk and waiting wolves. The images of fighting are unconventional. The hand-to-hand fighting emphasises faces rather than actions – actions are seen from beneath horse or wagon. When a riderless horse disappears, music begins, and the wolves rush forward. Adam's initial slingshot that precipitates the action hits its target to the sound of choral chanting.

Even Boček finds fault with the film's opening and, citing Gorky, notes the importance of establishing characters and action in the minds of the audience. But, poetically, the disorientation creates a mood, a state of mind, as if one has suddenly been parachuted into an alien world. Here, one can also point to Vláčil's 'poetic' approach to images, and the combination of action with subsidiary images (the hawk, the wolves), the victim hit by slingshot to music, the throwing of a cross on a chain to Adam.

While the film always maintains its narrative links, it is difficult to find any scenes that present their subject matter in an orthodox manner. This is not so much because Vláčil is 'opposing' classical narrative (like Godard or Jancsó), it seems more a function of poetic thought, the desire to 'see' or 'present' feelings or images that are repressed through conventional presentation. He seems to be working in the tradition of Viktor Shklovsky's *ostranenie* and *zatrudnenie*, that of 'making strange' and 'making difficult'. Here, it should be remembered that Shklovsky saw this as the function of art as such, even though such ideas have subsequently been linked mainly to the avant-garde.

In a number of scenes, Vláčil juxtaposes image and dialogue (telling one 'story' with words and another with images) but there is, in any case, little correlation between what people say and what they do. After the Kozlíks return to their camp with the captured Kristián, there is the lengthy argument between Old Kozlík and Mikoláš, in which Mikoláš is berated for allowing Lazar to rob him and for sparing the lives of Kristián and his servant. Most of the dialogue takes place off-screen and the camera focuses on Adam listening. The castle gives the sense of a lived environment with women, children and dogs moving around in the snow like a Breughel painting. Gradually, the attraction between Kristián and Alexandra is signalled, and triggers a flashback to her love-making with Adam. All of this is presented as a continuous evolution.

Of course, the film's showpiece is the madness of Kristián or 'Where love led the Bishop of Hennau and about the soliloquy of madmen'. Here, Kristián's journey is combined with a whole range of images: progression through different landscapes, images of his bloodstained father, flashbacks to the battle where his father demands that he give up Alexandra, the attack on Alexandra, dismembered bodies, a white horse caught in marshland, Kristián firing an arrow and piercing an eye, a mound of naked corpses, his search for Alexandra, her naked body hung by its feet in a courtyard. While this mad and delirious search echoes the style of Jan Němec's

Démanty noci (*Diamonds of the Night*, 1964), it here forms part of a wider tapestry. Kristián's hallucinations in most cases re-present material previously seen from the viewpoint of other characters.

Despite the consistent innovation in *Marketa Lazarová*, one never has the sense that Vláčil is seeking anything other than the most authentic form of expression for his subject. It seems to be quite clear that, behind what we experience, there is a complex web of relationships that coherently interact, an almost documentary reconstruction. The viewer, however, is a visitor to this world, and even with the help of the titles, has difficulty in recreating its coherence. Admittedly, he or she shares in the subjective experiences of characters, frequently in scenes of watching, but only in their 'half understanding' of what they observe (Marketa, Bernard) or the physical sensations of action or love. It marked, suggests Boček, a new chapter in the spirit of the nation, a time to be adult. History was no longer the source for contemporary needs and moral lessons, but a continuous process interacting with the force and wills of individuals.

Peter Hames

REFERENCES

Boček, Jaroslav (1967) 'Na okraj Markety Lazarové', *Film a doba*, 591–4, reprinted in Stanislav Ulver (ed.) (1996) *Film a doba: antologie textů z let 1962–70*. Prague: Sdružení přátel odborného filmového tisku, 133–9.

____ (1968) 'En marge de Marketa Lazarová', *Image et Son*, 221, 70–81.

Menefee, Emory and Ernest Callenbach (1969) '*Marketa Lazarová*', *Film Quarterly*, Summer, 35–7.

Pavliček, František and František Vláčil (1998) *Marketa Lazarová* (screenplay). Prague: FAD.

Škapová, Zdena (1998) 'Literární a filmová podoba *Markety Lazarové*', in František Pavlíček and František Vláčil, *Marketa Lazarová* (screenplay). Prague: FAD, 7–21.

Vláčil, František (1974 [1969]) Interviewed in Antonín J. Liehm, *Closely Watched Films: The Czechoslovak Experience*. New York: International Arts and Sciences Press.

VTÁČKOVIA, SIROTY A BLÁZNI BIRDS, ORPHANS AND FOOLS

JURAJ JAKUBISKO, CZECHOSLOVAKIA/FRANCE, 1969

Due to his early period of experiment and the deliberate development of his own auteurist style, which peaked in the work *Vtáčkovia, siroty a blázni* (*Birds, Orphans and Fools*, 1969), the films of Juraj Jakubisko are among the most significant creative achievements of Slovak cinema. From the beginning of his career, he attracted attention not only through his unbounded imagination and expressive power, but also by his testing of new possibilities for the film image and an 'unreasonable' straining of the traditional rules of narrative. As early as 1968, during a nostalgic reflection on his Film School years, he admitted, 'All that time in school, I struggled with the suspicion that I was unable to make a normal film.'

An extravagant visionary, Jakubisko is today one of the best-known Slovak directors and the most popular at home – and it was films like the historical saga from the time of the Habsburg monarchy, *Tisícročná včela* (*The Millennial Bee*, 1983), the spectacular fairy tale *Perinbaba* (*The Feather Fairy*, 1985) featuring Giulietta Masina, and the comedy *Nevera po slovensky* (*Infidelity: Slovak Style I–II*, 1981), which attracted the most attention. Jakubisko's film style is instantly recognisable and his films are regularly included in film festivals and retrospectives of Slovak cinema. After the split of Czechoslovakia in 1993, he decided to return/escape to Prague. One of his latest features, *Nejasná správa o konci sveta* (*An Ambiguous Report About the End of the World*, 1997), is an allegoric portrait of humankind on its way to self-destruction, produced in the Czech Republic. In 'Survey 2000', organised by Slovak film journalists and critics, he was declared the best Slovak director of the century.

At the end of the 1960s, three directors, graduates of the only Czechoslovak Film Academy (FAMU, the Prague Film School), entered Slovak cinema with feature debuts. The first to attract attention was Jakubisko with his *Kristove roky* (*Christ's Years* aka *Crucial Years*, 1967). Two years later, he was joined by two other directors of similarly ground-breaking films – Dušan Hanák (*322*, 1969) and Elo Havetta (*Slávnosť v botanickej záhrade/Party in the Botanical Garden*, 1969). Their appearance represented a generational shift, and their films marked the revival of a peripheral, 'forgotten' cinema – but only for a short time.

Although Jakubisko, Hanák and Havetta were developing divergent film styles, they all reacted to the new political, social and cultural situations. They avoided recycling the successful film styles of their colleagues of the Czech New Wave. In fiction as well as documentary, they had the courage to reveal 'fresh' points of view, fusing the contemporary tendencies of modernist aesthetics with sharp social criticism. Hanák was distinguished by his sophisticated collages of optical and sound images, Jakubisko by bizarre politicised parables and the magical use of spectacle, Havetta by his discovery of the carnival grotesque and impressionistic and luminous imagery.

The ambitions of the new generation of filmmakers competed with those of the older generation of directors. The works of older directors had become acts of remembering. They wanted to reveal the functioning of the regime, its tragic failures in the 1950s, and the widespread practice of suspicion, public reproach and exclusion. The increased political activity of artists and the increase in engaged cinema, drama and literature reflected the relaxing of the regime's control during the 1960s. Peter Solan, one of the most inspiring Slovak exponents of this line, said that he was trying to make 'civic films' and case studies from the the point of view of a witness, documenting the weaknesses of human character under different forms of pressure. This continuous development of critical change involved not just filmmakers but playwrights and writers as well (Peter Karvaš, Dominik Tatarka, Ladislav Mňačko). The cleansing of social life achieved primary importance not through confrontational accusation but by the constant inquiry into issues of personal responsibility. This line of film production included *Obžalovaný* (*The Accused*, 1964) by Ján Kadár and Elmar Klos, *Tri dcéry* (*Three Daughters*, 1967) by Štefan Uher and *Prípad Barnabáša Kosa* (*The Case of Barnabáš Kos*, 1964) by Peter Solan, and others.

On the one hand, it was a 'time of confessions', engagement and testimonies of past experience. On the other, it was the beginning of a period of 'flight films', surreal or impressionistic fantasies, and playful experimentation in film form. Emphasis on truth was juxtaposed with an emphasis on the filmic. From the 1960s on, the Czech and Slovak film critics led by Antonín J. Liehm cherished this differentiation. We find its 'schoolbook' confirmation in *Dejiny slovenskej kinematografie* (*The History of Slovak Cinematography*): 'Predecessors included in their unwritten manifestos the word truth, Jakubisko's generation introduced the term play.' Jakubisko's films and statements from the period following the Soviet invasion reflect the complex character of a creative process that was not built solely on separation from the older generation, but also on a new poetics and politics of the image.

After the invasion of 21 August 1968 and the Soviet occupation of Czechoslovakia, Jakubisko energetically reshaped his position: he wanted to be engaged and to mediate what he saw, thought and felt without self-censorship. That summer, he was finishing his second feature, *Zbehovia a pútnici* (*The Deserter and the Nomads* aka *Deserters and Pilgrims*). In its flow of apocalyptic, colourful reminiscences and visions of the world and man in the wars of the twentieth century, we find his famous black-and-white documentary on the invasion of the Russian tanks. The making of this film about the absurdities of war had been interrupted by direct personal experience. Later, in an interview with Liehm, Jakubisko admitted that he knew no greater pleasure than being able to tell the truth. From his viewpoint, however, this would result in the 'biggest absurdity and biggest cruelty I ever managed to film'. He started shooting his fourth film, *Dovidenia v pekle, priatelia!* (*See You in Hell, Fellows!*), in 1970, but he could not finish it before the fall of the regime in 1989. Jakubisko's creative position becomes most apparent in his third film *Birds, Orphans and Fools*. According to Czech critic Milan Klepikov, it is, both politically and formally, one of most radical films of the Czech and Slovak New Waves.

The shooting of *Birds, Orphans and Fools* began in October 1968. In the atmosphere of the Soviet occupation, Jakubisko sharpened and intensified its focus. This absurd reality reappears in his bizarre story of love, death and insanity and creates a contemporary background for the film. He originally drafted the story in 1967, with the title *Vyskočiť z kože* (*Being Beside Oneself*). In it, he asked the question that preoccupied his generation: why are we all fools and why do we find craziness the only possible way of existence? This was more than a simple conflict between man and society or the rejection of a one-dimensional world. The conflict was within man himself. The real issue was the creation of an alternative – an extraordinary, uncertain life-line (of flight). Jakubisko was interested in a man who wanted to be different, to 'fly out of the skin' of mundane reality. Here he builds on the commonly-held notion of the unbounded nature of life, but treats it with a scepticism linked to ideas of helplessness and worthlessness. A key example in the film is the scene in which he portrays a little bird imprisoned in a tight glass bottle, desperately trying to break free.

In his introduction to the film, Jakubisko presents himself as the director of the performance and, through voiceover, declares his intention of talking 'about people who wanted to be foolish but were prevented by love from fulfilling this desire'. Simultaneously, he presents an image of the film crew shooting in an asylum, surrounded by mentally handicapped children. In the detail of their innocent faces, he records the permanence of childhood and reveals their innocence and joy. His central characters, the voluntary fools Yorick, Andrej and Marta, can never be like them. In one shot, Jakubisko and his crew are shown in a photograph in the window of the institution, taken by photographer Andrej, a character in the film. Through this introduction, Jakubisko reveals that he also wears the fool's hat, and that we are all part of the same ship of fools.

At the beginning of the story with its preordained tragic ending, we are introduced to the friends, Yorick (Jiří Sýkora) and Andrej (Philippe Avron), who live in a large, abandoned and half-ruined house. Together with them lives a similarly lost, ageing landlord. One day, Yorick returns home with Marta (Magda Vašáryová), a strange and dirty girl, full of 'fleas'. Andrej's first reaction is to get rid of her because she is a Jew (his parents were killed by Jews). But, in their foolish exile, the three orphans become close, and she is initiated into the status of a fool. Her presence encourages them to compete in spontaneous fooling, joking and playful rebellion. They reflect on their happiness, love and freedom but also their fragility and transience. Thinking and confessions then replace games. One of the key scenes in the film is that in the leaking attic when Yorick describes, in words, his life experience: 'Everything besides yourself is vanity. So return into yourself. If they have demolished your house, start to build it again – but in your soul. Return into yourself. Build a house inside, live in it and you'll find happiness. [caption on a shroud: "The Word is a weapon of the powerless"]. They will call you a fool. But don't pay attention, if you are fine. You are fine because you are free. You are free because you are a fool.' At the same time, he plays pool with bottles, little birds and eggs. But while Jakubisko encourages laughter, he keeps in mind the other side of the coin, staging sequences of violence (the rape of a girl, guerrilla warfare). While his characters adopt an ironical approach to life and philosophical truth, they also show their anxiety and insecurity. What cannot be said becomes visible. Jakubisko defines his film as a strange, philosophical grotesque.

This story of shared craziness is intertwined with a story of shared love. Yorick loves Marta but does not want to lose Andrej's friendship and encourages him to share his love for her. Marta refuses such a relationship and, after fights with Yorick, decides to leave. Later, they find her again and re-establish their society of fools. During one of their rebellious trips, Yorick is arrested by the police and sentenced to prison. On his release, he learns of the romance between Marta and Andrej and her pregnancy. Yorick follows his impulses and his obsession with Marta leads to extreme cruelty. He kills her in a fit of jealousy and then commits suicide. He turns his death into a ritual. Standing on the Old Bridge over the Danube, he ties a statue of General Štefánik – his 'imaginary father' and the founder of Slovak independence – to his neck and jumps into the water.

In the first draft of the story, Yorick had been presented as 'unpredictable'. He lives a Bohemian life without perspective. A joker and a dreamer, his world is one of words rather than action. He enjoys his position as a sarcastic bystander, commenting on life. In the film the reference to the licenced (but dead) fool in Shakespeare's *Hamlet* is made explicit by readings from the play. Through decor, clothing and behaviour, the film also refers to similar figures from Cervantes and Rabelais, as well as to Sebastian Brant's *Ship of Fools* (1494) and Erasmus' *In Praise of Folly* (1512). But Jakubisko's Yorick is primarily a modern fool, governed by feelings of inferiority and uselessness that encourage his alienation from society.

Thanks to his mild and shy appearance and diligent character, Andrej, the other fool, complements Yorick's irrationality and masculine eccentricity. But neither Yorick nor Andrej are finished, clear-cut characters. They both reflect layers and dark corners of the fundamental 'foolish' human personality. Thus, as Jakubisko says, we meet two Yoricks, who are in certain moments both of them Andrejs: 'It is the very same character schizophrenically split into two roles.' On the one hand, he shows courage until death, and on the other he accepts reality. The third fool, the Jewish girl Marta, becomes the mediator in their discussions and arguments, a catalyst for their feelings and actions and a test of their changing craziness. She represents their future and during her initiation; they baptize her Sibyl.

The title *Birds, Orphans and Fools* embodies three facets of the ideal of liberated living common in the 1960s. Birds evoke freedom ('the birds of the air' who toil not but are nonetheless fed by God). Birds remind one of people without homes, 'brothers without shelter' (Kerouac), various nomads: tramps, wandering players and losers. Yorick, Andrej and Marta are all war orphans who rely only on themselves. They refuse to become part of a society in which their parents found reasons to 'kill each other'. As they say, they 'take photographs' only with their own eyes, recording and absorbing the unstoppable human recycling of evil and stupidity. All three of them want to be fools. As a drug, it is a game that helps them to survive and offers them a means of both escape and protest.

Jakubisko's first film, *Christ's Years*, had revealed the thematic direction of his work, his obsessive variation of 'waking into life'. However, his concern with the observation of this time of hesitation and uncertainty about joining the life of the majority required a loosening of narrative logic. Already, before 1970, he had developed his fantastic, magic realist – mosaic-like compositions that together targetted the viewer's emotions.

Jakubisko's film is also concerned with ambiguities – the complementary qualities of beauty and death, love and hate, tenderness and cruelty, laughter and pain, joy and sadness. For him, cruelty is not merely an unacceptable extreme of behaviour and death only the terrible end of life. In *The Deserter and the Nomads*, the absurdity of cruelty and killing is not restricted only to war. According to him, the film adopts the viewpoint of children. Within this perception of the world influenced by folk songs, ballads and poetry, he finds the exaggerated portrayal of cruelty almost beautiful.

Childlike perception became one of the primary inspirations of Jakubisko's work. He allowed mentally handicapped children to join his crew and handle the camera. He regards their viewpoint as an ideal of clear vision, which he clearly invokes in *Birds, Orphans and Fools*. The regular display and acceptance of death is closely related to the childlike and folk elements. Jakubisko is one of the few Slovak filmmakers to possess such an easy and familiar touch with death. He became death's filmic tempter. Death also stands for salvation from the pain of unfulfilled love and the loneliness of ageing. It can also attract by its beauty – as a sea of oblivion.

With Jakubisko, the theme of Christ's years and of a childlike film vision is closely related to the topic of fear of old age and helplessness. For his fools, the fists of the old age-related depression of their landlord serve as a warning. Their relation to him is mainly a relation to old age in general. A scene ends in the disgusted naming of the symptoms of old age (saliva, the smell of urine) and the scene in which they stage the cremation of the landlord provides a release for this anxiety. *Birds, Orphans and Fools* provides a double focus on an eccentric life style – it resonates as a joyful manifesto of life but also sends a shiver down the spine like a sceptical diagnosis. The pleasant drug of craziness becomes the indistinguishable poison of madness.

Jakubisko's refusal of the 'shallowness' of normal life is revealed in the film's spatial qualities. In addition to the windows and doors, the foolish residence has a number of other openings – holes in the walls, in the floor, in the roof. It represents an ideal of open living. There are many ways to enter the space. In a house like this, life as conducted in a normal living environment is impossible. The interior encourages useless and uncontrolled movement: sitting on the floor, sleeping on the top of the wardrobe, descending from the upper floor sliding down a pole. Another, even more crazy way of entering marks the strangeness of the abode more significantly. This is via the wooden beams leaning against the neighboring building (which is an island of un-reason par excellence – an institution for mentally handicapped children). The separation of the inner (house and asylum) from the outer (world of reason) makes up the basic spatial model for the film. In fact, this ruined foolish nest was the building of the former University of Humanities, Academia Istropolitana (established 1467), located in the centre of Bratislava. The Film and Television Faculty of the Academy of Performing Arts is located in the building today.

In Jakubisko's 'crazy 1968' film atmosphere, the building does not look only like Emmenthaler cheese where one can climb in and out – a tree also grows through it. Jakubisko clearly projects it as an oasis of winged life. The motif of flying and of bird life, the image of a man with wings, the joyful emphasis on our 'Daedalean origin' (Havetta) is the basis of the film poetisation of life (*Christ's Years*, 322, *Party in the Botanical Garden*, *L'alnie pol'né/Lilies of the Field*, 1972). A winged creature is the most obvious example of freedom and independence of movement in the world. In the open house full of holes we see many birds – parakeets, pigeons, sparrows flying around the three fools or hopping on tables, in beds, in closets. In some of the 'rooms' big branches stick out of the floor, as if a tree was growing through the building. The fools have organised the house as a bird's nest. The crazy world they live in is a real birds' world.

The only flyer repeatedly mentioned in the film is the French general, Slovak politician and diplomat Milan R. Štefánik. Together with the future presidents Tomáš G. Masaryk and Eduard Beneš, he founded the common state of the Czechs and Slovaks in 1918. In a number of scenes, Jakubisko organises a parodic accentuation of the legend of the famous Slovak founding father. He admits his fascination with this personality of modern Slovak history. In Štefánik's case too, his steep (career) flight was stopped by a tragic fall: his plane crashed under unclear circumstances near Bratislava in 1919. This rapid end to the hope of Slovak political emancipation led to some bizarre myths. At the beginning of the film, we see Yorick and Andrej at a commemoration event at Štefánik's memorial at Bradlo. They mock the need to glorify a hero, a nation's 'shepherd'. Yorick later claims to be his son, saying that all he has inherited from him is craziness and a statue of him. The statue becomes another figure in their games until finally the petrified father Štefánik helps Yorick to leave this world. For Jakubisko, the foolish treatment of Štefánik's character is not a sign of disrespect. He only unmasks false glorification. To emphasise their irreverence, he deliberately arranges for Yorick and Andrej to have their picture taken naked with Štefánik's statue.

The sarcastic commentary on Slovak national and cultural mythologies or 'state traditions' – besides Štefánik, they include the Slovak National Uprising of 1944 – is not the only sign of Jakubisko's art-film politicisation. He builds on those radical positions of political modernism, which in the 1960s were represented mainly by the films of Jakubisko's model, Jean-Luc Godard. He does so by showing an absurd guerrilla band of old women shooting machine-guns, and the scene of Yorick and Andrej coaxing the handicapped children into taking another bite for 'uncle Mao', and also by references to suppressed signs of homosexuality. It is not mere coincidence that, as Viera Protušová has stated, at that time Jakubisko admired Godard's way of 'political thinking through fantastic film form'.

Jakubisko is not interested in a traditional realistic imitation of reality, nor is he bound by the rules of classical film narration – traditional motivation, causality, continuity and so forth. That was one of the reasons why he chose Igor Luther – who shot Alain Robbe-Grillet's *L'Homme qui ment* (*The Man Who Lies*, 1968) in Slovakia – for his cinematographer. On the basis of the time- and space-concentration of the story, Jakubisko and Luther succeeded in outlining the characters' fragmentary conscience through 'un-premeditated' dynamics of framing and editing (including use of the 'dynamic frame'). In close-ups, the camera watches the characters' bizarre discussions and uncontrolled gestures, and moves, floating between them, revelling in joy. It thus problematises the distance between the viewer and the fools in the shot. Jakubisko does not expect audience identification, but at the same time he wants us to be touched by their performed absurdities. The camera seems to be one of them as they confide to it. Important points of the discourse are thus underlined by shots (medium close-ups, close-ups) of characters looking into the camera and declaiming their beliefs and impressions.

Visual stylisation is a characteristic feature of the film, thanks to Jakubisko's visual art training (graphic design) and also because he is one of the few Slovak directors who has also worked as a director of photography. His visual conception is implemented in the interior shots, scene structure, still-lifes, make-up and costumes of his characters, the intertextual variation of different poses and faciality, and the emphatic use of various intensities of light, luminosity and colour (for example, the Godardian solution of bloodiness as an intensity of red). The dialogic links to various visual art movements – quoting Dalí, paraphrasing Chagall, the original filmic use of not only avant-garde but also visual folk art tendencies – are reflected in the often critical search for stylistic relations un-restricted by connections to the arts of the twentieth century. As Václav Macek and Jelena Paštéková stated, 'Havetta is a Breughel of the Slovak cinema, Jakubisko [its] Bosch.' On the other hand, Jakubisko does not rely solely on the visualisation of the fluidity of mental states. The music of Zdeněk Liška transforms attempts at stepping outside oneself into the sphere of the audible: merriness, carelessness, the euphoria of fooling becomes contagious thanks to an accompanying music similar to that of the old film grotesques. In other sections, a modernistic assimilation of folk singing and music attracts our attention. When descending to the depths of passion, the sounds of folklorisation or carnivalisation ('indecent' sounds) withdraw, and feelings of loneliness, emptiness and hopelessness are reflected by piano solos supported and developed by women's choirs and orchestral music.

From the very beginning of *Birds, Orphans and Fools* Jakubisko foregrounds his role as director. He creates a film that revels in drawing attention to itself and the medium of film. During one of their last trips, Yorick, Andrej and Marta end up at a big dump consisting of used film stock. In the sea of film strips they again quote, and undermine the splendour and fame of the big dream factories that is soon to be destroyed. Wrapped in the stock, they stage the statues of Laocoön and then the logos of the large film companies (RKO, Mosfilm, MGM). Jakubisko does not aim solely at breaking the film's 'illusion of reality' in order to provide the viewer with a more critical insight. He doubts the value of film as a medium of communication and also its expressive potential. Just like the word, the film image has become only the vain expression of the helpless. Marta finally sets the dump on fire. It grows bigger and bigger through the purely filmic device of rapid montage. The climax of the scene confirms Jakubisko's sceptical and sarcastic viewpoint. His fools urinate on the burning film and announce the coming of the stream of urine by shouting: 'Watch out! The new wave!'

Birds, Orphans and Fools had its world premiere at the festival of Czechoslovak cinema in Sorrento, Italy in 1969. Jakubisko was awarded the Golden Siren for the direction of his first three features. Even at the time of the film's approval for production, the supporters of traditionalism feared its deviation from realism and its shocking imagery. They found nothing encouraging in the film and reproached it for its depressive, hopeless and gloomy atmosphere. Showing perversion, ugliness and the bizarre was said to have changed the image of our society – it was something unhealthy and fashionable, imported from outside. The consolidation of the regime after 1970, the so-called 'normalisation' of socialist culture meant the propagandistic discharge of such films on to the 'garbage dump' of decadent and harmful 'art'. It remained on the list of banned films until the very end of the communist regime in 1989. After its renewed premiere, it made a successful comeback and was perceived as one of the most progressive works of Slovak cinematography. Jakubisko's original film poetics, his fantastic penetration of the absurd and admirable aspects of human behavior and affectivity, and the playfulness and vision of his films are an inseparable feature of the common, as well as separate, Czech and Slovak film culture.

Martin Kaňuch

Translated from the Slovak by Zuzana Dudášová

SZERELEM LOVE

KÁROLY MAKK, HUNGARY, 1970

As with most great films, the story of *Szerelem* (*Love*, 1970) can be summed up in a few lines. A fragile, querulous, bedridden old lady is visited daily by her daughter-in-law, Luca, who fabricates letters which purport to come from America, recounting the glamorous adventures, as film director, of the absent son and husband, János. In truth, however, János is a political prisoner in a Hungarian jail. The old lady dies. János is released from prison, learns of the death of his mother, and hesitantly begins to rediscover his love for Luca.

The private concerns, feelings, anxieties and stratagems of these three people ultimately encapsulate the national trauma of Hungary (and of a large sector of the rest of the world) in the years of Stalinist oppression and its lingering and pervasive heritage. The precise period of the film's setting is not quite clear, but some glimpsed newspaper headlines suggest that the action takes place in the final years of Mátyás Rákosi's brutal regime, which was only checked in 1953 – though Rákosi continued in power as First Secretary of the Hungarian Communist Party until 1956. However it is not without significance that both the writer of the film, Tibor Déry, and the principal actor, Iván Darvas, had served substantial prison sentences after the revolution of 1956. (In 1957, Déry was sentenced to nine years' imprisonment but was released in 1960 after the formation of 'Tibor Déry committees' in many countries.) Political repression did not end with Stalin and Rákosi.

Even in 1972 it was a startling breakthrough for a film from Socialist Eastern Europe to acknowledge the existence of political prisoners. In the 1970s, however, Hungarian cinema sustained a role as a political avant-garde for Eastern European filmmakers, constantly testing the permitted limits of openness. An intelligent cultural authority always endeavoured to keep its reins upon the artists as slack as possible, given due regard to the ever-watchful eyes of Moscow. 'Difficult' films were sometimes delayed for months or even years, but few Hungarian films were ever banned outright.

Love was destined to mark the highpoint of the career of Károly Makk, one of Hungarian cinema's most gifted and durable directors. Born in 1925, his career in film began in 1943 when he was assistant on an experimental expressionist film, *Ketso Kettö* (*2 x 2*), starrng a prominent fascist actor, Lászlo Szillassy. After the war he found himself working again on the same film, which had passed to the Peasant Party. The scenes with Szilassy were reshot with Zoltán Várkonyi in the role, but Makk recalls, 'Nothing could save the picture. It was a terrible flop.'

2 x 2 nevertheless brought him into contact with leftist filmmakers like István Szőts and László Ranódy, who recommended him to the Peasant Party. Enrolled in the Budapest Academy of Dramatic and Film Art, he studied under Géza Radványi. Along with Félix Máriássy, Makk worked as assistant on Radványi's *Valahol Európában* (*Somewhere in Europe*, 1947), scripted by the well known film theorist, Béla Balázs, and a landmark in Hungarian film history.

On graduation, Makk was assigned to the newsreel studios along with Imre Féher. He first encountered the hazards of Socialism when he disagreed with his manager and was promptly sent off to work on a farm. He was forced to plough the fields for six months, until summer 1950 when Félix Máriássy, then shooting his second film, fell ill and asked for Makk as his assistant. Makk subsequently made a couple of shorts, *Ármány és szerelem* (*Cabal and Love*, 1952) and *Képzett beteg* (*The Trained Patient*, 1952), and went on to work as co-director with Zoltán Fábri on *Életjel* (*Signs of Life* aka *Fourteen Lives Saved*, 1954) and with Zoltán Várkonyi on a memorable adaptation of *Simon Menyhért születése* (*The Birth of Menyhért Simon*, 1954) which first introduced him to the book's author and the future writer of *Love,* Tibor Déry (1894–1977).

Makk finally had the chance to direct his first feature film, *Liliomfi*, in 1954. This was a significant stage in Hungarian cinema's liberation from the stricter dogma of Socialist Realism, in having no message except delight. The success of *Liliomfi* enabled him to make *A 9-es kórterem* (*Ward No 9*, 1955), an early film of social criticism, about hospital services under the Stalinist period. His talent for comedy was exploited in *Mese a 12 találatról* (*Tale on the Twelve Points*, 1956), a comedy about football-pools hopefuls. His first film after the events of 1956 was one of his best, *Ház a sziklák alatt* (*The House Under the Rocks*, 1958), a minutely observed psychological portrait of the emotional crisis of a peasant.

Following a 'monumental' film in celebration of the fortieth anniversary of the 1919 Hungarian Republic, *A 39-es dandár* (*Brigade No 39,* 1959), Makk's career throughout the 1960s proved to be less than successful. None of his films were well received either officially or critically, though *Megszállottak* (*The Fanatics*, 1961) was an interesting precursor of a group of Hungarian films that spoke of individual talent suppressed by the prevailing bureaucracy. The films alternated with periods of inactivity or work in television. He accepted a doomed Hungarian-Romanian co-production, *Bolondos vakácio* (*A Cloudless Holiday*, 1967) to win the chance to make *Isten és ember előtt* (*Before God and Man*, 1968), the dramatic tragedy of a family of Greeks who stayed in Hungary after the war, and which he believed provided his best subject since *The House Under the Rocks*. The reception of the film was unenthusiastic, and by the start of the 1970s Makk's morale was at a low ebb. He was to be saved by *Love*.

Makk had the script ready for several years before he was able to make the film. Since *The Birth of Menyhért Simon* he had remained friendly with Tibor Déry, though he had known him since the late 1940s. Makk recalls that he was then one of the most highly regarded Hungarian writers and was considered a major artistic figure by the Communist Party. Then, in the way of those times, he was attacked by a Party official just returned from Moscow, who charged him with not writing positively enough about the working class. Eventually, in 1953, he was thrown out of the Communist Party. 'I remember how upset he was. I was just a young guy and he was about fifty, but we formed a very close friendship.' Then they collaborated on Várkonyi's version of Déry's *Menyhért Simon*, for which Déry himself wrote the script.

They met a few times during the 1956 revolution, when Makk was filming events in the streets, and around that time Déry wrote the short story, 'Love', which was published in a literary newspaper. 'It was a very short but very touching story that simply described a political prisoner – a man jailed under the pretext of anti-communist propaganda – coming out of jail and being reunited with his wife.' Then, in 1960, after his own release from jail, Déry published another short story, based on a real incident, called 'Two Women'.

Makk thought of combining the two stories in a single screenplay in which the first part would examine the two women waiting for János to come out of jail, and the second part would show what happens when he comes out. When he first put the idea to Déry in the early 1960s, he was completely opposed. 'You are crazy. The stories are two different things. In "Love" the couple have a child, but in "Two Women" they have no child. In "Love" the woman has short hair but my wife has fantastic red hair. So there is no way you can make the combination.'

Makk persisted and gave Déry a crash course in cinema. Frequently, the septuagenarian writer would take his friend György Lukács, the great Marxist philosopher, with him to see a film. The two old gentlemen liked Italian Neorealism, loved *The Gold Rush*, but walked out of Alain Resnais. After six months, Déry telephoned Makk out of the blue and announced that he had written a script. From this beginning, the writer and director worked together to arrive at the final screenplay.

Déry's script was mostly based word for word on the two stories. Makk recalled in an interview that if he made changes, adding more scenes to try to make it more filmic, it was always wrong: 'When I came to make the film I simply took the two novels and shot them straight, because the dialogues were so perfect that there was no need to change anything. And through the dialogues the characters were so strong that there was no need for any manipulation'.

Makk first proposed the project to the studio in 1964, but it was firmly rejected on the grounds that Déry was an anti-communist writer. Two or three years later a German television production company bought the rights of the screenplay from Déry and planned to shoot the film in Budapest. The authorities soon saw the absurdity of a German company being allowed to make a film in Hungary written by Déry and directed by Makk when the same project was forbidden in Hungary. István Dosai, the head of Hungarofilm, made a report to the Minister of Culture. They informed the German company that there was a problem with the rights, which Déry had already assigned to a state company, and that it would not be possible to make the film in Budapest.

Every year after that, Makk said that he would like to shoot the film. Finally, in 1969 – 'they were probably just tired and bored with it all, or maybe they had some other current scandal with Jancsó or someone else' – they agreed. But they also wanted to include some 'positive' scenes showing that the authorities also had the power to bring these people out of the jails. Makk wrote the 'positive' scenes together with his close friend, György Konrád. 'But we never shot them. The film would have made no sense if I had made it like that.'

They had a precise script and the shooting of the film went well, but some ideas came later. Déry mentioned in a single line of the story that the old lady remembered a carriage and horses from her youth. The cinematographer János Tóth went on location and made a series of scenes that would look like old photographs without any reference to the script. 'The shots he created were marvellous. I just had to find the right places to put them. I always do the editing. Again, in the second part, I realised that it was too correct and literate, the sequences too logical. There was no play with time. But I found ways to intimate different ideas and memories, remembering how János first met his wife.'

These near-subliminal memories – the old lady's visions of former imperial elegance that blend into her fantasies of János' transatlantic adventures; János' memories of Luca, or momentary nightmares of the arrest – blend easily and naturally into the texture of the film, without any sense of imposed stylistic effects. That texture owes much to the virtuoso cinematography of Tóth, which uses black-and-white and an infinitely subtle intermediate range of greys, with impressive dexterity. The first part of the film has a bleak wintry light, with warmer tones for the cluttered interior of the old lady's house; János' return home is illuminated by a watery spring sunlight. The camera lingers on faces, capturing every nuance of Luca's resignation, despair and concealed exasperation with the testy old lady; of János' paranoia and apprehension, thrown back into the world after the guessed-at torment and humiliation of prison.

With infinite delicacy, Déry, Makk and Toth conspire to convey the games of deception between the women. Despite all obstacles, Luca arrives each day with flowers (when she cannot afford new ones she rearranges yesterday's), smiling, concealing irritability and the humiliations that are the lot of a prisoner's wife (she is dismissed from her job and forced to share her apartment with strangers). She teases the old lady out of her crabbiness, and simulates total belief in the absurd boasts of the faked letters, with their description of János's luxurious life in America, with bodyguards to protect him. How, asks the servant, can an old lady who has read so much, be so easily deceived? But is she deceived, or is she playing along with the game? The pretence seems strained for a moment when the old lady breaks down and sobs uncontrollably at the thought that she will never see her son again. Luca fools her – she says that she will ask him to come home this very day and let the film go hang. The bluff works and the old lady re-enters the pretence and forbids her to do anything of the sort, to risk spoiling his career. But everyone joins in these deceptions, which are the only means of spiritual survival – even the sceptical servant and the doctor who tells the old lady she will live to be a hundred, when he knows she has only days left. These are the sweet, benign deceptions that are an essential defence against the official lies that have sent János to jail.

The film's exquisite visual sensibility supports a trio of impressive performances. The old lady is played by Lili Darvas (1902–74), the widow of the internationally known dramatist, Ferenc Molnár (*Liliom*, *The Swan*). Darvas' career began with overnight success as Juliet at the Budapest Summer Theatre in 1920, instantly establishing her as a leading figure of the Budapest stage. In 1925, she was recruited by Max Reinhardt for the Josephstadt Theatre in Vienna, and this launched her international career. From 1938 she and her husband Molnár established themselves permanently in New York. Before *Love*, she had made one film appearance in Austria, in the title role of Hermann Kösterlitz's (Henry Koster) *Marie Bashkirtseff/Tagebuch der Geliebten* (1936), and played supporting parts in Hollywood in *Meet Me in Las Vegas* (Roy Rowland, 1956) and *Cimarron* (Anthony Mann, 1961), though she was frequently seen in American television dramas between 1947 and 1964.

Lili Darvas was not in fact Makk's first choice. His assistant had recommended Helene Weigel, the widow of Bertholt Brecht. 'I had seen a fantastic picture of her. I sent her the script and rushed to Berlin – where I met this dark, ugly, aggressive old lady. She said, "Károly, thank you! it's a great idea – it's lovely – I like it very much." I said to myself, "Oh my God, what shall

I do?" "But," she went on, "I don't want to leave this bloody dirty East Berlin, though I will never forget the idea." I ran back to the hotel and took a flight home immediately, in case she should change her mind … Two years earlier I had met Lili in Budapest when she was playing in a Molnár play; so I called her in New York, and she made her conditions. She was very fine, elegant, clever, a little ironical, a little sarcastic, with a great heart. When we first rehearsed she spoke very loud. I said, "Lilika, just hold back, just speak to me or to Mari." It was the first instruction I gave her, and from that moment she had a fantastic talent to feel the camera and to use her own real voice, with her marvellous Wienerisch accent. At that time every Hungarian film was dubbed because sound techniques were not good. She had never experienced looping before. After a short, simple take she asked to work without headphones. And after that it was perfect. She had such a feeling for the rhythm. She never watched the mouth on the screen, but just used this incredible feeling for rhythm … The shooting went very well. Lili Darvas was very correct. She never left the set – just sat there and watched everything. She had a good relationship with the rest of the unit. After *Love* I made a secret test with her for *Macskajáték* [*Cat's Play*, 1974] but we did not agree on which part she should play. I found her too elegant for the main part, which is what she wanted … It was my greatest adventure to work with such an intelligent, talented, fantastic artist.'

Mari Törőcsik, who played Luca, has remained one of Hungary's best-loved actresses since her debut at the age of nineteen in Zoltán Fábri's *Körhinta* (*Merry-go-round*, 1955) and has worked with almost every major Hungarian director in the half-century since then. She first worked with Makk in *Elveszett paradicsom* (*The Lost Paradise*, 1962). Iván Darvas was born in 1925 and made his film debut in 1949. He first worked with Makk on *Liliomfi* and had made two more films with him, *Ward No. 9* and *Tale on the Twelve Points*, before the events of 1956 and his subsequent imprisonment resulted in a seven-year absence from the screen. His comeback was again with Makk, in *Mit csinált felséged 3-tó l5-ig?* (*His Majesty's Dates*, 1964). In October 2002, Darvas was awarded the Imre Nagy Order along with former president Árpád Göncz and writer Tibor Méray: all three had served prison sentences for their part in the 1956 revolution.

Even when production began Déry retained some doubts: 'After two weeks of shooting I arranged a screening of rushes for him – a mixture from different scenes; at that stage I didn't want to show him the logical story. That evening he called me, very upset. He didn't like Darvas at all, and complained, "Mari has very short hair but my wife has fantastic red hair. Everything is false". Then later that same evening he called again: "I am an old, stupid writer. Don't care what I say. You have to do what you want." And finally, when we were in Cannes, someone at the press conference asked him how he felt the film compared with the stories; and he said, simply, "The film is better."'

Finally came the test of submitting the finished film for approval. It was screened for the chief of the Dialog Studio, a member of the Party, who had himself been in jail in the 1950s. Then after two or three weeks the chief called Makk and said, 'It's OK. The film is lovely, amazing, fine.' And it seems that when the Minister of Culture and all his people watched the film, it was particularly the women who said, 'You have to have the courage to tell the truth of what is happening to us.' It was the revolution of the females, who pushed the comrades to say yes. After that the *New York Times*' correspondent in Yugoslavia went to Budapest, saw the film and wrote a leading article – it was the first step that eventually led to Cannes and the Special Jury Prize.

Love gave Makk his first major critical success since *The House Under the Rocks*. The Cannes Festival Special Jury Prize led to world-wide distribution for the film, re-established his international reputation, and gave a new stimulus to his career, though subsequently his production has been irregular, with breaks of several years between films. His major successes were *Egy erkölcsös éjszaka* (*A Very Moral Night*, 1977) and the remarkable *Egymásra nézve* (*Another Way*, 1982), the story, based on real-life events, of a lesbian love affair in Stalinist Budapest. Two English-language productions, *Lily in Love* (1984) and *The Gambler* (1997), called into play much of the old finesse, but failed to win an international public.

In 2003 Makk was reunited with Iván Darvas and Mari Törőcsik to make *Egy hét Pesten és Budán* (*A Long Weekend in Pest and Buda*), relating the encounter of an elderly couple who were lovers in the 1950s. The couple have the actors' names: Iván had left at the time of the 1956 revolution and now lives with his English wife in Switzerland. Mari, who is revealed to have been a spy for the Communist authorities, stayed behind, bore his child, and now, dying, asks him to visit her. 'I never anticipated that this film would have any relation with *Love*. True it has the same actors, but it is a very different story. Everyone pushed me to connect the films, but though I was always against it, just out of curiosity I used some very short shots from *Love* as flashbacks. Now I would admit that it is somehow of the same family. A memory … The era of *Love* was a very interesting time of the cinema and of my life also.'

David Robinson

REFERENCE

Robinson, David (2003) Interview with Károly Makk (unpublished).

CZŁOWIEK Z MARMURU MAN OF MARBLE

ANDRZEJ WAJDA, POLAND, 1977

'I would have been a different man', Andrzej Wajda once said when commenting on how his life would have changed had he been allowed to film Stefan Żeromski's early twentieth-century novel *Przedwiośnie* (*Pre-Spring*); doubtless because it dealt explicitly with Polish reactions to the Russian revolution. Wajda had proposed this project in the 1960s, during which he also sought approval for a film based on a script by Aleksander Ścibor-Rylski, entitled *Człowiek z marmuru* (*Man of Marble*). So important was the impact of this film when it was finally released in the mid-1970s that its possible completion in the 1960s might have affected Wajda's life even more deeply than the abortive *Przedwiośnie* project. The development of Polish cinema – and perhaps even of Polish history – might also have been different. Even in the relatively liberal, late Gierek years, which oversaw the production, only an exceptionally open-minded Culture Minister – Józef Tejchma – could secure its approval. This was not from any secret sympathies with subversion, but because of his own memories of the erection of Nowa Huta – the prestige heavy industry construction sited near Kraków as a deliberate counterweight to that university town's venerable traditionalism – and desire to see its builders memorialised. *Man of Marble* would cost Tejchma his job and encountered a strenuous official campaign to marginalise it, which used the media to deny its veracity and consigned it to out-of-the-way cinemas. If *Man of Marble* is the story of the passing of the hot brick that broke the career of an exemplary 'shock-worker', it was itself a 'hot potato'. What gave it this status? A plot summary can help suggest some of the reasons.

It opens with film student Agnieszka (Krystyna Janda) hunting down material for her diploma film. Her subject is a 1950s shock worker, Mateusz Birkut (Jerzy Radziwiłowicz), whose star fell almost as rapidly as it had risen. *Man of Marble* uses a fragmented quest structure that echoes *Citizen Kane* (Orson Welles, 1941), showing Agnieszka hearing portions of Birkut's life recounted by friends, false friends, acquaintances and his wife, Hanka Tomczyk, now as much an alcoholic as Welles' Susan Alexander Kane became. It resembles *Citizen Kane* from the outset in its construction of a pastiche period newsreel as an orienting overview of Birkut's life that anchors the rest of the film. One of Agnieszka's first interviews is with the feted careerist film director Burski (Tadeusz Łomnicki), who achieved prominence by building up the propaganda image of Birkut. Birkut himself proves to be both idealistic and naïve. He sees Stakhanovite work-norms as an effective solution to the post-war housing shortage and is shocked when a hot brick is passed to him, doubtless by workers less enamoured of the gruelling work-schedules imposed on construction sites after a Birkut visit. Birkut is also courageous, too honest for his own good: not just the false, manipulated image of the hero, but a genuine hero who refuses to be used when he begins to grasp the nature and potential viciousness of state propaganda. When his friend and co-worker Witek (Michał Tarkowski) is accused of participating in an imperialist conspiracy to attack socialist construction by nobbling Birkut, Birkut assiduously seeks and is denied justice, then mocks the show-trial at which he is called as a prosecution witness. No wonder his star falls, his poster drifting down in sad, ignominious silence towards the mud. No wonder also that Agnieszka's project encounters insuperable obstacles, and that her camera is confiscated. The ending of *Man of Marble* is strangely upbeat, however, as she discovers Birkut's son and thereby in a sense recovers the untraceable Birkut, as the same actor plays both parts. As the two stride together down the long corridor of the television building in which her quest had begun, there is an air of triumph, even of a militant marriage. If our spirits rise, for all our rational scepticism regarding Agnieszka's ability to finish what she has begun, it is not only a testimony to the power of Wajda's art but also because we know that we have just seen 'Agnieszka''s film, albeit signed by Andrzej Wajda. She becomes Wajda's double as both of them banish the spectre of the safe, self-aggrandising path of a Burski.

Things had begun innocently enough, though, in 1963, when Wajda and Ścibor-Rylski first sought the approval of the State's Script Assessment Commission, describing their script as a homage to the common worker. The transcript of the meeting records a lengthy, sometimes stormy session. Controversy bubbled up at the very outset, when one speaker declared the primacy of political considerations over artistic ones and doubted 'that the political climate for the making of such a film exists'. Even his feeling that certain elements were treated too much in the manner of the grotesque can be read politically rather than aesthetically, as what he meant was the presentation of the Security Service. This speaker also doubted the probability of the mechanism of the passing of the hot brick. The next one weighed in with worries about the effect on the young of the ostensible lack of clarity in Agnieszka's attitude to what she learns. Indeed, the whole work was perturbingly open to various readings. Krzysztof Teodor Toeplitz, the well-known critic and social commentator, replied that since the ending shows Birkut's further development as positive (in a major divergence from the 1977 film, this script ended with Birkut beginning to better himself through study), any final indifference in Agnieszka is merely apparent. Toeplitz then became the first critic to note the indebtedness to *Citizen Kane*, and pronounced it a wise, understanding and pro-Party film. Approval would demonstrate the Commission's commitment to contemporary, engagé filmmaking. The discussion then reverted to a less favourable tone, with praise of the script's accomplishment leavened with deadly worries about the degree of its optimism and Birkut's attitude to socialism. Ścibor-Rylski and Wajda reacted strenuously to the criticisms, the former objecting particularly strongly to accusations of the mixing of truth and falsity, and Wajda frustratedly listing a series of other proposed projects denied approval. Jerzy Bossak, head of the Kamera Film Unit, was similarly scathing. All were put in their places by Wincenty Kraśko, one of the political appointees to the commission, who felt that bitterness had dictated the words of Wajda and Bossak. As far as he was concerned, Birkut was no communist but merely an honest man caught up in a mechanism. Culture Minister Tadeusz Zaorski noted the divergence in the positions of the politicians and the artists and advised further work on the script.

It is perhaps significant that the script's rejection did not prevent its publication in the same year in the 4 August edition of the Warsaw weekly *Kultura*, perhaps because it was in a medium that lacked the sizeable financial outlay and – perhaps more importantly – the potentially dangerous popular impact of the cinema. Come the 1970s, when a renewed attempt was made to secure approval for the script, the fact that the Script Assessment Commission had ceased to exist may have facilitated the film's making, rendering its approval less dependent on the hesitations of fearful *nomenklatura* bureaucrats.

As remarked above, its approval can be attributed to a single person, the mid-1970s Culture Minister Józef Tejchma, who decided not to consult the Central Committee, well aware that – as he put it in his diary on 24 January 1976 – 'there would probably – or even certainly – be no common ground and the screenplay would go on lying in the drawer'.

When Wajda finally gained permission to film Ścibor-Rylski's story, he decided to alter it in various ways, some of them involving its simple updating, others giving it an even more aggressive tone. If it was deemed unfilmable in 1963 for reasons that are not entirely clear, Wajda established clear-cut grounds for an active rejection linked to far-reaching changes in the characterisation of Agnieszka. Her opening dialogue with the television producer establishes the subject as dynamite, and Agnieszka vents her frustration with an obscene gesture at the television headquarters on Woronicza before heading off to pursue her transgressive project anyway. If some changes entailed simple updating – the addition of a prologue taking account of the role of alternative patron assumed by television in the 1970s, and an epilogue showing us Birkut's son and informing us of his father's death – the change in Agnieszka is fundamental and reverberates through the entire script. Janda's Agnieszka moves like a scissor woman, striking angular poses, limbs snapping shut to scythe her way through opposition. The Gdańsk dockyard cranes that appear near the end can seem like a further abstraction of the poses of a figure who is already to some extent cartoon-like.

The pulsing rhythms of the opening music set up a film that will fully exploit the love of speed Wajda had once shown when he rejoiced in the unprecedented rapidity with which the actors delivered their lines in *Popiół i diament* (*Ashes and Diamonds*, 1958). This speed will be one of the 'American' features of a work that sees itself as iconoclastic investigative reporting, a hybrid of *Citizen Kane* and *All the President's Men* (Alan J. Pakula, 1976). The air of transgression established by the television producer's initial statement that the footage Agnieszka wants will never be shown echoes the 'banned in perpetuity' label affixed to various Czech and Slovak New Wave films by the Czechoslovak authorities after 1968, somewhat misleadingly and self-servingly creating the straw-man of a 1970s Poland as oppressive as its southern neighbour. It is followed by Agnieszka's entry into a forbidden section of the National Museum's basement collections, her sound-man distracting the guide as she deftly employs a hair-pin to pick the lock to the Socialist Realist-era statues.

Where Ścibor-Rylski's Agnieszka takes small steps and wears tweed, Wajda's sports the leggy jean-suit of rebellion, disrespectfully and hurriedly munching – eating on the run – as the wide-angle lenses enlarge her big strides. Her transgression may be primarily political, but it is also subliminally sexual, as she becomes mannish in a man's world; she becomes, as it were, a politicised version of the predatory shark-mouthed student of Wajda's earlier *Polowanie na muchy* (*Hunting Flies*, 1969). Thus she bestrides the prone statue of Birkut, leans back upon it and gasps for breath near-orgasmically upon completion of her hand-held camera shot.

Since the film follows Ścibor-Rylski's original dialogue quite closely, it is worth noting that one or two lines are redistributed to accentuate Agnieszka's power and agency: for instance, it is she who has obtained the final clip of Birkut shown in the first screening room session, not the female editor, and she who persuades Hanka to speak of her former husband, not the sound-man. Wajda shows us an Agnieszka who surmounts obstacles to make her film, using cunning to tape the ex-security service man Michalak, whereas in the Ścibor-Rylski story he is a talking head fully aware of the camera. Wajda's Agnieszka winkles her way into Burski's car, and is not politely directed towards it, as in Ścibor-Rylski's story.

Agnieszka's ambition parallels Burski's, making it not entirely surprising that Party Secretary Jodla should attribute her drive to investigate the 1950s to a self-promotional sensation-seeking (note her opening statement that any old subject will not do for *her* diploma film). She is, after all, also a stand-in for Wajda himself, something hinted at in the opening sequence when the television producer declares that this material calls for an experienced director. Her use of the hand-held camera parallels Burski's on the project that launched his reputation, *Architects of Our Happiness*, a work whose assistant directorship Wajda ascribed to himself. The *mea culpa* also suggests the fraught nature of the choices demanded of all Stalinist-era directors and so may surreptitiously complicate the text's surface denunciation of Burski's later time-serving. (After all, had not even *Ashes and Diamonds* been 'politically correct' on one level, that of the plot depiction of the futility of resistance to the new, Soviet-backed authorities?)

Agnieszka, however, will strive to make the kind of filmmaking Burski abandoned when he – in his own words – 'wised up': the dark, critical work suggested by the unused shots of workers trudging through mud or pelting the site manager with fish in a manner ironically reminiscent of Sergei Eisenstein's flagship Soviet film, *Bronenosets Potëmkin* (*The Battleship Potemkin*, 1926). If Ścibor-Rylski's Agnieszka, like Wajda's, does not complete her film, it is for vastly different reasons: out of tact and hopefulness, not because she has hit a brick-wall of History. Ścibor-Rylski's Agnieszka makes this decision after seeing Birkut at night-school near the end: it is as if his story cannot yet be told, for a great deal may still lie before him. The significantly later production date of Wajda's film allows him to establish Birkut as dead, though with a hint of hope in the survival of his spirit in the manifest double who is his son, and the latent double who is Agnieszka. As in Walter Benjamin's theory of oral – one might add in this context, legendary – storytelling in general, Birkut's story becomes transmissable through the death that sets a seal upon it, rounds it out. Wajda may have been prevented from giving the cause of death, as Culture Minister Tejchma compelled him to remove a shot of a headstone bearing the date of the still-sensitive suppression of the Gdańsk workers in 1970, but he would be able to insert it into *Człowiek z żelaza* (*Man of Iron*, 1981), a mere five years later.

But if Wajda loses one chunk of his film to a censoring Cerberus, Agnieszka's is swallowed completely. So how can one explain – or even justify – the victorious air of her final walk down the television headquarters corridor, arm-in-arm with Birkut's son? A partial justification is her discovery of a key element (a mascot?) that may turn the tide and get her film reinstated. This suggestion is underwritten by the confidence exuded by the walk and the music; by the echo of the opening, the rhyme breathing an atmosphere of completion and simultaneous possible reversal; and the producer's craven retreat to the toilet. At the same time, though, a mere moment's thought will remind us that the authorities who feared the making of a film about Birkut are unlikely to be swayed by the production of his son as evidence. They will still have vested interests to defend intransigently. If a feeling of triumph survives our rational doubts, however, it is because we have indeed just seen a film about Birkut: not Agnieszka's, but Wajda's own. And because she is his double on one level – in the realm of the solidarity of filmmakers – a sense that her film has indeed been made emerges quasi-mystically. It may not be now, yet it will come, to echo Hamlet; youth will not be done down.

Tejchma's diary shows him fully aware of the dangers posed by the project. If, on 24 January 1976, he had seen his approval of the film as 'perhaps my most important decision as minister', upon its completion he records his apprehensions before discussion of the finished product with Wajda, and in a note for 11 December plans to request the following changes:

The main one: remove from the ending the Gdańsk cemetery, which refers to the events of December 1970. Tone down the scenes concerning the activities of the police authorities in the 1950s; remove the sentence 'what ghastly architecture!' (which concerns Nowa Huta, but is associated with the Lenin monument). Remove the scene of the smashing of the security office's windows.

It is worth noting that Wajda felt secure enough to comply only with the first. It is almost as if – in line with the practices of many Polish directors – he had inserted the Gdańsk cemetery sequence as a bargaining chip he knew would have to be deleted, and whose excision could then be used as a sign of compliance in important matters that would enable him to retain other elements that would become minor in comparison.

Given the intensive negative press campaign that would greet the film, the generally favourable tenor of its *kolaudacja* (Approving Committee) may seem remarkable, though it becomes less so when one realises that its discussions occurred behind closed doors. The first voices were all strongly approving, the first speaker apparently deciding to quash possible criticism at birth by declaring that 'there is no reason to fear that such a work of art could cause undesirable effects' and hoping that it would be the harbinger of similar works – a prophetic remark immediately echoed by its description by Aleksander Jackiewicz (one of Poland's best-known and most-respected film critics) as an 'inaugural work' in the vein of *Ashes and Diamonds*.

The first notes of disapproval are simply aesthetic and concern Agnieszka, whom one speaker described as engaged in a 'St Vitus dance'. In arguing that 'one would need a larger number of facts and proofs' to secure a proper judgement of the period of 'errors and distortions', another raised an issue central to socialist aesthetics, as it is to all didactic art: that of the typicality of a single concrete case. Various speakers voiced unease over such moments as Birkut's voting, the courtroom scene, or the ex-security man's move to managing strippers – one (Krzysztof Teodor Toeplitz) managing both to object to this and to add 'I know of such cases', all of which prompted Jackiewicz to take the unusual step of speaking a second time, underlining both the film's significance and Wajda's good taste, and arguing against any imposition of the sort of cuts and changes normally required by a *kolaudacja*.

When Ścibor-Rylski came to reply, the difference in reception since the Script Assessment meeting of 1963 led him to thank the meeting 'for its understanding of our intentions', and to make only two points. Stressing the film's novelty, despite some speakers' statements that it contained nothing new, he argued 'it is one thing to know such things, another to follow them on the screen'. Wajda remarked that he had rendered past and present interdependent in order to reach contemporary viewers, of whom Agnieszka was a typically neurotic representative. The energy he attributes to her is what he would like to see in the young, for whom he sees her as a model. Wajda defended Janda's acting as 'very genuine', warning against premature criticism: after all, it might be as successful with viewers as Zbigniew Cybulski's had been in *Ashes and Diamonds*. The summary from the chair pointed out the work's status as a 'landmark attempt to initiate a serious conversation about the 1950s', and noted the degree to which the screenplay had changed since 1963. Its value lay in Birkut's truth to his ideals 'despite being wronged', his transmission of his values to his son, and Agnieszka's evolution towards identification with Birkut. He asked Wajda to note the meeting's comments on particular sections of the film, but emphasised that there was no need to change anything, for 'we accept the film in this form'.

The simultaneous emergence and hounding of Wajda's film, however, indicates how deeply unacceptable it was to many sectors of the authorities. Reviews would seek viewers' assent by conceding tactically that it was artistically accomplished, but would then seek to demolish the accuracy and representativeness of its image of People's Poland. The youth paper *Walka młodych* (*Struggle of the Young*), for instance, organised a round table discussion entitled 'Kryształowy bohater – tendencyjne realia' ('A Crystal Hero – Tendentious Details') involving its editorial team and former activists of the ZMP (Union of Polish Youth) and ZSMP (Union of Socialist Polish Youth). Speaking for the paper, Józef Grabowicz began by stating the impossibility of such a 'noble, salt-of-the-earth character' as Birkut being launched by manipulators, careerists and cynics; the shock worker movement did not come from them. This comment was endorsed by a female former ZMP activist, who recounted an example of youth activists in Zabrze whose enthusiasm for work emulation, ironically, was deemed excessive and condemned as 'anarchy' by their management. Grabowicz stated that 'the film's creators needed an accumulation of demons and shady characters in order to achieve sharp contrasts and a clear delineation of the profile of the main protagonist. Thus this conception could be explained through the laws of drama, 'the drive to intensify conflicts'. All the more reason to conclude therefore that the 'triumph of the rogues and careerists' shown by the film 'has little in common with the complicated optimism of our most recent history'.

Man of Marble would become the most oppositionally potent film in the history of Polish cinema, kick-starting the late 1970s' 'Cinema of Moral Anxiety' whose strongest hotbed was Wajda's own X film unit. That movement would underline the depth of the disparity between the authorities' socialist rhetoric and their private self-enrichment and profound indifference to the corruption coursing through society. *Man of Marble*, however, would have a wider and more tonic epic sweep than any of the smaller-scale Moral Anxiety films, which could only follow up one or the other of its strands: the groundbreaking dissection of 1950s Stalinism, given extra bite by Wajda's first-hand experience of the period, or that of the official subterfuges of the present. Wajda's film became even more penetrating as its parallel structure suggested a continuity between the present and events the Polish 'United Workers' Party' hoped had been safely buried as 'the period of errors and distortions'. *Man of Marble* evokes a Poland still haunted by the repression of the memory of its Mateusz Birkuts and their unmarked headstones. Birkut arguably becomes all the more haunting an absent presence through the enforced excision of those images of his grave and date of death – in December 1970, during the authorities' violent suppression of the unrest of the workers of Gdańsk. That footage, of course, would turn up again in Wajda's *Man of Iron* made during the brief, uncensored heyday of Solidarity's sixteen-month overground existence. The man of marble would be as finally irrepressible as the Solidarity movement that itself came back from the dead to triumph in 1989, a mere eight years after General Wojciech Jaruzelski's imposition of martial law.

Paul Coates

REFERENCES

Grabowicz, Józef, *et al.* (1977) 'Kryształowy bohater – tendencyjne realia', *Walka młodych*, 8 May, 10–11.

Ścibor-Rylski, Aleksander (1972) '*Człowiek z marmuru*', in Aleksander Ścibor-Rylski, *Ich dzień powszedni: opowiadania filmowe.* Warsaw: Iskry, 183–251.

Tejchma, Józef (1991) *Kulisy dymisji: Z dzienników ministra kultury 1974–1977.* Kraków: Oficyna Cracovia.

NAPLÓ GYERMEKEIMNEK DIARY FOR MY CHILDREN

MÁRTA MÉSZÁROS, HUNGARY, 1982

Born in Hungary in 1931, Márta Mészáros is the daughter of the sculptor Lászlo Mészáros, who emigrated with his family to Kirghizia in the former Soviet Union in 1936; in 1938, he was arrested and imprisoned there and was never seen again. In 1942, her mother died of typhoid. Mészáros returned to Hungary in 1946. She went back to Russia to study at Moscow's film academy, VGIK, which she graduated from in 1956, moving back to Romania, to begin as a director of documentary films. From 1959 to 1968 she made some thirty documentaries, popular science films and educational short films, before directing her first feature, *Eltávozott nap* (*The Girl*, 1968). Living in Budapest and Warsaw when she is not on location, the trajectory of her film career underscores her conceptual and visual ability to link the personal with the political in order to depict individuals and the ways in which their efforts shape history, perhaps as much as they are constructed by it. Her fiction films are grounded in an aesthetics of realism, be it in their unsentimental re-creations of working-class environments, in the insightful delineation of details that weave together complex psychological portraits or in their dissection of the anatomy of relationships among women or between women and men. Her style embodies a distillation of emotions and places that depicts on an intimate level the impact of social issues and political changes on women in East Central Europe.

Among the few filmmakers who have consistently addressed the intersections of state ideology, sexuality and everyday life – rural and urban, workplace and domestic – Mészáros has explored the highly-charged intersections of gender and nationality. After a distinguished career as a documentary filmmaker trained in Moscow, her first feature films appeared in the late 1960s, catapulting her to a degree of international celebrity then unequalled by any other female East European director, and establishing the concerns that continue to interest her: the representation of working women and men attempting to create a new society against the background of modern political and socioeconomic life in post-war Hungary. Mészáros' films raise issues of class relations and gender, love and sexuality, deception and honesty in an unsentimental and at times even ruthless fashion. They have been particularly troubling for Hungarian audiences and critics discomfited by her uncompromising meditations on national and gender identity in post-Stalinist and post-communist Europe by confronting conflicts between men and women, whether factory workers and Communist Party officials or bourgeois intellectuals and new capitalists. Intimacy and sensuality are evident primarily between female co-workers or in solitary moments of respite from the rigours of contemporary life, regardless of the regime currently in power. 'I am an East European director,' she said in a 1993 interview, 'and my whole life, unfortunately, has been filled with politics. It is a tradition that, good or bad, you must deal with politics, especially for my generation educated under Stalinism … An independent woman – one who finds herself in a situation where she must make a decision on her own – is the central character in each of the pictures I have made so far.'

One of the country's supremely accomplished women directors, Mészáros has been particularly concerned to portray the generational effects of the communist period and the uprising of 1956. In the 1980s she began a series of 'diary' films, *Napló gyermekeimnek* (*Diary for My Children*, 1983), *Napló szerelmeimnek* (*Diary for My Loves*, 1987) and *Napló apámnak, anyámnak* (*Diary for My Father and Mother*, 1990). By using the diary format intended, as indicated in the titles, for her children, lovers and friends, she perfected a form that was to serve her admirably. Because her own father was a victim of Stalin's purges, her intergenerational articulation of Stalinism generated a particular authenticity that continues to reverberate today in the films of younger filmmakers.

As a leading figure of her generation, Márta Mészáros has, for over five decades, been directing films that resonate with the spirit and the struggles of her time. Her masterful trilogy, produced before the collapse of Communism of the 1990s, constitutes an ensemble of studies that narrate the evolution of a young woman facing the major historical moments of the twentieth century. They are passionate yet critical studies of personal development and political awakening, at once autobiography, confession, document and credible historical source material. Her project was clear, as she stated in a 1999 interview: 'I intended to make a trilogy from the very beginning. Ever since I began to see the world around me I had had a desire to do something on the screen that is similar to a saga, a family novel in literature. Where the stories continue, the characters return after certain changes, enriched or burdened with historic and private experiences.'

The most renowned of this trio, *Diary for My Children* (awarded the Special Jury Prize at the 1984 Cannes Film Festival) breathes an air of authenticity and a finely wrought urgency into its realistically unsentimental re-creations of working-class environments; in the insightful delineation of historical and political material, stitching together complex psychological portraits of protagonists in socialist East Central Europe; and in its dissection of the anatomy of relationships among women, between men and women and between parents and children. By foregrounding the voice of the narrator/director, *Diary for My Children* focuses on the interplay of an individual's own trajectory against the backdrop of traumatic historical events. The continuous interweaving of images from successive chronological periods and the insertion of archival footage and reconstructed documentary sequences have contributed to the film's status as a paradigm of groundbreaking visual strategies used to serve the filmmaker's long-censored story of familial loss, intergenerational tension and the struggle for artistic and personal identity.

Mészáros' principal strength remains her gift for connecting the personal with the political by portraying the impact of individual subjectivity upon history, and of historical forces upon individual lives. She has commented on her preference for a kind of pseudo-realism in her work, and her style confronts, on a scale at once intimate and epic, the impact of social issues and political changes on gender and identity in East Central Europe. The past was especially politicised during the socialist period and the force of history invoked to legitimate authority: 'collective memory' was activated to contest distortions in the historical record. Memory and history were often counter-posed in what Václav Havel described as the struggle to 'live in truth'.

The opportunity to revisit one of Mészáros' most accomplished films reveals an acute observation of Hungarian culture from the perspective of a director fluent in many languages and visual styles whose work has been honored by international retrospectives, such as New York City's Museum of Modern Art 1999 tribute, the first US survey of Mészáros' films. From its hard-line post-Stalinist period in the early 1950s through the Kádár regime (sometimes called 'goulash communism' in reference to the country's persistently Western-oriented economy and outlook in the 1970s and 1980s), Hungary's emergence from its Stalinist past is dramatically inscribed here; little wonder, then, that this film played such an important role in provoking public and critical opinion. *Diary for My Children* poses questions pertinent to the challenge of the cinematic representation of history: what becomes of the historical record of lives when they are recorded in images, rather than words? How do images convey ideas and information that are beyond the scope of words? In what ways can filmed history be measured against written history? How does cinema function as a way of thinking historically? And finally, what ways do depictions of private and public space interact and resonate?

As its title indicates, *Diary for My Children* is above all a personal film: the idea of 'diary', after all, presupposes a notion of intimacy and privacy. Although its genesis was motivated by historical and political circumstances, the film is neither purely fictional nor entirely autobiographical, nor, for that matter, strictly speaking a product of what has been called 'women's cinema'. Rather, by maintaining an intricate balance between personal exploration on the one hand and historical investigation on the other, Mészáros' cinematic method transforms and expands its autobiographical dimension by alternating sequences in which the historical context, marked by the use of archival footage, is dominant. This structure positions the viewer in a way that refuses both the more complete distancing of documentary and the more individually-motivated conventions of autobiographical cinema. In directorial motivation and structural composition, then, *Diary for My Children* transcends traditional categories of genre, yet it functions as a kind of history in the style of the French *Annales* school, a '*mise-en-regard*' in which different angles of vision operate to analyse micro-history in order to generate ideas about a larger, macro-historical vision – a private message, in other words, which, in the public mind, becomes a collective one. Its point of view is that of the director's younger alter-ego, Juli, played by Zsuzsa Czinkóczi, who had been cast in two previous films of Mészáros and who occupies the principal role in all three parts of the *Diary* trilogy.

The film was rejected by Communist censors for over a decade, doubly censored, one might say, by ideological repression and the director's own internal struggle with the powerful personal and political material that is its subject. The opening scenes take place in 1947 as Juli, the adolescent narrator-protagonist, is returning to Hungary from the Soviet Union with a group of Hungarian Communists, comrades of her parents exiled there before the Second World War. As the plane lands in Budapest, we see aerial shots of the city, its former Habsburg splendor diminished by war and poverty. In that stark setting, Juli's taut features and toneless voice betray her reluctance to embark upon the paradoxically privileged life offered her by Magda Egri, the loyal member of the Stalinist élite under whose sponsorship this return has been made possible. This repatriation is clearly not to be a joyous homecoming, scarred as it is by the wounds of the past – her parents' death, her country's suffering, her own contained sadness. But Juli quickly establishes herself as an independent young woman, unwilling to be seduced by Magda's efforts to win her over either to the cause of Stalin or to her own emotional needs for a comradely family. As she looks out of the window of Magda's sombre yet well-appointed apartment in the first few moments of this new life, Juli's memory is triggered by a glimpse of a ruined building just outside, about to be demolished by the wrecker's ball. In the first of many brief flashbacks, she recalls herself as a child with her real mother, a woman whose physical beauty and youth stand in stark contrast to Magda's middle-aged severity. To her friend Tomi, Juli describes her mother as having 'red hair, green eyes, tall, sad, happy, unlucky and lovely … she drew, sang and spoke four languages … we were always together.' Photographs of Mészáros's mother resemble this description: in the film, we see mother and daughter together at an outdoor movie projection in the Soviet Union (István Szőts' *Emberek a havason/People of the Mountains*, 1942), Juli being affectionately reassured that the actors who have been killed will reappear again in another film. Cinema is privileged as a special space, the movie theatre as a zone that promotes dream and fantasy, linking an adolescent girl's desire with her eventual choice of profession.

The visual juxtaposition of women of different ages and class backgrounds, frequent in Mészáros's films, is here brought into especially sharp focus within the framework of familial and political interrelationships. A former member of the anti-fascist Comintern movement, Magda has meanwhile become a high-ranking member of the new Stalinist Hungarian Communist Party, whereas the older couple accompanying Juli have remained embattled yet faithful devotees of socialism, but critical of Hungarian Stalinism. Magda's stern appearance – severe coiffure, tall leather boots and tailored uniform – contrasts sharply with Juli's sensual, rapturous recollections of her biological mother, and is drawn from the director's own foster mother, a rigidly punitive woman for whom her feelings were equally ambivalent. These contrasting images evoke an inner-world split between longing, idealised images of the 'good' (dead) mother and starker views of the 'bad' persecutory one, as if to embody Juli's guilt for having survived her mother's death and her resistance to Magda's seductive offer of a new life in the powerful party élite.

Magda's efforts to behave maternally toward Juli arouse in her a vehement resistance that takes several forms: repeated flashbacks to childhood memories, fantasies and reveries of her parents; a surreptitious and obsessive love for the cinema (in the interest of which Juli steals Magda's official movie passes, viewing as many as three films a day instead of going to the school for children of the party élite, to which she has undesired access through Magda's influence); and a proclivity for friends of whom Magda disapproves, in particular her new boyfriend Tomi. Only with Tomi is Juli gradually able to speak of the past. As Tomi's mother sleeps in the adjoining room of their crowded communal flat, Juli and Tomi steal a few moments of precious privacy, and in that intimate atmosphere Juli describes her parents in loving detail. Both were artists, like Mészáros' own parents – her mother a talented painter, her father a brilliant sculptor; both are visualised as ideally attractive and passionate. Like László Mészáros, Juli's father is arrested by the political police and presumably executed during Stalin's reign of terror. At the same time, Juli grows deeply attached to János, a chief engineer and Communist resistance member whose resemblance to her own lost father is consistently underscored by the fact that both roles are acted by Mészáros's companion and frequent leading man, Jan Nowicki.

Under the pressure of her increasing estrangement from Magda, Juli fails at school; János also finds himself in violent confrontations with Magda on account of her intensified detachment from the values he represents. Magda's acceptance of a new appointment as a prison warden symbolises a dangerous betrayal of her friends and the causes for which they have fought. Juli's efforts to find her father's brothers, ostensibly still living in the countryside, are undermined by Magda, whose henchmen forcibly return the girl to her self-appointed guardian. With the beginning of the Stalinist purges of 1949, another wave of disappearances sweeps the country, and János is arrested at his home in the presence of Juli and his wheelchair-bound son András, to whom Juli has meanwhile grown attached through her love for János. Her tolerance of the privileged life of a party cadre no longer manageable, Juli informs Magda that she is leaving to work, like János, in an industrial plant. When, at the end of the film, she and András visit János in prison, they are separated from him by the omnipresent surveillance, their conversations reduced to brief, highly-charged everyday phrases, their expressions marked by the sadness and suppressed anger of a long-enforced estrangement. Mészáros' use of the musical motif that continues long beyond the final credits is linked to Juli's prolonged periods of waiting, underscoring the agony of her uncertainty and capturing, perhaps even more palpably than the images, the suffering of those who risked opposing Stalinist power and paid with their lives.

As Magda's position weakens with the new regime, she eventually resigns from the Security Forces. Determined to uncover the truth of her father's fate, in a scene that conveys the damage wrought on honest human communication by decades of official prevarication and disinformation, Juli learns from an unctuous bureaucrat that, having been unjustly sentenced, her father has subsequently been 'rehabilitated'. The camera discloses her figure dwarfed by the building's massive Stalin-era architecture, emphasising the powerlessness of those seeking such information from party members whose concern lies elsewhere.

The falsification and distortion of language that came to typify life under Stalin in the Soviet Union and Eastern Europe of the 1950s (the target of much black humour among ordinary people, intellectuals and artists alike) is embodied by the exaggerated courtesy and feigned sincerity of apparatchiks: when Juli, like Mészáros herself, tries to discover her father's whereabouts, she is led through vast corridors and into the rooms whose faded elegance has not yet been wholly destroyed by the kitsch Communist-era décor of their new owners. The disparity between Juli's genuine sorrow and the fake politeness of the officials is made more grotesque still by their subsequent revelation that her father is in fact dead. The film's narrative displacement to the 1950s does little to disguise the director's critique of the Kádár regime that remained in power when the film was made, and it is meant to convey opposition to the film's temporal present as well as the past, as was often the case in works by East European artists denied the right to overt denunciation or even indirect critique of the political world in which they lived. Less accustomed to deciphering such codes, the Western viewer must take care not to misread these highly-coded inferences that permeated film production in the Stalin and post-Stalin eras, but whose meanings were instantly recognisable to a native audience. Indeed, the consequences of a missing generation of fathers continue to be explored by contemporary filmmakers. Mészáros' male characters often seem to thematise the false paternalism of Stalin and his associates whose propaganda was specifically directed toward the vulnerabilities of those who sought the security of surrogate paternal strength in the Party's ideology. Mészáros reinforces the alliance between lovers and fathers by casting the same actor, Jan Nowicki in both kinds of roles throughout the *Diary* trilogy.

Juli's exhausting struggle against this massive official obfuscation is conveyed by the determined posture and expressionless face of public compliance typical of East European cinema. As she leaves the office building with its monumental spatial proportions, she sees herself in flashback as a vivacious, freckle-faced child eating fruit in her father's studio, rapturously watching him at work as a sculptor. In the following scene, she is an adult observing him from outside his studio window, and, in the next, embraces him tenderly. Mészáros's use of this kind of temporal condensation recalls the language of dreams and fantasy, the timelessness of unconscious stimuli in the present fusing with long-buried psychic material that the cinematic apparatus achieves so seamlessly. In so doing, she provides a strategy for the visualisation of emotions for which no words seem adequate. Living in Magda's elegant apartment, Juli attends the school reserved for privileged children where students arrive in chauffeur-driven limousines, resort to elaborate cheating in class, entertain their friends extravagantly with imported wines and food, and dramatise Communist youth rituals in the hallways under a triptych that alternately reflects the faces of Stalin, Lenin or the 'Hungarian Stalin', Mátyás Rákosi, depending upon the viewer's position. Heroic party anthems ring out over the loudspeaker, while at home the *nomenklatura* dine on fine china and a Russian samovar is displayed on the table as Magda proudly demonstrates the lighting of a crystal chandelier, once the property of counts and bankers. But Juli struggles to preserve the familial identity she is urged to forget, clinging to her own feelings and the memories that enable her to resist attempts to suppress her personal history.

In contrast, Magda, having withstood the rigours of prison and torture in the radical communist underground, stands for historical revisionism: 'We've won', she says, 'but our enemies are everywhere … they smile and nod but they're awaiting their chance. But we're not giving an inch.' Juli asks Dezsö, a former fighter in the working-class movement and hero of the proletarian revolution of 1919, to clarify what happened to him and to Magda in 1949. Defeated and enraged by years of duplicity, he strikes Juli, ostensibly in punishment for her repeated truancy but more obviously for her dogged insistence on learning the truth of a past so insistently distorted by what some writers have called 'organised forgetting'. Magda intervenes, only to be accused in turn of committing torture as a member of the secret police. Dezsö confesses to having been beaten as a child by his father, and in this way Mészáros reveals enough of the history of these protagonists of her parents' generation to indicate – for the benefit of younger viewers uninformed of these events, her 'children' – the complex psychological bonds of power between victim and victimiser, the subtle mélange of pleasure and fear that characterises their protective stance toward the very actions of which they are also ashamed. This familiar litany of evasion, guilt and complicity in deception is, she suggests, shared by others of their generation, as Magda demonstrates: 'The Red Army arrived in Hungary not as a conqueror, but as the friend of the Hungarian people, their liberator from the yoke of German fascists … The Soviet commanders brought order and organisation to the villages and towns…'

Emerging concurrently with this narrative are flashbacks of Juli's childhood memories and dreams that increase in duration and frequency as the film progresses. At times the screen grows eerily bright as a haunting melody, the signature of Juli's past, replaces diegetic sound, suggesting the fallibility of memory and the helplessness of the five-year-old witness to a father's brutal arrest. These sequences are arranged to suggest that the process of grief and mourning is linked to Juli's fondness for movies and her stubborn refusal to surrender to authoritarian demands. The comforting anonymity of her role as spectator allows Juli to escape from the present through her indulgence in screenings of the Greta Garbo films and exotic newsreels that appear so far removed from the dreary oppressiveness of the present. Mészáros solicits the viewer's participation in the self-constructing dynamic of cinematic autobiography:

her own memory, articulated through Juli, conflates with the socio-political circumstances of national history as when Juli confides to János: 'I don't want to forget my mother and father, and that's what Magda wants. She acts as if they never existed. And I can't forget them.' Janos agrees: 'You're right, you shouldn't forget them … I think of my family, too – they were killed in an air raid in a bomb shelter near the factory where I worked during the war…'

Addressed primarily to the post-1950s generation, these intergenerational and retrospective narratives are intended to educate by countering the silencing indifference of Hungarian youth toward officially-sanctioned versions of their own political culture in the late-socialist period. The illusion of unequivocal ideological commitment is purchased, the director suggests, by zealots such as Magda at the expense of a double repression: denial of the complexity of the past, and pretence of knowledge of history, symbolised in a conversation among party cadres in Magda's apartment as Ilonka speaks of her experience in the Soviet Union when political exiles were forced to work in factories: 'I talked with the women weavers there: they clean the house, cook, raise their children after nine-hour shifts, but they accept it … they have an unbelievable self-awareness.' István responds, 'But it's only unbelievable if you don't know they have faith in the Party and are forming it … The workers understand the tense international situation. They support the party unconditionally. Comrade Rákosi, too, of course…'

Coercive political solidarity, Mészáros suggests, is in conflict with individual subjectivity: propagandistic documentary footage of celebrations of Stalin's seventieth birthday, when Stakhanovites extol their production quotas far in excess of required output, is inserted as ironic commentary, as are the ubiquitous busts of Lenin, statues of Stalin and the red star atop official Communist Party buildings. Still in pursuit of information about her father and uncles (whom she has reason to believe are in the countryside), Juli completes another futile application, a bust of Lenin perched on Magda's desk continuously visible in the frame. This narrative turning point foregrounds Juli's steadfastness in the face of official amnesia.

The tension culminates in a scene that casts into bold relief Magda's desperate suppression of the facts and Juli's opposition to the charade of denial which implicates her – and the spectator – in the fate of her nation. The factory machines are temporarily stilled as a backdrop for a lunchtime encounter between Juli and János as he reminisces about the young Magda, a 'lovely girl, just as we imagined the word "woman": full of life and all brains … how we believed in the future then!' As he reminisces about the idealism of young militants in the flowering of the early movement, János recounts the story of his arrest and imprisonment together with Magda in 1929, their escape in 1932, and his departure for Paris and hers to Moscow – two divergent paths that led both back to Budapest. Their conversation recalls an elegant dinner at Magda's apartment when István tells János, in a critique of Western bourgeois tendencies, 'You aren't aware that ideological commitment is the most effective force', to which János counters: 'An émigré life in the West was no bed of roses, either...' In the totalising ideology of Stalinism, Mészáros argues, those who deviate are dispensable.

Diary for My Children was shelved after production for over a year and released only following the excision of two scenes deemed unacceptable by Hungarian censors. The first was a sequence from Mikhail Chiaureli's Soviet epic, *Padenie Berlina* (*The Fall of Berlin*, 1949, scored by Dmitri Shostakovich), a massive fresco produced at the height of the 'cult of personality' in which Stalin, dressed in pristine white uniform, his arms filled with red roses, descends from a white airplane to the outstretched hands of peasant maidens. In his condemnation of Stalin at the 1956 Party Congress, Nikita Khruschev exhorted: 'Let us recall the film *The Fall of Berlin*; in it, only Stalin acts, issuing orders from a hall in which there are many empty chairs ... Stalin acts for everyone.' The second excision was a sequence portraying the funeral of László Rajk, the Communist politician and Minister of Foreign Affairs who was hanged after a show trial in 1949. According to Mészáros, this was taken to be an indirect reference to the secrecy surrounding the burial of Imre Nagy, martyred leader of the Hungarian uprising of 1956. She wished to bring to light the period between 1948 and 1956 – the Rákosi era – that 'has been erased from Hungarian history: my protagonist carries a deep wound, as I do – her missing parents. These people became communists in an age in which it was a common, basic philosophy: they truly believed in it and remained faithful to it and to themselves, even when it became unfashionable. That is why they were always in conflict with the state apparatus.'

As currents of nationalism, nostalgia and triumphalism circulate through post-communist societies, *Diary for My Children* offers contemporary viewers an ethically and politically sensitive re-reading of the socialist period informed by the specificities of Central European history.

Catherine Portuges

REFERENCE

Horton, Andrew James (2002 [1999]) 'Ordinary Lives in Extraordinary Times: Márta Mészáros Interviewed', *Senses of Cinema* (September). Available at http://www.sesnesofcinema.com/contents/02/22meszaros

REDL EZREDES COLONEL REDL

ISTVÁN SZABÓ, HUNGARY/WEST GERMANY/AUSTRIA, 1984

Critics have chosen to regard István Szabó's *Mephisto* (1981), *Redl ezredes* (*Colonel Redl*, 1984) and *Hanussen* (1988) as an integrated trilogy. Each is an impressionistic and speculative biography of a historical figure whose personal ambitions and dilemmas reflect and illuminate aspects of twentieth-century European history. *Mephisto* is based on Klaus Mann's novel, in turn based on the career of the celebrated actor Gustav Gründgens and his accommodations with the Nazi regime. *Hanussen* tells the story of Erik Jan Hanussen (born Karl Schroeder), a First World War soldier who became a hypnotist and seer, embraced by the Nazis until he indiscreetly predicted the Reichstag fire. Each of the protagonists is played by the same actor, Klaus Maria Brandauer (born 1944), an Austrian stage actor of dominating charisma, who first achieved international fame with *Mephisto*.

Szabó, however, denies absolutely any intentional link between the films: 'I never thought for a moment of a trilogy. I don't think about one film when I make another. I just make it for the audience and I don't expect them to take into consideration any other films … The greatest part of the audience will be unaware of the previous film.' After *Mephisto*, Klaus Maria Brandauer suggested that they do another film together and Szabó searched for a story that would suit Brandauer's cultural background, thinking immediately of the period of the Austro-Hungarian Empire: 'I found the story of Colonel Redl. This story of the Empire and the military establishment, of manipulation and betrayal seemed very good for Klaus. I read the Osborne play, *A Patriot For Me*, and somebody showed me a screenplay which I didn't like because it was centred on the sexual aspect. To me the story was much more about political manipulation than sexuality – though that played its part, of course.' He wrote the screenplay, gave it to Brandauer, and then to Peter Dobai, 'who polished it and added energy to the dialogue'. Manfred Durniok, who had produced *Mephisto*, helped set up the film, which was a Hungarian-West German-Austrian co-production.

The greater part of the film was shot on location in Hungary, with additional locations in Prague and about 20 per cent filmed in Vienna. 'The story, of course, is essentially Viennese; but there are enormous similarities between Vienna and Budapest and Prague. In the golden period they were very near to each other in style and architecture.' From the disparate settings, Szabó's regular cinematographer Lajos Koltai creates a coherent and richly evocative visual texture for the story. Liszt, Schumann, the Strausses and 'The Honeysuckle and the Bee' provide an aural complement.

Colonel Alfred Redl (1864–1913) is a famous and controversial figure in Austrian history. Born into a poor family in Lemberg, Galicia (between the wars Lwów in Poland and now L'viv in Ukraine), his intelligence, talents and energy won him a commission in the Austrian army, and the protective favour of General von Giesl. In 1900 he was appointed chief of the counter-intelligence corps, and went on to create a modern intelligence service, pioneering the use of hidden cameras and interrogation rooms bugged with gramophones. He set up an intelligence-sharing agreement with Germany and gathered fingerprints that brought about the apprehension of a network of Russian spies.

According to the official accounts of the affair, Redl became victim of his own weaknesses and vanities. He loved Daimler cars, fine clothes, parties, luxury apartments and the affection of young men, particularly a certain handsome lieutenant, on whom he lavished extravagant gifts. The Russian security services used his homosexuality to blackmail him into becoming a counter-spy within his own intelligence organisation, and from 1902 until 1913 he continued in this role, supplying Russia with a wealth of strategic information. At the same time he was maintaining his reputation for brilliant counter-intelligence by falsifying evidence against fellow officers and, for the sake of plausibility, exposing dispensable Russian agents.

Redl was finally exposed when von Giesl moved to Prague as commander of the Eighth Army Corps, taking Redl with him as chief of staff. Redl was succeeded as intelligence chief by Maximilian Ronge, whose postal censors intercepted two packets of money traced back to the French and Russian intelligence services, and eventually claimed from the post office by Redl. Confronted by his fellow-officers, Redl asked for a loaded revolver and retired to a hotel room, where he shot himself. The case definitively established the long-enduring principle that homosexuals are unsuitable to intelligence work as presenting special security risks.

This has remained the official story of the shame of Colonel Redl, and had already provided the subject for two earlier films, Karel Anton's Czech film *Aféra plukovnika Redla* (*The Affair of Colonel Redl*, 1931; German version: *Der Fall des Generalstabs-Oberst Redl*), adapted from E. E. Kisch's articles and the play by E. A. Longen, and Franz Antel's *Spionage* (1955). In 1964, John Osborne's play *A Patriot For Me* recounted the story with an emphasis on social and sexual pressures as the cause of Redl's fate. At the time the play, with its frank discussion of sexuality and its depiction of transvestism, was not permitted public performance in Britain.

Szabó, however, brought to the Redl affair the scepticism of someone who had grown up under Stalinist socialism and the show trials of the Cold War era. The Redl affair had first been made public by the Prague-born Jewish journalist Egon Erwin Kisch (1885–1948), and the way that Kisch had come by his scoop put Szabó uneasily in mind of later techniques of leaking incriminating evidence:

It was very peculiar. Kisch was watching a football game in a stadium in Vienna, and next to him was an Austrian officer. He paid no attention to the officer, because he was interested in the football. When the game ended, the officer had disappeared, but beside Kisch was a sealed package. He assumed someone had dropped it, and opened it up to try to trace the owner – only to find all the documents about Colonel Redl. Why would these documents land up at a football stadium? And why next to Egon Erwin Kisch, already an important news reporter? Who had had the idea of leaking this information to Kisch, knowing that he would be sure to publish it? In such a case one begins to ask, were the documents authentic, or was it a prefabricated affair with manipulated documents?

The story instantly reminded me of the machinery used for the show trials organ-ised by the Stalinist regimes in the USSR, Hungary and Czechoslovakia – the trial of László Rajk in 1949, for example. And then Redl's suicide recalls the 'confessions' and self-incrimination and apparent self-destruction that was part of those trials. The only version we have of his death is that issued by the Austrian War Office ... But did Redl commit suicide? They say he did, of course, but perhaps his last words before shooting himself were, 'Don't shoot!' It was always very significant to me also that Redl was essen-tially an outsider, coming from one of the many minorities within the Austro-Hungarian empire. The existence of so many minorities caused a lot of confusion in the Austrian army before the First World War. The generals needed to keep the army together; and maybe a scapegoat helped. And if a scapegoat was needed, it was obviously important to find him from a minority.

The film was made when Hungary was still under Socialist rule, but Szabó encountered no official problems with the script: 'By the 1980s we could do pretty well what we wanted to. But in any case, nobody cared about a historical film about the old Austro-Hungarian Empire. Even twenty years before, Jancsó had succeeded in describing the system in *Szegénylegények* [*The Round-Up*, 1965], which had a big success both in Hungary and abroad. He was able to do it because it appeared to be a period film. It was a kind of flower language. *Colonel Redl*, too, is much more about our problems under Socialism – the machinery employed by a feudal society to dominate a people – than *Mephisto* was'.

To avoid any subsequent difficulties, the film's German producer, Manfred Durniok, bought the rights of *A Patriot For Me*, but there are no obvious influences from the Osborne play. An opening title clearly declares Szabó's revisionist intent, something much broader and more probing than a simple historical reconstruction:

> We do not tell Colonel Redl's story from authentic documents. The actions of the characters are freely devised. Our work is inspired by John Osborne's play *A Patriot For Me* … and by the historical events of our century.

Szabó's approach is epic, covering the whole of Alfred Redl's life, from his childhood as a poor railwayman's son, fanatically inspired by loyalty to the Austrian Hungarian Empire. Accepted into the royal military academy he is befriended by a patrician fellow-cadet, the Hungarian Christoph von Kubinyi, and is awed to be accepted as a visitor to his family home. Redl later fails to prevent Kubinyi killing a fellow officer – a Czech Jew – in a duel, his efforts being compromised by his own concern to deny his own possible Jewish heritage. The fatherly commanding officer, Von Roden, recognising Redl's merit, allows him to take Kubinyi with him to Vienna. Despite his obvious love for Kubinyi, Redl allows himself to be seduced by Kubinyi's married sister Katalin. His own subsequent marriage is a matter of convenience, to counter growing smears of his homosexual inclination. Redl demonstrates his zeal and loyalty in combating the indifference and indiscipline of a border outpost in Galicia and Kubinyi is sent to the War Minstry in Vienna where he rises to the General Staff.

With the Empire disintegrating and war inevitable, Redl is taken up by the scheming heir to the throne, Archduke Franz Ferdinand, and is appointed head of military intelligence. In Vienna he is instructed by the Archduke to uncover – or invent – a plot amongst his fellow officers. The ensuing prosecution and scandal will be engineered to stiffen the loyalty of the officer corps. Redl exposes Baron Ullman as a spy for the Russians. Ullman commits suicide, but Redl discovers that Kubinyi is implicated in the plot, which had involved passing the plans of the Przemyśl fortress to St Petersburg. The Archduke, however, refuses to hear anything against a member of the general staff, dismissing Przemyśl as being of no strategic significance, and Redl realises that he is now himself destined to be the required scapegoat. Prompted by her brother, Katalin introduces Redl to the handsome young spy Alfredo Velocchio. Redl succumbs to the young man, and reveals the secrets of the Empire's Eastern defences. He is arrested and held in a hotel room, where he is shunned by his old friends and comrades. The Archduke instructs Kubinyi to hand him the revolver with which he will commit suicide, and promotes Kubinyi so that he shall not do this as Redl's inferior in rank (and cannot refuse the order). Later, at Sarajevo, Franz Ferdinand is assassinated; and the film ends with documentary images of the First World War.

In a 1985 interview Szabó said that for him Redl was not a con-man:

He really and truly wants to become another person … It's a basic, universal problem: without security you can't live. Different people find it in different ways: in love, in family, in work, in power. Sometimes, however, in war, at important historical moments, you can see the fight to achieve security more accurately. In *Bizalom* [*Confidence,* 1979], for example, the people who have to go underground against the Nazis find it defensively. Mephisto on the other hand goes on the offensive – he thinks that by having everybody's love he will achieve security. Redl tries to find it by seeking to become a member of the ruling élite.

My earlier films were about several characters, but this did not give me the opportunity to go deeply into one character. The psychological analysis remained on the surface. In *Mephisto* and *Colonel Redl*, I was really interested in finding out a lot about one person. I tried to use a literary method, the so-called development narrative. I wrote the script for Brandauer. It was a kind of Christmas present.

The extraordinary complexity of the Redl characterisation is throughout based on contradiction and doubt. Not only is the audience denied any easy understanding of his character but his own sense of self identity seems both constructed and ambiguous. The suspicion is that he is homosexual and a Ruthenian Jew, but while the overt practice of his homosexuality is delayed until the film's ending and leads directly to his downfall, his Jewish identity is denied even then. Redl's characteristic response to both charges is silence.

While Szabó confirmed his desire not to emphasise the film's sexual theme, it is made more explicit than other aspects of Redl's character. His lifelong friendship with Kubinyi remains key (although it also reflects the relationship between a social and ethnic inferior and a member of the ruling elite). But while the relationship remains close, Kubinyi's overt heterosexuality means that it can never progress further. When Redl sleeps with Katalin, who confesses her love for him, he reveals that he had been thinking about her brother.

Before his seduction by Lt Vellochio, Redl's previous relationships have been with women – a prostitute, with Katalin and his wife Clarissa. The episode with the prostitute first suggests his problems with women and is matched by the surprise kissing of Redl by a fellow officer. He marries at Katalin's suggestion, in order to counter rumours of his homosexuality, but by then seems to have accepted the inadequacy or impossibility of heterosexual relations. Interestingly, it is Katalin who seems to be the one person in whom he can confide.

Sexuality is presented as a kind of continuum in which all the overtures are made to Redl. When he visits Kubinyi's family as a cadet, the older Kubinyi places his hand over Redl's and the gesture is later repeated by Von Roden. During the same visit to the Kubinyis, Katalin places her hand on his leg (in adult life, she reminisces to him about an affair with a 'stable boy'), and the movement is repeated by his male piano teacher. His musical abilities are later equated with his supposed homosexuality and his infatuation with Vellochio is symbolised by their 'duet' on the piano. But the development of this explicit relationship with Vellochio is the result of a betrayal organised by others. If homosexuality is not approved (Redl's earlier commanding officer asks him if the dissident Czech, Lt Schorm is an 'invert' and Von Roden later addresses the same question to him), the sexual approaches made to him suggest that his case is not exceptional. Indeed, the story of the real Colonel Redl confirms this.

The question of ethnicity is rendered with much greater ambiguity. When asked by the Kubinyis if he is Polish, he replies that he is Ruthenian but is careful to point out that his father is part-German and his mother, as far as he knows, part-Hungarian. When Franz Ferdinand asks if he is of Hungarian descent, he again replies that he is Ruthenian. It is a Ruthenian scapegoat for whom he is required to search – a scapegoat that he ultimately accepts will be himself.

Here, it is worth considering the significance of his birthplace, Galicia, now part of Ukraine. As border country, it lay at the centre of historical disputes between Poland, Russia, Austria and Hungary and Lemberg, birthplace of the real Colonel Redl, was at the time a centre of Ukrainian nationalism. When Redl's commanding officer welcomes him and his fellow officers to Galicia, they are reminded that it is an area where 'you will find Poles, Jews, gypsies, thieves and whores'. It is rumoured later in the film that Kraków and Galicia may 'choose Poland' and that the Ruthenians 'prefer the Tsar'.

Previously part of Poland, Galicia was attached to Austria after the partition of Poland in 1772, with the Republic of Kraków added in 1846. Kraków, Eastern Galicia and Lemberg (as Lwów) became part of Poland after the First World War. After the Second World War, Lwów (now L'viv) and Eastern Galicia were attached to Ukraine while Kraków and Western Galicia remained part of Poland. Sub-Carpathian Rus (Ruthenia), which formed part of Hungary before the First World War, became part of Czechoslovakia between the wars, was re-annexed by Hungary in 1939, and became part of Ukraine after the Second World War. Redl, however, is a Ruthenian from Galicia, one of the most economically backward areas of the Empire. Ruthenian was also the term used to refer to Galicia's Ukrainians and was used as a synonym for peasant. For the Jewish community of Galicia, the period of Austrian rule was relatively progressive and many Jews were able to enter state employment. The Austro-Hungarian army also had more Jewish officers than any other in Europe. Redl's origin in a region of shifting allegiances and identities was clearly a significant factor in the development of the film's theme.

In the search for a scapegoat, Franz Ferdinand rules out Austrians and Hungarians as the dominant nations of the Empire and, for political reasons, Czechs, Serbs and Croats. A Jew cannot be selected because of the Empire's reliance on the Rothschilds and possible international reaction. But a Ruthenian, a nationality without power or aristocracy, suspected of sympathy with the Russians – that is another matter.

Redl is almost certainly Jewish, although he never admits this. The clearest evidence lies in scenes during his posting to Galicia. Here he visits a Jewish shop where the owner asks him if he is Jewish on his mother's side. A Jewish man invites him to supper but he recoils in a horror verging on hysteria when he is simultaneously approached by a gypsy woman. He also has an extreme reaction to a visit from his sister which, although not explicitly signalled as racial, provokes a similar fear of contamination. In a lecture to his fellow officers, Redl demands that they avoid contact with the local Jewish community, reminds them that they are officers in the army, and that their identities as 'Slovaks, Ruthenians, Jews' must be suppressed. At the end of the film, Redl tells the Jewish Dr Sonnenschein that the Empire will need other scapegoats and that the Jews may be next.

Like the themes of sexuality and ethnicity, the Jewish theme is reflected in the lives of other characters. Von Roden notes that every other Jewish factory owner is a Baron and counted among His Majesty's most loyal subjects. The part-Jewish Lt Schorm refuses a duel with Sonnenschein because he is Jewish. When Redl is questioned about Schorm's subversive articles about the officer corps in a Prague newspaper, the commanding officer asks if he is homosexual, a Jew and a Czech. This mirrors the questions around Redl himself – a homosexual, a Jew and a Ruthenian. Three undesirables linked. And, if he is not a Jew, Franz Ferdinand agrees that he has a 'Slavic' face.

But, if the film queries Redl's identity from the outside, he also engages in his own self-analysis. When, as a cadet, he finds himself manipulated into informing on his colleagues after being addressed as 'a bright peasant lad', he reflects on himself as 'a peasant traitor' and a Judas. Later, when he examines secret reports on himself describing him as an admirer of power and a poseur, he adds the quality of 'insincerity' in his own hand. But the film also shows Redl to be talented and as a man of physical courage.

Redl's desire to identify with the Empire reflects Szabó's perennial theme of the search for security. The child's poem in praise of the Emperor at the beginning and end of the film provides its own comment, as does Redl's excitement when he first glimpses the Emperor Franz Josef in Vienna. As a member of a minority – 'peasant', homosexual, maybe Jewish – it is in this greater cause that security may be found. It is worth noting that the nineteenth-century ethno-linguistic concept of the nation saw its final European realisation in the disintegration of the Habsburg Empire. Redl holds rather to the traditional political-territorial concept with loyalty directed towards the ruler. In a conversation with Katalin, he argues that the concept of the Monarchy is good despite its faults and preferable to the alternatives.

Throughout the film, the disintegration of the Empire and of the officer corps is foregrounded. Corruption within the corps is recognised by Redl, who tries to eliminate it, but also by Schorm (who dies because of his revelations), Kubinyi and, ultimately, Franz Ferdinand. In Galicia, Kubinyi defends the attitudes of the other officers and describes them as 'waiting for the end'. Redl constantly emphasises loyalty to the Empire and the need to suppress ethnic identities in the greater cause.

The film was condemned by the English historian, Ian D. Armour, as a pointless fiction that built a fantasy around a framework of real events and it also led to political controversy in Austria. Others have pointed to historical errors in the portrayal of the officer corps and the fact that Szabó suggests too easy a parallel between feudalism and totalitarianism. While rumours circulated around the real Redl's Galician background, and he was rumoured to be Jewish, he was in fact German-Austrian. He was, however, a practicing homosexual and had systematically betrayed military secrets. But Szabó's Redl is a victim – a defender of the monarchy who becomes its scapegoat. His explicit practice of homosexuality is the result of a trap laid by his friend, Kubinyi, and his betrayal of secrets – a list of statistics – only occurs after he has accepted this reality. It is true that the film uses the name of Redl, which suggests that it aims at historical reconstruction. On the other hand, Szabó is very clear about its story being 'freely devised' and its deliberate parallels with the Stalinist era. Historical figures are normally treated with dramatic licence and, even if the name of the central figure had been changed, the same implications would have been drawn.

The film's parallels with Stalinism lie in the theme of the political scapegoat and a lack of concern with the truth of Redl's case. This is made most apparent when he is offered lenient treatment if he confesses and co-operates with the proposed trial (such lenient treatment was almost never forthcoming in the political trials of the 1950s). Various scenarios are offered when he refuses to collaborate, including a closed trial, a verdict issued after execution and suicide followed by a press leak (which is, of course, what happened in reality). The whole accusation and its discovery is presented as a set-up like its 1950s equivalents when committed communists were eliminated and there was a strong emphasis on 'Jewish origin'.

The film touches on issues of historical and individual identity in a profound manner. If the narrative is resolved, the portrait of Redl maintains its shifting focus. One is left with a series of questions about Redl – about sexuality, race, power and identity but the shifting emphases reflect those of the Empire itself. Perhaps, it suggests, all identities are thus. As Schorm observes earlier in the film, 'Everybody here's playing a part'. From these perspectives, it is arguably one of the best films made about the last years of the Habsburg Empire, constantly raising issues that link it to the Second World War, Stalinism, anti-Semitism, and the relationship between the personal and the political.

Szabó has argued that he has no interest in the development of a personal style – although others would disagree. His objective is rather 'to tell of experiences … to help people think about their problems'. However, one cannot but note the importance of close-ups in films such as *Confidence*, *Mephisto* and *Colonel Redl*. If *Mephisto* ends with Brandauer wearing the mask of the actor, *Colonel Redl* begins with the mask of the man, a face barely moving, like a portrait. While the emphasis on the close-up reflects Szabó's notion of the cinema's distinctive quality – 'the living human face with emotions and ideas' – the close-ups in *Colonel Redl*, which are often close to head on, constantly pose the question of identity.

Szabó also delights in recreating the elegant surfaces of Imperial grandeur, the balls and palaces and prancing horses that mask the putrefaction of deception, deceit and decay. The use of the *Radetzky March* for the credits and the omnipresence of Johann Strauss waltzes are used to telling effect. Three key sequences set at balls present the official face of the monarchy, the differing status of Redl, the masks of the participants (literally, in the case of the masked ball), but they also reflect the process of disintegration. The film is rich in marvellous set-pieces – the child Alfred's panic of embarrassment when he cannot turn off the tap of the Kubinyi tea-urn; the dawn duel; Redl's bewitchment at his sight of the Emperor; the meeting in the snow with the beautiful Vellochio and the subsequent symbolic played out on the keyboards of a piano; Redl's desperate, retching panic at the moment of suicide.

The part of Redl is ideally suited to Brandauer's ability to show both arrogance and abject insecurity at the same moment. His Redl is a supremely self-conscious man, at once knowingly guiding his own destiny and at the same time blinding himself to his coming fall. There are some notable supporting performances. Armin Müller-Stahl makes Franz Ferdinand an unimposing, watery-eyed, unshaven creature, grinning and whistling as he weaves his complex plots. Redl's paternal commanding officer is the German actor Hans-Christian Blech (1925–93). An actor better known for his work in television, Jan Niklas, makes a dangerously charming Christoph von Kubinyi, and Gudrun Landgrebe is Katalin Kubinyi. There is a private joke, in the appearance of a number of Szabó's peer filmmakers – including Gyula Gazdag, Pál Sandor, Pál Zolnay and the film's co-writer Péter Dobai – as members of the Austrian General Staff. András Bálint, the lead actor in Szabó's earliest films, plays Dr Sonnenschein, looking forward to Szabó's subsequent confrontation with history in *Sonnenschein* (*Sunshine*, 1999).

Istvan Szabó may rightly deny an overall plan to his choice of subjects, but he has described his subject as Central Europe, and the Central European experience as 'the struggle of the individual amid the storms of history'. He is an artist with a phenomenally acute feeling for history and its effect upon individual lives. The body of his best work – *Apa* (*Father*, 1966), *Szerelmes film* (*Love Film*, 1970), *Tuzoltó utca 25* (*25 Firemen's Street*, 1973), *Confidence* (1979), *Mephisto* (1981), *Colonel Redl* (1984), *Hanussen* (1988), *Sunshine* (1999) and *Taking Sides* (2001) – stands as an incomparable portrait of the life and mind of Central Europe in the first half of the twentieth century.

David Robinson and Peter Hames

REFERENCES

Palmer, Jerry (1985) 'Don't shoot! *Colonel Redl* and the search for security', *Sight and Sound*, 54, 3, 158.

Robinson, David (2003) Interview with István Szabó (unpublished).

NĚCO Z ALENKY ALICE

JAN ŠVANKMAJER, SWITZERLAND/FRANCE/UK/ CZECHOSLOVAKIA, 1987

By fluidly shifting from one diverse discourse to another, showing the interrelation of art, philosophy, science, spirituality and so forth, Novalis (1772–1801) reconciled seemingly disparate ways of appropriating the world. He recorded his observations and his reflections on the true nature of things, including fairy tales and magic. Novalis suggests that fairy tales resemble dreams as their creators animate them with mystery and the marvellous, and that all of nature contains higher and unseen forces. With the topsy-turvy worlds depicted in *Alice's Adventures in Wonderland* and *Through the Looking-Glass,* Lewis Carroll (Reverend Charles Lutwidge Dodgson) charmingly distils Novalis' conception of fairy tale logic. This transportation to other nonsensical realms not unlike our own has prompted many artists to filter Wonderland through their own sensibilities. Everyone from the likes of Walt Disney, who presented an almost verbatim translation of *Alice's Adventures in Wonderland,* to the Wachowski Brothers, who infused *The Matrix* with Wonderland allusions, have been drawn to Carroll's world and the dream realm that lies just on the other side of our mirrors. With *Něco z Alenky* (*Alice* aka *Something From Alice,* 1987), Jan Švankmajer maintains his uncompromising vision as he explores a world inspired by Carroll's tales whilst demonstrating the interconnectedness of dream with waking life.

Švankmajer's body of work defies the conformity, lyricism and sentimentality that characterise many of the films made after the rise of Stalinism in Czechoslovakia. Despite the brief reprieve from Stalinism, felt during the Prague Spring of the late 1960s, which encouraged the experimentation evident in the films of the Czech New Wave, many of these filmmakers subsequently emigrated to places with more tolerant governments or stifled their true voice to avoid the censor's wrath, once Stalinism was again firmly in place. For Švankmajer, freedom is the absolute pursuit of desire. His embrace of freedom and irrationality proved far more threatening than any overt and rational protest against Stalinism. Whereas animators in Poland and the former Soviet Union could smuggle political statements past Communist censors under the guise of fairy tale folklore, Švankmajer was criticised on every occasion as censors imaginatively interpreted each film as subversive. With its rebellion of objects, *Zvahlav aneb Šatičky Slaměného Huberta* (*Jabberwocky, or Straw Hubert's Clothes,* 1971) was banned along with most of his other titles. Švankmajer was banned entirely from filmmaking between 1973 and 1980 after he made *Leonardů denik* (*Leonardo's Diary*, 1972).

Since Švankmajer's films embody marginal traditions unique to the city of Prague, he best represents the quintessence of Czech culture in his obsession with alchemy, animation by hand, magic, natural history, puppetry and Surrealism. *Alice* serves as an exemplar of Bohemian film in that it presents all the historical and cultural undertones that pervaded, despite political repression, in a form that is, in its very essence, subversive. Coincidentally, Jan Švankmajer was born in 1934, the same year that the Czech Surrealist Group formed. The fourth and fifth generations of this group still thrive creatively, based on a solidarity no doubt inspired by the need to bond together to protect their work from oppressive regimes.

During the Velvet revolution of 1989, Švankmajer's Mannerist films invoked the permissive spirit of the rule of the Habsburg Emperor, Rudolf II. The court of Rudolf II embraced the search for, and collection of, all things exceptional. As eloquently suggested by Peter Hames, with Švankmajer 'living in a former alchemist's house and among other echoes of Rudolfine Prague, it is not surprising that [André] Breton's "magic city" should also assert itself'. Although Švankmajer is not a practising alchemist, he does read alchemical texts and approaches his art with a comparable attitude in attempting to find a universality of matter despite inherent, yet unsettlingly beautiful discontinuities. Many alchemists pursue the philosopher's stone yet it is their spiritual journey and inner transformation along with the external processes employed that prove just as important as the stone itself. More than the creation of elixirs or transmutation of base metals into gold, alchemy is the art of bringing the hidden attributes of objects to the surface. This process finds analogy in many poetic quests evident in Romanticism, Symbolism and Surrealism. Roger Cardinal indicates that 'the Romantic world-view envisions any given object as the threshold to the whole cosmos: the single modest thing represents a magical microcosm of the entirety of things, and as such sheds its anonymity and assumes a revelatory distinctiveness'. This view certainly existed as encapsulated by the *wunderkammern* of Rudolfine Prague. As the philosopher's stone serves as a microcosm of the world, the *wunderkammer* assumes an alchemical extension as it yields not only a sense of the world but also the connection of one object to another. The advent of *wunderkammern* marks the merge of society and science as well as featuring the fluid mix of fantasy with reality:

In containing both man-made and natural objects, the Habsburg collections of the second part of the sixteenth century, like other *Kunstkammern*, thus reflected the contents of the universe in all its variety … In containing samples of all that was to be found in the macrocosm, the greater world, the *Kunstkammer* can be thought to represent the world in microcosm.

Švankmajer is an avid collector of all kinds of objects that possess potentialities for his art. His cinematic power lies in arranging objects through a provocative juxtaposition that prods them to communicate their inner stories. The mundane can become magical through inspired groupings as Švankmajer reveals life in objects believed to be dead, inert or outmoded. Since children instil toys and other objects with life through imagination, childhood serves as a potent setting for Švankmajer's object resurrections, with Carroll's Wonderland as the most advantageous backdrop.

Švankmajer's first visual excursion into the pages of Carroll occurred in 1971 with *Jabberwocky, or Straw Hubert's Clothes*. Undoubtedly, he carried a Surrealist map to navigate Carroll's dream territory as Salvador Dalí and Max Ernst had before him. Ernst illustrated an edition of *La chasse au Snark* (*The Hunting of the Snark*, 1950) yet traces of a Carrollean heroine appear in Ernst's dazzling collage novel *Rêve d'une petite fille qui voulet entrer au Carmel* (*A Little Girl Dreams of Taking the Veil*, 1930) as Ernst follows a young girl through a Sadean dream journey. Likewise, Dalí created his own Chiricoesque Alice in *Alice au pays des Merveilles* (1969) with a rope-skipping figure appearing as a ghostly logo in each image; he suggested this form in an engraving for Paul Eluard as early as 1935. The Paris-based Surrealists considered Lewis Carroll to be one of their precursors based on his dialogue with dream and employment of black humour, a major component of Surrealism that Švankmajer often liberally applies in his work. André Breton includes Carroll in his *Anthologie de l'humour noir* (*Anthology of Black Humor*), in which he describes black humour as 'the mortal enemy of sentimentality'. Many of Breton's other entries read identically to Švankmajer's key 'conspirators' including Edgar Allan Poe, D.-A.-F. de Sade, Alfred Jarry, Comte de Lautréamont (Isidore Ducasse) and Villiers de l'Isle-Adam. In the 1941 issue of *View,* Max Ernst – the Surrealist with whom Švankmajer most closely aligns his creative principles – names Carroll, Poe, Jarry, Novalis and Lautréamont as his favourite poets of the past. Canto Six of Lautréamont's *Les Chants de Maldoror* (*The Songs of Maldoror*, 1869) contains the oft-quoted 'As beautiful as the chance meeting upon a dissecting-table of a sewing-machine and an umbrella!' This passage implies destruction to yield new hybrid entities and a strange beauty within this irreversible alteration. Alchemical transformation arises through destructive forces that produce hybrids as part of the process.

Švankmajer structures *Jabberwocky* with sequences of destruction as toys in the nursery change in shape or usurp other toys as the new favourite objects for play. In addition, *Jabberwocky* shows a child (represented visually by a boy's sailor suit) approaching the threshold of adulthood as his games grow in sophistication and his puzzle-solving attempts cease to be thwarted by a mischievous black cat. This process parallels the path of the occult neophyte that transforms through experimentation into the adept.

Animation is merely one of many means with which Jan Švankmajer expresses his creative impulses. Initially, he constructs a collage or a poem that may eventually turn into a film. Švankmajer applies this collage technique to his films as he combines the manipulation of puppets, dolls and objects with live action. Joining disparate pieces becomes viable through inventive layering as Max Ernst proves in his trilogy of collage novels. The practice of collage can act as a unifying agent for evocative fragments as well as creating psychic disruptions. As well-crafted collages yield new associations, rhythmic edits produce potential connections. Not only does Švankmajer visually assault us with his rapid-fire editing style but he also emphasises tactility through visual repetitions and close-ups. To serve as an intermediary between conscious and unconscious thought, Ernst created the birdman hybrid Loplop as his alter ego. In *Spiklenci slasti* (*Conspirators of Pleasure*, 1996), Švankmajer pays homage to Loplop, and tableaux featuring Loplop in Ernst's *Une Semaine de Bonté* – Švankmajer's lead character, Pivoňka, constructs a rooster's head that energises him with supernatural powers only when he wears it.

Švankmajer, however, allows childhood to pose as his alter ego, which makes his intersection with Carroll a charmed encounter. In both *Jabberwocky* and *Alice*, Švankmajer juxtaposes the exterior forest of reality and the fabricated interior populated by objects from the everyday world. The strength of Švankmajer's textural rendition of Wonderland lies in its mundane appearance as rooms that anyone of us could have been in at one time or another. Švankmajer engages in a dialogue with dream rather than losing himself in a fantasyland. In *Alice*, the space does not constitute the visible leap, it is the creatures, objects and activities within them that do. By constructing Wonderland from the recognisable materials of reality and dream, Švankmajer removes the psychedelic reading from Carroll that has been such an easy lapse for other artists. The mind-expanding elements in Švankmajer's take on Carroll involve a deep investigation into the nature of dream and the unconscious state rather than filtering the hallucinatory passages of Carroll through a hookah or mushroom-induced haze. Švankmajer verifies that 'indeed, my *Alice* is partly about the point where reality merges with dream – is Alice awake at the end or not?'

Alice begins near a stream where Alice and her older sister sit side by side. She throws stones into the stream as her sister reads. Once she has discarded all of her stones, Alice flicks through the pages of her sister's book, which earns her a reprimanding slap on the hand. As the opening credit sequence rolls, the titles are intercut with Alice's dialogue. Švankmajer films her mouth in extreme close-up (a distancing device that he employs for all of Alice's voiceover narration, to indicate which character voices particular lines, since Alice speaks the lines for every character). Alice announces, 'Alice thought to herself, now you will see a film for children, perhaps; perhaps, but I forgot, now you must close your eyes, otherwise, you won't see anything.' This line proves extremely telling in that it prepares the audience not only for the beginning of the film but for the dream that follows. Film and dream become analogous entities. This harks back to Poe's poetical line, 'All that we see or seem is but a dream within a dream.' Although Švankmajer's structure implies that Alice's dream commences directly after the credits, Švankmajer does not make clear demarcations in order to increase ambiguity. The end instruction of Alice's line telling us to close our eyes to see suggests that we should attempt to see in a way reaching back to Romanticism, with an interior sight that heightens our other senses. One is reminded of Caspar David Friedrich's injunction to 'close your physical eye that you might first see your picture with the eye of the mind'.

Max Ernst reinterpreted this approach as he looked for ways to irritate his visionary faculties, resulting in his automatic techniques including collage and decalcomania that lead to a tangible image of hallucinatory visions comparable to amorous desire and dreams. In recounting his creation of his version of the collage process, Ernst recounts that collage intensified his sight to allow him to transform figures in a convulsively beautiful manner by placing them in foreign surroundings. In an essay on 'Gestural Sculpture' from 1979, Švankmajer explains in a manner echoing the influence of alchemical writing, Ernst and Friedrich on his artistic vision that gesture must be perceived by touch as the artist's immediate emotion works directly on the viewer:

> If we are to believe what the old hermetical books tell us, strong emotions leave an indelible impression on objects touched, which are capable of passing on these emotions to sensitive perceivers and even allow them to visualise them … The tension which occurred at the birth of a gestural sculpture should be transferred, by touch … to the psyche of the perceiver; and there provoke visual associations. The whole process of perceiving should therefore take place before our *inner eye*, which is still the domain of our psyche and does not fall prey to aesthetic conventions.

Back at her nursery, Alice replays the day's activities with dolls. She casts pebbles into a filled teacup from the lap of a porcelain doll that resembles her down to the detail of her dress. This repetition sets the stage for later recurrences of activities as Alice's dream continues. Švankmajer's camera roams through this scene to take inventory of the objects from her nursery. These curious objects serve as the impetus for images in her dream. Familiar, banal objects acquire new significance whilst demonstrating the interconnection of dream with reality. This technique exists also in Neil Jordan's fantasy film *The Company of Wolves* (1984) based on Angela Carter's nightmarish reworking of such fairy tales as 'Little Red Riding Hood'. *The Company of Wolves* includes an older sister at the start, who taunts the heroine, Rosaleen. As Rosaleen sleeps restlessly, the toys and other objects (a mirror and so forth) from her room become integrated into the dream. The end of this film implies that Rosaleen's nightmare might not actually be over when she awakens as a howling wolf-pack crashes through her window-pane into the waking world.

The White Rabbit disrupts Alice's playtime, as he breaks free from his glass encasing. As we see him for the first time, he seems less like a preserved pet and more like a specimen from a natural history museum as his case is marked Lepus Cuniculus no. 23. Although he adorns himself in regal finery, his abdomen splits open. He leaks sawdust throughout the rest of the film, despite attempts to secure this rupture with a safety pin or to replace his innards by eating a bowl of sawdust. In a creepy fashion, he keeps his pocket-watch in his chest rather than a waistcoat pocket and licks sawdust from its face with a protruding tongue before declaring, 'Oh dear, oh dear, I shall be late'. The White Rabbit's worry over time serves as a typical device common to an uneasy anxiety dream and fuels the chase. With the character of the White Rabbit, Švankmajer injects the grotesque into his filmic world.

In her examination of the miniature, Susan Stewart argues, 'The miniature world remains perfect and uncontaminated by the grotesque so long as its absolute boundaries are maintained. Consider, for example, the Victorian taste for art (usually transformed relics of nature) under glass or Joseph Cornell's glass bells. The glass eliminates the possibility of contagion, indeed of lived experience.' The glass environment from which the White Rabbit escapes contrasts vividly with his house in Wonderland. A façade of brightly-coloured building blocks mask the interior that is part hatch, part dollhouse strewn with excremental pellets.

Just as Alice's chase after the White Rabbit initiates her deep descent into Wonderland, the White Rabbit's escape from his vitrine complete with secreted clothes and scissors in a hidden drawer sets the stage for the discovery of contaminated containers housing unexpected contents. In an ingenious display of editing as superb as the creative geography of early Soviet masters, Buster Keaton, Luis Buñuel and Maya Deren, Švankmajer pans from the confines of Alice's nursery to a desolate field with uneven terrain where Alice follows the White Rabbit to a desk. With finesse comparable to Ali Baba, the White Rabbit claps once to open the desk drawer. Without a hitch, he springs into the drawer then disappears into a space that should be too small to accommodate his form. Švankmajer bestows the desk with the magical faculty for transportation and transformation.

The desk initially thwarts Alice's attempts to gain entry at every turn as its knob comes off in her hand, forcing her to fall onto the ground. This running sight gag continues for each of the half-dozen occasions that she encounters a desk of any size. Alice crawls into the drawer filled with compasses and a protractor that pricks her finger. The area shifts into a corridor strewn with larger versions of these geometric instruments. This oscillation of size represents a motif that pervades the film whether in the change in Alice's dimensions or the wild fluctuation of objects.

Alice's eventual entry into Wonderland possesses all the violent comedic energy of early Mack Sennett films as she steps on a rake that smacks her in the forehead causing her to be knocked off-balance. As she lands in a bucket, the bottom drops out and she begins to descend in a lift. Alice travels past three levels that contain a myriad of objects that range from the authentic to the fantastical. The first floor houses all the toys from her nursery that will later reappear in various permutations. The second level looks like a larder with jars filled with wondrously strange specimens. Alice takes a look, then selects a jar of marmalade from the shelf. But it has been rendered inedible with drawing pins mixed in with bits of orange. In *Alice,* the larder transforms into a *wunderkammer* on the way to Wonderland before Alice crashes through a crack in a ceiling that seals itself and she lands in a pile of autumn leaves. Alice slips by taxidermal animals that progress from creatures found in nature to bizarre amalgams of mismatched bones and human glass eyes. Švankmajer later animates similar hybrids as 'the animals' in Alice's narrative. A few hatch out of jam jars and eggs whilst 'the animals' pursue Alice after she has wrecked the White Rabbit's house and cabbage garden by spontaneously growing to a monstrous size after drinking ink. Before eating a tart and shrinking to a smaller version of herself played by the porcelain doll from the beginning of the film, she kicks and nearly kills Bill who tries to get inside through the chimney to fight Alice. Once outside, 'the animals' gang up on Alice in her doll form. She falls into another pail filled with milky, mercurial liquid that encapsulates Alice in an enormous, alembic-like *papier-mâché* shell resembling her smaller porcelain form. The mob drags her into the nearby larder in a scene reminiscent of the Lilliputians' capture of Gulliver. Locked inside, Alice penetrates her encasing like a hatchling. In an attempt to escape, she opens a sardine tin finding the key to the door. With distaste, she licks the brine from the key.

As in the other automatic techniques innovated by Max Ernst, decalcomania involves dreaming an imaginative reality back onto a found form revealed by the process itself. Ernst used decalcomania to create the beautiful and terrifying painting *The Temptation of Saint Anthony/Die Versuchung des hl. Antonius* (1945). A menagerie of hybrid forms torturously attacks the saint. When one sees 'the animals' in *Alice*, Švankmajer's menacing hybrids and striking caterpillar resemble the bird-like, aquatic and crustacean creatures made of talons, fangs and eyes from Ernst's painting. In Carroll's version of Wonderland, the caterpillar in the forest instructs Alice that one side of the mushroom where he sits will make her grow taller and that the opposite side will make her grow shorter. After she eats the half in her right hand, she shrinks as her chin hits her feet. She instantly eats the opposite half and grows sky-high. Švankmajer resourcefully changes this part to have Alice encounter the caterpillar in a forest of serpentine socks that bore their way through the floorboards of a room. The caterpillar is an old sock that constructs itself out of glass eyes and dentures found in a desk drawer as he perches on a wooden darning mushroom. After his advisory statement about the shrinking and growing properties of the mushroom, she snips two pieces off with scissors. He tells Alice to leave him alone so that he may sleep. The caterpillar sews both eyes shut to close them. Outside of the room, fake plastic Christmas trees shrink and grow as Alice nibbles the mushroom halves. As she admits, the mushroom works quite well but not quite as she or we would have expected.

Alice stumbles upon the Mad Hatter's tea party. This scene best illustrates the repetitions that are integrally linked to the nature of dream. As she initially enters, the Mad Hatter gruffly and repeatedly informs her that there is no room – yet she can see otherwise. The Mad Hatter declares that he wants a clean cup. They all move around one space each time that he demands a new cup in this variation of musical chairs without the music. The rest of this scene launches into a segment of vigorously rhythmic editing that shows a rapid succession of the following actions: the turning of the March Hare's key to enable him to move, pulling his dangling eye back into its socket, his placing of watches on the Mad Hatter's chest as if they were metals, pouring tea, moving around one space, drinking tea, buttering the watch workings and so forth. Alice leaves the room after all of this nonsense punctuated by the Mad Hatter's insults and silly riddles. Alice peeks back in the room and the actions of the Mad Hatter and March

Hare replay themselves showing the finite number of tasks that toys can perform and the Mobius loop character of this sequence. The Mad Hatter conjures up the White Rabbit out of his hat. Amusingly, the White Rabbit serves as magician and magic trick all at the same time. Once more, she chases the White Rabbit who ultimately leads her to the Queen of Hearts and a possible beheading.

In *Alice,* Švankmajer emphasises the materiality of the puppets he employs by allowing us to see the wind-up gear of the March Hare and the marionette strings and hollow interior of the Mad Hatter. Peter Hames illuminates this practice by explaining that puppets give tangible form to the world of imagination whilst invoking a sense of touch. Švankmajer's use of puppets steeps *Alice* in the realm of magic extending from Carroll, a source rich in irrationality, a quality that exists in magical ritual, dream and child's play. In addition, children think in analogy as they equate the effigy (or in this case puppet) with its real representation. Returning full circle to Novalis, he writes in 'Logological Fragments I', 'Magic is the art of fusing the world of the senses at will.' In this manner of synaesthetic fusing intensified by hyper-real sound effects, Švankmajer proves himself as the highest form of magus. *Alice* remains one of the finest trick films of all time. His awakening of the stirring in the souls of dormant objects to animate Wonderland is Švankmajer's grandest illusion.

Tina-Louise Reid

REFERENCES

Cardinal, Roger (2001) 'The Eloquence of Objects', in Anthony Shelton (ed.) *Collectors: Expressions of Self and Other*. London/Coimbra: The Horniman Museum and Gardens/ Museu Antropologico da Universidade de Coimbra, 23–31.

Hames, Peter (2003) 'The Core of Reality: Puppets in the Feature Films of Jan Švankmajer' (unpublished paper).

Stewart, Susan (1993) *On Longing*. Durham: Duke University Press.

Švankmajer, Jan and Eva Švankmajerová (1998) *Anima, Animus, Animation*. Prague: Slovart Arbor Vitae Foundation.

DEKALOG THE DECALOGUE 21

KRZYSZTOF KIEŚLOWSKI, POLAND, 1989

It seems that the 10-episode television series *Dekalog* (*The Decalogue*), probably the most notable production of Polish cinema in the 1980s, was conceived out of sheer despair. As Krzysztof Kieślowski recollects: 'After *Bez końca* [*No End*, 1984] we were trashed by everybody. Obviously, that didn't make us feel any good. The weather was nasty, it was chilly and rainy, I'd lost one of my gloves. I met Piesiewicz. We were in a horrible mood. What's worse, a passing car splashed water all over us, and then Piesiewicz said: "We must write something new."'

Putting this story in a wider context, Kieślowski wrote in 1993:

Chaos and disorder ruled Poland in the mid-1980s – they were everywhere, dominated everything, interfered in practically everybody's life. Tension, a feeling of hopelessness, and a fear of yet worse to come, were obvious. By that time I had already occasionally travelled abroad and observed a general uncertainty in the world at large. I'm not thinking of politics here but of ordinary, everyday life. I sensed mutual indifference behind polite smiles and had the overwhelming impression that, more and more frequently, I was watching people who didn't really know why they were living. So I thought Piesiewicz was right, but filming the Ten Commandments would be a very difficult task.

These words aptly reflect the circumstances in which *The Decalogue* was made. After a succession of political films, such as *Blizna* (*The Scar*, 1976), *Amator* (*Camera Buff*, 1979), *Przypadek* (*Blind Chance*, 1981) or *No End*, Kieślowski openly declared his disappointment with politics, ostentatiously turned his back on social and political turmoil and began making films about the mysteries of human spirituality. And yet, all its universal values notwithstanding, *The Decalogue* is undoubtedly an extraordinarily faithful portrayal of Poland and Polish society in the late 1980s. Although critics like to draw a firm line between 'early' and 'late' Kieślowski, it is beyond doubt that *The Decalogue*, as we know it, could not have been made without the early, documentary period of Kieślowski's career. Out of all his films, it is this series where the synthesis of the specific and the universal, of extraordinary perceptiveness rooted in documentary practice and ability to imperceptibly transform a specific object into an intense, meaningful symbol, reached its culmination.

The housing estate, which constitutes a backdrop for all the stories unfolding in the series, is a huge Le Corbusierean 'machine for living', a predictable component of the urban landscape in all Eastern Bloc countries. The drab setting was provided by Ursynów, a big housing project in Warsaw. The living conditions are portrayed with great skill: residents cramped into claustrophobic apartments, shortages of hot water supply, unsettling noises from the staircase, violation of privacy, impersonal, often bleak and squalid surroundings, cold and depressing light, malfunctioning elevators. From *The Decalogue* one could easily compose a documentary film about survival in a dismal architectural wasteland.

The series is pervaded with sorrow, melancholy and hopelessness, interspersed with occasional outbursts of feverish action. This mood reflects the social mores that pervaded most of the Polish society at the end of the 1980s. After the remarkable soaring of hope and outburst of high expectations at the beginning of the 1980s, followed by the brutal freeze of 13 December 1981 with the institution of martial law, Poland found itself in a frustrating clinch. The awareness of impending civilisational implosion, of technological regression, of dropping behind, was omnipresent. It was accompanied by a nostalgic yearning for the West and increasing emigration, fostering the impression that those who elected to stay in the country were weaklings deprived of will power, courage and inventiveness. This mood of burnout, disaster and captivity, combined with hidden or manifest hostility to other people, was the hallmark of Poland in the late 1980s. As Józef Tischner noted during the 1997 Paris colloquium devoted to Kieslowski's work: 'Kieślowski's camera shows us a destroyed world – not just the physical landscape, but the human. In terms of Polish art, this is a form of melancholy – not despair, but a deep melancholy where every act is drained of meaning.'

According to Véronique Campan, a characteristic trait of practically all protagonists of *The Decalogue* is the fact that 'their existence has been stuck in a form governed by certain rules, and they don't want to or are unable to step outside them. These rules, marked by living space and a rigid schedule of everyday activities, have become "narrow format rules", hemming in all those who comply with them. In the ethical context, evoked by the Ten Commandments, their imprisonment takes the form of a dilemma. The binary logic of the Law (obedience or breach), hitherto willingly accepted, suddenly turns out to be irrational, unbearable.'

The impression of imprisonment is overwhelming. Trapped in the small cubicles of their apartments, in the boxes of their tower blocs, in elevators and mazes of corridors, the protagonists additionally lock themselves in, cut themselves off from the outside world with bars (episode X) and bolts (episode I). In the staircases, on the paths winding among tower blocks, they occasionally meet characters known from other episodes, as if the whole universe consisted of a limited number of elements. This claustrophobic mood is enhanced by framing and lighting, which privileges close-ups and darkness, tightly enveloping the silhouettes of the protagonists.

The characters are also trapped in time. The stifling stigma of some event from the past hangs over most of them, disfiguring their lives and crippling their development. Death and illegitimate love are most common: the sudden death of the doctor's family (episode II), of Jacek's sister (episode V), of a stamp-collector (episode X), an extramarital love affair (episodes II and III), an affair between a teacher and a schoolgirl (episode VII). In episode IV we have both of these motifs: the death of the heroine's mother and a suggestion of her infidelity. Sexual promiscuity, although not so precisely anchored in the past, is also hinted at in episodes I, VI and IX. Sometimes this is tantamount to a breach of the commandment referred to in a given episode (episode VII and VIII). Sometimes the past does not take the form of a discrete, separable event, but is more diffused, like a childhood spent in an orphanage (episode VI). In any case, the past is like a curse hanging over vulnerable characters. The protagonists are plagued by irreversible memories of bygone events, tainted with original sin, haunted by feelings of guilt and remorse. They lurch in a net cast on them by the past, a net which they had cast on themselves.

This overwhelming impression of entrapment in space, time and everyday routine is contrasted with a peculiar potential for freedom and change. Most of the protagonists represent liberal professions which, interestingly enough, are called 'free' in Polish. They are artists, doctors, scientists, lawyers, i.e. professionals whose calling is to penetrate or to transcend boundaries. Moreover, many of them are in a state of transition. A telltale sign of this predicament – although today not exactly transparent even to Polish viewers – is a passport. In communist countries it was a scarce commodity, a pass to a better world, jealously guarded, granted to few. Many of *The Decalogue* protagonists belong to this elect group, which in reality was never large. This means, however, that they are neither from here, nor from there. (Incidentally, another important feature of most episodes is contact between protagonists and Western countries; not only people, but the whole country is in a state of transition; frozen into a depressing reality, mentally and spiritually it is elsewhere.) A perfect example of this is Dorota, the heroine of the second episode; a subtle musician and a die-hard mountaineer, a female yuppie, living in a cold, impersonal apartment.

Other protagonists lack stabilisation, because they are homeless. This is the case of the young murderer from episode V, who, in his own words, was forced to leave his native village; of the voyeur from episode VI, who grew up in an orphanage; or the singer from episode X, who says that he does not have a home.

This innermost changeability is also visible in Kieślowski's obsessive urge to portray alternatives (present in his other work, such as the three versions of events in *Blind Chance* and the two versions of Véronique's life in *La Double vie de Véronique/The Double Life of Véronique*, 1991); the two versions of episodes V and VI. In *The Decalogue*, this obsession adopts visual forms. Kieślowski and his cameramen created frames containing countless alternate looks –reflections of the protagonists in mirrors, windows, glasses, sleek surfaces. They indulged in shooting through flawed windows, drapes or other objects that distorted the view. The lighting very often split faces, rendering one part bright (one profile, lower or upper part) and plunging the other part into darkness, or painted different parts of the various bodies in different colours (for instance, in episode V, before the murder scene, one hand of the murderer is orange, the other one – the green of decay). As Véronique Campan noted 'every hero is doubled – confronts his other part, this part of darkness, which drags him from the 'straight way' and deprives him of his identity'. Consequently, such splits and multiplications visually suggest the relativity, instability and malleability of the protagonists' identities.

Typical traits of human relationships are aggression, hostility, indifference and lack of communication. The series abounds in scenes depicting aimless aggression, such as pouring cold water over naked, drunk people (episode III), throwing stones into cars, verbal insults and rude misbehaviour (episodes VI and VIII). Apart from such apparently aimless aggression between strangers, which seems only to unleash frustration, there are numerous instances of instrumental aggression, resulting from a mounting conflict between the protagonists. 'I wish I had run you over', Dorota says to the doctor in episode II; 'I dreamt that you had your neck broken, tongue outside, and I looked at you and smiled' says Ewa to her former lover (episode III); Magda humiliates Tomek and inspires beating him up (episode II); and Majka watches her mother's despair with joyous vengeance (episode VII). The protagonists also often display indifference to each other, in some cases hovering on the brink of an almost autistic remoteness. They do not react to greetings, fail to answer questions and seem not to understand what other people say. This is enhanced by the defectiveness of their communication. They eavesdrop (episodes IV and IX) or peep (episodes VI and IX), see but do not hear (in many scenes of looking through the window) and hear, but do not see (in telephone conversations or listening to voice mail).

Human interactions in *The Decalogue* invariably yield suffering and pain. People hurt each other by resorting to aimless or instrumental aggression, to mutual indifference, to badly located affection. Hurting each other, however, at the same time they seek each other. According to Véronique Campan, characters in *The Decalogue* go from confrontation to dialogue, but it is the former that prevails. The French critic finds only three scenes of genuine dialogue, in which the protagonists really try to understand each other. But lack of understanding is only one of a number of factors involved. The role of emotions must be also emphasised. In five episodes out of ten (III, IV, VI, VII, IX), conflict originates from the fact that someone demands love from his or her partner; others are rejected, and the desired love is refused. In some cases we have both situations at the same time. Even in the three episodes in which we do not encounter a clearcut variant of this situation (I, II and VIII), the motif of love and rejection emerges.

According to Christopher Garbowski, *The Decalogue* should be analysed in terms of two dimensions: horizontal and vertical. The former refers to relationships among characters, the latter – to relations between characters and God. Vertical and horizontal lines make up a cross, the symbol of Christianity: 'The horizontal plane has got a great deal of bitterness for them: their love has gone through the crucible of suffering, and no doubt suffering will remain a component of it for the foreseeable future. The vertical plane represents the axis of hope through which all things are possible, although hope can be dim at times.' Through suffering to God – this very Christian concept seems to lie at the heart of Kieślowski's oeuvre.

Taking into account the fact that *The Decalogue* is founded on the Ten Commandments, it is hardly surprising that it has often been regarded as a religious series. Many authors writing about the series have argued for its immanent religious quality and amassed evidence to confirm it. For many critics, the mere fact of founding the series on the commandments carved on the tables of stone bequeathed to Moses is sufficient proof of its religiousness. It has often been noted, however, that the relationship between given commandments and the episodes 'built around' them may be viewed with some ambivalence: only occasionally is it fairly straightforward (as in episode V, about killing), more often than not, it is hazy and remote, sometimes even contradictory and perverse. Some episodes seem to refer to several commandments simultaneously. In addition, Kieślowski employs the canonical ordering of commandments in the Roman Catholic and Protestant traditions. The order of commandments in the Church of England or in Judaism is different, however, which makes the relationships between them and given episodes even more complex and ambiguous.

In three episodes (I, II and VIII), the existence of God is the subject of important conversations between the protagonists. In others, Christian symbolism manifests its presence quite openly, for example the weeping Madonna in episode I, a ladder brought into a death chamber in episode V, or water, symbol of baptism, which appears in numerous forms and guises throughout the whole series. According to the Russian Orthodox priest Michał Klinger a dark hole in the ice is a visible sign of God. Furthermore, even the symbolic dimension of the protagonists' names has not remained unnoticed. The seductress from episode III bears the name Ewa, like the biblical Eve, her former lover who cheats on his wife is Janusz, which is reminiscent of 'Janus face', the misbehaving heroine of episode VI is Magda (the short form of Magdalena), the professor of ethics from episode VIII is Zofia (Sophia), the murderer from episode V is Łazar, and 'like the evangelical Lazarus he is a dead man'.

Another commonly highlighted sign of the religious character of *The Decalogue* is the mysterious character played by Artur Barciś, often called 'the Guardian Angel'. He appears in every episode except episode VII, usually in critical moments, when some crucial decision is about to be made. Never saying a word, he remains an apparently passive onlooker, but an intense feeling of sympathy emanates from his face and eyes. Viewers unanimously regard him as a messenger of God, the sign of the existence of some metaphysical order. The origins of this character also hint at his metaphysical nature. Kieślowski was inspired by a story about a Polish writer Wilhelm Mach. After some screening, Mach said he liked the film very much, especially the scene at the cemetery with the guy in the black suit. Despite the film director's protestations that there was no such character in the movie, Mach held on to his view: 'How come? He stood on the left-hand side of the frame, in the foreground, in a black suit, white shirt and black tie. Then he walked across to the right-hand side of the frame and moved off.' Ten days later Mach was dead. 'I understood', Kieślowski noted, 'what was missing: this guy in a black suit whom not everyone sees … He doesn't have any influence on what's happening, but he is a sort of sign or warning to those whom he watches, if they notice him.'

Other signs of the existence of some metaphysical order are unruly objects: an ink bottle breaking without any visible reason, a painting stubbornly going awry, a glove compartment in a car opening out of the blue, and many other objects apparently living their own lives. They obey some order independent of the human will, suggest the finger of God, or at least the intervention of something 'beyond and above physics'. Also in *No End*, produced immediately before *The Decalogue*, Kieślowski suggested the intervention of an apparition in exactly the same way. Some critics commented upon it sarcastically, regarding it as a naïve discovery of the beyond.

The presence of some higher order may also be inferred from the structure and style of the entire series. Some structuring devices, such as flash-forward or parallel editing, contribute to the aura of fatalism. The son from the first episode is dead before he even appears on the screen. We alternately look at people who do not know each other. Their paths are bound to intersect, but they do not know it yet. These devices create an impression that the events can unfold only in one, specific way, that their itinerary has been prepared in advance. Dead animal corpses found at the outset of episodes I, II, V and X also play the roles of omens. More generally, the omnipresence of such topics as death and birth invokes fundamental questions.

The rhythm of *The Decalogue* is slow, trance-like. It is a well-established fact that 'dead moments' in a film, when the action slows down, may induce a state of meditation in the viewers. Kieślowski was one of very few directors who were capable of representing the weight of life, the hardship of everyday existence, its monotony, in a way evoking transcendental, religious feelings. It is not accidental that this style was employed by those film directors regarded as the main representatives of the religious trend of European cinema: Robert Bresson, Carl Theodor Dreyer, Andrei Tarkovsky, Ingmar Bergman … and Krzysztof Kieślowski.

The sturdy foundation of the Ten Commandments, the mysterious 'Guardian Angel', unruly objects, symbols from Christian tradition, fatalistic structure, transcendental style, all these pieces of evidence have been carefully stockpiled to corroborate the case of *The Decalogue* as a decisively religious comment on the existence of God. And yet, in spite of their abundance, this thesis has not been accepted or recognised unanimously. Some critics noted that his voice was that of a Protestant, or even a Quaker, rather than a Catholic, that he perpetuated 'agnostic spirituality', that stressing the private, spiritual dimension of religion, Kieślowski edged uncomfortably close to New Age ideas, in which spirituality is everything and institutional religion nothing. Some Polish critics interpreted the widespread popularity of *The Decalogue* in Western Europe as an effect of spiritual impoverishment stemming from many years of secularisation. The pervasive conviction about the religious nature of *The Decalogue* was not supported by any equally common agreement concerning the nature of this religiousness and its relationship to institutional religion, its creeds, icons and myths. According to Annette Insdorf, 'Kieślowski was neither overly nor overtly fond of organised religion, but his later work emanates a belief in the life of the spirit … If Kieślowski still seems so present to many of us, maybe it's because of the transcendence in which he seemed to believe – his "impression that there must be more things beyond what we can see". If this is true, Kieślowski's series is metaphysical rather than religious, its Catholicism stems rather from tradition and cultural milieu than from genuine commitment and, really in a New Age vein, it is rather *a way* than *the way* to spirituality.

Metaphysical questions pave the way to the ethical dimension of *The Decalogue*. Many commentators suggest that Kieślowski did not follow the path staked out by Moses. He used to say in interviews that he did not want simply to illustrate commandments, but to induce the viewers to reflect on the ethical dimension of their lives. It seems, however, that there is more to it than just that, that at least in some episodes one can find thoughts which coincide with the commendations carved in the tables of stone. Véronique Campan pointed out that for many of the protagonists, obeying the letter of the law would be self-destructive: 'If Anka, Majka or Romek still complied with the moral rules, they would have to commit suicide, for their situation would be unbearable. Some others – the doctor, the lecturer, the postman – if they reject the temptation to break the law, will be strangled by a hopeless existence.' In other cases, obeying commandments would lead to somebody's death or harm. If Janusz (episode III) had appropriately observed the holy day instead of driving around the whole city with his former lover and cheating on his wife, he would have unintentionally contributed to Ewa's death. In episode II, the perjury, which the doctor in all probability committed, saved an unborn life. In both cases breaching the law saved a life; observing it would have led to death. Episode VIII depicts a similar situation: rigid observance of the law means the almost certain death of a Jewish child. On the other hand, when the son of the scientist who believes in a 'false god' (the computer) falls under the ice and dies (episode I), we do not identify with the letter of the Law; on the contrary, we are horrified by the harshness of the inflicted punishment.

One possible conclusion is that *The Decalogue* revives an old conflict between the concepts of law in the Old and New Testaments, between the letter and the spirit where, according to St Paul, 'the letter killeth, but the spirit giveth life' (II Corinthians, 3:6), where strict observance of the law is called the 'ministration of death, written and engraved in stones' (II Corinthians II, 3:7) and juxtaposed to the 'ministration of spirit' (II Corinthians, 3:8). Commenting upon Kieślowski's confession that he feels closer to the demanding, cruel God of the Old Testament, Paul Coates stated: 'If this is so, *The Decalogue* may benefit from the possible tension between Kieślowski's own Old Testament God and the New Testament one of the Catholic Piesiewicz – the tension between law and love. For the Christian, love finally triumphs over law, mercy over judgement, and the old covenant becomes obsolete (Hebrews 8:13).'

Tension between love and law, so pronounced in *The Decalogue*, is not, however, the only point of dispute with Christian tradition. Another one is the idea of sacrifice. Insdorf quotes her American student who, commenting upon the scene in the church (episode I), in which the Holy Mother 'weeps' with wax tears, stated that 'Her story, and that of Christianity, is that of the sacrificed child to a greater cause.' While it is disputable whether a 33-year-old man can be still called a child, it is beyond doubt that the idea of sacrifice, which constitutes the cornerstone of Christianity, and which can probably be found in all known religions, is one of the most important themes of *The Decalogue*. It has obtained a most elegant, almost exemplary shape in episode II. The heroine's husband is severely sick. She, being pregnant by another man, approaches the doctor asking him to decide if the husband is to die or not. If he survives, she has to abort her pregnancy; if he is going to die, the child will live. The doctor is thrust into the position of God, who decides about life and death, or even more accurately – into the position of a priest, who sacrifices one life on behalf of another.

Such a sense of symmetry pervades the whole series. In almost every episode there are scales, and a man's life is weighed against some other life or an important cause. In episode I the son's life is paired with his father's faith; in episode II the child's life is set against the husband's life; in episode III the heroine's life hinges upon the night with her former lover; in episode V Jacek's life is paired with the driver's life (or, to put it another way, he loses his life on the altar of justice); in episode VI Tomek sacrifices his life on the altar of his love to Magda; in episode VIII the child's life is set against the safety of a resistance organisation; in episode IX a child the couple did not want to have is juxtaposed with an easy, comfortable life; in episode X their father's death conditioned the brothers' closeness. Even in the remaining two episodes (IV and VII) one may talk about sacrifice in a more metaphorical sense. In episode IV, depicting a play of desire between a daughter and her father, one may say that the heroine must kill the daughter in herself in order to become a woman for her father, and that he rejects this sacrifice. In episode VII a small child's well-being is sacrificed on the altar of a love/hate game between mother and daughter.

If this is so, we can truly say that the idea of sacrifice constitutes the main structural and conceptual axis in *The Decalogue*. Certainly, each of the above situations is different, each has its own unique background and psychological conditioning. And yet, if we tried to infer one simple conclusion which would apply to all of them, it would take the form of an 'it should not' clause: the son should not die because of his father's 'misguided' faith; the unborn's life should not be set against the husband's life; Ewa's life should not hinge on the circumstances of the Christmas night, and so on. 'No idea, no concept, nothing is more important than a child's life' says the professor of ethics in episode VIII and this statement may truly be regarded as the answer to all the difficult situations depicted so masterfully in *The Decalogue*. The idea of sacrifice is, if not totally ill-conceived, then at least problematic. In this way Kieślowski's series, so strongly rooted in the Christian tradition, makes one of its fundamental concepts disputable.

Mirosław Przylipiak

REFERENCES

Campan, Véronique (1997) 'Dziesięć krótkich filmów: od pojedynku do dialogu', in Tadeusz Lubelski (ed.) *Kino Krzysztofa Kieślowskiego*. Kraków: Universitas, 59–88.

Coates, Paul (1999) 'The Curse of Law: *The Decalogue*', in Paul Coates (ed.) *Lucid Dreams: The Films of Krzysztof Kieślowski*. Trowbridge: Flicks Books, 94–115.

Garbowski, Christopher (1997) *Krzysztof Kieślowski's Decalogue Series: The Problem of the Protagonists and Their Self-Transcendence*. Lublin: Maria Skłodowska-Curie University Press.

Insdorf, Annette (1999) *Double Lives, Second Chances: The Cinema of Krzysztof Kieślowski*. New York: Hyperion.

Klinger, Michał (1997) 'Strażnik wrót. Rzecz o *Dekalogu* Krzysztofa Kieślowskiego', in Tadeusz Lubelski (ed.) *Kino Krzysztofa Kieślowskiego*. Kraków: Universitas, 51–8.

Stok, Danusia (ed.) (1993) *Kieślowski on Kieślowski*. London: Faber.

SÁTÁNTANGÓ

BÉLA TARR, HUNGARY/GERMANY/SWITZERLAND, 1994

Sátántangó (1991–94) is the most spectacular achievement of Hungarian art cinema of the past twenty years, and one of the most important works of European art cinema after the decline of modernism. Since the 1970s it has been the most radical accomplishment of what can be called the Antonioni-form, an important feature of which is the almost real-time representation of the disappearance of human contact, or the representation of the psychological recognition of this disappearance.

Sátántangó was Béla Tarr's sixth feature film and the second part of his 'black-and-white' series in collaboration with Hungarian writer László Krasznahorkai, which started with their film *Kárhozat* (*Damnation*, 1988). Tarr began his career as a director of documentary-style fiction films on people living in poor financial conditions against a lower-class cultural background. However, he had no interest in the description of social reality for its own sake; he preferred to focus on the human relationships that were partly informed by those conditions. From the beginning, the focus of his interest was on the question of how it was possible to preserve human dignity in the midst of the most miserable social conditions. For him, hopeless social conditions were just the manifestation of a universal moral degradation. Helplessness is, for Tarr, not solely social nor solely moral. His heroes could be wealthy and powerful. In his world, they would get no mercy anyway. He chooses socially-deprived heroes, because their defencelessness is accentuated. At the end of the 1950s, Antonioni placed his heroes in an upper-middle-class milieu, so that no one made the mistake of thinking that estrangement could be avoided, when financial needs were met. The reason for Tarr placing his characters so low is to show that there are no depths of misery from which one could not sink even lower, for this deprivation is not primarily a financial question. Tarr's world is as hopeless as Antonioni's, but he embraces the world from underneath rather than from above. No one can claim that Antonioni's problems are those of the rich, and no one can claim that Tarr's films only represent the misery of the poor.

Sátántangó consists of several loosely connected events, each of which is in one way or another connected to a single central plot line. The location is a little village somewhere in the great plain of Hungary. The village as well as its inhabitants is extremely run down, poor and hopeless. All they dream of is how to get away from there in one way or another. A mysterious person named Irimias and his helper, Petrina, have promised to help them. Irimias is considered as a sort of a saviour, but he has not shown up for more than a year, and he was reported to be dead. The villagers try to save some money in order to leave and start a new life, but two of them decide to steal the savings and flee. Just as they are planning this, Irimias suddenly shows up and promises them that he will provide them with proper jobs and with better conditions if they give him all the money they have. He manages to convince them again to continue believing in him and to give him the money. He orders them to leave the village together, leaving everything behind. The villagers follow his orders and they all go to the agreed meeting point, a railway station. There Irimias tells them that due to certain circumstances, his original plan cannot be realised for the moment. He sends each of them to different places where they are supposed to settle down temporarily, and wait for his next order to reunite again to go to the promised new place where they will get work and proper conditions.

This central plot takes up less than the half of the film. The rest is filled by scenes representing the moral, psychological and physical misery of the characters' lives. We learn also – what the villagers do not know – that Irimias is a petty criminal used by the police to spy and report on the villagers, but the concrete reason for this assignment remains unknown. This seems to be just the general practice of a certain political system. Another central character of the film is the village doctor, who is constantly observing the lives of the villagers, and taking notes of what they are doing. He is the one who knows everything, but never intervenes and does not take part in their lives. The film's main plot elements, repeated over and over again in different variations, are concerned with faith, cheating and deception, loss of belief and confidence, and how to take account of this.

In Tarr's oeuvre, *Sátántangó* is the result of a conscious search for a certain style. His main purpose was to find a form that could create an atmosphere of social realism which was at the same time a manifestation of constant moral degradation. It was clear for Tarr that a continuous composition of space and time had to play a key role in this. But what is a camera movement like, what is the time like that renders the image universal, with the world remaining at the same time very concrete? Tarr knew he had to go beyond the abstract set stylisation of *Őszi Almanach* (*Autumn Almanac*, 1985), and return to a seemingly realistic portrayal of the world, while keeping the feeling of the universality of the entire world and not letting it fall back to the level of social realism. Andrei Tarkovsky and Robert Bresson were his main models. Bresson's static and impassive camerawork characterised by a fixation on a partial visual motif with no regard for what happens around it, so that much of the action takes place in off-screen space, is combined here with Tarkovsky's extreme long-take monotone camera movements, which evoke the time experience of eternity going beyond the physical nature of things. One thing, however, had to be different in this film from both Bresson and Tarkovsky: unlike them, Tarr wanted to evoke the *lack* rather than the presence of the metaphysical dimension of the world.

Kraszhahorkai's novel was meant to solve this problem. The human situations in it are very similar to those in Tarr's earlier films. He found the social environment (worn down characters on the verge of misery and corruption) very close to his heart, while the structure of the book is based on a time game with composition. It seemed that Krasznahorkai provided the answers to Tarr's problem of the treatment of time. The answer was the Nietzschean eternal return. Monotonous repetition, and infinitely slow and ruthless seclusion can raise even the most earthly, most worn down, most extreme and most unique-seeming world from its concrete historical and social situation and create a whole world from it. So it became possible for Tarr to bring back his naturalistic world-portrayal, while standing on the borderline between artificiality and reality. This was the most important characteristic of the human world portrayed by him. Krasznahorkai saw in the world the same thing as Tarr did: endless destruction and misery disguised as redemption and elevation.

In his early films Tarr related this process to a concrete social environment or to the selfish and uncaring nature of the human soul; but the fact that cheating is inherent in the world itself, in its false nature, never became a central theme, except in the case of *Autumn Almanac*, where the emphatically artificial set alluded to it. Without leaving his realistic portrayal of the world too far behind, without having to give up portraying real misery and ruin, he could now show that this is the reality of a false world, a result of cheating and conning. The world is constructed so that people believe in redemption and love. Trust is a way to redemption. And when people believe this and leave themselves unshielded for a moment, they are struck down mercilessly and what little they still have is taken from them. The misery of the world is not a result of the financial or political situation, but derives from an abuse of the last remnants of faith in humanism. Krasznahorkai's novel was special in that it depicted the process of deterioration rather then the static condition of misery. Not a disrupted world, but continuous disruption. This became the key for Tarr. Monotonous slowness is the time of this ruthless crash, the form of inevitability is the eternal return, which became the basic element of the three great films Tarr made with Krasznahorkai.

Tarr's film provides a consistent application of the formal principles laid down in his previous film *Damnation*, and a consistent adaptation of the novel's main compositional principle, which is to document not facts nor a story, but a general process of unstoppable degradation. In *Sátántangó* Tarr uses the principles found and elaborated in *Damnation* in a much easier and more chiselled manner. The basic set elements remain the same, but the smalltown scene has changed into an indefinable village-like settlement, which is talked of as the 'block'. In *Damnation* the characters still had social status, whereas here, no one except the doctor has any. We do not know who they are, what they do, how they got here, or when and where the story takes place. The motor of the story here is the same as in most Tarr films: faith, appearance and deception. In the portrayal of this world, however, there is no stylisation at all. Tarr did not need the set to allude to the background of the story as directly as in *Damnation*. This world does not promise anything good, it just keeps the people living in it captive, while they desperately try to get out; the story is much more straightforward and direct.

It is essentially a criminal story about the tricks of two con-men, embezzlers, one of them an informant, who cheats the inhabitants of the village out of their last savings in the vilest possible way, making them believe that they will help them to a better life. The villagers see the Messiah in the two crooks; they follow them blindly and even lose their homes. While the story is perfectly fictional and structured step by step, the characters are incredibly precise and authentic. Tarr uses all the knowledge he gained from his experience of direct filming and creates an elaborate scale of misery that can represent a whole society. All intellectual and spiritual types are to be found in this micro-environment, all variations of human and existential ruin. The doctor, the policeman, the cleaning-woman, the pensioner, the worker, the inn-keeper, the whore, the poet and the philosopher create an entire world, conveying the whole scale of human relationships, emotions, desires and beliefs, while converging monotonously on the same place. Tarr creates a dichotomy of the real and the unreal now – for the first time – not through different motifs (set, dialogue) but in the same milieu, that of humankind. Therefore he does not need an over-stylised set or a too-poetic dialogue. Where the latter appears still, it is strictly functional.

Irimias, the con-man, is successful with those living in perfect uncertainty, because his angelic face, his earnestness and prophetic speeches discover the last remnants of faith and trust in them. He is a real fake prophet; he sucks the blood of the most desperate, most defenceless people, who still have something to lose, who still have dreams and who are therefore happy to grab at all the possibilities that might promise a better life. This character is diabolical, while all he appeals to is his own suggestive power. He does not try to convince people, but – with his appearance, his secretiveness, his abstract, philosophical and poetic speeches – makes them believe that he is from another world. People trust him, because they believe him to be the messenger of another world. His secret is the same as that of many real and fake prophets. And an evil irony of fate is that, in a way, they are right to believe him.

Irimias is a petty criminal and police informant on parole. He has really been sent from 'up above', from the police. However, he is 'unreal', and that is why he can play his part. The way people approach him is also unrealistic – and this unreality provides the film's most important statement. Men and women, even in their utter defencelessness, can always find something above them, which seems greater and in which they can believe. That is why their defencelessness can offer no hope. The more unrealistic something seems, the more likely is the prospect that empty appearances may govern these defenceless people of faith. The dichotomy of semblance and reality comes from one single character, Irimias. He represents the superior world as the great con. One scene in the film symbolises this clearly: the bells the characters hear tolling are not in the church, and only come from a cheap belfry, whose rope is pulled by a half-wit.

That is why it is a mistake to use the concept of metaphysics in connection with Tarr's films, though his portrayal, which superficially resembles that of Tarkovsky, tempts us to this explanation. But Tarr's statement about the other world is very clear in this film, about the domain beyond the senses; this metaphysical territory, is none other than a shelter from utter despair, and belief in it is the final proof of human defencelessness. It's only good is to enable people to hide their own misery from themselves. Tarr's and Krasznahorkai's way of thinking is mostly inspired by Nietzsche. Their closed, circular time-concept is a proof of that, too.

All analyses of *Sátántangó* have to first account for why seven and a half hours were needed to tell this story, what the reason may be for its improbable, slow pace, and how the film can still be enjoyed. Here I can only hint at the reasons. First of all the slow monotony and circulation of time is a central topic in Krasznahorkai's novel. The inevitability of a fulfilling fate is what Tarr and Krasznahorkai meant to express with this slow monotony. This was no arbitrary choice on their part. One can portray the inevitability of fate in many ways, depending on what we think fate owes its power to. A sentimental melodrama, a tense tragedy, a fast-paced action movie can all become means. Tarr does not find fate dramatic. According to Tarr and Krasznahorkai it is not the result of fatal or contrived events. It is not inevitable, because of something that happened, whose consequences are unavoidable. Fate – in their view – is that of the unchanging, of the eternal return. There is no crime needed for it, nor a blow of fate. It applies to everyone, regardless of where we are in the social hierarchy.

In Tarr's world, deconstruction is slow, but unstoppable and finds its way everywhere. The question therefore is not how to stop or avoid this process, but what we do in the meantime. Tarr asks this question of the audience, but if the audience wants to understand the question, they first have to understand the fatality of time. And in order to grasp that, they have to understand that in surviving the present moment there is no escape: time is empty. It is an infinite and undivided dimension, in which everything repeats itself the same way.

The other and most important motivation for *Sátántangó* being so slow and of an extraordinary length is the emptying of time-experience. Quite contrary to Tarkovsky, who uses slowness to build a transcendent experience, Tarr uses the same technique to rid us of the illusion of the transcendent experience. A little frivolously we could say that knowing the reflexes of the audience used to the art film's search for the transcendent, Tarr needs a little more time and an even slower pace to reach his goal than Tarkovsky. Tarr empties time by creating the constant illusion that what is happening moves the plot forward. The great bravado of the film is that it manages to maintain a state of suspense for seven and a half hours. This could not be achieved through the plot alone. It is necessary that all objects, all landscapes and figures create such a colourful diversity, that they awaken curiosity in themselves.

One element in this is the fact that most characters are played not by professional actors, but by artists, with distinctive faces and characters: film directors, cinematographers, composers, set-designers, writers, painters. Most of Tarr's characters create the tension necessary for the audience's interest with their faces, voices and movements. One cannot know who they are since all the characters remain secret. They all look unbelievably miserable in a miserable environment, but still they show some fine qualities, some sign of intellect. They are not descendants of this world; they just arrived here somehow and now cannot escape. They are wretched people with a serene countenance, and we still believe that they might have dreams. In *Damnation*, the past was carried by the outer and inner surfaces of buildings, here history is condensed in human faces.

Sátántangó is Tarr's modernist masterpiece, which – with a brave gesture – not only continues, but also radicalises, the tradition of modern film which has been most overshadowed in contemporary film culture: the world-forming contemplation and meditation of Yasujiro Ozu, Michelangelo Antonioni, Andrei Tarkovsky and Jim Jarmusch. In their own ways and in their own cultural contexts they all created something radical, but from a technical viewpoint it is Tarr who went the furthest and who reached an unsurpassable endpoint. This in itself is no value judgement, but it has to be said. It is hard to imagine how one could go any further on this road, which, however, does not mean that it is a dead end. The extraordinary length and slowness was a means of telling a story and not an end in itself. Tarr did not have to give up the essence of his style in order to return to a more traditional, an almost classical form in his next film, *Werckmeister Harmóniák* (*Werckmeister Harmonies*, 2000).

Sátántangó constitutes a provocation and a challenge for the whole of contemporary film culture. The undertaking was grand, perhaps the greatest gamble in film history. Tarr has made a film, which is, in practical terms, unsuitable for distribution, for the film's length of seven and a half hours does not consist of parts which can be seen days or weeks apart, like Fassbinder's *Berlin Alexanderplatz* (1980) for example. It is a single huge composition, which has to be seen in a single viewing since it depicts one single process. What is more, this length is not justified by a long or complicated story. What happens in the film is not more than could be told in 90 minutes.

By the beginning of the 1990s, the hegemony of American films in Europe had become overwhelming. This was not only due to their numbers, but a certain Americanisation had also appeared in European film: readily comprehensible, emotional stories, impetuous narration, colourful and grand imagery, fast rhythm. It seemed reason enough for concern that the kind of filmmaking once characteristic of the 'new waves' and the whole of modern film art had become completely isolated by the 1990s. Another response to the same phenomenon was the manifesto of the Dogme95 group and the sequence of films that followed. They also wanted to return to personal expression, to a denial of the conventions dictated by commercial profit and to a use of a film language seeking new paths. It seemed likely that European filmmakers were in danger of forgetting all this and would only survive in the battle with Hollywood by becoming more Hollywood-like themselves. Tarr's radical gesture was a challenge for cinemagoers in favour of European culture. It was as if – through shock-therapy – he was trying to lead them back to the recognition of what real film art is about. Black-and-white was the answer to the over-coloured mayhem of today's visual culture. The style of long takes and no cuts was a response to the raging pace sieving through from commercials and video-clips. Seven and a half hours were a response to today's film style of superficial, quick reactions and subliminal effects. The story of little plot was a response to the action-packed, aggressive plot-structures. *Sátántangó* in all its elements is an extreme counterpoint to the developments that started in the film culture of the 1990s and remain prevalent today.

András Bálint Kovács

ZÁHRADA THE GARDEN

MARTIN ŠULÍK, SLOVAKIA/FRANCE/CZECH REPUBLIC, 1995

Martin Šulík, the director of *Záhrada* (*The Garden*, 1995), became known to the public after the fall of the Berlin Wall and the political upheaval in November 1989, and after the spontaneous changes that swept most countries of Central and Eastern Europe. Thanks to his extraordinary integrity and creativity, he was able to draw inspiration, quite naturally, from domestic sources and soon became the most distinctive representative of Slovak cinema of the 1990s. His poetic films, modest in their setting and rich in light irony and humour, won remarkable international success, simultaneously fascinating critics and audiences in Slovakia and abroad.

Šulík made his debut with *Neha* (*Tenderness*, 1991), telling the story of the loss and disintegration of values at a time when old rules ceased to be valid and new ones were only beginning to form. His second film *Všetko, čo mám rád* (*Everything I Like*, 1992) is also set in the period of dissolving communication barriers. He sought a new hierarchy of values in a changed world, realising that the balance has been disrupted; the recent past has changed into history and one is suddenly on the threshold of a new historical epoch. His third feature, *The Garden*, further develops the theme of the two previous films and brings something akin to good news to our unstable world. However, it does not continue the story of his first two films, but rather offers another modification of Šulík's hero – 'a patient nomad on the path to knowledge', as critics called him – and thus it carries on a loose 'trilogy of relationships' connected through their inner logic.

Even in *Tenderness* Šulík tenaciously departed from everything that was common in Slovak cinema, restricted as it was by the ideological constraints of the 1970s and 1980s and by the unwritten laws of classic dramatic composition. By creating the unbalanced Šimon, a hero seeking the key to what is right at the cost of disillusions and mistakes, falling under the spell of a cruel *ménage à trois* with a much older couple, he provocatively ignored the psychosocial classification of characters and the precise identification of place and time. Šulík realised his first work from an unwritten duty to 'truthfully reflect reality' and created a film that was stylised and abstract in form. It did not directly reflect social reality but rather a certain feeling of the period – connected loosely with the political and economic changes determining the development of society.

In *Everything I Like*, Šulík was again preoccupied with expressing his message through personal relationships, rather than through the pseudo-real world, although compared with *Tenderness*, it was much more related to the contemporary social and cultural context. Its main hero, Tomáš, hesitating as to whether he should emigrate and flee from responsibility, intuitively turns to positive values from his old life and is reluctant to abandon them even after unanticipated political changes. The film emphasised the need to continue all the positive elements in life and pointed to the imminent danger in searching for a new modus vivendi, that one may throw the baby out with the bath water. In *The Garden*, Šulík proceeds from personal to universal themes; from an inner and real emigration from a frustrating reality and the search for a footing in new social relationships to the universal problems of the future of civilisation. His hero Jakub approaches consciously the point at which 'everything is as it should be'.

Although Jakub (Roman Luknár) looks brawny, we know nothing about him except the fact that he is a teacher. This man in 'Christ's years', with the astonished face of a child, looks more abstract and naïve than the protagonists of Šulík's previous films. His story seems to be simple. We meet him at the moment when he faces one problem after another. He is unable to become independent and resolve the lingering conflict with his father nor is he satisfied with his work as a teacher or with his passionate affair with Tereza, a married woman. Bored, disgusted and 'sick' of his life, he goes to his grandfather's cottage, situated in an isolated garden, in order to sell it and buy a flat of his own. Contrary to the logic of his previous lifestyle, he remains there. The place begins to fascinate him with its magic. The garden turns into a stage invaded and deserted by curious characters from the surrounding world. Jakub decodes the message of his grandfather's diary that he finds accidentally and learns to perceive his environment in a new way, to understand the real needs and contents of words and acts. He meets young Helena, a mysterious visitor to the garden, who becomes the catalyst for his path to maturity. Thanks to her, Jakub redefines his attitude to primary values and relationships.

The film is a mosaic of 14 chapters, its form reminiscent of Voltaire's rationalist novels. Every chapter, introduced by the narrator, shows how the main character gains new knowledge. In this respect Šulík follows the form of his previous films. While in *Tenderness* integrated sequences were separated by a cathartic fadeout underlined by music, in *Everything I Like* each part is introduced by subtitles set against a dark background as in silent film. They create a rhythm for the narrative and add meaning to every single sequence. In a similar spirit of literary convention, something like a medieval introduction enters *The Garden*, a brief account of the content of the following chapter in old stylised speech resembling the language of the Bible.

Šulík often accentuates the historic aspect of an old narrative, referring at the same time to the dual phenomenon of the Slovak cultural environment: the heritage of the fairy tale myth and the medieval pilgrimage form of the *Bildungsroman*, the most remarkable among them being *René mládenca príhody a skúsenosti* (*The Adventures and Experience of René, the Young Man*) by Jozef Ignác Bajza and *Pilný domajší a polný hospodár* (*The Industrious Domestic and Field Farmer*) by Juraj Fándly. The repeated introduction parodies the action of individual chapters and produces a permanent comic effect. The language of the grandfather's journal is created similarly: written backwards, it is to some degree an ironic paraphrase of Leonardo's diaries.

Jakub struggles to get into the enclosed garden through a dilapidated gate and at that very moment it suddenly opens by itself. The fence draws an imaginary line separating the garden from the outer world. Thus Jakub's invasion of the garden changes his 'urban life of debauchery' into the initiatory silence of Robinson Crusoe's solitude, into the mystical space of genuine knowledge, and he remains there. He rids himself of formal clothes in a ritual, returning to traditional values, manual labour and intellectual innocence in order to put an end to his old life and make a new start. However, his 'purgation' paradoxically, and typically of Šulík, begins with a fall into his grandfather's cesspool. Here we can perceive the old initiation genre and a direct influence of the broad stream of lyrical prose in Slovak inter-war literature, particularly the works of Dobroslav Chrobák, *Drak sa vracia* (*The Dragon Returns*) and František Švantner, *Nevesta hôľ* (*The Bride of Pastures*) who – like the Scandinavian or French Naturists – often drew on myth and its characteristic form marked with lyricism, advocating a departure from urban decadence and a return to the restorative power of nature. At the same time we can appreciate Šulík's need to make everything relative, humorous and distanced, in order to obscure the essence of his message in spontaneous humour and purifying self-irony.

Typical, in this respect, is the scene reminiscent of the quest for heritage in which Jakub, following his grandfather's old map, digs out a bottle of vintage plum schnapps. Paraphrasing the motifs of a fairy tale, after drinking it all, the director lets him listen to – and perhaps finally understand – the sounds of nature. The director treats in a similar way the bizarre initiation scenes of three master philosophers who take turns to visit the garden. Jakub, woken up by a flock of sheep, one of them eating his straw mattress, finds himself face to face with a shepherd, representing St Benedict (Ján Melkovič). The old man shakes his head with dissatisfaction over Jakub's inactivity. St Benedict, one of the founders of new European culture, is the symbol of activity, responsibility and humility: this particular place is the world you live in and you must cultivate it until your last days. When the intruder challenges him to wash his feet, he hesitates awhile and then crouches humbly to wash the shepherd's skinny feet covered with mud. The situation evoking the gospel ends in a small theft: on his departure, the shepherd steals a funnel from the windowsill and then, knocking over the fence and the natural borders of Jakub's world, walks away surrounded by sheep. The second spiritual visitor is Jean-Jacques Rousseau (Stanislav Štepka) – the philosopher's car goes out of control and hits Jakub's fence, interfering again with the borders of his world. Rousseau the sensualist, advocates a return to nature and innocence, invoking the forces that deny Descartes' reason and its influence on an increasingly alienated society. He tells Jakub about the destructive effects of progress and the beneficial bliss of poverty, but Jakub is unable to repair his old smashed car. Rousseau therefore transfers his noisy family to his Peugeot and sets off without thanking him. Only the third magus, Ludwig Wittgenstein (František Kovár), in the eyes of critics 'a prudent prophet of the future', offers Jakub a tempting choice. If he wants to get rid of the garden – and the path to knowledge studded with thorns that it brings – then his father, a real estate dealer in Vienna, can help him. Leaving the garden, he jumps over the fence – but thanks to the metaphorical comparison, he leaves the imaginary gate open. His gesture refers directly to the scene of Jakub's unnecessarily complicated entrance into the garden. The significance of all three characters from history is altered; the actors perform their roles with comic exaggeration. Despite a philosophical undertone, every line they say is immediately slapped down with a small gag or joke to avoid the thesis dominating. This produces a naïve philosophical tract that ironically reflects on our gloomy state of mind, but acquires a lightened expression of comedy through the counterpoint of jokes.

Thus the enclosed garden fulfils the model of an isolated idyllic place with reference to many cultural sources, including the Garden of Eden. Even in the mediaeval initiation *Roman de la Rose* by Guillaume de Lorris for instance, the garden is defined as the place (topos) of initiation, an inner space of genuine life. Yet it is a paradox that Jakub is not in fact initiated into inner life by any one of the masters, but by the third element of the initiation triad typical for a medieval initiation novel – the virgin, in this case 'the Miraculous Virgin', as the narrator calls Helena. The character of Helena is a direct descendent, an embodied archetype of all the mysterious, independent women behind the Marian tradition, the basis of the Slovak cultural context. Here we should mention the heroine of *Panna zázračnica* (*The Miraculous Virgin*), the story by Dominik Tatarka, the personified paradigm of Slovak surrealists, which was adapted for the screen by Štefan Uher in 1966.

The Miraculous Virgin, embodied by Zuzana Šulajová, looks like a frail girl with the confidence of a mature woman. She is the bearer of miracles, an intuitive guardian of purity and truth, the woman who opens the door to the magic of being for Jakub and accompanies him to the unexplored spontaneity of love. Jakub gradually begins to understand that the world is not a simple, easily recognisable machine operated by remote control. He begins to perceive it as a mystery in which the intuitive merges with the rational and the female principle interpenetrates the male. Helena is the personification of this mystery, a counterbalance to Tereza, a lustful woman shamelessly following Jakub to his exile.

The self-indulgent Tereza (Jana Švandová), a regular customer of Jakub's plump father (Marián Labuda) who makes his living as a dressmaker and platonically fulfils his dreams about beautiful women while trying on their clothes, seduces Jakub in the next room at the very beginning of the film. Their passionate lovemaking is interrupted when Jakub's father suddenly enters the room. This leads indirectly to Jakub's banishment from home. After Tereza's first visit to the garden, Jakub again succumbs to temptation and curiously measures her well-built body with a tape measure as he saw his father do. Then he gives her a lift and drops her at the bus stop, refusing intuitively to return to the town. Tereza, humiliated, provokes a new invasion. She quarrels with her rich husband in front of her children, to whom Jakub had sent a case of fruit. However, Jakub's life and attitudes have long changed and, without a twinkle in his eye, he denies any relationship with his wife to the saddened husband, refusing to become a public trophy of Tereza's fear of ageing. Yet what seems to be a flat lie becomes a metaphorical truth. Meanwhile Jakub has turned into someone else. He belongs to Helena, who remains hidden in the house.

Nevertheless, after the departure of his visitors, he finds the house deserted and looks for the Miraculous Virgin at her mother's. He discovers with horror that, as a result of his behaviour, she has been cursed with an unknown disease. He takes her lifeless body in his arms and carries her into the garden solitude to take care of her and redeem her with his dedication and suffering. This symbolic reference to fairy tale motifs is the test of Jakub's maturity, but redemption only comes in the guise of Jakub's old tomcat with the symbolic name Baruch (Spinoza); his presence cures Helena. Similar citations and layers of other semantic 'texts' penetrate *The Garden* and create an unrepeatable mosaic in the story, a polyphonic dialogue without hierarchy: a dialogue between the traditional and the modern, popular wisdom and philosophy, the empirical and the intellectual.

Initially, the main motif of Jakub's departure from town was his unwillingness to face problems, but in the garden he has to learn alone that every flight from problems is temporary. In fact, he is unable to completely banish his worries and they gradually return as unexpected encounters.

After Tereza and Helena's mother denounce Helena as completely mad, Jakub's unhappy father appears unexpectedly. He tries 'to bring his son to his senses' and to remind him of his duties at school; he is not at all interested in metaphysical problems, but instead he asks practical questions. A new conflict arises in a strangely nostalgic atmosphere amid memories of the grandfather. Jakub's father also goes through his first ritual purgation: they both shave each other's heads. Changing the appearance connected to their previous life, they experience the symbolic death that follows initiation, a transition to a new status quo and, at the same time, on the second plane of action, symbolically expose their minds in order to be reconciled. Critics agreed that their trip beyond the gates of the garden, ending on the neutral ground of a motel, may be the most beautiful sequence of the film: a short plump ageing dressmaker suddenly performs an animated dance to the rhythm of Latin American music. Yet complete reconciliation between father and son comes only on another visit, when he meets the Miraculous Virgin. Although Jakub's father puts on his boxing gloves, he merely feels obliged to 'awaken' his son with a straight punch; as soon as he remembers his own father he stops forcing him into anything. When Helena begins to feed the dressmaker with the symbolic bird's milk, a ritual change occurs, opening the way for him to initiation. This daily act again conceals a reference to Marian symbolism, connected with the topos of the garden, overshadowed by the evening scene of going to bed. This time the father measures Helena's supple young body in order to forget his age, yet in contrast to his son, he does not interfere in the relationship. The theme of the fear of transience and unfulfilled life pervades *The Garden* as its secondary motif.

Another characteristic motif connecting all three protagonists of Šulík's respective films is the generation gap. His heroes feel an urge to free themselves from their father's authority, to escape from everything it represents and simply 'roll away' as far as possible from the 'tree'. Only the reconciliation has a different quality in each of the three films. Although *Tenderness* began with the vapid statement: 'you beat your father', a precise laconic connection of words emphasising the physical aspect of the painful conflict between father and son, no solution was found. In *Everything I Like*, the conflict rather turns into emotional blackmailing and psychological pressure leading to mutual spiritual fatigue and disillusionment. In this film, however, the father/son conflict is extended to the triad grandfather/father/grandson. As a result, the protagonist acquires the knowledge that we often repeat the mistakes of our parents and in the process lose the thread of conversation with our own children.

In *The Garden* the conflict turns into a ridiculous 'fight' between father and son. It takes the form of a patient and gradual definition of the borders and rules of communication vital for good relationships. Grandfather's diary and the return of the grandson to a traditional life-style links Jakub with his father. He, too, ran away to the town, an act of defiance, to finally go through the ritual of initiation in his native garden, to reconcile and concede that 'everything is as it should be'. His final words, hanging in the air together with the levitating Miraculous Virgin, symbolise the return of order.

Marián Labuda, cast in the role of father, developed his comic acting to the point of blending contemporary genres and offers a deeply humane performance. His character is able to abandon his fatherly authority in favour of a balanced relationship with his son.

The reversed relationship between Helena and her mother, though merely outlined, forms a specific chapter in this film. Helena was born when her mother (Katarína Vrzalová) was in her fifties and therefore remains an accompaniment to her ageing: she shifts Helena to the social periphery and inspires the others to do so. This merely disguises her helplessness as a drinker unable and unwilling to take responsibility for someone else. Helena, much more mature in emotional relationships than her mother, is endowed with magic vitality and natural wisdom.

The stage of *The Garden* uses a minimum number of actors and following Šulík's experience in theatre direction, his films are never crowded with characters. Critics noticed that his characters are somewhat reminiscent of marionettes: as if they were unable to enter the conflict between their internal experience and external acting. A concise theme and focus on a small number of characters is quite common in theatre, and convention enables the main characters to resolve only those situations which are directly connected with the theme. Šulík tries not to expand the story of *The Garden*, concentrating as much as possible on its fictional core. Like Ingmar Bergman, he exploits a model dramatic composition: life penetrates into his films through actors, not through contemporary local colour. However, with Šulík, banal shifts in the everyday change into universal gestures of the grotesque.

The rhythm gradually slackens when Jakub begins to adapt to the pace of the idyllically enclosed garden and the meanings of individual encounters build up until time comes to a halt in the final scene showing Helena levitating. Under the influence of the unity of place, the borders of time diminish, creating an illusion that time passes in cycles. However, real time passes in nature: summer turns into autumn, the viewer can see the changes in the cycle of the seasons – instead of the sunny garden of 'paradise' and trees loaded with apples, the characters are suddenly surrounded by a grey and brown silence amidst bare tree trunks.

The director tells the stories of his films in long takes, which significantly influence their rhythm. The change of tempo and interference with their continuity through rhythmical division and splitting into images or chapters blurs the viewer's perception and disrupts his identification with the first plane of action. In contrast with commercial films, Šulík's features require the active participation of the viewer. In *The Garden*, the world of the viewer's experience and the linear spectacle are continuously intersected with metaphor, which evokes the inner continuity of communication and co-creates the viewer's mental perspective. Despite the broken narrative, the creation of a parallel 'initiatory' space enables the director to create the illusion of an independent world and provide the emotional intensity of co-experience. By means of double coding, he promotes the transference of ideas.

The palimpsest nature of Šulík's narrative in which original images show through the 'text', the toying with genres as well as double coding, and the parodic aspect of the narrative suggest a broader reference to postmodernist streams in world cinema. Nevertheless, Šulík's film is somehow much more playful and compassionate than the majority of films from the 1990s as if it was saying: if it is impossible to speak seriously, let us simply play…

The screenplay was written by the director in collaboration with Marek Leščák, a debut scriptwriter, who is credited with the poetic diction of this film. However, the final shape of the script was made in co-operation with Ondrej Šulaj, who also co-operated with Šulík on the scripts for *Tenderness* and *Everything I Like*. This shared experience enabled him to provide the screenplay with a much more consistent form and structure.

The stunning photography of Šulík's films is the work of Martin Štrba and a team of other regular collaborators. His sensitive shooting of the changeable light and dreamy moods of Indian summer in *The Garden* makes the film a tempting and visually appealing work. František Lipták, who also co-operated on Šulík's other features, designed the sets. Experienced in stage design, unlike other film architects, he always builds reality from the foundations. The hauntingly simple music, written by Vladimír Godár, is reminiscent of the tides of human life: tension alternates with relaxation, sounding like a child's violin practice. Often it suddenly subsides to give space to the sounds of nature. The soundtrack creates a compact emotive structure, providing the film with an overall integrity.

After the premiere of *The Garden* in 1995, the film gave rise to controversy and divided the public. Some maintained that the film was an end in itself and deliberately formalistic, like Šulík's later feature films *Orbis Pictus* (1997) and *Krajinka* (*Landscape*, 2000). Others welcomed it with enthusiasm, willing to accept Šulík's rules of the game or disregard the fact that he plays a game with the viewer. Critics appreciated Šulík's ability to create a unique narrative style and plot, emphasising the fact that he does not try to please the public by imitating blockbusters.

The film succeeds because it appeals to the viewer through presenting a universal problem and offering an archetypal model in which the traditional blends with the contemporary. It is this postmodernist inter-alliance, which most appeals to the public.

After the release of *The Garden* the situation became more complicated for other Slovak filmmakers reflecting the present. Many filmmakers from the late 1990s were labelled as merely followers of Šulík and were attacked by the critics. The reviewers forgot to realise that the hesitating, weak, always questing male characters of Slovak films are not just Šulík's discovery. If we leave aside the literary sources mentioned above and national classic literature, it is enough to mention *Ružové sny* (*Rose-Tinted Dreams*, 1976) or other films by the director Dušan Hanák, particularly his full-length documentary *Obrazy starého sveta* (*Pictures of the Old World*, 1972). Some of Hanák's heroes discovered the beauty of simple objects, rural mischief based on common sense, and mature humanity earlier in the 1960s and 1970s, long before the hero of *The Garden*. In the moral disintegration of that period, they concealed beneath the compliance and inactivity of men shaped by socialism, an empathy and eternal boyhood, though they were observers rather than actors in life.

This also provides the answer to what the 'gardens' of cinematic Slovakia are in reality; the gardens in which someone always continues the quest for himself. Their stories concern the individual character of the heroes as much as the national mentality in general. They do not merely reflect the atmosphere of the period, but conceal a national self-reflection and the need to continue traditions from a new perspective. Šulík tried to make *The Garden* a film which would be an essay about an escape from a destroyed environment, about defiance against everything that happens there. Although it is apparent that a return to nature is impossible because we cannot live without the achievements of civilisation, he succeeded in making a film which does not avoid reality but seeks a constructive and dignified way of survival. Šulík succeeds in making elements of the deepest subconscious visible by appealing to our inner world, and accentuating the values that strengthen human identity. He emphasises that man has to rely solely on his own resources rather than on institutions. The numerous prizes awarded to this 'lyrical comedy on the mysterious life in the garden' prove that it also appealed to audiences beyond the region of Central Europe.

Zuzana Gindl-Tatárová

Translated from the Slovak by Beata Havelská

BOLSE VITA BOLSHE VITA

IBOLYA FEKETE, HUNGARY/GERMANY, 1996

In the name of Truth I am willing to sacrifice beauty.

– Sándor Petőfi to János Arany, 1847

Bolse Vita (*Bolshe Vita*, 1995) belongs to a genre of its own: a postmodern collage of documentary and fiction, whose original vitality was confirmed by the international success of *Chico* (2001), director Ibolya Fekete's second feature film. Upon its release, *Bolshe Vita* made quite an impact worldwide, winning, among others, the prestigious Gene Moskowitz Foreign Critics' award. At a time when post-Communist cinema and societies were still in the grips of crises triggered by the transition to democracy and market economy, Fekete took festival audiences by surprise with her bold tackling of sociological issues, usually considered to be the domain of documentary cinema. Equally challenging was the audacity of the film's form and style, based on – or rather a fictionalised version of – Fekete's own two-part documentary, *Az Apokalipszis gyermekei* (*Children of Apocalypse*), released in 1992.

The generic roots of Fekete's style can be found in the Hungarian tradition of literary and cinematic 'sociography'. András Kovács – one of the masters of the Hungarian 'direct' cinema – admitted that sociographic literature or 'sociography', this typically Hungarian literary genre has determined to a large extent' his work in cinema, especially the 'form and style of *Nehéz emberek* [*Difficult People*, 1964]'. The sociological reportage – a mixture of documentary observation, confession, sociological document and *belle lettre* – was defined as the 'most impressive outcome of the *népi* (populist) writers' movement' from the 1930s, and the writers who 'cultivated this genre were called village explorers (*falukutatók*). The 'explosive popularity of Zoltán Szabó's *A tardi helyzet* (*The Situation at Tard*, 1936) describing the day-to-day existence of a village in the Mátra Mountains, together with the relevant sociological, historical, ethnographic and demographic background' prompted the literary series *Magyarország Felfedezése* (*The Discovery of Hungary*). Here is how Jósef Darvas formulates sociography:

It could be defined both as a documentary prose and a 'literature of fact', and yet it is something completely different. The raw actuality of life provides the material; the methodological approach is based on documentary contemplation and analytical conceptualisation, but the focus is on the social environment … Sounds like sociology? That too, but the method of reflection is predominantly literary, not scientific.

Inspired by landmark documentary works like *Difficult People* and under the pressure of students, who wanted to have a more substantial rapport with 'real' life, the Academy of Drama and Film in Budapest introduced an obligatory exam in documentary cinema for film production and cinematography students. The Béla Balázs Film Studio followed suit in 1969, and launched its five-year programme of sociological documentaries, like the famous *Nevelésügyi sorozat* (*Educational Series I–V*, 1973), directed by a collective of young directors, led by István Dárday.

A package of fictionalised documentaries (known in Hungary as documentary-fiction or DF) also emerged at that time, most notably Gyula Gazdag's *A Sípoló macskakö* (*The Whistling Cobblestone*, 1971) and Pál Zolnay's *Fotográfia* (*Photography*, 1972), followed by István Dárday's *Jutalomutazás* (*The Prize Trap* aka *Holiday in Britain* (1974) and Béla Tarr's *Családi tűzfészek* (*Family Wasp's Nest* aka *Family Nest*, 1977). The DF aesthetics can roughly be defined as structuring footage, shot in a rough documentary manner according to the laws of narrative fiction, and featuring amateur actors or simply workers or peasants in their everyday environment.

In spite of its inherent iconoclastic impetus, sociographic cinema evolved relatively undisturbed into the 1980s. The high professionalism of Hungarian filmmakers and their strong social awareness played a key role in the long-standing compromise they reached with the authorities, known as 'goulash Communism' or 'Kádárism' after János Kádár, Hungary's long standing Communist leader (1956–88). His famous slogan, 'Who is not against us, is with us', came to play a decisive role in the ongoing negotiation and re-negotiation of artistic freedom after the national uprising of 1956. As a result, a loose unspoken consensus ensued: filmmakers were not to discuss taboo subjects such as the Hungarian revolution, the role of the Soviet Union or the leading role of the Communist Party, and they would be left more or less to their conscience and talent.

The sociographic films remained little known outside of Hungary as it was difficult for an outsider to pick up the subtleties, and this was a good reason why such a close and frank look at the raw actuality of 'real socialism' was allowed to persist under the nose of authorities. Even Béla Tarr, currently enjoying a near cult-status in the West, was just an obscure name until *Öszi almanach* (*Autumn Almanac*, 1984) and especially *Kárhozat* (*Damnation*, 1988) – works of sophisticated psychological symbolism, significantly removed from the docu-dramatic roughness of his first films – propelled him into fame. Western audiences did welcome Márta Mészáros's films from the 1970s as her feminist stance, knowable social issues and professional actors reduced the cultural barrier.

With its organic fusion of fictitious narrative and authentic, documentary look at people and cultures in the brief moments of hope, spanning the euphoric upheaval after the collapse of Communism and the dawning era of new disappointments, *Bolshe Vita* fits comfortably into Jósef Darvas' description of literary sociography as creative eclecticism, defined nowadays as a postmodern collage. It is also related to the ideological and aesthetic iconoclasm of Béla Tarr and Pál Erdöss who took the DF aesthetics one step further with their films from the early 1980s (*Panelkapcsolat/Prefab People*, 1982, and *Adj király katonát/The Princess*, 1982, respectively), blending professional and non-professional actors in improvised, real-life situations. Most of Fekete's characters play the roles they perform in real life, but follow a meticulously, even geometrically organised script based on her documentary *Children of the Apocalypse*.

Fekete's vision is fundamentally *chronotopic*, in Mikhail Bakhtin' terms, where time and space are intrinsically connected and 'definite and absolute concrete localities serve as the starting point of creative imagination'. True to the unprejudiced historical approach of sociography, she examines her selected *chronotopes* along three well-informed paths of analysis, which merge time and space into a single geographical, socio-political and psychological unity. The current study therefore consists of three parts, prompted by the three aspects of this unity: from a wide angle panorama of East Central Europe on the move, outlining the outer limits of the endemic 'Post-Communist Pilgrimage of Hope', Fekete zooms in on Hungary and Budapest to reveal 'the Topography of Social Change', and through the destinies of half a dozen people, shaped directly by the evolving events, she sketches a precise 'Socio-Psychological Typology of the Post-Communist Transition'.

The opening credits of *Bolshe Vita* roll on two men, one tall one short, staring at the ocean, fantasising about life in the West but leisurely concluding that if they go further East they would end up in the West, and vice versa. The subtitles identify the harbour as Vladivostok, a Russian city on the Pacific, the tall man is Vadim (Igor Csernyevics) and the short one is Yura (Yuri Fomichyov as himself). In the light of the ensuing images and events, their conversation transcends the above topographical truism, and acquires the ethical and philosophical dimensions of an epigraph to the film.

The subsequent montage episode immerses the viewer in the volatile atmosphere of a turbulent 1989. The voiceover steers us through the ups and downs of 'the short but memorable period when East Europe was happy': the storming of the Austro-Hungarian border by German tourists in their Trabis, the riot police and water cannon unleashed on demonstrators in Prague and the Romanian street riots in Tirgu-Mures. The celebratory mood in the streets of Budapest is captured in the words of a popular song, chanted by the crowds: 'We have had enough of the "temporary occupation" of our country … of not owning our own country … of being the "happiest barrack" of the Socialist camp.' The archival video footage is followed by excerpts from Fekete's own *Children of the Apocalypse*, featuring huge line-ups of Eastern European fortune-seekers at the main check-points on the westbound roads of Hungary. A shell of a solitary Trabant, rotting alongside the Hungarian-Austrian border stands as a solitary monument to the downfall of Communism, marking the site where the first hole in the formidable Iron Curtain was punctured. It could also be seen as a nostalgic reminder of the cheap, but secure socialist comfort, which, as we shall see, many would soon come to lament.

Catapulted by the energy of those memorable events, the narrative begins to take shape, outlining in subtitles the diegetic time and space. It is at the 'Soviet-Hungarian Border, 1990', where we catch up with the westward-bound Vadim and Yura. A guitarist and a saxophone player, they are the only musicians of 'Trio Fomich', an ill-designed cover for a ragbag group of young men trying to get into Yugoslavia via Hungary. Impressed by the Hungarian countryside, the charmingly inexperienced Yura is surprised to hear that Hungary is just another socialist country. The 'tour' bus is turned back first at the Czechoslovakian-Hungarian and then at the Hungarian-Yugoslav border, where the Yugoslav guards remain unimpressed by the presented touring 'contract'. At that point Yura decides he has 'already arrived' in the West, and Vadim, in truly Brechtian manner, turns to the camera and announces that they 'spat on the collective and left'. Next we see them in Budapest, playing in the streets and enjoying spring and freedom, oscillating between two centres of power – Western Europe and the Soviet Union – and their competing poles of attraction.

At that point the third principal character makes his appearance. The subtitles introduce him as 'Sergei' (Aleksei Serebryakov), and inform us that he 'has got knives'. Soon this ominous statement is demystified, and we learn that Sergei is a mechanical engineer, also on his way to Yugoslavia, hoping to sell his kitchen knives in Hungary to pay his passage to the 'real' West.

The three Soviet Russians, once feared and resented and now mere asylum claimants seekers meet at Erzsi's (Agnes Mahr), a former teacher of Russian, who survives by running a crowded bed and breakfast and helping illegal Russian immigrants. The intertextual reference to István Szabó's poignant drama *Édes Emma, drága Böbe vázlatok, aktok* (*Sweet Emma, Dear Böbe*, 1992), represents yet another postmodern distancing device, undermining the illusion of reality. By contrasting Erzsi's down-to-earth practical sanguinity to the dismal failure of Szabó's heroines to fit into the brutal post-Communist reality, the film demonstrates the explanatory advantages of sociographic observation *vis-à-vis* the metaphorical extrapolations of classical tragedy.

In 'Crossroads at Erszi's', one of the twelve titled episodes, the Russians meet with Maggie (Helen Baxendale), a teacher of English from the UK and later with her room-mate Susan (Caroline Loncq), a Texan. Both have ended up in Hungary where all the excitement is. Predictably, Yura and Maggie fall for each other, and so do Vadim and Susan, albeit briefly. Although Susan believes that 'freedom is a state of mind' and one does not have to move in space to feel free, she extends her pilgrimage even further East, chasing the elusive spectre of excitement as far as Moscow and Tashkent. Similarly (or symmetrically), Sergei overcomes his attraction to Erzsi and, ignoring her feelings and sensible advice, continues further West determined 'not to stop half way' and to test 'his limits'. Unfortunately, his aspirations are frustrated in a most humiliating manner at the Hungarian-Austrian Border. It is impossible to overestimate the meaning of this final border episode: the Eastern European 'Pilgrimage of Hope' has come full circle, making it painfully clear that the New Europe is not much different from the old one.

Paradoxically, only Yura, who is perfectly happy in Budapest, ends up in the 'real' West as Maggie gets pregnant and they move to the UK as a married couple. Although prone to flamboyant bouts of nostalgia as the episode titled 'Russia is Big' shows, the quiet Vadim practices what Susan preaches, and finds solace in his internal pilgrimage towards the meaning of life and perfection in art. Significantly, the film closes with snap-shots of a somewhat solemn-looking Yura and Maggie with their little girl, taken on a Brighton beach on a dark autumn day.

The trajectory of the post-Communist 'Pilgrimage of Hope', oscillating between the geographical home and the desired one 'where the heart is', allows Fekete, as Catherine Portuges has elegantly put it, to 'slyly challenge national and cultural stereotypes: Russians speak of Hungarians in much the same way that Hungarians speak of the West, alluding to Budapest's reputation under state socialism as the "Paris of the East" ... The issue of shifting Russian identity is addressed through repeated references to Russia as misinterpreted and unappreciated, its image at odds with the reality of modern Russian life'. The pilgrimage of Yura, Vadim and

Sergei, on the other hand, is 'symbolic of the desire to escape from the violence – at once physical and cultural – that has become a part of that reality'.

The film's second trajectory is socio-political, highlighting the flea market and the night rock-club Bolse Vita as *chronotopes* of Social Change, encapsulating the drama of the rise and fall of post-Communist expectations. True to the iconoclastic legacy of sociographic literature and cinema, Fekete challenges the enthusiasm of neophyte laissez-fairists, and exposes in a concise manner the anti-social logic of the market institution and its damaging effect on the unprotected society. This layer of 'analytical conceptualisation' is undoubtedly influenced by the versatile Hungarian school of social and political thought, known in the late 1970s and early 1980s for its merciless scientific exposure of the totalitarian mechanism and its detrimental effect on society. Building on the revolutionary work *The Great Transformation* (1944) by the renowned social philosopher Karl Polanyi, Hungarians were amongst the first to warn of the dangers of laissez-fairism in the late 1980s and early 1990s. The intrinsic links of literary sociography to the social sciences is confirmed most eloquently by the fact that Polanyi also co-edited *The Plough and the Pen: Writings from Hungary* (1930–56), one of the first representative collections of sociographic work to be published in English.

The market place *chronotope* might as well be inspired by Polanyi's opus, privileging the socially benign 'market pattern … of barter, truck and exchange' over the aggressive institution of the so-called 'self-regulating' market. The huge sun-lit space is a kind of post-Communist – kinder and gentler – common market. Dominated by a friendly spirit, the market reminds one of Bakhtin's idea of the *carnivalesque* as a popular opposition to officialdom. Indeed, in spite of officially-declared divisive allegiances, Yugoslavs, Poles, Russians, Vietnamese and Hungarians seem to enjoy sharing and mingling more for the sake of socialising than for turning a profit.

During the second act the atmosphere is still friendly and Sergei receives a beautiful Ukrainian farewell song for the road to Yugoslavia, but a few thugs are already lurking ominously in the crowd. If we are to refer to Polanyi again, the logic of the 'market pattern' that ignores 'social relations' leads to 'running the society as an adjunct to the market'. In other words, whoever controls the market, controls society. In the social, political and moral interregnum of the early post-Communist transition, the controlling body seems to be that of organised crime, or the so-called Mafia.

In tune with the rules of classical dramaturgy, the plot thickens in the brief third act with the arrival of a young Mafioso, a squat man with a heavy look (Eduardo Rózsa Flores who would make his major appearance as Chico in Fekete's second film). Informed by the thugs at the gate that the market is 'no one's', he declares himself its Master without even getting out of his chauffeured limousine.

The fourth act shows the Mafiosi in action, 'encouraging' the spontaneity of laissez-faire initiative through extortion, beatings and terror. Through the eyes of Sergei who has just returned from his ill-fated journey to the Hungarian-Austrian border, it becomes clear that the self-proclaimed Master is already trading in dangerous, radioactive 'stuff', and Sergei's friend, the adventurous and wisecracking Correspondent (Leonid Maximov) is unceremoniously chased out for being too intelligent for the Mafiosi's taste.

In an eloquent demonstration of the market economy's dire logic, the Mafiosi – in an attempt to tighten control – take over the deserted Soviet Army barracks and the market place drama culminates in Sergei's death from the Mafiosi's bullets.

Fekete's Bolse Vita *chronotope* represents, in Bakhtin's terms, another 'piece of human history, historical time condensed into space', following a dramaturgical pattern similar to that of the market, and founding its analytical conceptualisations on what Polanyi calls 'protective movements of society' against the 'onslaught of the market'.

Introduced much later into the film, the bar – whose title name reflects *l'air du temps*, referring simultaneously to the ominous Bolshevik party of Lenin and to Federico Fellini's 1964 masterpiece *La Dolce Vita* (or *Sweet Life*) – is a happy place. Patrons drink and discuss loudly the present and future of the New Europe in German, Serbo-Croat, English and Hungarian. And the statement about 'broken down societies' and the 'absence of civil societies in this region', made by a German journalist for the camera, rings false and pseudo-scientifically pretentious against the complexity of real life we have witnessed so far. As usual, it is well off the mark, reflecting the resilient East/West cultural divide that would keep lingering on long after the Iron Curtain is forgotten.

The second bar episode is transitional, signalling a turning point in the lives of the personages and in the film's mood – from romantic euphoria to mundane realism. Susan shows up in Bolse Vita to inform the heartbroken Vadim she is getting married in Tashkent; Maggie and Yura are already planning their future with the baby; and shortly after the embarrassed Sergei will return to Erszi, and she will let him stay but only 'on her terms'.

The 'short but memorable period when East Europe was happy' comes to a sad end in the third bar episode, as patrons are terrorised by the already familiar Russian thugs. Yura is assaulted on grounds of 'principle' for entertaining 'undeserving foreigners' with his Russian ballads – a preview of the chauvinist xenophobia and aggressive intolerance that were soon to plague parts of the region. The last Bolse Vita episode merges time and space into the image of a menacing-looking mugger replacing the front sign 'Bolse Vita' with a poisonous-pink 'Sex Shop', epitomising the triumph of the predatory laws of marketised pornography over freedom of cultural exchange, thus bringing up to date our contemplation on the future of post-Communist Europe. This episode is also transitional, marking the beginning of the film's dramatic finale.

As a fitting conclusion to this study, the third and final trajectory of *Bolshe Vita* outlines a brief 'Socio-Psychological Typology of the Post-Communist Transition'. True to the spirit of the 'psychological authenticity' of István Dárday, one of the founders of sociographic cinema and producer of *Bolshe Vita*, this trajectory links the texture of everyday experience to C. G. Jung's analytical psychology of archetypes. The three principal personages represent a post-modern triptych of the hero archetype in its classic (Sergei), romantic (Yura) and existential (Vadim) variations, where the 'Pilgrimage of Hope' can be read as a serendipitous quest for self-actualisation. Fittingly for a specialist in Russian literature – Fekete's original profession – the heroes are linked intertextually to forms of dissent in Soviet art: Sergei's dramatic hero, for example, comes straight from the literature and film of the thaw in the 1960s, where his likes met self-sacrificial ends in the name of principle rather than motherland. The flamboyant extrovert Yura is a 'bard', also related to the 1960s by way of his profession – a singer with a guitar who lives off and for the artistic appreciation of his underground verse. The phlegmatic introvert Vadim is a jazz-playing saxophonist, which in itself amounted to ideological misde-meanour in Soviet times.

Erszi's intertextual cinematic and social lineage was mentioned above, while Maggie and Susan belong to the most popular Western female types that used to 'wash up' on those shores – a teacher of English and an adventurer. Albeit on the move and equally unsettled, they repre-sent points of stability, activating the archetypal notions of family, romantic love and home.

The six of them eagerly respond to the call to adventure, which draws them, in Joseph Campbell's terms, 'into a relationship with forces that are not rightly understood' and there-fore frustrating. Once having 'traversed the threshold' of the Western borders of their country, the three Russians undergo trials of initiation 'through the grace' of the three women. In a feminist twist, instead of continuing on their own towards the triumphant return, the men become increasingly dependant on them. Once left to his own devices, Sergei's quest stalls at the threshold of the new life and his senseless death in the barracks' inner yard symbolises the futility of the dramatic Hero's quest for the Brave New World. Albeit Yura's quest seems to have ended with his 'return' to Brighton with Maggie, its challenging continuation is captured in the second part of *Children of the Apocalypse*. 'Through the grace' of his patient and loving (real life) Maggie, Yura continues to chase the spectre of artistic fulfilment in the West.

After the departure of Susan and Yura, Vadim withdraws even deeper into his music, and the last glimpse of him is playing a sad piece on the bank of an unidentified river – the Volga, or the Danube or maybe the mythical Styx. It is a most fitting backdrop for the final collage of disturbing documentary footage from the first Bosnian war and Sarajevo.

The Correspondent is the only one to return from the westbound quest with the life-altering wisdom (or disillusionment) of what the Brave New World is all about. A secondary personage and an ambivalent Trickster figure, he leaves for St Petersburg minutes before the bullets that kill Sergei start flying. The place of the Hero – tragic, existential or romantic – is gradually arrogated in literature and film by the postmodern Trickster, born in the no-man's-land between Communism and post-Communism.

The camerawork of the final part of *Bolshe Vita* evokes the films of György Somjas and Ferenc Grunwalsky, with whom Fekete had worked in the late 1980s, where cinematic sociography became a 'realism of the extremes'. Jean-Pierre Jeancolas described them as '*films noirs* in the French sense of the term, implying violence … and a tragic end', a cinema related to the fatalistic vision of the French films made on the eve of the Second World War.

The last images we see are of Albanian refugees pleading with Hungarian border guards not to send them back, clinging to them with the words 'you are our West'. The quest for the mythic West continues.

Christina Stojanova

REFERENCES

Bakhtin, Mikhail (1990) *Speech Genres and Other Late Essays*. Austin: University of Texas Press, Slavic Series, no. 8.

Campbell, Joseph (1949) *The Hero with a Thousand Faces*. New York: Princeton University Press.

Jeancolas, Jean-Pierre (2001) *L'oeil hongrois: Quatre décennies de cinema à Budapest 1963–2000*. Budapest: Magyar Filmunió.

Polanyi, Karl (1944) *The Great Transformation*. Boston: Beacon Press.

Portuges, Catherine (1997) '*Bolse Vita*', *The American Historical Review*, 102, 3, 938–40.

FILMOGRAPHY

HEJ-RUP! HEAVE-HO! 1934
Czechoslovakia
Production Company: Meissnerfilm (Prague)
Director: Martin Frič
Screenplay: F. Formen (=Jiří Voskovec, Jan Werich, Václav Wasserman, Martin Frič)
Photography: Otto Heller (b& w)
Editing: Martin Frič
Music: Jaroslav Ježek
Art Direction: Arnold Reiman
Set Decoration: Guido Lagus, Rudolf Wels
Sound: Bedřich Polednik
Producer: František Jerhot
Cast: Jiří Voskovec (Filip Kornet), Jan Werich (Jakub Simonides), Helena Bušová (Marta), Josef Skřivan (Mr. Worst), Theodor Pištěk (Mr. Brown), Zvonimir Rogoz, Alois Dvorský (Philatelist), Václav Trégl, František Černy, Miroslav Svoboda, Jan W. Speerger, Jan Richter, František Filipovský, Bohuš Záhorský, Filip Balek-Brodský, Jiří Hron, Jaroslav Průcha (Newscaster), František Paul, Alexander Třebovský, Ferdinand Hart, Jaroslav Bráška, Miloš Šubrt, Anna Švarcová (Kateřina, doss-house keeper).
Running time: 104'

DER DIBUK THE DYBBUK 1937
Poland
Production Company: Phoeniks Film
Director: Michał Waszyński
Screenplay: Alter Kacyzne and Mark Arnstein from Solomon Ansky's play *The Dybbuk* or *Between Two Worlds*
Photography: Albert Wywerka (b&w)
Music: Henikh Kahn
Ritual songs: Gershon Sirota
Art Direction: Jacek Rotmil and Stefan Norris
Choreography: Judith Berg
Producer: Ludwig Prywes
Cast: Lili Liliana (Leah), Leon Liebgold (Khonon), Gershon Lamberger (Nissen), Moyshe Lipman (Sender), Avram Morevsky (tsaddik from Miropolye), Isaac Samberg (Messenger), Dina Halpern (Freyde), Max Bozyk (Nute), Shmuel Landau (Zalmen), David Lederman (Meyer), Samuel Branecki (Najhman), M. Messinger (Menashe)
Running time: 125'

EMBEREK A HAVASON PEOPLE OF THE MOUNTAINS 1942
Hungary
Production Company: Modern Film Kft, Hunnia Studio, Budapest.
Director: István Szőts
Screenplay: Jószef Nyírő, István Szőts (from the collected stories *Kopjafák* by Nyírő)
Photography: Ferenc Fekete (b&w)
Editing: Zoltán Kerényi.

Music: Ferenc Farkas.

Art Direction: Imre Sorés.

Sound: Ferenc Lohr.

Assistant Director: Mihály Morrell.

Production Manager: Pál Siklóssy

Cast: Alice Szellay (Anna), János Görbe (Gergő Csutak Erdei), Ferenc Péterke (Gergő, their son), József Bihari (Márton Üdő), János Makláry (conductor), Lenke Egyed (landlady), Lajos Gárday (Ádám Ülkei),Oszkár Borovsky (steward), Imre Toronyi (doctor), György Kürthy (medical professor), János Pásztor, Elemer Baló, Jenő Danis (woodcutters), Sándor Hidassy, László Misoga, Endre C. Turáni, Nándor Bihary (train passengers).

Running time: 103'

DALEKÁ CESTA DISTANT JOURNEY 1949

Czechoslovakia

Production Company: Československý státní film (Czechoslovak State Film) [Production team Řezáč-Fábera-Šmída]

Director: Alfréd Radok

Screenplay: Mojmír Drvota, Erik Kolár, Alfréd Radok, based on Erik Kolár

Photography: Josef Střecha (b&w)

Editing: Jiřina Lukešová

Music: Jiří Sternwald

Art Direction: Jan Pacák

Set Design: František Tröster

Costume Design: František Mádl, Jan Kropáček

Sound: Josef Vlček

Production supervisors: Bohumil Šmída, Miloš Mastník

Cast: Blanka Waleská (Dr. Hana Kaufmannová), Otomar Krejča (Dr. Antonín Bureš), Viktor Očásek (Oskar Kaufmann), Zdeňka Baldová (Hedvika Kaufmannová), Eduard Kohout (Professor Reiter), J.O. Martin (Rudolf Bureš), Josef Chvalina (Pepa Bureš), Anna Vaňková (Margit), Jiří Plachý (Abrahamovič), Saša Rašilov (Mošeles), Jiří Spirit (Honzík Kaufmann), Rudolf Deyl junior (Jarda Noha).

Running time: 108'

EROICA 1958

Poland

Production Company: Film Polski ZAF 'Kadr' (Łódź) / WFD (Warsaw)

Director: Andrzej Munk

Screenplay: Jerzy Stefan Stawiński, based on his short stories *Węgrzy* (*The Hungarians*) and *Ucieczka* (*Escape*)

Photography: Jerzy Wójcik (b&w)

Editing: Jadwiga Zajiczek, Mirosława Garlicka

Music: Jan Krenz

Art Direction: Jan Grandys, Zdzisław Kielanowski

Sound: Bohdan Jankowski

Producer: Stanisław Adler

Cast: *Scherzo alla polacca*: Edward Dziewoński (Dzidziuś Górkiewicz), Barbara Połomska (Zosia Górkiewicz), Ignacy Machowski (Major Grzmet), Leon Niemczyk (Hungarian officer), Kazimierz Opaliński (Commander of Mokotów); *Ostinato lugubre*: Kazimierz Rudzki (Lieutenant Turek), Henryk Bąk (Lieutenant Krygier), Mariusz Dmochowski (Lieutenant Korwin-Makowski), Roman Kłosowski (Szpakowski), Bogumił Kobiela (Lieutenant Dąbecki), Józef Kostecki (Lieutenant Żak), Tadeusz Łomnicki (Lieutenant Zawistowski), Józef Nowak (Lieutenant Kurzawa), Wojciech Siemion (Lieutenant Marianek)

Running time: 87'

POPIÓŁ I DIAMENT ASHES AND DIAMONDS 1958

Poland

Production Companies: ZAF 'Kadr' at WFF 1 (Łódź), WFF 2 (Wrocław)

Director: Andrzej Wajda

Screenplay: Andrzej Wajda and Jerzy Andrzejewski, from the novel by Jerzy Andrzejewski

Photography: Jerzy Wójcik (b&w)

Editing: Halina Nawrocka

Music: Jan Krenz, Michal Kleofas Ogiński (*Polonez*)

Art Direction: Roman Mann

Sound: Bogdan Bieńkowski

Producer: Stanisław Adler

Cast: Zbigniew Cybulski (Maciek Chełmicki), Ewa Krzyżewska (Krystyna), Wacław Zastrżeżyński (Szczuka), Adam Pawlikowski (Andrzej), Bogumił Kobiela (Drewnowski), Jan Ciercierski (porter), Stanisław Milski (Pieniążek), Artur Młodnicki (Kotowicz), Halina Kwiatkowska (Mrs Staniewicz), Ignacy Machowski (Waga), Zbigniew Skowroński (Słomka), Barbara Kraftówna (Stefka), Irena Orzecka (Grandmother Jurgiełuszka), Aleksander Sewruk (Swięcki), Józef Pieracki, Mieczysław Łoza, Tadeusz Kalinowski, Zofia Czerwińska, Grażyna Staniszewska.

Running time: 108'

NÓŻ W WODZIE KNIFE IN THE WATER 1962

Poland

Production Company: ZRF Zespół 'Kamera', WFF Łódź

Director: Roman Polański

Screenplay: Roman Polański, Jerzy Skolimowski, Jakub Goldberg

Photography: Jerzy Lipman (b&w)

Editing: Halina Prugar

Music: Krzysztof Komeda-Trzciński

Art Direction: Bolesław Kaykowski

Sound: Halina Paszkowska

Producer: Stanisław Zylewicz

Cast: Jolanta Umecka (voice of Anna Ciepielewska) (Krystyna), Zygmunt Malanowicz (voice of Roman Polański) (Hitchhiker), Leon Niemczyk (Andrzej)

Running time: 94'

RĘKOPIS ZNALEZIONY W SARAGOSSIE THE SARAGOSSA MANUSCRIPT 1964

Poland

Production Company: Zespol filmowy 'Kamera', Film Polski, WFF Wrocław, WFF Łódź

Director: Wojciech Jerzy Has

Screenplay: Tadeusz Kwiatkowski, from the novel by Jan Potocki

Photography: Mieczysław Jahoda (b&w)

Music: Krzysztof Penderecki

Art Direction: Jerzy Skarżyński and Tadeusz Myszorek

Sound: Bogdan Bieńkowski

Cast: Zbigniew Cybulski (Alphonse Van Worden), Kazimierz Opaliński (Hermit), Iga Cęmbrzyńska (Princess Emina), Joanna Jędryka (Princess Zibelda), Franciszek Pieczka (Pascheco), Adam Pawlikowski (Cabbalist), Gustav Holoubek (Velasquez), Beata Tyskiewicz (Rebecca), Bogumił Kobiela (Toledo)

Running time: 179'

OBCHOD NA KORZE A SHOP ON THE HIGH STREET 1965
Czechoslovakia
Production Company: Film Studio Barrandov, Prague (Production Group Feix-Brož)
Directors: Ján Kadár and Elmar Klos
Screenplay: Ladislav Grosman, Ján Kadár, and Elmar Klos, based on the novel by Ladislav Grosman
Photography: Vladimír Novotný (b&w)
Editing: Jaromír Janáček
Music: Zdeněk Liška
Sound: Dobroslav Šrámek
Executive Producer: Ladislav Hanuš
Cast: Ida Kamińska (Rozália Lautmannová), Jozef Kroner (Tóno Brtko), František Zvarík (Kolkocký), Hana Slivková (Evelyna), Martin Hollý senior (Kuchár), Elena Zvaríková-Pappová (Ružena), Martin Gregor (barber).
Running time: 120'

ZSEGÉNYLEGÉNYEK THE ROUND UP 1965
Hungary
Production Company: Mafilm (Studio IV)
Director: Miklós Jancsó
Screenplay: Gyula Hernádi
Photography: Tamás Somló (b&w)
Editing: Zoltán Farkas
Music: (none)
Art Direction: Tamás Banovich
Cast: János Görbe (János Gajdor), Zoltán Latinovits (Veszelka/gendarme), Tibor Molnár (Lovas-Kabai sen.), András Kozák (Lovas-Kabai jun.), Gábor Agárdy (Torma), János Koltai (Béla Varju), Géza Tordy (officer), István Avar, Lajos Öze, Rudolf Somogyváry, György Bárdy, Zsigmond Fülöp (investigators)
Running time: 95'

OSTŘE SLEDOVANÉ VLAKY CLOSELY OBSERVED TRAINS 1966
Czechoslovakia
Production Company: Film Studio Barrandov (Production Group Bohumil Šmida-Ladislav Fikar)
Director: Jiří Menzel
Screenplay: Bohumil Hrabal and Jiří Menzel, from the novel by Bohumil Hrabal
Photography: Jaromír Šofr (b&w)
Editing: Jiřina Lukešová
Music: Jiří Sust
Art Direction: Oldřich Bosak
Sound: Jiří Pavlík
Producer: Zdeněk Oves
Cast: Václav Neckář (Miloš Hrma), Josef Somr (Hubička), Vladimír Valenta (stationmaster), Vlastimil Brodský (Zednìček), Jitka Bendová (Maša), Jitka Zelenohorská (Zdenička Svatá), Libuše Havelková (stationmaster's wife), Ferdinand Krůta (Uncle Noneman), Květa Fialová (countess), Naďa Urbanková (Viktoria Freie), Jiří Menzel (Dr. Brabec)
Running time: 92'

SEDMIKRÁSKY DAISIES 1966
Czechoslovakia
Production Company: Film Studio Barrandov, Prague (Production Group Bohumil Šmida-Ladislav Fikar)
Director: Věra Chytilová
Screenplay: Věra Chytilová and Ester Krumbachová, from a story by Pavel Juráček
Photography: Jaroslav Kučera (c)
Editing: Miroslav Hájek
Music: Jiří Šlitr, Jiří Šust
Art Direction: Karel Lier
Costume Design: Ester Krumbachová
Sound: Ladislav Hausdorf
Artistic collaboration: Ester Krumbachová, Jaroslav Kučera
Cast: Jitka Čerhová (Marie 1), Ivana Karbanová (Marie II), Jan Klusák (man with the butterfly collection), Julius Albert (elderly 'playboy'), Marie Češková, Jiřina Myšková, Marcela Březinová, Oldřich Hora, Václav Chochola, Josef Koníček, Jaromír Vomáčka.
Running time: 75'

O SLAVNOSTI A HOSTECH THE PARTY AND THE GUESTS 1966
Czechoslovakia
Production Company: Film Studio Barrandov (Production Group Erich Švabík-Jan Procházka)
Director: Jan Němec
Screenplay: Ester Krumbachová and Jan Němec
Photography: Jaromír Šofr (b&w)
Editing: Miroslav Hájek
Music: Karel Mareš
Art Direction: Oldřich Bosák
Costume Design: Ester Krumbachová
Sound: Jiří Pavlík
Production Manager: Ladislav Kalaš
Cast: Ivan Vyskočil (The Host), Jan Klusák (Rudolf), Jiří Němec (Josef), Zdena Škvorecká (Eva), Pavel Bošek (František), Karel Mareš (Karel), Evald Schorm (The Husband), Jana Prachařová (The Wife), Helena Pejsková (Marta).
Running time: 70'

MARKETA LAZAROVÁ 1967
Czechoslovakia
Production Company: Film Studio Barrandov (Production Group Erich Švabík-Jan Procházka)
Director: František Vláčil
Screenplay: František Pavlíček and František Vláčil, from the novel by Vladislav Vančura
Photography: Bedřich Baťka (b&w)
Editing: Miroslav Hájek
Music: Zdeněk Liška
Art Direction: Oldřich Okáč
Artistic collaboration: Theodor Pištěk, Jan Koblasa, Zbyněk Sekal, Jaroslav Vožniak, Miloslav Hotový
Sound: František Fabián
Cast: Josef Kemr (Old Kozlík), František Velecký (Mikoláš), Magda Vašáryová (Marketa), Ivan Palúch (Adam), Pavla Polášková (Alexandra), Michal Kožuch (Lazar), Vladimír Menšík (Bernard), Zdeněk Kryzánek (Pivo), Vlastimil Harapes (Kristián), Harry Studt (Old Kristián)
Running time: 162'

VTÁČKOVA, SIROTY A BLÁZNI BIRDS, ORPHANS AND FOOLS 1969

Czechoslovakia / France

Production company: Štúdio hraných filmov Bratislava-Koliba (Production Group Albert Marenčin - Karol Bakoš) /
COMO Film (Paris)

Director: Juraj Jakubisko

Screenplay: Karol Sidon and Juraj Jakubisko from a story by Karol Sidon

Photography: Igor Luther (c)

Editing: Maximilián Remeň and Bob Wade

Music: Zdeněk Liška

Set Design: Anton Krajčovič

Costume Design: Helena Anýžová

Sound: Alexander Pallós

Producer: Samy Halfon

Executive Producers: Ján Svikruha and Ján Tomaškovič

Cast: Philippe Avron (Andrej), Jiří Sýkora (Yorick), Magda Vašáryová (Marta), Mila Beran (Landlord), Françoise
Goldité (Sasha), Mikuláš Ladižinský (Partisan), Augustin Kubán (Sailor).

Running time: 82'

SZERELEM LOVE 1971

Hungary

Production Company: Mafilm Studio 1

Director: Károly Makk

Screenplay: Tibor Déry, based on his two stories *Két asszonyok* (*Two Women*) and *Szerelem* (*Love*)

Photography: János Tóth (b&w)

Editing: György Sivó

Music: András Mihály

Art Direction: József Romváry

Sound: János Réti

Costumes: Piroska Katona

Dramaturg: Péter Bacsó

Producer: Lajos Gulyás

Cast: Lili Darvas (The Old Lady), Mari Törőcsik (Luca), Iván Darvas (János).

Running time: 92'

CZŁOWIEK Z MARMURU MAN OF MARBLE 1977

Poland

Production Company: PRF Zepoły filmowe and Zespól filmowy 'X'

Director: Andrzej Wajda

Screenplay: Aleksander Ścibor-Rylski

Photography: Edward Kłosiński (c)

Editing: Halina Prugar

Music: Andrzej Korzyński

Art Direction: Allan Starski

Sound: Piotr Zawadzki

Producer: Barbara Pec-Ślesicka

Cast: Jerzy Radziwiłowicz (Mateusz Birkut), Krystyna Janda (Agnieszka), Tadeusz Łomnicki (Burski), Jacek Łomnicki
(Young Burski), Michał Tarkowski (Witek), Piotr Cieślak (Michalak), Wiesław Wójcik (Party Secretary Jodla),
Krystyna Zachwatowicz (Hanka Tomczyk), Magda Teresa Wójcik (Cutter), Bogusław Sobczuk (TV Programme
Director), Leonard Zajączkowski (Cameraman), Jacek Domański (Soundman), Irena Laskowska (Museum

Functionary), Zdisław Kozień (Agnieszka's father)
Running time: 165'

NAPLÓ GYERMEKEIMNEK DIARY FOR MY CHILDREN 1982
Hungary
Production Company: Mafilm
Director: Márta Mészáros
Screenplay: Márta Mészáros
Photography: Miklós Jancsó jr (b&w)
Editing: Eva Kármentö
Music: Zsolt Döme
Sound: György Fék
Cast: Zsuzsa Czinkóczi (Juli), Anna Polony (Magda), Jan Nowicki (János), Tamás Tóth (János' son), Mari Semes (Grandmother), Pál Zolnay (Grandfather)
Running time: 107'

REDL EZREDES OBERST REDL COLONEL REDL 1984
Hungary/West Germany/Austria
Production Companies: Mafilm-Studio Objektiv/Mokép (Budapest)/Manfred Durniok Produktion für Film und Fersehen (West Berlin)/ZDF (Mainz)/ORF (Vienna)
Director: István Szabó
Screenplay: István Szabó, Péter Dobai
Photography: Lajos Koltai (c)
Editing: Zsusza Csákány
Music: Zdenkó Tamássy
Sound: György Fék
Cast: Klaus Maria Brandauer (Alfred Redl), Hans-Christian Blech (Colonel von Roden), Armin Müller-Stahl (Archduke Franz Ferdinand), Gudrun Landgrebe (Katalin von Kubinyi), Jan Niklas (Christoph von Kubinyi), László Mensáros (Colonel Ruzitska)[?],
András Bálint (Dr. Sonnenschein), László Gálffy (Lt Vellochio), Dorotya Udvaros (Clarissa), Károly Eperjes (Lt Jaromil Schorm), Róbert Rátonyi (Baron Ullmann).
Running time: 149'

NĚCO Z ALENKY ALICE 1987
Switzerland/West Germany/UK
Production Companies: Condor Film (Zürich), Hessicher Rundfunk (Germany), Film Four International (UK)
Director: Jan Švankmajer
Screenplay: Jan Švankmajer, from themes by Lewis Carroll
Photography: Svatopluk Malý (c)
Editing: Marie Zemanová
Animation: Bedřich Glaser
Art Direction: Jan Švankmajer
Artistic collaboration: Eva Švankmajerová
Sound: Ivo Špalj
Producer: Peter-Christian Fueter
Production Manager: Jaromír Kallista
Executive Producers: Keith Griffiths, Michael Havas
Cast: Kristyna Kohoutová (Alice) (English version spoken by Camilla Powers)

DEKALOG THE DECALOGUE 1988

Poland

Production Company: Polish Television/Sender Freies (Berlin) (I, II, III, IV, VII, VIII, IX, X); Polish Television/TOR (V, VI)

Director: Krzysztof Kieślowski

Screenplay: Krzysztof Kieślowski, Krzysztof Piesiewicz

Photography: Wiesław Zdort (I), Edward Kłosiński (II), Piotr Sobociński (III, IX), Krzysztof Pakulski (IV), Sławomir Idziak (V), Witold Adamek (VI), Dariusz Kuc (VII), Andrzej Jaroszewicz (VIII), Jacek Bławut (X) (c)

Editing: Ewa Smal

Music: Zbigniew Preisner

Art Direction: Hanna Dobrowolska

Costume Design: Małgorzata Obłoza, Hanna Ćwikló

Sound: Małgorzata Jaworska (I, II, IV, V), Nikodem Wołk-Łaniewski (III, VI, VII, IX, X), Wiesława Dębińska (VIII)

Decalogue I

Cast: Henryk Baranowski (Krzysztof), Wojciech Klata (Paweł), Maja Komorowska (Irena), Artur Barciś (young man), Maria Gładkowska (girl), Ewa Kania (Ewa Jezierska), Aleksandra Kisielewska (woman), Aleksandra Majsiuk (Ola), Magda Sroga-Mikołajczyk (journalist), Anna Smal-Romańska, Maciej Sławiński, Piotr Wyrzykowski, Bożena Wróbel

Running time: 53'

Decalogue II

Cast: Krystyna Janda (Dorota), Aleksander Bardini (doctor), Olgierd Łukasiewicz (Andrzej), Artur Barciś (young man), Krystyna Bigelmajer, Karol Dillenius, Ewa Ekwińska, Jerzy Fedorowicz, Stanisław Gawlik, Krzysztof Kumor, Piotr Siejka, Aleksander Trabczyński

Running time: 53'

Decalogue III

Cast: Daniel Olbrychski (Janusz), Maria Pakulnis (Ewa), Joana Szczepkowska (Janusz's wife), Artur Barciś (tram driver), Krystyna Drohocka (aunt), Zygmunt Fok, Jacek Kalucki, Barbara Kołodziejska, Maria Krawczyk, Krzysztof Kumor, Włodzimierz Musiał, Jerzy Zygmunt Nowak, Piotr Rymszkiewicz, Włodzimierz Rzeczycki, Dorota Stalińska.

Running time: 56'

Decalogue IV

Cast: Adrianna Biedrzyńska (Anka), Janusz Gajos (Michał), Artur Barciś (young man), Adam Hanuskiewicz (professor), Jan Tesarz (taxi driver), Andrzej Blumenfeld (Michał's friend), Tomasz Kozłowicz (Jarek), Elżbieta Kilarska (Jarek's mother), Helena Norowicz (optician), Igor Śmiałowski.

Running time: 55'

Decalogue V

Cast: Mirosław Baka (Jacek Lazar), Krzysztof Globisz (Piotr Balicki), Jan Tesarz (taxi driver), Zbigniew Zaposiewicz (bar examiner), Barbara Dziekan-Vajda (girl in cinema box office), Aleksander Bednarz (executioner), Jerzy Zass (court official), Zdzisław Tobiasz (judge), Artur Barciś (young man).

Running time: 57'

Decalogue VI

Cast: Grażyna Szapołowska (Magda), Olaf Lubaszenko (Tomek), Stefania Iwińska (godmother), Artur Barciś (young man), Piotr Machalika (Roman), Stanisław Gawlik (postman), Rafał Imbro (bearded man), Jan Piechociński (blond man).

Running time: 58'

Decalogue VII

Cast: Anna Polony (Ewa), Maja Berełkowska (Majka), Władisław Kowalski (Stefan), Bogusław Linda (Wojtek), Bożena Dykiel (ticket woman), Katarzyna Piwowarczyk (Ania), Stefania Błońska, Dariusz Jabłoński, Jan Mayzel, Mirosława Maludzińska, Ewa Radzikowska, Wanda Wróblewska.

Running time: 58'

Decalogue VIII

Cast: Maria Kościałkowska (Zofia), Teresa Marczewska (Elżbieta), Artur Barciś (young man), Tadeusz Łomnicki (tailor), Wojciech Asiński, Marek Kępiński, Janusz Mond, Marian Opania, Krzysztof Rojek, Bronisław Pawlik.
Running time: 55'

Decalogue IX

Cast: Ewa Błaszczyk (Hanka), Piotr Machalica (Roman), Artur Barciś (young man), Jan Jankowski (Mariusz), Jolanta Piętek Górecka (Ola), Katarzyna Piwowarczyk (Ania), Jerzy Trela (Mikołaj), Renata Berger, Małgorzata Boratyńska, Janusz Cywiński, Joanna Cichoń, Sławomir Kwiatkowski, Dariusz Przychoda.
Running time: 58'

Decalogue X

Cast: Jerzy Stuhr (Jerzy), Zbigniew Zamachowski (Artur), Henryk Bista (shopkeeper), Olaf Lubaszenko (Tomek), Maciej Stuhr (Piotrek), Anna Gronostaj, Cezary Harasimowicz, Dariusz Kozakiewicz, Henryk Majcherek, Ezżbieta Panas, Jerzy Turek, Grzegorz Warchoł.
Running time: 57'

SÁTÁNTANGÓ 1994

Hungary/Germany/Switzerland
Production Companies: Mozgókép Innovációs Társulás (Budapest), Von Vietinghoff Filmproduktion GmbH (Berlin), Vega Film AG (Zürich); supported by Magyar Mozgókép Alapítvány, Filmfördering Berlin, Eurimages, Magyar Televízió, Television Suisse Romande.
Director: Béla Tarr
Screenplay: László Krasznahorkai and Béla Tarr, from the novel by László Krasnahorkai
Photography: Gábor Medvigy (b&w)
Editing: Ágnes Hranitzky
Music: Mihály Vig
Cast: Mihály Vig (Irimias), Dr. Putyi Horváth (Petrina), Erika Bok (Estike), Peter Berling (the doctor), Miklós B. Székely (Futaki), Éva Almási Albert (Mrs Schmidt), László Lugossy (Mr Schmidt).
Running time: 450'

ZÁHRADA THE GARDEN 1995

Slovakia/France/Czech Republic
Production Companies: CHARLIE'S (Bratislava), ARTCAM INTERNATIONAL (Paris), SFT Koliba (Bratislava), STV (Bratislava), ČTV (Prague)
Director: Martin Šulík
Story and Screenplay: Marek Leščák and Martin Šulík
Screenplay collaboration: Ondrej Šulaj
Photography: Martin Štrba (c)
Editing: Dušan Milko
Music: Vladimír Godár
Art Direction: František Lipták
Costume Design: Mona Hafsahl
Sound: Peter Mojžiš
Producers: Rudolf Bierman, Joel Farges
Cast: Roman Luknár (Jakub), Marián Labuda (Jakub's father), Zuzana Šulajová (Helena), Jana Švandová (Tereza), Katarína Vrzalová (Helena's mother), Dušan Trančík (Tereza's husband), Ján Melkovič (Saint Benedict), Stanislav Štepka (Jean-Jacques Rousseau), František Kovár (Wittgenstein), Marta Rašlová (Rousseau's wife), Marián Labuda jr (waiter), Pavol Trančík (boy)
Running time: 95'

BOLSE VITA BOLSHE VITA 1996

Hungary/Germany

Production Company: M.I.T. Studio; Zweites Deutsches Fernsehen (ZDF)

Director: Ibolya Fekete

Screenplay: Ibolya Fekete

Photography: András Szalay (c)

Editing: Klára Majoros

Music: Yuri Fomichyov, Ferenc Muk

Art Direction: Zsolt Juhász Buday

Costume Design: Zsusza Pártényi

Sound: István Sipos

Producer: István Dárday

Cast: Yuri Fomichyov (Yura), Igor Csernyevics (Vadim), Aleksei Serebryakov (Sergey), Helen Baxendale (Maggie), Caroline Loncq (Susan), Agnes Mahr (Erzsi), Iván Kamarás (Árva), Sándor Badár (Hosszúlépés), Eduardo Rózsa Flores (Mafia boss)

Running time: 97'

BIBLIOGRAPHY

GENERAL

Balski, Grzegorz (1991) *Directory of Eastern European Film-Makers and Films 1945–1991*. Trowbridge: Flicks Books.

Berend, Ivan T. (2001) *Decades of Crisis: Central and Eastern Europe Before World War II*. Berkeley: University of California Press.

Biró, Yvette (1982) *Profane Mythology: The Savage Mind of the Cinema*. Translated by Imre Goldstein. Bloomington: Indiana University Press.

_____ (1983) 'Pathos and Irony in East European Films', in David W. Paul (ed.) *Politics, Art and Commitment in the East European Cinema*. London: Macmillan, 28–48.

Caute, David (2003) *The Dancer Defects: The Struggle for Cultural Supremacy During the Cold War*. Oxford: Oxford University Press.

Downing, John D. H. (1996) *Internationalizing Media Theory: Transition, Power, Culture: Reflections on Media in Russia, Poland and Hungary, 1980–95*. London: Sage.

Dyer, Richard and Ginette Vincendeau (eds) (1992) *Popular European Cinema*. London: Routledge.

Eagle, Herbert (1992) 'Czechoslovak, Polish, and Hungarian Cinema Under Communism', *Crosscurrents 11: A Yearbook of Central European Culture*. New Haven: Yale University Press, 175–92.

_____ (1998) 'Eastern European Cinema', in Sabrina P. Ramet (ed.) *Eastern Europe: Politics, Culture, and Society since 1939*. Bloomington: Indiana University Press.

Eidsvik, Charles (1991) 'Mock Realism: The Comedy of Futility in Eastern Europe', in Andrew S. Horton (ed.) *Comedy/Cinema/Theory*. Berkeley: University of California Press, 91–105.

European Commission (1998) *The Development of the Audiovisual Landscape in Central Europe Since 1989*. Luton: ULP/John Libbey Media.

Falkowska, Janina (ed.) (1996) 'National Cinemas in Postwar East-Central Europe', special issue of *Canadian Slavonic Papers*, XLII, 1–2.

Finney, Angus (1996) *The State of European Cinema: A New Dose of Reality*. London: Cassell.

Garton Ash, Timothy (1983) *The Uses of Adversity: Essays on the Fate of Central Europe*. London: Cape.

Giorgi, Liana (1995) *The Post-Socialist Media: What Power the West? The Changing Media Landscape in Poland, Hungary and the Czech Republic*. Aldershot: Avebury/Ashgate.

Glenny, Misha (1990) *The Rebirth of History: Eastern Europe in the Age of Democracy*. London: Penguin.

Głowa, Jadwiga (ed.) (1999) *Zooming in on History's Turning Points: Documentaries in the 1990s in Central and Eastern Europe*. Kraków: Jagiellonian University.

Goldman, Eric A. (1988) *Visions, Images and Dreams: Yiddish Film Past and Present*: Ann Arbor: UMI Research Press.

Goulding, Daniel J. (ed.) (1989) *Post New-Wave Cinema in the Soviet Union and Eastern Europe*. Bloomington: Indiana University Press.

_____ (ed.) (1995) *Five Filmmakers: Tarkovsky, Forman, Polański, Szabó, Makavejev*. Bloomington: Indiana University Press.

_____ (1998) 'East Central European Cinema: Two Defining Moments', in John Hill and Pamela Church Gibson (eds) *The Oxford Guide to Film Studies*. Oxford: Oxford University Press, 471–7.

Harászti, Miklós (1989) *The Velvet Prison: Artists Under State Socialism*. Translated by Katalin and Stephen Landesmann. London: Penguin.

Havel, Václav (1985) *The Power of the Powerless: Citizens Against the State in Central-Eastern Europe*. Edited by John Keane. Translated by Paul Wilson and A. G. Brain. London: Hutchinson.

Hendrykowska, Małgorzata (1997) 'East Central Europe Before the Second World War', in Geoffrey Nowell-Smith (ed.) *The Oxford History of World Cinema*. Oxford: Oxford University Press, 383–9.

Hendrykowski, Marek (1997) 'Changing States in East Central Europe', in Geoffrey Nowell-Smith (ed.) *The Oxford History of World Cinema*. Oxford: Oxford University Press, 632–40.

Hibbin, Nina (1969) *Eastern Europe*. London: Zwemmer.

Hoberman, J. (1991) *Bridge of Light: Yiddish Film Between Two Worlds*. New York: Museum of Modern Art; Schocken Books.

Hoffman, Eva (1994) *Exit into History: A Journey Through the New Eastern Europe*. London: Minerva.

Insdorff, Annette (1989) *Indelible Shadows: Film and the Holocaust*. Cambridge: Cambridge University Press.

Iordanova, Dina (1999) 'College Course File: Eastern European Cinema', *Journal of Film and Video*, 51, 1, 56–77.

____ (2000) 'The New Russians in Film: Nostalgia for the Occupier, Commiseration for the Immigrant', in Janina Falkowska (ed.), 'National Cinemas in Postwar East-Central Europe', special issue of *Canadian Slavonic Papers*, XLII, 1–2, 113–31.

____ (2003) *Cinema of the Other Europe: The Industry and Artistry of East Central European Film*. London: Wallflower Press.

Johnson, Lonnie R. (2002) *Central Europe: Enemies, Neighbors, Friends*. Second Edition. New York and Oxford: Oxford University Press.

Jones, Derek (ed.) (2001) *Censorship: A World Encyclopedia*. 4 volumes. London and Chicago: Fitzroy Dearborn.

Kundera, Milan (1984) 'A Kidnapped West or Culture Bows Out', trans. Edmund White, *Granta*, 11, 93–118.

Liehm, Mira and Antonín J. Liehm (1977) *The Most Important Art: Soviet and East European Film After 1945*. Translated by Káča Poláčková-Henley. Berkeley: University of California Press.

____ (1989) *Les Cinémas de l'Est*. Paris: Editions du Cerf.

Miłosz, Czesław (1980) *The Captive Mind*. Translated by Jane Zielonko. Harmondsworth: Penguin.

Nemes, Karoly (1985) *Films of Commitment: Socialist Cinema in Eastern Europe*. Translated by András Boros-Kazai. Budapest: Corvina.

Paul, David W. (ed.) (1983) *Politics, Art and Commitment in the East European Cinema*. London: Macmillan.

Petrie, Graham and Ruth Dwyer (eds) (1990) *Before the Wall Came Down: Soviet and East European Filmmakers Working in the West*. Lanham: University Press of America.

Portuges, Catherine (1992) 'Border Crossings: Recent Trends in East and Central European Cinema', *Slavic Review*, 51, 3, 531–5.

____ (1997) 'Hidden Subjects, Secret Identities: Figuring Jews, Gypsies and Gender in 1990s Cinema of Eastern Europe', in Gisela Brinkler-Gabler and Sidonie Smith (eds) *Writing New Identities: Gender, Nation, and Immigration in Contemporary Europe*. Minneapolis: University of Minnesota Press, 196–215.

Quart, Barbara (1988) 'Eastern European Women Directors', in Barbara Quart, *Women Directors: The Emergence of a New Cinema*. New York: Praeger, 191–239.

____ (1993) 'Three Central European Women Directors Revisited', *Cineaste*, 19, 4, 58–61.

Rupnik, Jacques (1988) *The Other Europe: The Rise and Fall of Communism in East Central Europe*. London: Weidenfeld and Nicolson.

Schöpflin, George and Nancy Wood (eds) (1989) *In Search of Central Europe*. Cambridge: Polity Press.

Slater, T. J. (ed.) (1992) *Handbook of Soviet and East European Films and Film-makers*. New York: Greenwood Press.

Sparks, Colin and Anna Reading (1998) *Communism, Capitalism and the Mass Media*. London: Sage.

Splichal, Slavko (1994) *Media Beyond Socialism: Theory and Practice in East-Central Europe*. Boulder CO: Westview Press.

Stoil, Michael Jon (1974) *Cinema Beyond the Danube: The Camera and Politics*. Metuchen NJ: Scarecrow Press.

Stojanova, Christina (2000) 'Ars longa, Politica Brevis: Overseas Sketches on the Newest History of the East European Cinema', in 'East of Eden: Countries in Transition, Cinema in Experiment. Special issue of *Kino* (Bulgaria), 3-15.

Taylor, Richard., Nancy Wood, Julian Graffy, and Dina Iordanova (eds.) (2000) *The BFI Companion to Eastern European and Russian Cinema*. London: British Film Institute.

Tscherkassky, Peter (ed.) (1998) *Avant-Garde Films and Videos from Central Europe*. Vienna: Sixpack Film.

Vincendeau, Ginette (ed.) *Encyclopedia of European Cinema*. London: Cassell/British Film Institute.

Whyte, Alistair (1971) *New Cinema in Eastern Europe*. London: Studio Vista.

Wolff, Larry (1994) *Inventing Eastern Europe: The Map of Civilization on the Mind of the Enlightenment*. Stanford: Stanford University Press.

CZECHOSLOVAKIA, CZECH REPUBLIC AND SLOVAKIA

Anděl, Jaroslav (1989) 'Artists as Filmmakers', in Jaroslav Anděl, Anne Wilkes Tucker, Alison de Lima Greene, Ralph Mckay and Willis Hartshorn (eds) *Czech Modernism 1900–1945*. Houston: Museum of Modern Art/Boston: Bulfinch Press, 165–81.

_____ (2000) *Alexandr Hackenschmied*. Translated by Derek Paton. Prague: Torst.

Anděl, Jaroslav, Anne Wilkes Tucker, Alison de Lima Greene, Ralph Mckay and Willis Hartshorn (eds) (1989) *Czech Modernism 1900–1945*. Houston: Museum of Modern Art/ Boston: Bulfinch Press.

Asociace producentů v audiovizi/Audiovisual Producers' Association (2002) *České filmy Katalog 1991–2001/Czech Films Catalogue 1991–2001*. Prague: Asociace producentů v audiovizi.

Bartošek, Luboš (1985) *Náš film. Kapitoly z dějin*. Prague: Mladá fronta.

_____ (1989) *Československý filmy 1981–1985*. 2 volumes. Prague: Československý filmový ústav.

Bartošková, Šárka and Luboš Bartošek (1983) *Československé filmy 1977–1980*. 2 volumes. Prague: Československý filmový ústav.

_____ (1986) *Filmové profily: Českoslovenšti scénáristé, režiséři, kameramani, hudební skladatelé a architekti hraných filmů*. Prague: Československý filmový ústav.

_____ (1990) *Filmové profily 2: Českoslovenští filmoví herci*. Prague: Československý filmový ústav.

Bartošková, Šárka (1959) *Československé filmy 1945–1957*. Prague: Československý film.

_____ (1960) *Československé filmy 1958–59*. Prague: Československý film.

_____ (1966) *Československý film 1960–65*. Prague: Filmový ústav.

_____ (1970) *Československé filmy 1966–68*. Prague: Český filmový ústav.

_____ (1973) *Československé filmy 1969–71*. Prague: Český filmový ústav.

Bartošková, Šárka, Myrtil Frída and Jan Kolár (1965) *Československý zvukový film, 1930–45*. Prague: Filmový ústav.

Bernard, Jan (1994) *Evald Schorm a jeho filmy: Odvahu pro všední den*. Prague: Primus.

Buchar, Robert (2004) *Czech New Wave Filmmakers in Interviews*. Jefferson and London: McFarland.

Burian, Jarka (2000) *Modern Czech Theatre: Reflector and Conscience of a Nation*. Iowa City: University of Iowa Press.

Boček, Jaroslav (1965) *Modern Czechoslovak Film*. Translated by Alice Denešová. Brno: Artia.

_____ (1967) *Looking Back on the New Wave*. Prague: Československý Filmexport.

_____ (1968) *Kapitoly o filmu*. Prague: Orbis.

Brázda, Marián, Martin Kaňuch and Peter Michalovič (eds) (2000) *Svet v pohyblivých obrazoch Martina Šulíka*. Bratislava: Slovenský filmový ústav.

Bregant, Michal (1989) 'Několik poznámek na téma Jiří Voskovec a film', *Iluminace*, 1, 95–125.

_____ (1990) 'The Devětsil Film Dream', in Rostislav Švácha (ed.) *The Czech Avant-Garde of the 1920s and 30s*. Oxford: Museum of Modern Art/London: Design Museum, 70–3.

_____ (1992) 'Avantgardní tendence v českem filmu', in *Filmový sborník historický*, 3. Prague: Čs. Filmový ústav, 137–74.

_____ (1998) 'Czech Republic', in Peter Tscherkassky (ed.) *Avant-garde Films and Videos from Central Europe*. Vienna: Sixpack Film, 19.

_____ Brož, Jaroslav (1967) *The Path of Fame of the Czechoslovak Film*. Prague: Československý Filmexport.

Brož, Jaroslav and Myrtil Frída (1959) *Historie Československého filmu v obrazech, 1898–1930*. Prague: Orbis.

_____ (1964) *Historie Československého filmu v obrazech 1930–1945*. Prague: Orbis.

Brumagne, Marie-Magdeleine (1969) *Jeune cinéma tchécoslovaque*. Lyon: SERDOC.

Černý, Oldřich and Gerald O'Grady (eds) *The Banned and the Beautiful: A Survey of Czech Filmmaking, 1963–1990*. New York: The Public Theater.

Daniel, František (Frank) (1983) 'The Czech Difference', in David W. Paul (ed.) *Politics, Art and Commitment in the East European Cinema*. London: Macmillan, 49–56.

Dewey, Langdon (1971) *Outline of Czechoslovakian Cinema*. London: Informatics.

Eagle, Herbert (1977) 'The Syntagmatic and Paradigmatic Axes in *Closely Watched Trains*', in Ben Lawton and Janet Staiger (eds) *Film Studies Annual*, part one. New York: Redgrave, 45–57.

____ (1991) 'Dadaism and Structuralism in Věra Chytilová's *Daisies*', in *Cross Currents 10: A Yearbook of Central European Culture*. New Haven: Yale University Press, 223–34.

Forman, Miloš and Jan Novák (1994) *Turnaround: A Memoir*. London: Faber.

French, Alfred (1982) *Czech Writers and Politics, 1945–1969*. Boulder CO: East European Monographs.

Frühauf, Jiří and Vlasta Svobodová (1977) *Československé filmy 1972–76*. 2 volumes. Prague: Československý filmový ústav.

Goetz-Stankiewicz, Marketa (1979) *The Silenced Theatre: Czech Playwrights Without a Stage*. Toronto: University of Toronto Press.

____ (ed.) (1992) *Good-bye, Samizdat: Twenty Years of Czech Underground Writing*. Evanston: Northwestern University Press.

Golan, Galia (1971) *The Czechoslovak Reform Movement: Communism in Crisis 1962–1968*. Cambridge: Cambridge University Press.

____ (1973) *Reform Rule in Czechoslovakia: The Dubček Era, 1968–1969*. Cambridge: Cambridge University Press.

Halada, Andrej (1997) *Český film devatesátych let: Od Tankového praporu ke Koljovi*. Prague: Nakladatelství Lidové noviny.

Hames, Peter (1979) 'The Return of Věra Chytilová', *Sight and Sound*, 48, 3, 168–73.

____ (1985) *The Czechoslovak New Wave*. Berkeley: University of California Press.

____ (1989) 'Czechoslovakia: After the Spring', in Daniel J. Goulding (ed.) *Post New Wave Cinema in the Soviet Union and Eastern Europe*. Bloomington: Indiana University Press, 102–42.

____ (1994) 'Forman', in Daniel J. Goulding (ed.) *Five Filmmakers: Tarkovsky, Forman, Polański, Szabó, Makavejev*. Bloomington: Indian University Press, 50–91.

____ (ed.) (1995) *Dark Alchemy: The Films of Jan Švankmajer*. Trowbridge: Flicks Books.

____ (2000a) '*The Good Soldier Švejk* and After: The Comic Tradition in Czech Film', in Diana Holmes and Alison Smith (eds) *100 Years of European Cinema: Entertainment or Ideology?* Manchester: Manchester University Press, 64–76.

____ (2000b) 'Czech Cinema: From State Industry to Competition', in Janina Falkowska (ed), 'National Cinemas in Postwar East-Central Europe', special issue of *Canadian Slavonic Papers*, Vol XLII, 1–2, 63–85.

____ (2000c) 'Czechs on the Rebound'. *Sight and Sound*, 10, 7, 32–4.

____ (2001a) 'Enfant Terrible of the Czech New Wave: Jan Němec's 1960s films', *Central Europe Review*, 3, 17: Available at http://www.ce-review.org/01/17/kinoeye17_hames.html

____ (2001b) 'Bringing Up Baby' [Jan Švankmajer], *Sight and Sound*, 11, 10, 26–8.

____ (2004) 'Down from the Mountain' [Juraj Jakubisko], *Sight and Sound*, 14, 3, 8–9.

____ (2005) *The Czechoslovak New Wave*, second edition. London: Wallflower Press.

Havelka, Jiří (1967) *Kronika našeho filmu, 1898–1965*. Prague: Filmový ústav.

____ (1977) *Československé krátké filmy 1945–1970*. 3 volumes. Prague: Československý filmový ústav.

Heiss, Gernot and Ivan Klimeš (eds) (2003) *Obrazy času: Česky a rakouský film 30. let/Bilder der Zeit: Tschechischer und österreicher Film der 30er Jahre*. Prague: Národní filmový archiv; Brno: Österreichisches Ost- und Südosteuropa-Institut.

Holy, Ladislav (1996) *The Little Czech and the Great Czech Nation: National Identity and the Post-Communist Transformation of Society*. Cambridge: Cambridge University Press.

Horton, Andrew James (ed.) (2001) 'Pure Film: The Art of Jan Němec', special issue of *Central Europe Review*, 3, 17, 14 May: Available at http://ce-review.org

____ (ed.) (2002) 'Strach: Czech Film's Love Affair with Fear and Horror', special issue of *Kinoeye*, 2, 1, 7 January: Available at http://www.kinoeye.org

Hrabal, Bohumil (1990) *Closely Observed Trains*. Translated by Edith Pargeter. London: Abacus.

Image et Son: La Revue du Cinéma (1968) 'Cinéma tchécoslovaque', special issue. November.

Jachnin, Boris (1990) *Jan Werich*. Prague: Čs. filmový ústav.

Jaros, Jan (1991) *Juraj Jakubisko*. Prague: Čs. filmový ústav.

Janoušek, Jiří (1965) *Tří a půl*. Prague: Orbis.

____ (1969) *Tří a půl podruhé*. Prague: Orbis.

Jasný, Vojtěch (1999) *Život a film*. Prague: Národní filmový archiv.

Ježek, Svatopluk (1946) *Panorama českého filmu*. Prague: Filmový ústav.

Juráček, Pavel (2003) *Deník (1959–1974)*. Edited by Jan Lukeš. Prague: Národní filmový archiv.

Klevan, Andrew (2000) 'Delays Around Events: Miloš Forman's *Loves of a Blonde*', in Andrew Klevan, *Disclosure of the Everyday: Undramatic Achievement in Narrative Film*. Trowbridge: Flicks Books, 103–34.

Kolár, Jan S. and Myrtil Frída (1957 and 1962) *Československý němý film 1898–1930*. 2 volumes. Prague: Československý filmový ústav.

Kopaněva, Galina (2000) 'The Czech Film: Searching for New Ways of Survival', in 'East of Eden: Countries in Transition, Cinema in Experiment', special issue of *Kino* (Bulgaria), 45–50.

Kosík, Karel (1976) *Dialectics of the Concrete: A Study of Problems on Man and World*. Translated by Karel Kovanda and James Schmidt. Dordrecht and Boston: Reidel.

Košuličová, Ivana (ed.) (2002) 'Věra Chytilová: Permanent Rebel', special issue of *Kinoeye*, 2, 8, 29 April: Available at http://www.kinoeye.org

____ (ed.) (2003) 'Ať žije film! (Long Live Film!): Karel Kachyňa's 50 Years in Cinema', special issue of *Kinoeye*, 3, 9, 15 September: Available at http://www.kinoeye.org

Král, Petr (1993) *Voskovec a Werich čili Hvezdy klobouky*. Prague: Gryf.

Kroupa, Vladimír, and Milan Šmid (1998) 'The Limitations of a Free Market: Czech Republic', in *The Development of the Audiovisual Landscape in Central Europe Since 1989*. (European Commission in association with Eureka Audiovisuel. Luton: ULP/John Libbey Media, 61–109.

Kučera, Jan (1937) 'V & W ve filmu', in *10 let Osvobozeneho divadla V+W*. Prague: Nakladatelství Fr. Borový, 49–54.

____ (1971) *Pokrokové tendence v českém filmu v období 1920 až 1938*. Prague: Čs. Federace filmových klubů.

Kusin, Vladimír V. (1971) *The Intellectual Origins of the Prague Spring: The Development of Reformist Ideas in Czechoslovakia 1956–67*. Cambridge: Cambridge University Press.

____ (1978) *From Dubček to Charter 77: A Study of 'Normalisation' in Czechoslovakia 1968–1978*. Edinburgh: Q Press.

Laura, Ernesto (ed.) (1960) *Il film Cecoslovacco*. Rome: Edizione dell'Ateneo.

Liehm, Antonín J. (1968) 'The Reckoning of a Miracle: An Analysis of Czechoslovak Cinematography', *Film Comment*, 5, 1, 64–9.

____ (1973) *The Politics of Culture*. Translated by Peter Kussi. New York: Grove Press.

____ (1974) *Closely Watched Films: The Czechoslovak Experience*. New York: International Arts and Sciences Press.

____ (1975) *The Miloš Forman Stories*. Translated by Jeanne Němcová. NewYork: International Arts and Sciences Press.

____ (1993a) *Příběhy Miloše Formana*. Prague: Mladá fronta.

____ (1993b) 'Czech and Slovak Cinema', *Cineaste*, 19, 4, 62.

____ (2001) *Ostře sledované filmy: Československá zkušenost*. Prague: Národní filmový archiv.

Lukeš, Jan (1993) *Orgia střídmosti aneb Konec československé státní kinematografie*. Prague: Národní filmový archiv.

Lukeš, Jan and Ivana Lukešová (eds) (2002) *Nová Nová Vlna? Rozprava o české a francouzské kinematografii/Nouvelle Nouvelle Vague? Débats sur le cinéma tchèque et français*. Prague: Národní filmový archiv.

Macko, Jozef (1992) 'Slovak Alternative and Experimental Film', *Moveast*, 2, 25–37.

Macek, Václav (1992) *Slovenský film 1970–1990*. Bratislava: Slovenský filmový ústav-Narodné kinematografické centrum.

____ (1998) 'Slovakia', in Peter Tscherkassky (ed.) *Avant-Garde Films and Videos from Central Europe*. Vienna: Sixpack Film, 24–5.

Macek, Václav and Jelena Paštéková (1997) *Dejiny slovenskej kinematografie*. Martin: Osveta.

Menzel, Jiří and Bohumil Hrabal (1971) *Closely Observed Trains* (script). Translated by Josef Holzbecher. London:

Lorrimer.

Montmarte, Danièle (1991) *Le Théâtre Libéré de Prague: Voskovec et Werich*. Paris: Institut d'études slaves.

Musil, Jiří (ed.) (1995) *The End of Czechoslovakia*. Budapest: Central European University Press.

Národní filmový archiv (1995) *Český hraný film I: 1898-1930/Czech Feature Film I: 1898-1930*. Prague: Národní filmový archiv.

____ (1998) *Český hraný film II: 1930-1945/Czech Feature Film II: 1930-1945*. Prague: Národní filmový archiv.

____ (2001) *Český hraný film III: 1945-1960/Czech Feature Film III: 1945-1960*. Prague: Národní filmový archiv.

____ (2004) *Český hraný film IV 1960-1970/Czech Feature Film IV 1960-1970*. Prague: Národní filmový archiv.

Navrátil, Jaromír (ed.) (1998) *The Prague Spring 1968*. Translated by Mark Kramer, Joy Moss, Ruth Tosek. Budapest: Central European University Press.

Parrott, Cecil (1989) 'The Liberated Theatre: Voskovec and Werich', in Alan Ross (ed.) *The London Magazine 1961-1985*. London: Paladin/Grafton, 242-60.

Pavliček, František and František Vláčil (1998) *Marketa Lazarová* (screenplay). Prague: FAD.

Přádna, Stanislava, Zdena Škapová and Jiří Cieslar (2002) *Démanty všednosti: Český a Slovenský film 60. let*. Prague: Pražská scéna.

Pynsent, Robert B. (1994) *Questions of Identity: Czech and Slovak Ideas of Nationality and Personality*. London and Budapest: Central European University Press.

Sayer, Derek (1998) *The Coasts of Bohemia: A Czech History*. Princeton: Princeton University Press.

Schonberg, Michal (1989) 'The Theatre and Films of Jiří Voskovec and Jan Werich', in Jaroslav Anděl, Anne Wilkes Tucker, Alison de Lima Greene, Ralph Mckay and Willis Hartshorn (eds) *Czech Modernism 1900-1945*. Houston: Museum of Modern Art; Boston: Bulfinch Press, 183-91.

____ (1992) *Osvobozené*. Prague: Odeon.

Šimečka, Milan (1984) *The Restoration of Order: The Normalization of Czechoslovakia*. Translated by A. G. Brain. London: Verso.

Škvorecký, Josef (1971) *All the Bright Young Men and Women: A Personal History of the Czech Cinema*. Translated by Michael Schonberg. Toronto: Peter Martin Associates.

____ (1982) *Jiří Menzel and the History of the Closely Watched Trains*. Boulder CO: East European Monographs.

____ (1991) *Všichni ti bystří mladi muži a ženy: osobní historie českého filmu*. Prague: Horizont.

Skwara, Janusz (1968) *Nowy film czechoslowacki*. Warsaw: W.A.i.F.

Slater, T. J. (1987) *Miloš Forman: A Bio-Bibliography*. New York and London: Greenwood Press.

Smatlák, Martin and André Zmecek (1998) 'Market Intentions Restrained: Slovak Republic', in *The Development of the Audiovisual Landscape in Central Europe Since 1989*. European Commission in association with Eureka Audiovisuel. Luton: University of Luton Press/John Libbey Media, 307-51.

Smatláková, Renata (1999) *Katalóg slovenských celovečerných filmov 1921-1999 (The Catalogue of Slovak Full-Length Feature Films)*. Bratislava: Slovenský filmový ústav (Slovak Film Institute).

Steiner, Eugen (1973) *The Slovak Dilemma*. Cambridge: Cambridge University Press.

Šulaj, Ondrej, Marek Leščák, Dušan Dušek, Martin Šulík (2003) *5 Scenárov [Neha; Všetko čo mám rád; Záhrada; Orbis Pictus; Krajinka]*. Bratislava: Slovenský filmový ústav, Charlie's s.r.o.

Švankmajer, Jan (1996) *Faust: The Script*. Trowbridge: Flicks Books.

Švankmajer, Jan and Eva Švankmajerová (1998) *Anima Animus Animation: Between Film and Free Expression*. Prague: Slovart, Arbor Vitae Foundation.

Taussig, Pavel (1989) 'On the Sunnyside of Film', in Jaroslav Anděl, Anne Wilkes Tucker, Alison de Lima Greene, Ralph Mckay and Willis Hartshorn (eds) *Czech Modernism 1900-1945*. Trans. Jitka Salaquarda. Houston: Museum of Modern Art; Boston: Bulfinch Press, 193-207.

Ulman, Miro and Peter Ulman (2001) *Sprievodca klubovým filmom*. Bratislava: Asociácia slovenských filmových klubov.

Ulver, Stanislav (ed.) (1996) *Film a doba: Antologie textů z let 1962-1970*. Prague: FAD.

Williams, Kieran (1997) *The Prague Spring and Its Aftermath: Czechoslovak Politics, 1968-1970*. Cambridge: Cambridge University Press.

Žalman, Jan (1967) 'Question Marks on the New Czechoslovak Cinema', *Film Quarterly*, Winter 1967–68, 18–27.

_____ (1968) *Films and Film-makers in Czechoslovakia*. Prague: Orbis.

_____ (1993) *Umlčený film: Kapitoly z bojů o lidskou tvář československého filmu*. Prague: Národní filmový archiv.

Zaoralová, Eva and Jean-Loup Passek (eds) (1996) *Le Cinéma Tchèque et Slovaque*. Paris: Centre Georges Pompidou.

HUNGARY

Antal, István (1998) 'Hungary', in Peter Tscherkassky (ed.) *Avant-Garde Films and Videos from Central Europe*. Vienna: Sixpack Film, 38.

Armes, Roy (1976) 'Miklós Jancsó: Dialectic and Ritual', in Roy Armes, *The Ambiguous Image: Narrative Style in Modern European Cinema* (London: Secker and Warburg), 141–53.

Békés, Csaba, Malcolm Byrne and János M. Rainer (eds) (2002) *The 1956 Hungarian Revolution: A History in Documents*, National Security Archive Cold War Readers. Budapest: Central European University Press.

Biró, Yvette (1968) 'The Hungarian Film Style and its Variations', *New Hungarian Quarterly*, 9, 32, 3–8.

_____ (1977) *Miklós Jancsó*. Paris: Editions Albatros.

Bori, Erszébet (2001) '"Cold Spell": Béla Tarr: *Werckmeister harmóniák* (*Werckmeister Harmonies*)', *The Hungarian Quarterly*, 42, 162, 155–60.

Burns, Bryan (1996) *World Cinema: Hungary*. Trowbridge: Flicks Books.

Clark, George and Travis Miles (eds) (2003) *The Cinema of Miklós Jancsó*. London: Hungarian Cultural Centre, Canadian High Commission, Italian Cultural Centre, Riverside Studios.

Cunningham, John (2004) *Hungarian Cinema: From Coffee House to Multiplex*. London: Wallflower Press.

Czigány, Lórànt (1984) *The Oxford History of Hungarian Literature*. Oxford and New York: Oxford University Press.

Diszeri, Eszter (1999) *Kockáról Kockára: A Magyar animácio krónikája 1948–1988*. Budapest: Balassi Kiadó.

Estève, Michel (ed.) (1969) *Le nouveau cinéma hongrois*. Paris: Minard.

Fábri, Zoltán and István Nemeskürty (1994) *Fábri Zoltán, a képalkotó művész*. Budapest: Szabad Tér.

Forgacs, Éva (1995) 'Image in Motion: László Moholy-Nagy and Film', *Hungarian Quarterly*, 36, 139, 139–40.

Garai, Erzsi (1969) *A Magyar film a tanácsköztársaság idejen*. Budapest: Magyar Filmintézet.

Gervai, András (2001) '"Making Films is My Only Pleasure": An Interview with Miklós Jancsó', *The Hungarian Quarterly*, 42, 163, 151–60.

Gyertyán, Ervin (1975) *Miklós Jancsó*. Budapest: Magyar Filmtudományi és Filmarchívum.

György, Péter and Hedvig Turai (1992) *Art and Society in the Age of Stalinism*. Budapest: Corvina.

Hames, Peter (2001) 'The melancholy of resistance: The films of Béla Tarr', *Kinoeye*, 1, 1, 3 September: Available at http://www.kinoeye.org/01/01/hames01.php

Haudiquet, Philippe, Jean-Pierre Jeancolas and István Nemeskürty (1979) *Le Cinéma Hongrois*. Paris: Centre national d'Arte and de Culture.

Horton, Andrew James (ed.) (2003a) 'Images of Power and the Power of Images: The Films of Miklós Jancsó'. (Part One), special issue of *Kinoeye*, 3, 3, 17 February: Available at http://www.kinoeye.org

_____ (ed.) (2003b) 'Images of Power and the Power of Images: The Films of Miklós Jancsó' (Part Two), special issue of *Kinoeye*, 3, 4, 3 March: Available at http://www.kinoeye.org

_____ (ed.) (2004) 'Focus on Hungarian Film', 4, 2, 29 March: Available at http://www.kinoeye.org

Jaehne, Karen (1978) 'István Szabó: Dreams of Memories', *Film Quarterly*, 32, 1, 30–41.

Jeancolas, Jean-Pierre (1989) *Miklós, István, Zoltán et les autres: Vingt-cinq ans de cinéma hongrois*. Budapest: Corvina.

_____ (2001) *L'Oeil Hongrois: Quatre décennies de cinéma à Budapest*. Budapest: Magyar Filmunió.

Kósa, László (2000) *A Cultural History of Hungary in the Nineteenth and Twentieth Century*. Budapest: Corvina; Osiris.

Kovács, András Bálint (2001) 'The World According to Tarr', in *Béla Tarr*. Budapest: Magyar Filmunio.

Lendvay, Judit (1985) *Jancsó Miklós a Magyar közvéleményben*. Budapest: Tömegkommunikációs Kutatóközpont.

Lengyel, Emöke (1998) 'The Art of Careful Power Balancing: Hungary', in *The Development of the Audiovisual Landscape in Central Europe Since 1989*. European Commission in association with Eureka Audiovisuel. Luton:

University of Luton Press/John Libbey Media, 139–202.

Levenson, Claude B. (1966) *Jeune cinéma hongrois*. Lyon: SERDOC.

Macartney, C. A. (1956) *October 15th: A History of Modern Hungary, 1929–1945*. Edinburgh: Edinburgh University Press.

Magyar Filmintézet/Hungarian Film Institute (1985) *Játékfilmek 1970–74*. Budapest: Magyar Filmintézet.

_____ (1987) *Játékfilmek 1980–1984*. Budapest: Magyar Filmintézet.

_____ (1999) *Játékfilmek 1931–1998/Hungarian Feature Films 1931–1998*. Budapest: Magyar Filmintézet/Hungarian Film Institute.

Magyar Filmtudományi és Filmarchívum (1973) *Játékfilmek 1945–1969*. Budapest: Magyar Filmtudományi és Filmarchívum.

_____ (1980) *Játékfilmek 1970–1974*. Budapest: Magyar Filmtudományi és Filmarchívum.

Micciche, Lino (1974) *Viaggio attraverso il cinema ungharese*. Rome: Avanti.

Micheli, Sergio (1982) *Cinema ungherese. Tradizione, idée, forme*. Rome: Bulzoni.

Nagy, Moses M. (ed.) (1990) *A Journey Into History: Essays on Hungarian Literature*. New York: Lang.

Nemeskürty, István (1961) *A mozgóképtol a filmművézetig 1907–1930*. Budapest: Magveto.

_____ (1965) *A magyar film története, 1912–1963*. Budapest: Gondolat.

_____ (1968) *Word and Image: History of the Hungarian Cinema*. Translated by Zsuzsanna Horn. Budapest: Corvina.

Nemeskürty, István and Tibor Szántó (1985) *A Pictorial Guide to the Hungarian Cinema*. Budapest: Helikon.

Orr, John (2001) 'Béla Tarr Circling the Whale', *Sight and Sound*, 11, 4, 22–4.

Passek, Jean-Loup (ed.) (1979) *Le Cinéma hongrois*. Paris: Centre Georges Pompidou.

Paul, David (1989) 'Hungary: The Magyar on the Bridge', in Daniel J. Goulding (ed.) *Post New Wave Cinema in the Soviet Union and Eastern Europe*. Bloomington: Indiana University Press, 172–214.

_____ (1994) 'Szabó', in Daniel J. Goulding (ed.) *Five Filmmakers: Tarkovsky, Forman, Polański, Szabó, Makavejev*. Bloomington: Indiana University Press, 156–208.

Péternak, Miklós (1989) 'A Short History of the Avant-Garde in Hungarian Cinema', *Undercurrent*, 18, Autumn, 31–5.

Petrie, Graham (1978) *History Must Answer to Man: The Contemporary Hungarian Cinema*. Budapest: Corvina.

_____ (1997) 'Hungarian Silent Cinema Rediscovered', *Hungarian Quarterly*, 38, 147, 152–60.

_____ (1998) *Red Psalm*. Trowbridge: Flicks Books.

Pinter, Judit and Vince Zalan (eds) *Szőts István: Szilánkok és gyaluforgacsok. (István Szőts: Splinters and Shavings)* Budapest: Osiris.

Polanyi, Karl (1957 [1944]) *The Great Transformation*. New York: Beacon Press.

Portuges, Catherine (1993) *Screen Memories: The Hungarian Cinema of Márta Mészáros*. Bloomington: Indiana University Press.

_____ (1995) 'Post-Transition Hungarian Cinema and its National Imaginary', *Slavic Review*, 54, 4, 1004–9.

_____ (1997) 'Bolse Vita', *The American Historical Review*, 102, 3 June.

_____ (2000) 'Sunshine', *Cineaste*, 26, 1, 56–7.

_____ (2001) 'Home Movies, Found Images and "Amateur Film" as a Witness to History: Péter Forgács's *Private Hungary*', *The Moving Image*, Fall, 107–25.

Reynaud, Bérénice (2001) 'Two Variations for a Theme', in *Béla Tarr*. Budapest: Magyar Filmunio.

Rez, Pál (1993) 'Tibor Déry and Two Women', *The Hungarian Quarterly*, 34, 129, 39–42.

Robinson, David (1972) 'The Case of Károly Makk', *Sight and Sound*, 41, 2, 67–8.

Romsics, Ignác (1999) *Hungary in the Twentieth Century*. Budapest: Corvina/Osiris.

Rosenbaum, Jonathan (1995) 'A Bluffer's Guide to Béla Tarr', in *Placing Movies: The Practice of Film Criticism*. Berkeley: University of California Press, 54–8.

Sadoul, Georges (1952) *Panorama du cinéma hongrois (1896–1953)*. Paris: Les Editeurs Français Réunis.

Sándor, Tibor (1992) *Örségváltás: A Magyar film és szélsőjobboldal a harmincas-negyvenes evekben*. Budapest: Magyar Filmintézet.

_____ (1996) 'Popular Film in Hungary (History, Politics, Film: A Workshop Study)', *Moveast*, 3, 3–27.

_____ (1997) *Örségváltás utan: zsido kérdés és filmpolitika, 1938–1944*. Budapest: Magyar Filmintézet.

Somogyi, Lia (ed.) (1984) *Hungarian Film Directors 1948–1983*. Budapest: Interpress.

Székely, István (1978) *Hippolytöl a Lila akácig*. Budapest: Gondolat.

Szilágyi, Gábor (1994) *Életyel: A Magyar filmművészet megszületese 1954–1956*. Budapest: Magyar Filmintézet.

Tökés, Rudolf L. (1967) *Béla Kun and the Hungarian Soviet Republic*. Stanford: Hoover Institution.

_____ (1996) *Hungary's Negotiated Revolution: Economic Reform, Social Change, and Political Succession, 1957–1990*. Cambridge: Cambridge University Press.

Véronneau, Pierre (ed.) (1976) *Le cinéma hongrois d'après 1968*. Quebec: Cinémathèque Québécoise.

Zsuffa, Joseph (1987) *Béla Balázs: The Man and the Artist*. Berkeley: University of California Press.

POLAND

Amiel, Vincent (1995) *Kieślowski*. Paris: Rivages/Cinéma.

_____ (ed.) (1997) *Krzysztof Kieślowski*. Paris: Editions Jean-Michèle Place.

Andrew, Geoff (1998) *The 'Three Colours' Trilogy*. London: British Film Institute.

Ansky, Solomon (1992) *The Dybbuk and Other Writings*. Edited by David G. Roskies, translated by Golda Werman. New York: Schocken Books.

Armatys, Barbara (1988) *Historia filmu polskiego 1930–1939*. Vol. II. Warsaw: W.A.i.F.

Ascherson, Neal (1987) *The Struggles for Poland*. London: Michael Joseph.

Belmans, Jacques (1971) *Roman Polanski*. Paris: Editions Seghers.

Bereda, Jerzy, Jan Słodowski, Oskar Sobański, Jacek Tabęcki and Konrad Zarębski (1986) *Twórzy polskiego filmu leksykon*. Warsaw: WFPDF.

Bird, Daniel (2002) *Roman Polanski*. Harpenden: Pocket Essentials.

Bren, Frank (1986) *World Cinema: Poland*. Trowbridge: Flicks Books.

Brossard, Jean-Pierre (ed.) (1980) *Le Nouveau Cinéma polonais*. Locarno: Cinédiff.

Butler, Ivan (1970) *The Cinema of Roman Polanski*. London: Tantivy Press.

Campan, Véronique (1993) *Dix brèves histoires d'image: Le Décalogue de Krzysztof Kieślowski*. Paris: Presses de la Sorbonne Nouvelles.

Coates, Paul (1985) *The Story of the Lost Reflection: The Alienation of the Image in Western and Polish Cinema*. London: Verso.

_____ (1996a) 'The Sense of an Ending: Reflections on Kieślowski's Trilogy', *Film Quarterly*, 50, 2, 19–26.

_____ (1996b) 'Revisiting *Ashes and Diamonds* with Andrzejewski and Wajda', *Canadian Slavonic Papers*, 38, 3–4, 288–303.

_____ (ed.) (1999) *Lucid Dreams: The Films of Krzysztof Kieślowski*. Trowbridge: Flicks Books.

_____ (2000a) 'Observing the Observer: Andrzej Wajda's *Holy Week*', in Janina Falkowska (ed.) 'National Cinemas in Postwar East-Central Europe', special issue of *Canadian Slavonic Papers*, 42, 1–2, 25–33.

_____ (2000b) 'Shifting Borders: Konwicki, Zanussi, and the Ideology of "East-Central Europe"', in Janina Falkowska (ed.) 'National Cinemas in Postwar East-Central Europe', special issue of *Canadian Slavonic Papers*, 42, 1–2, 87–98.

_____ (2002) 'Dialectics of Enlightenment: Notes on Wocjiech Has's *Saragossa Manuscript*', in E. S. Schaffer (ed.) *Comparative Criticism: Fantastic Currents in Comparative Literature: Gothic to Postmodern*. Cambridge: Cambridge University Press.

_____ (2005) *The Red and the White: The Cinema of People's Poland*. London: Wallflower Press.

D'Agostini, Paolo (1980) *Zanussi*. Florence: Il Castoro Cinema.

Davies, Norman (1981) *God's Playground: A History of Poland – 1795 to the Present*. Oxford: Clarendon Press.

Eagle, Herbert (1982) 'Andrzej Wajda: Film Language and the Artist's Truth', in *Cross Currents: A Yearbook of Central European Culture*. Ann Arbor: University of Michigan, 339–52.

_____ (1994) 'Polański', in Daniel J. Goulding (ed.) *Five Filmmakers: Tarkovsky, Forman, Polański, Szabó, Makavejev*. Bloomington: Indiana University Press, 92–155.

Estève, Michel (ed.) (1965) *Andrzej Munk* (Études Cinématographiques). Paris: Minard.

_____ (ed.) (1967) *Jerzy Kawalerowicz* (Études Cinématographiques). Paris: Minard.

_____ (ed.) (1968) *Andrzej Wajda* (Études Cinématographiques) Paris: Minard.

____ (ed.) (1987) *Krzysztof Zanussi* (Études Cinématographiques). Paris: Minard.

Estève, Michel and Yvette Biró (1994) *Krzysztof Kieślowski*. Paris: Lettres Modernes.

Falkowska, Janina (1996) *The Political Films of Andrzej Wajda: Dialogism in Man of Marble, Man of Iron and Danton*. Oxford and Providence: Berghahn Books.

Falkowska, Janina and Marek Haltof (eds) (2003) *The New Polish Cinema*. Trowbridge: Flicks Books.

Fogler, Janusz (ed.) *Wajda. Films*. 2 volumes, Warsaw: W.A.i.F.

Fuksiewicz, Jacek (1973) *Polish Cinema*. Trans. Ewa Gromek-Guzińska. Warsaw: Interpress.

____ (1981) *Film i telewizja w Polsce*. Warsaw.

____ (1989) *Le Cinéma polonais*. Paris: Editions de Cerf.

Furdal, Małgorzata and Roberto Turigliatto (eds) (1988) *Dalla scuola polacca al nuevo cinema 1956–1970*. Milan: Ubulibri.

____ (eds.) (1989) *Kieślowski*. Turin: Museo Nazionale del Cinema.

Gambetti, Giacomo (ed.) (1988) *Settimana del Cinema Polacco 1988*. Rome: Ministero degli Affari Esteri; Ente dello Spettacolo.

Garbowski, Christopher (1996) *Krzysztof Kieślowski's Decalogue Series: The Problem of the Protagonists and Their Self-Transcendance*. Boulder CO: East European Monographs.

Grzelecki, Stanislaw and Alicja Helman (1969) *Twenty Years of Polish Cinema, 1947–1967*. Warsaw: Art and Film Publishers.

Haltof, Marek (1995) 'A Fistful of Dollars: Polish Cinema After 1989', *Film Quarterly*, 48, 3, 15–25.

____ (2000) 'The Representation of Stalinism in Polish Cinema', in Janina Falkowska (ed.) 'National Cinemas in Postwar East-Central Europe', special issue of *Canadian Slavonic Papers*, 42, 1–2, 47–61.

____ (2002) *Polish National Cinema*. Oxford and New York: Berghahn Books.

____ (2004) *The Cinema of Krzysztof Kieślowski: Variations on Destiny and Chance*. London: Wallflower Press.

Haudiquet, Philippe (1963) *Nouveaux cineastes polonais*. Lyon: SERDOC.

Helman, Alicja and Tadeusz Miczka (1984) *Analizy i interpretacje. Film polski*. Katowice: Uniwersytet Śląski.

Helman, Alicja (2000) 'The Masters Are Tired', in Janina Falkowska (ed.) 'National Cinemas in Postwar East-Central Europe', special issue of *Canadian Slavonic Papers*, 42, 1–2, 99–111.

Hendrykowska, Małgorzata (1993) *Śladami tamtych cieni: Film w kulturze polskiej prze omu stuleci, 1895–1914*. Poznán.

____ (1999) *Kronika kinematografii polskiej 1895–1997*. Poznán: Ars Nova.

Horton, Andrew James (ed.) (2002) 'Women in Polish Film', special issue of *Kinoeye*, 2, 6, 18 March: Available at http://www.kinoeye.org

Insdorff, Annette (1999) *Double Lives, Second Chances: The Cinema of Krzysztof Kieślowski*. New York: Talk Miramax Books/Hyperion.

Jakobowicz, Karol (1998) 'Improving on the West – the native way: Poland', in *The Development of the Audiovisual Landscape in Central Europe Since 1989*. European Commission in association with Eureka Audiovisuel. Luton: University of Luton Press/John Libbey Media, 253–84.

Janicki, Stanisław (1977) *Film polski od A do Zet*, third edition. Warsaw: W.A.i.F.

____ (1985) *The Polish Film. Yesterday and Today*. Translatd by Emma Harris. Warsaw: Interpress.

____ (1990) *Polskie filmy fabularne 1902–1988*. Warsaw: W.A.i.F.

Karpiński, Maciej (1989) *The Theatre of Andrzej Wajda*. Cambridge: Cambridge University Press.

Kieślowski, Krzysztof and Krzysztof Piesiewicz (1991) *Decalogue: The Ten Commandments*. Translated by Phil Cavendish and Suzannah Bluh. London: Faber.

Kluszczyński, Ryszard W. (1998) 'Poland', in Peter Tscherkassky (ed.) *Avant-Garde Films and Videos from Central Europe*. Vienna: Sixpack Film, 43–4.

Kuszewski, Stanisław (1978) *Contemporary Polish Film*. Translated by Bogna Piotrowska. Warsaw: Interpress.

Leaming, Barbara (1981) *Polanski, A Biography: The Filmmaker as Voyeur*. New York: Simon and Schuster.

Leutrat, Paul (1973) *Andrzej Munk*. Lyon: CERT.

Lubelski, Tadeusz (1997) (ed.) *Kino Krzysztofa Kieślowskiego*. Kraków: Universitas.

_____ (2000) *Strategie autorskie w polskim filmie fabularnym lat 1945–1961,* second edition. Kraków: Rabid.

Marszałek, Rafał (1985) *Historia Filmu Polskiego.* Vol V. Warsaw: W.A.i.F.

Maurer, Monika (2000) *Krzysztof Kieślowski.* Harpenden: Pocket Essentials.

Mazierska, Ewa (2000) 'Non-Jewish Jews, Good Poles and Historical Truth in the Films of Andrzej Wajda', *Historical Journal of Film, Radio, andTelevision,* 20, 2, 213–26.

_____ (2001) 'In the Land of Noble Knights and Mute Princesses: Polish Heritage Cinema, *Historical Journal of Film, Radio and Television,* 21, 2, 167–82.

McArthur, Colin (ed.) (1970) *Andrzej Wajda: Polish Cinema.* London: BFI Education.

Michałek, Bolesław (1973) *The Cinema of Andrzej Wajda.* London: Tantivy Press.

Michałek, Bolesław and Frank Turaj (1988) *The Modern Cinema of Poland.* Bloomington: Indiana University Press.

_____ (1992) *Le Cinéma Polonais.* Paris: Centre Georges Pompidou.

Miłosz, Czesław (1983) *The History of Polish Literature,* second edition. Berkeley: University of California Press.

Morris, Neil (1970) 'The Uses of History: Eastern Europe' (extract), in Colin McArthur (ed.) *Andrzej Wajda: Polish Cinema.* London: BFI Education, 5–12.

Murri, Serafino (1997) *Krzysztof Kieślowski.* Milan: Il Castoro.

Nurczyńska-Fidelska, Evelina (1982) *Andrzej Munk.* Kraków: Wydawnictwo Literackie.

Nurczyńska-Fidelska, Evelina and Zbigniew Batko (eds) (1995) *Polish Cinema in Ten Takes.* Łódź: Łódżkie Towarzystwo Naukowe.

Oleksy, Elżbieta, Elżbieta Ostrowska and Michael Stevenson (eds) (2000) *Gender in Film and the Media: East-West Dialogues.* Frankfurt am Main: Peter Lang.

Orr, John and Elżbieta Ostrowska (eds) (2003) *The Cinema of Andrzej Wajda: The Art of Irony and Defiance.* London: Wallflower Press.

Pangon, Gérard (1994) *L'Itinéraire de Krzysztof Kieślowski.* Paris: Études Cinématographiques.

_____ (1997) *Andrzej Wajda.* Paris: Editions Mille et une nuits.

Pangon, Gérard and Vincent Amiel (1997) *Krzysztof Kieślowski.* Paris: Editions Payot and Rivages.

Passek, Jean-Loup (ed.) (1980) *Jan Lenica.* Paris: Centre Georges Pompidou.

Patocki, Jan (1996) *The Manuscript Found in Saragossa,* trans. Ian Maclean. London: Penguin.

Pirie, Donald, Jekatarina Young and Christopher Carrell (eds) (1990) *Polish Realities: The Arts in Poland 1980–1989.* Glasgow: Third Eye Centre.

Polański, Roman (1984) *Roman.* London: Heinemann.

Przylipiak, Mirosław (2000) *Poetyka kina dokumentalnego.* Gdańsk: Wydawnictwo Uniwersytetu Gdańskiego.

Skwara, Anita (1992) 'Film Stars do not Shine in the Sky over Poland: The Absence of Popular Cinema in Poland', in Richard Dyer and Ginette Vincendeau (eds) *Popular European Cinema.* London: Routledge, 220–32.

Stok, Danusia (ed.) (1993) *Kieślowski on Kieślowski.* London: Faber.

Sulik, Bolesław (1970) 'War and History: 1954–58', in Colin Mc Arthur (ed.) *Andrzej Wajda: Polish Cinema.* London: BFI Education, 13–30.

_____ (1976) *A Change of Tack: Making The Shadow Line.* London: British Film Institute.

Toeplitz, Jerzy (1974) *Historia Filmu Polskiego 1939–1956.* Vol III. Warsaw: W.A.i.F.

_____ (1980) *Historia Filmu Polskieho 1957–1961.* Vol IV. Warsaw: W.A.i.F.

Trinon, Hadelin (1964) *Andrzej Wajda.* Paris: Seghers.

Turaj, Frank (1989) 'Poland: The Cinema of Moral Concern', in Daniel J. Goulding (ed.) *Post New Wave Cinema in the Soviet Union and Eastern Europe.* Bloomington: Indiana University Press, 143–71.

Wajda, Andrzej (1984) *Three Films: Ashes and Diamonds; A Generation; Kanal.* (screenplays). London: Lorrimer.

_____ (1989) *Double Vision: My Life in Film.* London: Faber.

Wexman, Virginia Wright (1985) *Roman Polanski.* Boston: Twayne.

Zamoyski, Adam (1987) *The Polish Way: A Thousand-year History of the Poles and their Culture.* London: John Murray.

Žižek, Slavoj (2001) *The Fright of Real Tears: Krzysztof Kieślowski Between Theory and Post-theory.* London: British Film Institute.

INDEX

The Cinema of Japan and Korea

edited by Justin Bowyer
preface by Jinhee Choi

A unique companion to the cinema of both Japan and Korea, this collection includes in-depth studies of such films as Stray Dog, Godzilla, Killer Butterfly, Battle Royale and Audition and places in historical context the work of directors such as Kurosawa, Mizoguchi and Takeshi Kitano as well many prominent contemporary Korean filmmakers.

£16.99 pbk 1–904764–11–8
£45.00 hbk 1–904764–12–6
2004

The Cinema of Italy

edited by Giorgio Bertellini
preface by Gian Piero Brunetta

Placing Italian filmmaking traditions within the context of both Italian and Western film culture, this unique collection considers the wide range of masterworks from The Bicycle Thieves and La Strada to A Fistful of Dollars and Dear Diary and includes coverage of directors from Rosselini, Fellini and Visconti to Pasolini, Olmi and Moretti.

£16.99 pbk 1–903364–98–1
£45.00 hbk 1–903364–99–X
2004

The Cinema of the Low Countries

edited by Ernest Mathijs
preface by Harry Kümel

Identifying and celebrating the many connections between the Low Countries' films in terms of genre, representations and languages, this volume discusses such key films as Turkish Delight, The Vanishing, Rosetta and Man Bites Dog, and focuses on the varied works of directors such as Joris Ivens, Paul Verhoevan and the Dardenne Brothers.

£16.99 pbk 1–904764–00–2
£45.00 hbk 1–904764–01–0
2004

The Cinema of Latin America

edited by Alberto Elena and Marina Díaz López
preface by Walter Salles

Compiles 24 essays on the work of filmmakers such as Glauber Rocha, Luis Buñuel and Tomás Gutiérrez Alea. Films discussed include Amores Perros, Memories of Underdevelopment, The Hour of the Furnaces and Foreign Land, and includes coverage of the cinema of Brazil, Argentina, Cuba, Mexico.

£16.99 pbk 1–903364–83–3
£45.00 hbk 1–903364–84–1
2003

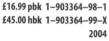

THE CZECHOSLOVAK NEW WAVE *2nd edition*

Peter Hames

This study of the most significant movement in post-war Central and East European cinema examines the origins and developments of the Czech New Wave against a background of the political and cultural developmements of the 1960s leading to the Prague spring of 1968. The book also surveys key aspects of the history of Czech and Slovak cinema from the 1930s onwards. This second edition has been fully updated to include more developed accounts of some films that were banned at the time of the origianl research and extends the analysis to the present day.

'Vividly evokes the most exciting and boistrous decade in the history of Czechoslovak filmmaking ... the most meticulous study of any national cinema to have appeared in recent years.'
Vaclav Taborsky, *Canadian Slavonic Papers*

'In analysing this complex artistic-social phenomenon, Mr Hames illuminates an important episode in modern film history ... his descriptions of the marvellously ageless films are accurate and exhaustive.'
Josef Skovorecky, *Sight and Sound*

2005
1-904764-42-8 £16.99 pbk
1-904764-43-6 £45.00 hbk

CINEMA OF THE OTHER EUROPE
The Industry and Artistry of East Central European Film

Dina Iordinova

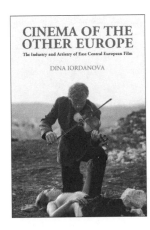

A comprehensive study of the cinematic traditions of Poland, Hungary, the Czech Republic and Slovakia from 1945 to the present day, *The Cinema of Other Europe* explores the major schools of filmmaking and the main stages of developement across the region during the period of state socialism up until the end of the Cold War, as well as more recent transformations post-1989. It is thus a timely appraisal of Film Studies debates ranging from the representation of history and memory, the reassessment of political content, ethics and society, the rehabilitation of popular cinema, and the rethinking of national and regional cinemas in the context of globalisation.

'An excellent and timely contribution to European Film Studies. The book's wide-ranging scope, its critical consideration of scholerly literature and the inclusion of a comprehensive resource guide make it an authoritative compendium on East Central European Film.'
Daniela Berghahn, Oxford Brookes University

'Its greatest innovation is the decidedly regional and cross-disciplinary approach, liberating East Central European cinema from the aesthetic-political analysis that traditionally considered these films within their isolated national contexts.'
Anikó Imre, University of Washington

2003
1-903364-61-2 £14.99 pbk
1-903364-64-7 £42.50 hbk

THE RED AND THE WHITE
The Cinema of People's Poland

Paul Coates

The Red and the White: The Cinema of People's Poland takes a fascinating look at the history of post-war Polish cinema, and how it was affected by the political, social and cultural upheavals throughout the period 1947–1989. This timely study re-evaluates the legacy of Socialist Realism, the representation of the war, cinematic portrayals of national myth and cultural history, literary adaptation and surrealism, and discourses of exile and national identity. Although paying particular reference to the work of Krzysztof Kieslowski and Andrzej Wajda, this book considers the contribution of a wide range of filmmakers, including Jerzy Skolimowski, Krzysztof Zanussi, Agnieska Holland, Andrzej Munk, Jerzy Kawalerowicz, Wojciech Has and Roman Polanski.

The volume also includes unique primary archival research into the role of state-sponsored censorship, and coverage of Polish-Jewish representations in film. Among the many films discussed are *A Generation* (1955), *Eroica* (1957), *Ashes and Diamonds* (1958), *Family LIfe* (1971), *The Promised Land* (1975), *The Hour Glass Sanatorium* (1973), *Hands Up!* (1981), *Decalogue 8* (1988), *Europa, Europa* (1990), *The Double Life of Veronique* (1991).

2005
1-904764-26-6 **£15.99 pbk**
1-904764-27-4 **£45.00 hbk**

HUNGARIAN CINEMA
From Coffee House to Multiplex

John Cunningham

In the 1960s Hungary entered a period of relative stability and increasing cultural relaxation resulting in an astonishing growth of film-making. Innovative and groundbreaking directors such as Miklós Jancsó (Hungarian Rhapsody, The Red and the White), István Szabó (Mephisto, Sunshine) and Márta Mészaros (Diary for My Children, Little Vilma) emerged and established the reputation of Hungarian films on a global scale. This is the first book to discuss all major aspects of the history of Hungarian cinema and its place in the development of Hungarian society. The book also focuses on film-makers as diverse and significant as Zoltán Fábri (The Storm, Fourteen Lives Were Saved) and Béla Tarr (Satan Tango, Werckmeister Harmonies) and includes coverage of under-explored areas of Hungarian cinema, including avant-garde film-making and animation, football films, and representations of the Gypsy and Jewish minorities.

'An accessible and enjoyable introduction to Hungarian cinema. I would not hesitate to recommend it to students of Central and East European Cinema and to others in search of approachable materials for undergraduates.'
– Catherine Portuges, University of Massachusetts, Amherst

'In this lively and highly readable volume, Cunningham employs historical rigour and colourful observation to bring to life the complex development of one of Europe's most interesting film cultures.'
– Andrew James Horton, Editor-in-Chief, Kinoeye

2004
1-903364-79-5 **£14.99 pbk**
1-903364-80-9 **£42.50 hbk**

THE CINEMA OF KRZYSZTOF KIESLOWSKI
Variations on Destiny and Chance
Marek Haltof

Since his death in 1996, Krzysztof Kieslowski has remained the best-known
contemporary Polish film-maker, and one of the most popular and respected
European directors. In this study Marek Haltof provides a comprehensive study of
Kieslowski's cinema, from his early documentaries and student films to television
projects and award-winning features. The book discusses industrial practices and
the context of Polish cinema from the late 1960s as well as wider European
film-making, and stresses that the director is more than merely a 'great East
Central European auteur', his films being as unique to Poland as elsewhere.

2004
1–904764–91–4 £14.99 pb
1–904764–92–2 £42.50 hbk

THE CINEMA OF ANDRZEJ WAJDA
The Art of Irony and Defiance
edited by John Orr and Elzbieta Ostrowska
preface by Andrzej Wajda

A major reassessment of the great Polish director Andrzej Wajda, who received
a Lifetime Achievement Academy Award in 2000, this timely new collection
covers all aspects of his work. From the early trilogy of the 1950s – *A Generation*,
Kanal, *Ashes and Diamonds* – to the 1999 epic *Pan Tadeusz*, the contributors
consider Wajda's daring innovations in style, his concern with Polish history
and nationhood, and his artistic defiance of authoritarian rule during the Cold
War, particularly in such films as *Man of Marble* and *Man of Iron*. It is a thus a
wide-ranging examination of a prolific film-maker whose work over four decades
reflects the changing nature of cinema itself.

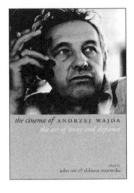

2003
1–903364–89–2 £14.99 pbk
1–903364–57–4 £42.50 hbk

THE CINEMA OF EMIR KUSTERICA
Notes From the Underground
Goran Gocic

The Cinema of Emir Kusterica is thhe first book to be published on Sarajevan
filmmaker in English. By comprehensively covering his career to date, the
book explores one of the most successful and celebrated European directors
working today. In thIs insightful and wide-ranging account, this study focuses in
particular on Kusterica's passionate dedication to the marginal and the outcast,
and includes exclusive interviews with the director as well as other artistic
collaborators.

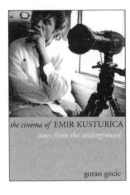

2001
1–903364–14–0 £14.99 pbk
1–903364–16–7 £42.50 hbk

**Forthcoming titles in the DIRECTORS' CUTS series include *The Cinema of Roman Polanski*
and *The Cinema of Theo Angelopoulos*. Please visit our website for details of further titles
in this series – www.wallflowerpress.co.uk**